D1512386

The Idea of the Canterbury Tales

The Idea of the

Canterbury Tales

Donald R. Howard

UNIVERSITY OF CALIFORNIA PRESS

BERKELEY   LOS ANGELES   LONDON

University of California Press
Berkeley and Los Angeles, California
University of California Press, Ltd., London, England
Copyright © 1976 by The Regents of the University of California
First Paperback Edition, 1978
ISBN 0-520-03492-9 (paperback)
0-520-02816-3 (clothbound)
Library of Congress Catalog Card Number: 74-81433
Printed in the United States of America
Designed by Dave Comstock

1 2 3 4 5 6 7 8 9 0

TO THE MEMORY OF

Francis Lee Utley

1907 – 1974

CONTENTS

ILLUSTRATIONS

ACKNOWLEDGMENTS

As best I can I have used the footnotes to document factual claims, to point the reader to books or articles I have mentioned or had in mind, to include peripheral details, sometimes to pick an argument or propose a toast. But I cannot claim to have acknowledged all my debts. For an example of the difficulty in doing so the reader may consult chapter 4, n. 14. So much has been written about *The Canterbury Tales* that I am pretty much convinced anything which follows resembling an original idea is a combination of preexisting ones. I wrote with a card file of Chaucer studies at my elbow, inefficiently added new items as they appeared, attended meetings, discussed Chaucer with students and colleagues. Any Chaucer critic, drifting in this sea of free-floating opinion, has to clutch at straws when it comes to writing footnotes.

I wish then to acknowledge in a general way the vast collaborative effort to understand *The Canterbury Tales* which preceded my own. I wish to acknowledge too my debt to the late A. O. Lovejoy, who introduced the study of the history of ideas into American intellectual life. Since Lovejoy's time the idea of an idea has changed, and I have been indebted to the writings of those who changed it, especially to Leo Spitzer, Erich Auerbach, Georges Poulet, and E. H. Gombrich.

The first draft of this book was written in 1969-1970 on

a Guggenheim fellowship, so I want to express my special gratitude to the John Simon Guggenheim Memorial Foundation. I am grateful for the hospitality of the British Museum, the Henry E. Huntington Memorial Library, and the libraries of the University of California; to the small, efficient, and infinitely helpful staff of the Milton Eisenhower Library at The Johns Hopkins University; to the Library of Congress; to the New York Public Library; and to a number of libraries, whose names I ungratefully did not record, for inter-library loans and brief visitations.

The first part of chapter 3 appeared originally in *ELH* and is reprinted here, revised and expanded, with the permission of the editors.

The whole manuscript was read by Morton W. Bloomfield, Stanley E. Fish, Herbert Lindenberger, Harry Sieber, Francis Lee Utley, and Barry Weller. I'm grateful for their care, patience, and encouragement. I'm especially grateful to Elizabeth Hatcher and Christian K. Zacher for reading the whole and commenting extensively: they were students of mine who quickly became colleagues and friends, and they afforded me a special pleasure by teaching their former teacher. The manuscript, revised as these readers suggested, was read by Anne Middleton for the University of California Press and by Ulrich Knoepflmacher of the press's Editorial Committee. I am deeply grateful to Professor Middleton for her responsive and acute analysis, and indebted to Professor Knoepflmacher for specific, practical recommendations which I wouldn't have thought of on my own. I want also to thank Susan Dresner, my scholarly and imaginative research assistant at Johns Hopkins; Susan Welling, my copyeditor at the University of California Press; and William J. McClung, that rare kind of editor who can see an author's idea more clearly than the author himself.

The dedication of the volume memorializes a friendship two decades old with a generous-spirited man more learned than anyone I know, who has given me more kindness and encouragement than I could ever return except by a gesture.

This much I wrote many months before Francis Lee Utley died on March 9, 1974, and I hope I may be permitted to add a brief memorial. He was a student of Kittredge's and like his mentor had a profound technical learning in philology, a vast knowledge of books, and an ability to see a literary work whole. He responded to people objectively, with a sense of justice; he had genuine compassion for his friends' sorrows and took genuine pleasure in their joys and successes. He was a fine companion to drink and talk with; one never came away without learning something, without imbibing his skeptical, humorous, and optimistic spirit. He was a humanist in the good old sense; it says something that in his last years he had turned to a close study of Petrarch and Boccaccio. He believed as few still do that scholarship is a joint enterprise. He gave of himself generously and his spirit lives in his students and colleagues who survive him, in his writings, and in the writings of others; I hope very much that it lives in the present book.

Baltimore, 1974

NOTE ON
QUOTATIONS AND
CITATIONS

PASSAGES quoted from *The Canterbury Tales* have been compared with *The Text of the Canterbury Tales*, ed. J. M. Manly and Edith Rickert, 8 vols. (Chicago: Univ. of Chicago Press, 1940). Passages quoted from Chaucer's other works have been compared with texts offered in *The Works of Geoffrey Chaucer*, ed. F. N. Robinson, 2nd ed. (Cambridge, Mass.: Houghton Mifflin, 1957). However, I have consulted textual notes and compared other editions, and have sometimes preferred the reading of another editor, usually explaining my preference in a footnote. Punctuation is my own. Numbered line references conform to the Robinson edition.

The Middle English spelling is normalized: I have as best I could removed non-functional old spellings according to the principles stated in *The Canterbury Tales: A Selection*, ed. Donald R. Howard with James Dean, Signet Classic Poetry Series (New York: New American Library, 1969), pp. xxxix–xl. My reason for quoting Chaucer this way is my conviction that his infinitely supple language is a living one too vibrant to be valued for its quaint appearance on a page. I have been fretfully mindful of Chaucer's warning in *Troilus*, V. 1793–1798 against miswriting or mismetering his poetry; but I have been mindful too of the "grete diversitee," greater than he could have imagined, in English speech and writing especially in the century after his death when extant manuscripts were copied—and mindful of his final and most earnest prayer, that his poetry be understood.

ABBREVIATIONS

Baugh	*Chaucer's Major Poetry*, ed. A. C. Baugh (New York: Appleton-Century-Crofts, 1963)
CE	*College English*
CentR	*Centennial Review*
ChauR	*Chaucer Review*
EETS	*Early English Text Society*
ELH	*Journal of English Literary History*
ES	*English Studies*
JEGP	*Journal of English and Germanic Philology*
LR	*Chaucer Life-Records*, ed. Martin M. Crow and Clair C. Olson (Univ. of Michigan Press, 1966)
M&H	*Mediaevalia et Humanistica*
MAE	*Medium Aevum*
MED	*Middle English Dictionary*, ed. Hans Kurath (Ann Arbor: Univ. of Michigan Press, 1956–)
MLN	*Modern Language Notes*
MLQ	*Modern Language Quarterly*
MLR	*Modern Language Review*
MP	*Modern Philology*
MS	*Mediaeval Studies*
N&Q	*Notes & Queries*
NLH	*New Literary History*

NM	*Neuphilologische Mitteilungen*
OED	*Oxford English Dictionary*
PL	Migne, *Patrologia Latina*
PLL	*Papers in Language & Literature*
PMLA	*Publications of the Modern Language Association*
PQ	*Philological Quarterly*
RES	*Review of English Studies*
Robinson	*The Works of Geoffrey Chaucer*, ed. F. N. Robinson, 2nd ed. (Boston: Houghton Mifflin, 1957)
SA	*Sources and Analogues of Chaucer's Canterbury Tales*, ed. W. F. Bryan and Germaine Dempster (Chicago: Univ. of Chicago Press, 1941; Rpt. New York: Humanities Press, 1958)
Skeat	*The Complete Works of Geoffrey Chaucer*, ed. W. W. Skeat, 7 vols. (2nd ed. Oxford: Clarendon Press, 1899)
SP	*Studies in Philology*
S&T	*Chaucer Criticism:* The Canterbury Tales, ed. Richard Schoeck and Jerome Taylor (Notre Dame, Ind.: Univ. of Notre Dame Press, 1960)
UTQ	*University of Toronto Quarterly*

In the footnotes full references are given only once, at the first mention of a title; thereafter short references are given throughout the book. Names of authors will be found in the index.

Abbreviations of the titles of Chaucer's works are the standard ones used in the Tatlock and Kennedy *Concordance* and in most editions.

Citations and quotations from the Bible are to the Douay-Rheims translation except for phrases commonly known to English-speakers in the King James version.

I

THE IDEA OF
AN IDEA

EVERYONE knows that Chaucer had not finished *The Canterbury Tales* at the time of his death. Much written about the work inquires or assumes how he would have done so, and it is often supposed he would have changed or added so much as to alter its character. Scarcely any work of English literature, including other unfinished ones, has been approached with such a supposition in mind. Why has *The Canterbury Tales* been approached this way?—because of the statement in the General Prologue that each pilgrim is to tell two tales on either leg of the journey. And yet this is not Chaucer's statement; it is the Host's, as reported by the narrator. It may or may not at some point have been Chaucer's idea—we do not know. What we know is that, like other ebullient men, the Host plans more than he and his "flock" can deliver; most of the plans laid in *The Canterbury Tales*, like most plans in life, go awry. If we consider this failure of the plan a feature of the story, not a fact about the author's life, we will be able to read the book as it is, not as we think it might have been. That is what I propose to do: to approach the work believing that "the work as produced constitutes the definitive record of the writer's intention," and to argue *that it is unfinished but complete.*[1]

1. Northrop Frye, *Anatomy of Criticism* (Princeton: Princeton Univ. Press, 1957), p. 87. I would be surprised if Frye did not allow that his

Chaucer, though a man of his age, was an exceptional man; one can fairly expect from him some amount of individuality.[2] When we approach his last and greatest work, we want to know what happened in his mind when he conceived and executed it. Of course one can never know fully what is in another's mind, yet we know a writer's mind in part when we read his work. An act of communication takes place. That is why I talk about the "idea" of *The Canterbury Tales*. Whatever ideas are, we know they can be shared and passed from one generation to the next. The idea of a literary work is not the same as its "intention"—an author's intentions can be frustrated or subverted, sometimes happily so, and they can be unconscious. The intention—like the form, unity,

---

remark applies to a work unfinished because of, or at the time of, the author's death; the work as produced would still be the best and is usually the only evidence of intention. For the distinction between "unfinished" and "uncompleted" see Frye, "The Structure of Imagery in *The Faerie Queene*," *Fables of Identity: Studies in Poetic Mythology* (New York: Harcourt, Brace & World, 1963), pp. 69–87.

Some of my predecessors in the effort to see the work as a whole, to whom I owe a particular debt, are Ralph Baldwin, *The Unity of the Canterbury Tales*, in *Anglistica*, vol. 5 (Copenhagen: Rosenkilde and Bagger, 1955); E. T. Donaldson, esp. *Chaucer's Poetry: An Anthology for the Modern Reader* (New York: Ronald Press, 1958) and *Speaking of Chaucer* (New York: W. W. Norton, 1970); Morton W. Bloomfield's articles on Chaucer, most of them rpt. in *Essays and Explorations: Studies in Ideas, Language, and Literature* (Cambridge, Mass.: Harvard Univ. Press, 1970); and Robert M. Jordan, *Chaucer and the Shape of Creation: The Aesthetic Possibilities of Inorganic Structure* (Cambridge, Mass.: Harvard Univ. Press, 1967).

2. Chaucer's originality and poetic individuality have hardly ever been denied. Even *SA* largely attests to the genius he brought to every adaptation. In recent years the study of medieval rhetoric has encouraged a tendency to dwell upon the stylized aspects of medieval literature and downplay the individuality or originality of poets. The most important influence upon this tendency is the monumental work of Ernst Robert Curtius, *European Literature and the Latin Middle Ages*, trans. Willard R. Trask, Bollingen Series 36 (New York: Pantheon Books, 1953). At a farther extreme, the urge to interpret all medieval poems as allegories has led some to deny any element of individual self-expression in medieval poems; e.g. see D. W. Robertson, Jr., *A Preface to Chaucer: Studies in Medieval Perspectives* (Princeton, N. J.: Princeton Univ. Press, 1962), pp. 16 – 17. A good case against Curtius and for individuality in medieval poetic art is made by Peter Dronke, *Poetic Individuality in the Middle Ages: New Departures in Poetry 1000–1150* (Oxford: Clarendon Press, 1970), pp. 1–32.

structure, style, or "world"—of a literary work is identifiable in the work and shares in the culture of the author's time. All are part of the idea of a work. The same is true of genre; genres are classifications imposed after the fact, but every author must have some idea of the kind of work he writes, though it is often found that literary works are not "generically pure."[3] Ideas are, I am afraid, like the ocean: they include much, change constantly, and are hard to scoop up. The idea of *The Canterbury Tales* in some of its aspects existed long before Chaucer's time. It appears to have changed somewhat as he got the work on paper. And, as it has been grasped and expressed by readers, it has gone through many permutations since his death.

I conceived of this book first as a history of a literary idea, then as an anatomy. I wanted first to know how the poem came to be, in its own time and milieu, to understand its creation as a unique event. If we could understand that we would understand a lot, but not everything. We might understand what the poet wrote for his contemporaries, but not necessarily what he wrote for himself or for posterity. And we would not understand why we still read his works or how it is that many of them retain the power to interest us and move us. Chaucer was not unaware of posterity: he showed an interest in Fame's house early on, addressed the *Troilus* to a literary tradition, worried about the accurate preservation of his text, and joked (in the Man of Law's Prologue) about his reputation. It is fair to say he wrote for us as well as for his contemporaries. So we want to know what the work *is*, not merely what it *was*. I set out *not* to write a linear "reading" which would proceed in the conventional way from tale to tale. I wanted somehow to see the whole "idea" of the work in a historical perspective, but a diachronic treatment would have left little to say about the fifteen years during which Chaucer was writing it. So I have written instead an anatomy.

When you write an anatomy it is an inconvenience that

3. On the place of genre in artistic creation, see Claudio Guillén, *Literature as System: Essays toward the Theory of Literary History* (Princeton: Princeton Univ. Press, 1971), esp. pp. 107–134.

an arm has so many things in common with a leg. The form
promotes repetition and discourages structure. But I believe
such an approach will further an understanding of *The
Canterbury Tales* better than historical or biographical approaches have done. Every historical study of *The Canterbury
Tales* has necessarily nibbled off one aspect of history,
finding in medieval thought a dominant idea, technique,
pattern, or style which may be discovered in the poem. Such
studies usually oversell their subject. Thus one scholar finds
Chaucer's poetry allegorical; another abstracts from Dante
"infernal" and "purgatorial" modes, which he projects upon
selected tales; another finds preexisting styles combined in
Chaucer's works; another finds allusions to Chaucer's contemporaries; several others find "tradition."[4] Taken together such books present a many faceted picture of an age
which was variegated and a work which is complex. Scarcely any of their authors has claimed to find the single key which
will unlock the secrets of Chaucer's works. How could they?
Everyone knows that the greatest poems confound the critic.
Literary criticism would be a sorry art—wouldn't be an art at
all—if critics chose only those works that yield themselves
compliantly to interpretation. The critics who have seen most
in the works they treat have seen, or glimpsed, their impene-
trability. There are those who believe that a great literary
work has the power to generate an indefinite number of valid
critical accounts, as many at least as there are critics. This
belief sounds as though it flies in the face of objective
historical inquiry, but it does not. History itself prompts rival
interpretations; probably everything does. It is possible to
delimit an area of "objective" historical interpretation, to
distinguish a group of meanings possible at one point in

4. I refer respectively to Robertson, *Preface to Chaucer*; Paul G. Rug-
giers, *The Art of the Canterbury Tales* (Madison and Milwaukee: Univ. of
Wisconsin Press, 1965); Charles Muscatine, *Chaucer and the French Tradi-
tion: A Study in Style and Meaning* (Berkeley and Los Angeles: Univ. of
California Press, 1957); George Williams, *A New View of Chaucer* (Durham,
N. C.: Duke Univ. Press, 1965); Ian Robinson, *Chaucer and the English
Tradition* (Cambridge: Cambridge Univ. Press, 1972) and P. M. Kean,
Chaucer and the Making of English Poetry, 2 vols. (London and Boston:
Routledge & Kegan Paul, 1972).

history from a host of impossible ones, but no one has persuaded me that the real meaning of a poem can be established from this sort of inquiry.[5] It depends on what you mean by "real."

One argument for historical understanding of medieval texts goes like this: "There are vast differences between modern and medieval thought, and the values we find in Chaucer are colored by our own modernity. Our notions of the unity of literary works are post-romantic, our ideas of narrative Jamesian, our view of character psychoanalytical. We must strip these scales from our eyes. We have been making mistakes, and these mistakes are to be laid at Hegel's door, at Coleridge's, Freud's, James's." There is no arguing with those who take this line. I claim that history is various, complex, and pluralistic, filled with struggle and contradiction; my opponent counters that this is a post-Hegelian idea. I argue that the ideals of the Church were one of several sets of values, often in conflict with such aristocratic ideals as that of chivalry or courtly love; my opponent retorts that courtly love is a *jeu d'esprit* of nineteenth-century French historians. I argue that Chaucer had great sensitivity as an observer of human conduct and great skill in ironic role-playing; my opponent taxes me with post-Freudian psychological relativism. Thus one writer thinks we should study the literature of the past in order to see how different it is from our own; he seems to think literary study is a form of therapy which permits us to see ourselves objectively.[6] But one objective fact about us is that *The Canterbury Tales*, though written six hundred years ago, can still make us laugh, make us ponder, make us look up sometimes from the page with a wild surmise. This is part of its "real" historical significance; and we can understand that significance better than men of Chaucer's time precisely because we have Hegel, Coleridge, Freud, and James behind us.

5. The case is stated in E. D. Hirsch, *Validity in Interpretation* (New Haven and London: Yale Univ. Press, 1967).
6. D. W. Robertson, Jr., "Some Observations on Method in Literary Studies," *NLH* 1 (1969): 21–33. For my reaction see "Medieval Poems and Medieval Society," *M&H*, n.s. 3 (1972): 99–115.

Another barrier to understanding is the biographical or personal estimate of poetic creation, what I will call the "workroom" view. One argument for the workroom view goes like this: "Chaucer did not finish *The Canterbury Tales* and we can see that he left many loose ends. Some of his tales are unsuccessful, some incomplete, some contain mistakes and oversights. He lived at a time when light was poor, pens and ink insufficient, paper expensive; and he was a busy public official with little time to spare. We admire him too much and so are blinded to his shortcomings. What lies before us must therefore be explained largely by the circumstances of the work's composition." Thus, for example, passages difficult to interpret are sometimes written off as leftovers from a previous version—Chaucer must have meant to delete them. A variant of this workroom view involves the oral delivery of the tales before the king's court: the audience did not have anything like the fancy expectations we have—they only expected a good story from time to time.[7] If the tales were written with such limited expectations in mind, how does one account for the presence of the General Prologue, for the work's overriding structure, for the dramatic interplay among the pilgrims, for the way the tales reflect the characters of their tellers—in short for the work's unity and complexity? Something of the same might be said to those who think Chaucer's age was a unilaterally Christian civilization with no inner conflicts, and that readers expected moral edification from all poems.[8] If the audience's expectations were that narrow, it would be hard to account for the extraordinary variety of the tales; for the work's enduring capacity to please and instruct even those to whom Christianity now seems only a boring mistake of history; and for the excitement over the narrative, rather

7. Many examples of this kind of approach might be offered; one is Paull F. Baum, *Chaucer: A Critical Appreciation* (Durham, N. C.: Duke Univ. Press, 1958); another, Bertrand H. Bronson, "Chaucer's Art in Relation to His Audience," *Five Studies in Literature*, Univ. of California Publications in English 8, no. 1 (Berkeley, 1940), pp. 1–53, or his *In Search of Chaucer* (Toronto: Univ. of Toronto Press, 1960).
8. Robertson, *Preface to Chaucer*, pp. 3–51 and passim.

than the moral, features of Chaucer's work expressed in, say, Henryson's *Testament* or the *Tale of Beryn*.

If we want to know what *The Canterbury Tales* is we should begin by looking at it very carefully and saying what we see. To such an enterprise we might bring a multitude of methods. If we are able to see in literature and in literary interpretation more than the medievals did, we serve Chaucer well to bring to his works every sophistication we can. We never balk at applying to his language the subtleties of modern linguistics, or at reading the manuscripts of his poems under ultraviolet light. I know Chaucer never applied the word "form" as I do to a literary work, never used the word "idea," never talked about mechanistic and dynamic models, or shared consciousness, or the rest of it; I agree it is important and interesting to understand how one or another of Chaucer's contemporaries would have understood his poems. But we have managed to understand many things better than they did. Perhaps this is so of poems: perhaps we do see more in their poetry than any fourteenth-century reader would have imagined, and perhaps what we see is there.

Let me give an example of the kind of critical approach I mean to take. And let me draw my example from the visual arts, where we can see the whole at once without having to read through it and hold it in memory as we do with literature.

The example is the Ellesmere portrait of Chaucer (Figure 1).

The portraits of the pilgrims in the margins of the Ellesmere manuscript were done by at least two artists, probably by three or even four. Most of the portraits are admired for their realism and life-like detail, for their fidelity to the text, for their feeling and mobility, for their use of colors, and so on. They are good illustrations. The portrait of Chaucer is probably by a separate artist. In all the illustrations except that of Chaucer, the horses are more or less in scale and suited to their riders—the Squire rides a good mount elegantly equipped, the Clerk a miserable nag (Figures 2 and 3). But Chaucer himself is mounted on a curious minia-

Figure 1. The "Ellesmere" portrait of Chaucer. Ellesmere ms., fol. 153^v.

ture horse scarcely bigger or more mobile than a hobby-
horse. How are we to explain this?

The most simplistic historical explanation might be that
horses and ponies were smaller in the Middle Ages,[9] that
men on pilgrimage rented horses and ponies from livery
stables, and that the artist was representing a fact: Chaucer's
horse was a small pony. But this is not supported by the text
of The Canterbury Tales or by the other illustrations, so there
is still something exceptional about our master's having a
mount smaller than anyone else's. Another explanation of a
historical kind might argue that the medievals had little
sense of scale and perspective, that these were inventions of
the Renaissance, and that until then art was more primitive
and naive. This makes a certain amount of sense, the more
so if we argue that proportion and perspective are modern
values which the medievals did not share with us, and that to
understand their art we must strip from our minds our own
preconceptions. But there are examples of good perspective
and proportion in fourteenth-century manuscript drawings;
and figures out of scale should not trouble a modern viewer
unless somehow he has been shielded from modern art.

Another explanation—a historical one of the "workroom" variety—might hold that the artist drew the horse
using a copybook or pattern. The horses of the Franklin,
Shipman, and Squire are so drawn; the indentation made by
the stylus is quite visible in the vellum.[10] No such indenta-

9. Large horses were used in battle, but for riding from London to
Canterbury a horse might have been used which would now be reckoned a
pony. The riders ride in the old way with knees not bent and heels not
down, very shocking to modern horsemen, but the seat can be seen in
eighteenth-century illustrations. If one looks at the place on the horse
where the rider's foot comes, and at the length of the rider's leg in
proportion to his body, one finds the scale pretty acceptable in most cases
(though the Reeve's horse is very small). As we shall see, the poet looks
bandy-legged or dwarfish.

10. Herbert C. Schulz, The Ellesmere Manuscript of Chaucer's Canterbury
Tales (San Marino, Calif.: Huntington Library, 1966), p. 4. These stylus
marks were not made later by someone tracing over the drawing; we know
this because in the case of the Franklin's horse the stylus mark goes
through the two preceding leaves to the beginning of the quire but no
trace appears on the last sheet of the previous quire. This shows that the
tracing from a copybook was done while the leaves were bound in quires

Figure 2.
The Squire. Ellesmere
ms., fol. 115ᵛ.

tions are to be seen about Chaucer's horse, but a copybook
still could have been used. A similar explanation would hold
that the bad proportions "could be explained by the use of a
conventional portrait of Chaucer to provide the artist with
an authentic likeness from which to copy the upper, more
crucial part of the figure, and his then adapting the lower
part to the riding position and to the limited space available

---

but before the quires had been put together as a book, which was normal
procedure in workshops. The needlessly heavy tracing suggests an
apprentice's hand. At the portrait of the Friar part of the illumination has
been scratched off to make room; this suggests that the illumination was
done first and the drawings put in later. Everything points to the
characteristic division of labor in a fifteenth-century workshop. At the
portrait of Chaucer the left margin of writing is flush down the page but
the marginal gold leaf line is set in at the beginning of the *Melibee*; this
suggests that the scribe did not know a portrait was to go here but the
decorator did. The fact that the initial has been moved presumably to
make room for Chaucer's portrait may indicate a collaborative effort or a
change of plan. I am much indebted to Mr. Schulz, the retired curator of
manuscripts at the Huntington Library, with whom I have discussed all
these matters at length and who arranged for me to see the Ellesmere
manuscript.

Figure 3.
The Clerk. Ellesmere
ms., fol. 88

in the margin of the leaf."[11] It is true, Chaucer's leg is also
out of scale—the knee is not bent, the leg hardly as long as
the arm, an improbable circumstance. The initial letter in
the text has been moved to the right of the tracing made for
it, presumably to make room for the drawing. Everything
indicates that the text, illumination, and drawings were a
collaborative effort done in a workshop. And the portrait
does bear a resemblance to the "Hoccleve" portrait (Figure 4).[12] Perhaps the horse would have been bigger if the
margin had been wider.

11. Schulz, p. 3. The bound volume leaves more space in the outer than
in the inner margins; only the drawing of the Miller appears in the inner
margin. The larger horses are in the right outer margin where there is
more space beside the lines in verse; but Chaucer's is in the left outer
margin beside the prose *Melibee*, and the prose lines leave less space.
12. The authenticity of the Hoccleve portrait rests on Hoccleve's claim
in the verse he wrote to accompany it; but the three manuscripts of the
Regement of Princes which contain the drawing are evidently copies of a lost
original—the best, Harley 4866, contains many copyist's errors. The
portrait shows Chaucer as short, rotund, and rather droopy eyed; but the
original artist might have had these details from his works rather than

Figure 4.
The "Hoccleve" portrait
of Chaucer. Harley ms.
4866, fol. 88.

Anyway, the horse *is* out of scale; and these explanations do not help us understand or interpret this fact. They
explain away, rather than account for, the curiosity we
notice. So we are back to the question of why medieval artists
and viewers did not expect scale and proportion as we do.
They could after all have had different sized patterns in
their copybooks. Besides, there *is* space in the margin for a
bigger horse—the artist could have turned and foreshort-
ened it as he did with the Monk's (Figure 5), or omitted the

from observation. As to his size, Chaucer's grave was opened in 1897
when Browning's grave was dug; the coroner of the Abbey measured his
remains and calculated that he was 5′ 6″, but men were smaller then, as we
may judge from suits of armor, and this would not have been much less
than average height. On the portraits of Chaucer see M. H. Spielmann,
The Portraits of Geoffrey Chaucer, Chaucer Soc., 2nd ser. 31 (London,
1900); Edwin Ford Piper, "The Miniatures of the Ellesmere Chaucer," *PQ*
3 (1924): 249–252; Aage Brusendorff, *The Chaucer Tradition* (1925; rpt.
Gloucester, Mass.: Peter Smith, 1965), pp. 13–27; and Roger Sherman
Loomis, *A Mirror of Chaucer's World* (Princeton, N. J.: Princeton Univ.
Press, 1965), nos. 1–6.

Figure 5.
The Monk.
Ellesmere ms., fol. 169

grass plot. And he could have made Chaucer smaller. Chalk it up to a slovenly apprentice or an ill-coordinated *atelier* if you like; but the Ellesmere manuscript is a handsome piece of work and the lack of scale could not have been reckoned a serious fault.

A more compatible explanation might fasten upon the artist: it might be thought that he made the horse small and stylized in order to attain a particular effect, that the drawing mitigates the importance of the horse to throw our attention upon the personage. This would be no original stroke on the artist's part, for there are many medieval drawings in which things are out of scale. We could compare a drawing of a wedding (Figure 6) held, like the Wife of Bath's, outside a church door; the church, from any realistic point of view, is scarcely bigger than a doghouse. We must conclude, using another historical sort of interpretation, that this was a "convention" of medieval art. In the Ellesmere drawing, as in the Hoccleve portrait, Chaucer is wearing a *pointel* or stylus around his neck to show he is a writer, which is conventional enough. But here we are again trying to explain why such conventions existed.

My way of "explaining" the drawing would be to say first

Figure 6. Marriage ceremony performed outside a church. Ms. Bodley 264, fol. 105.

that it is as it is. Chaucer the pilgrim is out of scale with his horse. This does not tell us anything exclusively about the pilgrim, about the horse, about the psyche of the artist who made the drawing, about artists in general or the state of art in the early fifteenth century, or about the society. It does not make the drawing primitive, or naive, or abstract, or iconographic. Probably the artist meant the drawing to look this way; probably neither he nor his viewers expected scale or proportion in all drawings. The reason why Chaucer's horse is small is that the artist experienced it this way and could count on others to experience it this way. If you asked him why he made the horse smaller than it "really is," he probably would have looked at you with squinty eyes. He could not have said—any more than we can say why figures in modern line drawings often lack hands or feet, why Orphan Annie has O's for eyes or Charlie Brown a single hair. True, it is a convention, but the convention cannot be understood except as a matter of style, and style expresses experienced reality. The drawing of Chaucer reveals how things seemed to contemporary viewers. Chaucer looks different from the other pilgrims in the Ellesmere drawings, as he does in the poem itself. *They* are fictional characters, real because he makes them so; *he* is a living presence, less real because he is not depicted as they are, yet more real because we engage ourselves directly with him, and with them only through him. The artist has made him part of the pilgrimage by showing him on a horse, but has made him bigger than the reality of the pilgrimage by reducing the horse in size, making it look somewhat unreal. It is a wonderful illustration! The man and poet loom over the fictional pilgrim precisely as in the work itself, one imposed on the other, neither one fully distinguishable from the other. The drawing is like an "optical illusion." Look at it one way and you see a comic figure on an incongruous mount; look at it another way and you see a presence larger than life. Who can doubt that the illustrator knew the poem well?

"Perhaps" (I hear the reader reply) "but can we be sure?" We can't, of course. But we can be as sure of this as of any other explanation, and the advantage is that this finds meaning where others do not. It tries to see the artist's work in its own terms, to assume that he did what he did because at some level of consciousness *he had an idea of it.* He got this idea from the conventions, attitudes, and myths of his culture, and expressed it through them. We have to experience what he experienced before we can explain that idea, but we don't need a "methodology" to do this; we need to see the drawings as the medievals saw them and experience reality as they experienced it. We can never wholly succeed in doing this: not every medieval viewer would have seen the drawings in the same way. Nevertheless, we can in some measure adopt their frame of mind and understand their myths, styles, and conventions without having to remove from our minds those styles or ways of thinking that have developed since. We have to get the hang of it or the feel of it. And once we've done that perhaps we do not need to say very much about it, but if we are going to say anything we need to talk about form, about style, about structure or proportion, about their modes of perception and ours, and, I suppose, about the medieval mind and the modern one. It would not have occurred to any medieval man to talk about any of these things; it would not have been necessary. If we could see it as he saw it we would not say or write anything about it, and perhaps that is our goal. But we seem to have to say and write a great deal to attain that goal, and perhaps in the process we manage to articulate some things with the advantage of hindsight which the artist's contemporaries would not have grasped at all.

Does such an approach, this imaginative and responsive appropriation of the past, really get us inside the unknown artist's mind, help us grasp the "idea" of the drawing? I say it does. I do not say it is an exact science. But neither is any other kind of interpretation. A critic who looks at the drawing and says "The artist botched it" cannot prove he is right; nor can the critic who tells us the horse is a symbol of the corruption of the flesh. The one has his eyes on the craftsman, the other on the church fathers; I have mine on the experience of being alive in those days *and now*. For the drawing after all lives among us: it is reproduced all the time—people think of it when they try to visualize Chaucer probably oftener than they think of the more authentic "Hoccleve" portrait or the more elaborate and elegant drawing of a middle-aged Chaucer reading aloud to the court of King Richard II. It commands our attention; if we think about it we may see that it conveys an idea, an idea with a history.

I do not know any name for such a critical approach when applied to literature, and do not offer one. We might as well call it humanism. It is an application of various methods. It is different from the work of those literary critics who tie analysis to the process of writing, or the "linear" experience of reading, or the historical background alone. Some of my contemporaries, during the time we received our formal education, were unsatisfied with the positivism and formalism of literary study prevalent then; we liked best those studies that saw literature as part of human experience, that explored the relationship between subject and object, the continuity between past and present. Most of us still think that studying literature "objectively" is limiting. When scholars conceive of themselves as being "objective" this very fact colors the tone and direction of what they study and write. So of course does being "subjective," but subjectivity isn't reckoned a virtue. The objective historical existence of a literary work is not very important; when it is read or performed, when it is experienced, when it has an effect, it is important. And we know that effect by discovering it in ourselves better than by observing or calculating it "objectively" in "the text itself" or "the contemporary audience." Responsive readers since Chaucer's time have in common not their "linear" experience of reading a work (ways of reading change) but the experience of recollection which permits them to see the work as a whole when they have read to the end. Not all see the same thing in the same way; but each shares the experience of putting it down and feeling that he then possesses it, that it belongs to his experience of the world, and that the experience makes him know the world and himself better than before. Chaucer, I will argue, introduced this kind of reading experience into English literature; he produced a kind of work which had never been produced before. Nothing quite like it has been produced since. If only we could know what he was thinking, could grasp the *idea* behind that experience and that work.

"Then are you making the outrageous claim that you have seen into the mind of Geoffrey Chaucer?" Well, I am. But I say it isn't so outrageous. We see but darkly into the minds of living people whom we know very intimately, may project ourselves upon them and may but slenderly know ourselves; yet we claim we communicate with them. Critics make the same implicit claim when they get an "insight"—or most do; you hardly ever hear anyone admit the possibility that the author had a vague idea but posterity understood a clear one, and posterity was right. We claim we understand "what the author meant" when we claim to understand his works. We say we should validate such claims by putting them in the realm of historical probability, yet where poetic genius is at work we know the improbable is possible. Besides, in Chaucer criticism it has always been claimed that we know what happened in the author's mind: it has been assumed that his original idea was the simple one he had the Host propose in the General Prologue, and that he did not execute it for want of time or interest or because he changed his mind. My thesis is that he had a far more complex idea and *did* in large measure execute it; and that we can at least in part grasp that idea.

But how? Partly perhaps by studying the history of ideas—by viewing literature as a movement of the ideas which have "affected man's imaginations and emotions and behavior," by viewing literary ideas as "growths from seed scattered by great philosophic systems which themselves, perhaps, have ceased to be," by looking to literature for "the inward thoughts of a generation."[13] Since scholars took an interest in the history of ideas, however, the idea of an idea has changed. In literary study it became clear that you cannot separate a literary idea from the style in which it is expressed, and that you cannot speak of style without speaking of the effect of that style on the reader or audience. This means being subjective enough to follow one's responses and intuitions unabashedly, being (in Leo Spitzer's phrase) "mentalistic." This natural way of understanding literature had been anathematized in America as a heresy, the "affective fallacy"; but those who know what a fallacy is have ignored the anathema and embraced the heresy. This has meant breaking down the traditional barrier between subject and object, inquiring in introspective or in psychological terms what happens *in us* when we experience a work of art. It has meant viewing an idea not as a pellet of intellection but as an event, something that once happened to an author, significant only in so far as it engages our interest, captures our imagination, provokes in us at least vicarious participation.

A literary idea, seen this way, involves the language, customs, institutions, values, and myths shared through a cultural tradition. Even dreams, though we may think of them as altogether individual experiences, contain much that is shared through culture or through universal human nature. If I said that I have set out to analyse *The Canterbury Tales* as if it were a dream I know I would send many readers bustling off murmuring "Freudian." But Chaucer's earliest

13. Arthur O. Lovejoy, *The Great Chain of Being: A Study in the History of an Idea* (1936; rpt. New York: Harper & Row, 1960), pp. 16–17.

poems *were* dream-visions. And not just "conventional" ones—they are powerfully like real dreams. In *The Canterbury Tales* the narrator presents his story as a memory rather than a dream, but the debt of *The Canterbury Tales* to the dream-vision has been established.[14] Poems, even those not presented as dreams or memories, are like dreams, memories, or fantasies in this respect: they happen in our heads, but they mean something in our conscious lives only when we reach the end and hold the whole in remembrance well enough to think and talk about it. We may not remember all the pieces from the signs or codes which have preserved them, but we want to know the whole from as many pieces as we retain. And the whole which was in the author's mind is nowhere now if it is not in ours.

This whole is an idea. The idea of a poem such as *The Canterbury Tales* must seem, like any difficult idea, "nebulous," but I ask the reader to consider the metaphor implicit in the word. How "nebulous" is a cloud? Can't we classify it, see what it is made of, observe its shape, even read a message in it before it passes from our sight? The nebulous quality which we attribute to a cloud is in us, not in the cloud. It might be more somber and "objective" to talk about the *ideas* in *The Canterbury Tales*, but the subject would not accomplish what I mean to accomplish. That is not to say the idea I am looking for isn't really a complex of associated ideas, models, feelings, attitudes; it can only be called *an* idea because the work in which it is embodied is *a* work, has *a* form and structure, is *a* way of organizing experience, is by *an* author, has *an* effect. We must piece the idea together the way we solve a puzzle, by reasoning, guessing, intuiting, by trial and error. The process may be like anatomy or archeology, but the idea is not a dead idea. If it were dead, we would not be reading Chaucer at all.

Some may say that the idea of an "idea" which was in the author's mind and embodied in his work is a modern idea.

14. J. V. Cunningham, "Convention as Structure: The Prologue to the Canterbury Tales," rpt. in *Tradition and Poetic Structure* (Denver, Colo.: Alan Swallow, 1960), pp. 59–75.

"Surely you have taken the romantic, Coleridgean notions about poetic inspiration and 'organic unity' and imposed these upon medieval poetic art." But that is not at all what I have done. Romantic images like the Aeolian harp and the poetic organism are as far from my thoughts as they were from Chaucer's. Rather, I am thinking about the image which medieval theorists had: that of the poet conceiving in his mind or heart an idea, purpose, or archetype, and planning within himself a process of executing this idea comparable to the manner in which a builder builds a house.[15] Art existed in this mental archetype or plan, in the artist's tools, and in the material which received its form from his art. Medieval poets saw themselves as craftsmen who could, like the painter or builder, *make a thing*. In Middle English "make" was used to mean "compose," "thing" sometimes to mean a poem. Behind that thing was an idea which existed in the artist's mind, and it was this which informed what he made.[16] We will see in chapter 4 that Chaucer held such a notion. So the idea we are looking for is one of whose nature and being Chaucer himself had an idea.

15. Edgar De Bruyne, *The Esthetics of the Middle Ages*, trans. Eileen B. Hennessy (New York: Frederick Ungar, 1969), pp. 138–148, 197–209. (I cite this admirable and accessible abridgement, made by the author himself, of his *Études d'esthétique médiévale* [3 vols., Bruges: De Tempel, 1946]; the abridgement is carefully keyed by volume and page to its original.)

16. Erwin Panofsky, *Idea: A Concept in Art Theory*, trans. Joseph J. S. Peake (Columbia, S.C.: Univ. of South Carolina Press, 1968), esp. pp. 35–43.

II

A BOOK ABOUT
THE WORLD

I N THE mid-1380s, probably about 1386-87, Chaucer
completed *Troilus and Criseyde* and turned his attention to *The Canterbury Tales*. For the rest of his life
he gave his major efforts to this work, leaving it unfinished at his death. Except for *The Legend of Good Women*
(whose prologue he revised in the early 1390s) and some
short lyrics, it was, as far as anyone knows, the only poem he
worked on in those years. He completed its beginning (the
General Prologue) and its end (The Parson's Tale and Retraction) but not its middle: there are only twenty-three inter-
vening tales, four unfinished. If Chaucer meant to do what
he has the Host propose—have each pilgrim tell two tales on
each leg of the journey—we have less than a fourth of the
projected work. But if he meant to do what he did—ignore
the return trip and have each pilgrim tell one tale—we have
all but the tales of the Yeoman, Guildsmen, Plowman, and (if
he was meant to tell a tale) the Host.[1] Chaucer put the

1. The notion that Chaucer meant to carry out his plan, show the
pilgrims at Canterbury, and have more tales told on the return trip goes
back to the anonymous fifteenth-century *Tale of Beryn* (ed. F. J. Furnivall
and W. G. Stone, Chaucer Soc., 2nd ser. 17, 24 [London, 1887]). In recent
years the foremost proponent of the return trip has been Charles A.
Owen, Jr., who has parceled out tales for the journey home; see "The Plan
of the Canterbury Pilgrimage," *PMLA* 66 (1950):820–826; "The Develop-

Knight's Tale first and linked most tales one to another; the order of the remaining unlinked tales or groups of tales is not always clear. Still, we have enough of the work to be able to say quite a few things about it. And the first thing we need to say is what kind of work it was meant to be.

There are not, as with modern poets, any journals, notes, letters, or drafts to clarify the poet's idea or its later mutations. We know Chaucer had an "idea" of the work because he suggested one in the General Prologue. This idea doubtless changed somewhat as he wrote.[2] Almost all the real evidence about the work is in the work itself, but I want to examine first some clues which come from outside it. I find only three:

1. Chaucer, apparently referring to *The Canterbury Tales* (in *Troilus*, V, 1786–88), called it "some comedye."

2. Chaucer dedicated the *Troilus* to John Gower (V, 1856–57) and almost certainly alluded to Gower in the Man of Law's Prologue (77–89); in both passages morality is brought up. Contemporary documents show that he and

---

ment of the *Canterbury Tales*," *JEGP* 57 (1958):449–476; and "The Earliest Plan of the *Canterbury Tales*," *MS* 21 (1959):202–210. More recently, conjectures about the two-way journey have been made by Daniel Knapp, "The Relyk of a Seint: A Gloss on Chaucer's Pilgrimage," *ELH* 39 (1972):1–26. Against this dominant view is the more moderate one, that Chaucer ran out of time or got sick or changed his mind—see for example W. H. Clawson, "The Framework of *The Canterbury Tales*," *UTQ* 20 (1951):137–154—or that, as Baum (*Chaucer: A Critical Appreciation*, pp. 11–13) thinks, he lost interest as times changed. To my knowledge, Ralph Baldwin, in *The Unity of the Canterbury Tales*, was the first to suggest that a one-way journey was intended. R. M. Lumiansky, "Chaucer's Retraction and the Degree of Completeness of the *Canterbury Tales*," *Tulane Studies in English* 6 (1956):5–13, shows how, for whatever reason, the plan stated in the work does change.

2. This has been the relentless theme of the "workroom" view, as presented for example in the books by Baum and Williams cited earlier. One could mention scores of books and articles which attempt to trace Chaucer's adaptation of sources, his use of living prototypes for his characters (a search begun by John Matthews Manly, *Some New Light on Chaucer* [New York: Henry Holt, 1926]), and his revisions or slips as they can be second-guessed from extant texts. Evidence of change and revision suggests to some critics that Chaucer was perpetually indecisive, but it can as logically suggest that he took great care to shape an artifice according to a design.

Gower were friends.[3] Gower was working on the *Confessio Amantis* at the same time Chaucer was working on *The Canterbury Tales*, so it is probable that the two poets compared notes. Their two works are similar in plan and kind, though worlds apart in execution.

3. Chaucer appended to *The Canterbury Tales* a retraction in which he revoked those of the tales that "sownen into sinne" (X.1085). In the same sentence he revoked other works, stating the title of each with the formula "The Book of. . . ." He did not apply this formula to *The Canterbury Tales*.

These scraps of evidence can fairly be called "extrinsic." The rest of this chapter will consider what they mean.

Most critics in recent years have eschewed biographical evidence and tried to determine everything from "the text itself." Biographical evidence inferred from the author's works has in particular been reckoned fallacious or heretical. But criticism of "the text itself," especially with older poets, almost always ends appealing to "the background." To explicate a text we must dredge up contemporaneous meanings of words, analogous forms or conventions, iconography, topoi, motifs, even here and there a real live historical event. This kind of "objective" criticism leaves one with the impression that "the background" gets silted into poems by natural erosion, though I doubt any critic believes it. Almost everyone feels or senses an author's unique mind present in and behind his work—not just when, as with Chaucer, we know the canon of his works, but even when we read an

3. Gower on some occasions had Chaucer's power of attorney; see *LR*, pp. 12 note 5, 54, 60. The fullest account of their personal relationship is by John H. Fisher, *John Gower: Moral Philosopher and Friend of Chaucer* (New York: New York Univ. Press, 1964), chaps. 2 and 5. Fisher shows that the legend of a quarrel between the two poets originated with Tyrwhitt and is based on conjectures about the allusion to Gower in the Man of Law's Prologue and the disappearance of a complimentary reference to Chaucer from later versions of the *Confessio Amantis* (pp. 26–28, 116–127); the disappearance of the complimentary reference had originally a political motive and was preserved in later versions by accident. Fisher (pp. 235–250) treats *The Legend of Good Women* as the companion to the *Confessio*, but *The Canterbury Tales* is a frame narrative too and was being written at the same time.

anonymous poem like *Pearl* or *Sir Gawain*. This is not a matter of biography in any narrow sense, for a writer gets some part of what is in his mind from other writers or their works, or from the culture they share. Work, style, and mind are inseparable; we never confront the one without confronting the others.

But to get inside the mind of Geoffrey Chaucer in the mid-1380s, we have to acknowledge the difficulties. These are grave but not insurmountable.

First we have to face the reasons why no real biography of Chaucer has ever been written or can be written. We do not know enough. To have a biography, even a "portrait," we need to know about a man's family and education, his marriage and domestic life, his beliefs, his attitudes, his friends, his work and amusements. With Chaucer we have to throw up our hands in almost all these matters. We know nothing about the personalities of his mother or father or the quality of his home life; we are not sure how many siblings he had, or, if he had a sister Katherine, whether she was younger or older; we do not know for sure where he got his early education, or when his wife died. We know who some of his friends were but do not know how intimate he was with them. We know a fair amount about his employment as a civil servant but can only guess how he viewed this position. We know he wrote poems for the king's court and was under the "patronage" of John of Gaunt, but we do not know the character of these acquaintanceships. From his works we can surmise a great deal about his learning and reading, yet scholars go on arguing about the gravity of his religion and about his tastes in reading or his understanding of what he read. Even the way he conceived of a poet's work or of poetry itself is the subject of a controversy. We get an impression of his personality from his writings, but knowing he was an ironist we cannot fully trust this impression. Any biography of Chaucer, trying to supply this missing evidence, must boggle in literary analysis and social history: we would be back again with the works and their "background."

And then, even if the skeletal idea of *The Canterbury Tales* can be pieced together from a few odd bones, we can never be sure what Chaucer did with it. We know too little about his habits of composition. About half his longer works as they come down to us from fifteenth-century manuscripts are unfinished. But we cannot be sure he left all of them so—his own drafts could have been complete, the endings never revised, or left off in copying. We know he did revise: there are earlier versions of the prologue to *The Legend of Good Women*, of the Knight's Tale, and (some think) of the *Troilus*.[4] We know he changed his mind in some matters: it appears, for example, that the Shipman's Tale was first meant to be told by a woman and the Second Nun's Tale by a man. We even know he had a scribe named Adam who copied, or miscopied, the "Boece" and the *Troilus*, and perhaps other works; from the same short poem addressed to this scribe we learn that Chaucer proofread these copies, rubbing and scraping errors and correcting them. He says he worried about the accurate preservation of his work when copied:[5] he was aware that English was spoken and written variously in various parts of England and that this could result in mistakes of words or meter. It looks as if he set many works aside before completing them or considering them complete: several of the Canterbury tales seem to be works first written in the 1370s,[6] and at least two of the tales

4. Evidence of revision based on manuscripts copied from a presumed earlier version of *Troilus* was presented by Robert Kilburn Root in *The Textual Tradition of Chaucer's Troilus*, Chaucer Soc., 1st ser., 99 (1916; rpt. New York: Johnson rpt., 1967), and in his edition, *The Book of Troilus and Criseyde* (Princeton: Princeton Univ. Press, 1926), pp. xii–xiii, lxx–lxxxi; Root acknowledges his indebtednesses and offers abundant new evidence along with conjectural explanations. Critics have often used this evidence of revision to scrutinize Chaucer's artistry; e.g. Charles A. Owen, Jr., "The Significance of Chaucer's Revisions of *Troilus and Criseyde*," *MP* 55 (1957–1958):1–5. But the evidence is now questioned by specialists in textual criticism who think it can be explained as scribal variants and errors—notably by George Kane in unpublished lectures. A study of the problem is being undertaken by Elizabeth R. Hatcher and Ardath S. McKee.

5. *TC* V:1793–1798. Cf. the remark on "pointing" in *RR* 2157–2161 which is not in the French original.

6. The Knight's Tale and the Second Nun's Tale, it is generally agreed, were written early. This is based on the testimony of *The Legend of Good Women*, F Pro 417–428. The Monk's Tale is usually thought to date from

are unfinished.[7] He evidently worked on several jobs at once: while writing *The Canterbury Tales* he wrote *A Treatise on the Astrolabe*, parts of *The Legend of Good Women*, perhaps other translations and poems. He says he read a great deal, and speaks so lyrically of books that we must believe him; besides, vast reading is revealed in his work.[8] He says he had trouble getting to sleep, but always says this when he is writing a dream-vision, so it is not necessarily factual; and he mentions once (*HF* 658) that he looked "daswed" from reading late into the night, a fact perhaps confirmed by early portraits of him. But we do not know what his handwriting, drafts, or fair copies looked like, or how much revision he normally made in his poems. We are uncertain, and still debate, how much he got his ideas from literary models and how much from life. We know the man almost entirely through his works, and what we learn of him this way is not "extrinsic" evidence in the way Keats's letters or Shelley's drafts are. But then, such evidence, when it *is* available, is almost always used on the assumption that a work can be explained by tracing the process of its composition; and there are better ways of explaining literary works. They only begin, but do not live, in the workroom.

----

the "Italian period" and the stanza on Bernabo (who died in 1385) thought to have been added later. Some think the tales in stanzaic form date from the early eighties, on the assumption that Chaucer gave up writing stanzas after finishing the *Troilus*. Some think the Man of Law's Tale and the Physician's Tale were written earlier because of their similarity to the stories in the *Legend*; but then, Chaucer seems to have continued puttering with the *Legend* during the *Canterbury Tales* period. Some assign the Clerk's Tale to the "Italian period" because of its Italian source. But all these conjectures are based on bromides about Chaucer's development—that he turned from stanzas to couplets, from literary tradition to realism, from pious to secular subjects. It is certain that he reworked some earlier materials for inclusion in *The Canterbury Tales*, but dating his works is guesswork.

7. The Cook's and Squire's tales, though we cannot be absolutely certain Chaucer didn't finish them; the endings might have been lost. *Sir Thopas* and the Monk's Tale are intentionally or avowedly unfinished: the pilgrims interrupt them because they are boring.

8. See R. W. V. Elliott, "Chaucer's Reading," in *Chaucer's Mind and Art*, ed. A. C. Cawley (Edinburgh and London: Oliver & Boyd, 1969), pp. 46–68.

Finally, because *The Canterbury Tales* was not finished, we can never know the idea in its final embodiment. This is a fact. There is no getting around it. It is not, however, such a grave or special problem as it seems. There is much to admire and say about many unfinished works—we read the *Summa theologica* or *The Faerie Queene* without thinking them the less imposing or the more inexplicable. The history—and the esthetics—of unfinished works would furnish an ambitious author with a promising topic. With all works of art there is a sense in which even "finished" ones are unfinished. Henry James in his later years undertook to improve the style of his works; are we to take the earlier published works or the later revised ones as "finished"?[9] The poems of Yeats and Auden, both tireless revisers, present even more complicated difficulties. Anyone who has edited a text, even of a comparatively recent writer, knows that twilight zone where the author's corrections to copy and proofs, or to succeeding printings and editions, shade off into the man-handling of editors, proofreaders, and typesetters. And can we be sure that an author's last-minute alterations represent the final embodiment of his idea? Might they not rather be blunders and losses of nerve made in the last moments of stagefright? Might not a work get finished out of impatience to "slay the beast" (as Winston Churchill put it) "and fling it abroad to the public"? The unfinished character of *The Canterbury Tales* is a more dramatic instance of the imperfect character of art, but the problems it raises are not of a different order: "Between the conception and the creation. . . . Falls the shadow."

When I talk about the unfinished character of *The Canterbury Tales* I have in mind the handful of missing and unfinished tales, some possible missing links between tales, and a few passages which might seem to call for revision. I do not have in mind another tale for each pilgrim on the way to Canterbury and two more for each on the return. By the time the Host is ready for the Franklin he is saying that each must "tellen atte lest / A tale or two" (V:697f.), and

9. Cf. James Thorpe, *Principles of Textual Criticism* (San Marino, Calif.: Huntington Library, 1972), pp. 42–45.

outside Canterbury he declares "Now lacketh us no tales mo than oon" (X:16). This is generally taken to mean that Chaucer changed his idea of the plan; yet it is the Host whose idea changes. What Chaucer's idea was *at first* we cannot know. Perhaps he meant to identify it with the Host's suggested plan in the General Prologue; if so, he ended up revealing a grandiose plan unfulfilled and his own control unsustained, which could be Chaucerian self-humor. The *fact* stated in the Parson's Prologue as the pilgrims approach their destination is, only one tale remains to be told.

With all this talk just outside Canterbury about knitting things up and making an end, one assumes the work is over. Here there are strong reasons for saying that Chaucer, far from having "changed his mind," never had any idea of depicting the return journey. The one-way "pilgrimage of human life" was a conventional metaphor and topos, and would have been an effective frame for the work. Still, what he wrote is not an allegory like the *Pèlerinage de la vie humaine* but a fictional account of a real pilgrimage. He chose to treat not the allegorical pilgrimage to the heavenly Jerusalem, nor the great pilgrimage (of which all others were mere types or imitations) to the Holy Land, but the familiar national pilgrimage to Canterbury. Moreover, he chose to depict the pilgrims busy with the very activity against which moralists always cautioned pilgrims: *curiositas*.[10] He depicted a tale-telling game, squabbles, practical jokes, "quitting" (getting even with), bawdry. Emphasis falls on the amusement of the trip.

This may seem like an original stroke on Chaucer's part. The pilgrimage setting and the way tales characterize their tellers make *The Canterbury Tales* unlike the *Decameron* or Sercambi's *Novelle* (which, incidentally, did not depict a pilgrimage).[11] Yet there was another tradition of writings

10. In what I say about *curiositas* I am heavily indebted to Christian K. Zacher for providing me with a copy of the manuscript of his study *Curiosity and Pilgrimage: The Literature of Discovery in Fourteenth-Century England*, forthcoming from the Johns Hopkins Univ. Press.
11. Pratt and Young (*SA* p. 32) refer to the "pilgrimage framework of the *Novelliero*," written ca. 1374 and now lost. Chaucer might have heard

against which *The Canterbury Tales* is never compared—the large number of guidebooks and realistic prose accounts of the Jerusalem pilgrimage.[12] But even those which focus on sightseeing and curiosity do not ever depict the return journey. Probably the first author who found any intrinsic interest in the return and the homecoming was Friar Felix Fabri, who wrote his long account in the 1480s. The first

---

about it or seen it in Lucca or Milan in 1373 or 1378 (*SA* p. 31f.). There are two accounts of the lost manuscript but neither says anything about a pilgrimage; one (*SA* p. 29) calls it "un viaggio per la Toscana." The later *Novelle* is assuredly not a pilgrimage: it has no shrine as its destination (nor even a destination) and does not have a religious purpose. The purpose is to escape the plague, as in the *Decameron*, and the trip is a tour, what the Italians now call a *giro*. They make a circle down the west coast of Italy, up the east coast, and through the north. They stop at interesting places, only some of which are shrines. Aluizi reminds the company that they should think to their souls as well as their bodies and do "nessuna dizonesta cosa tra noi nè tra altri"; they reply that they will behave with such *honestà* "che la mogle col marito nè con altri uzerà" (*SA* pp. 38–39), which I take for a joke. The journey is never called a pilgrimage and has nothing in common with accounts of pilgrimages. The incomplete manuscript ends with the company nearing Lucca, where they started.

12. There are 526 known accounts written between 1100 and 1500; see Reinhold Röhricht, *Bibliotheca geographica Palaestinae: Chronologisches Verzeichnis der von 333 bis 1878 verfasster Literatur über das Heilige Land mit dem Versuch einer Kartographie* (1890; rpt. Jerusalem: Universitas Booksellers, 1963). For the suggestion of studying these prose narratives as background to *The Canterbury Tales* I am indebted to Morton W. Bloomfield, "Authenticating Realism and the Realism of Chaucer," *Thought* 39 (1964): 348; rpt. in *Essays and Explorations*, see p. 188. It would make a long digression to present the results of my studies here, and it would be evidence about what the writers *didn't* write; I will publish it elsewhere when I can say without digressing what the writers *did* write.

Edmund Reiss, in "The Pilgrimage Narrative and the *Canterbury Tales*," *SP* 67 (1970):295–305, notes that *The Canterbury Tales* was "much influenced by the narrative tradition of the pilgrimage" but that it "makes concrete the usual allegorical figures of the pilgrimage . . . , giving them dramatic and worldly relevance by putting them in realistic garb and having them meet on a worldly stage" (299). By "narrative tradition" he means allegories and dream-visions; he does not mention factual itineraries and memoirs of pilgrimages. This metaphoric or "allegorical" aspect of the pilgrimage is amply documented by Charles P. R. Tisdale, *The Medieval Pilgrimage and Its Use in* The Canterbury Tales, Diss. Princeton, 1970, esp. chaps. 2 and 3, and by F. C. Gardiner, *The Pilgrimage of Desire: A Study of Theme and Genre in Medieval Literature*, esp. chap. 1. But one would never know from reading any of these authors that medieval men actually packed up and went on pilgrimages.

fictional account of a pilgrimage—like Chaucer's, drawn from books—was *Mandeville's Travels* (1356), a work widely read in Chaucer's time which I believe Chaucer knew; but even Mandeville does no more than mention the return journey. Some accounts do not even do that. In fact the custom was to declare the Jerusalem pilgrimage finished at the destination. The pilgrims, those who had survived the perilous journey, often went their separate ways rather than return as a group. We must conclude that medieval pilgrims conceived of and experienced a pilgrimage as a one-way journey; the return was a mere contingency. This was not a metaphor or topos, but the source of the metaphor and topos: it was their *idea* of a pilgrimage.

That idea of a pilgrimage is part of the idea of *The Canterbury Tales*. Of course Chaucer might have meant to depart from this tradition of travel writings and this habitual way of experiencing a pilgrimage, but the weight of evidence is against it. All the other parts of the Host's plan are violated too; neither narrator nor poet ever suggests he anticipates more tales on the return; and the Parson's Prologue outside Canterbury says the end is there. The pilgrimage, so conceived as a one-way journey, gave *The Canterbury Tales* an over-all unity, a "frame." It is a work, not "works"—disjointed, various, unaccountable, it still has a consistency of tone, of style, of tact, of mind. This conception and these arrangements were immanent in medieval culture and convention; they are preserved in the text of the work; but they *happened* in the mind of Geoffrey Chaucer in the 1380s and 1390s. If at some point during those years Chaucer had a bright vision, what he left us are shadows on the wall of a cave. But we will have to contemplate these, for they are all we have.

THE CANTERBURY TALES AS A COMEDY

At the end of the *Troilus* Chaucer promised a future work:

> Go litel book, go, litel myn tragedye,
> Ther God thy makere yet, ere that he die,
> So sende might to make in some comedye.
>
> (V:1786–1788)

This is surely a reference to *The Canterbury Tales*. The only other possibility would be a work he wrote which has not survived or one he planned but did not write. He could not have meant *The Legend of Good Women*, for he would have called it, as he did, by the generic term legend; besides, its subject matter is far from comedy as Chaucer would have understood the term.[13] *The Book of the Lion* which he mentions in the Retraction—if indeed he wrote it and if it was, as is generally thought, an adaptation of Machaut's *Dit dou Lyon*—could not be called a comedy. So if we knew what Chaucer meant by "comedy" we would know something important about *The Canterbury Tales*. It is, by the way, the only time he ever used the word.

The passage sets "comedye" against "tragedye" with such emphatic parallelism as to suggest they are opposites, and that was the medieval view. There was, after all, no classic form of medieval comedy, as there was of tragedy. To know what tragedy meant one can examine collections of *de casibus* narratives and even quote the definition Chaucer put in the mouth of the Monk; since Chaucer knew this definition of tragedy, he likely knew the traditional definition of its opposite. That of Evanthius (who died ca. 359) was quoted in editions of Terence and used in glosses and encyclopedias, and Professor Cunliffe points especially to the influence of this sentence:

> Inter tragoediam autem et comoediam cum multa tum inprimis hoc distat, quod in comoedia mediocres fortunae hominum, parui impetus periculorum laetique sunt exitus actionum, at in tragoedia omnia contra, ingentes personae, magni timores, exitus funesti habentur; et illic prima turbulenta,

13. It is true that Chaucer has just finished an allusion to *The Legend of Good Women*: "And gladlier I wol write, yif you leste, / Penelopees trouthe and good Alceste" (1777–1778). The stanza which follows, addressed to women, amusingly warns them against men's falseness. But the *Legend* is a collection of stories that end unhappily. It sounds as though he had already been assigned, probably by the queen in an ironic spirit, to write the *Legend*, and that he already had *The Canterbury Tales* in mind. Possibly at the time he wrote the lines he had in mind the earlier version of the Knight's Tale, drawn like the *Troilus* from Boccaccio and having a happy ending, as his proposed comedy; but then this was to become a key element of *The Canterbury Tales*.

tranquilla ultima, in tragoedia contrario ordine res aguntur; tum quod in tragoedia fugienda uita, in comoedia capessenda exprimitur; postremo quod omnis comoedia de fictis est argumentis, tragoedia saepe de historia (sic) fide petitur.[14]

[Between tragedy and comedy there is, among other things, this principal difference, that in comedy there are insignificant fortunes of men, small forces of danger, and happy outcomes of actions; but in tragedy everything is the contrary—there are great personages, momentous fears, and disastrous outcomes. In comedy things begin in turbulence and end in tranquillity; in tragedy things happen in the opposite way. Furthermore in tragedy the type of life to be avoided is represented, in comedy the type of life to be espoused. Finally, every comedy is about subjects which are invented, whereas tragedy is often taken from actual history.]

Here tragedy deals with significant "fortunes" of great men faced with great dangers, begins in tranquillity and ends in turbulence, treats historical subjects, and depicts a life to be fled. The *Troilus* fits this definition of tragedy nicely: it deals with significant fortunes (the Fall of Troy), involves great dangers and important figures, ends in disaster, and is taken from history. It does, to be sure, depict a "type of life to be espoused" in Book III; but it shows that life dissipate into a miserable one which the hero does indeed seek to flee. Troilus's laughter on the eighth sphere does suggest a kind of tranquillity; but the dominant movement rather than the ending itself is what the definition fastens upon, and Chaucer saw the dominant movement of the whole as "Fro woe to wele and after out of joye" (I:4) according to the movement of Fortune's wheel, a tragic rather than a comic movement.

If the *Troilus* (which Chaucer called a tragedy) fits the old definition, one might expect *The Canterbury Tales* (which Chaucer called a comedy) to fit it too. *The Canterbury Tales* deals with less significant fortunes: pilgrims gather in an inn and tell tales as they ride, and most (but not all) tales treat

14. John William Cunliffe, *Early English Classical Tragedies* (Oxford: Clarendon Press, 1912), pp. x–xi; translation mine. Cf. Wilhelm Cloetta, *Beiträge zur Litteraturgeschichte des Mittelalters und der Renaissance* I [Komödie und Tragödie im Mittelalter] (Halle: Max Niemeyer, 1890), esp. 14–46.

ordinary affairs of ordinary men. The pilgrims are from all walks of life, but most are from the "commons" and none from the rank of princes.[15] It begins in a sort of turbulence and ends with the Parson's words which may be thought tranquil. It treats for the most part invented subjects, though the author claims the pilgrimage really took place and the pilgrims often claim their stories really happened—a not unusual claim for storytellers. Whether it depicts "the type of life to be espoused" depends on the meaning of that phrase. Tragedy depicted a life falling into misery, a life to be fled, and so one to be held in contempt; comedy depicted its opposite. Perhaps *capessenda* here has a neutral connotation—not "enjoyed" or even "espoused" but only "entered into" or "taken up"; however you translate it, it refers to espousal of the world rather than contempt of it.[16] And surely the initial concerns of *The Canterbury Tales* are worldly—the pilgrimage as it starts out at the Tabard is very much of this world and so are most of the tales. The work contains pathetic tales and tragedies, but the whole does not seem pathetic or tragic. Finally, the definition seems to suggest a distinction of social class. In tragedy the personages are *ingentes*; in comedy men's fortunes are *mediocres*. The mention of fortunes suggests the fickle goddess and her wheel, which involved a movement toward and then away from

15. The Knight is not an exception. Despite some attempts to connect him with Henry, Duke of Lancaster or John of Gaunt, everything in the description of him suggests he is a lesser noble, a "soldier of fortune." If he were from among the "royals" he would have more of a retinue than just his son and servant. There is a sprinkling of royals in the pilgrim's tales (Theseus, figures in the Monk's "tragedies") and some baronial noblemen of high estate like the Marquis Walter. Even with these we are concerned with domestic or private cares rather than with public ones.

16. The entrenched notion that "comedy" has to do with espousal of the world may explain the absence of a set form of comedy during the Middle Ages. There was scarcely any explicit defense of espousing the world (as there was of contempt for the world) until the end of the fourteenth century. Many comic works or works with happy endings which would have fitted the traditional definition were not called comedies. For earlier uses of the term, see Cloetta, pp. 68–109. It might be added that the notion of a performance managed to cling to the two terms even when they were not used of plays, a fact applicable to *The Canterbury Tales*.

"high estate."[17] That men's fortunes in comedy are *mediocres* could mean we are turning our attention to the domestic and private cares of nobles rather than to their more significant public cares; but it probably means we are turning our attention to the lower classes who do not properly *have* public cares. The *Troilus* is about great nobles but about their private cares; *The Canterbury Tales* is chiefly about ranks of society beneath that of great nobles, and chiefly about private cares.

The *Canterbury Tales* squares with this medieval definition of comedy enough to convince me that Chaucer initially thought of it as that kind of work and said so at the end of the *Troilus*; but at this stage it was doubtless a vague idea— ask any author to describe the book he is going to write and you will get a lot of hemming and hawing. This vagueness is expressed by the phrase "some comedye." "Some" used with a singular noun can mean "one or another" (as in "lest they diden some follye," *LGW* 723) or "a quantity of" (as in "some mirth or some doctrine" CT VII: 935), or "a kind of" (as in "ye han some glymsyng" Merch. T 2383), or "a certain" (as in "of some contree / That shall not now be told for me" *HF* 2135–2136). These usages are on occasion hard to differentiate—when Pertelote recommends "some laxatif" she might mean any of them; when the Pardoner promises "some moral thing" he could mean "a certain" or "a kind of," but the other uses do not fit. At times, though, the sense can be narrowed: in the Miller's Tale, "In some woodness or in some agony" (3452) must mean "a kind of" because the speaker's casting about among various terms rules out the chance of a delimited notion in the speaker's mind, which the other uses seem to imply. "Some" was, and still is, a convenient obfuscating word. In the present line Chaucer meant either (1) a certain comedy already in mind which he would not reveal, or (2) a kind of comedy, something like or in the nature of a comedy, which he had not yet clearly

17. On the form of tragedy so conceived, see Willard Farnham, *The Medieval Heritage of Elizabethan Tragedy* (1936; rpt. Oxford: Basil Blackwell, 1956).

framed. The line tells us he had chosen a genre, but it obscures the specific matter or form.

"To make in some comedy" is a puzzling phrase, and it is still more puzzling that editors have not commented on it. Why "in"? Possibly it means "with respect to" (as when we say "succeed in business") or "in the realm of" (as when scholarly foundations announce awards for "creative writing in poetry"). The line could be paraphrased imaginatively "to compose in the manner (or, genre) of a certain (kind of) comedy." Skeat paraphrased it "to take part in composing some 'comedy.'" I do not find that Chaucer used "in" this way anywhere else with "make," and rarely with any other verb.[18] These difficulties have led one commentator to suggest that "make" is an early instance of its use in the old sense "to match";[19] Professor Robinson, abandoning his usual caution, accepted this suggestion. The lines would then mean "wherefore may God yet send your author the power, before he die, to match (it) in some comedy" or "to do equally well in some comedy." But "make" in this sense was a rare usage recorded only in the late fifteenth and early sixteenth centuries, and Chaucer used it nowhere else. These troubles could be erased if the line read "to maken some comedye," and this reading, which occurs in one manuscript, was nervously offered by Skeat in his textual notes with a question mark. The usual reading, "make in," is a more vague (or cautious) utterance: it is one thing to say you will write a comedy and another to say you will write in the *realm* of comedy.

There is a reason why Chaucer might have preferred the more cautious utterance: "comedy" suggests Dante's *Commedia*. We must therefore ask whether in 1386–1387 Chaucer had in mind a poetic conception comparable to Dante's.

18. He seems to use it with "seyn" in *TC* I:396–397: "I dare well seyn, in all that Troilus / Seyde in his song, loo! every word . . ." but here "seyn" has a direct object. "Make *on* some comedye" would be a possible emendation: cf. *LGW* F Pro 579—"right thus on my Legende gan I make." But "in" in this sense is attested.

19. Richard C. Boys, "An Unusual Meaning of 'Make' in Chaucer," *MLN* 52 (1937):351–353. See Robinson's note.

Chaucer had read the *Commedia*, and it is possible he had read as well the letter to Can Grande in which "comedy" is defined. The definition does not add much to Evanthius's: it repeats the notion that comedy begins in harshness and ends happily, but does not mention the stature of the personages, the gravity of their fears, or the kind of life depicted, and does not say whether its matter is invented or historical. It adds a fanciful etymology after the medieval fashion (*comus*, village, and *oda*, song; hence village song) without explaining what assistance this bit of intellection has to offer. It also adds a detail very pertinent to Chaucer—that the fashion of the speech in this comedy is "meek and humble, being the vulgar tongue" and that even females communicate in it. One thinks at once of the Reeve's dialect or the Wife of Bath's monologue.

That Chaucer could have received much edification from Dante's letter seems dubious, but from the *Commedia* itself he received, or so it is usually thought, the most startling impression. It was Dante's use of the word *Commedia* as the title of his masterpiece, rather than his definition of it, which would have given it some ring of awe when it fell from Chaucer's tongue. But here again we stumble into the thicket of our ignorance. We know Chaucer made two, and perhaps three, journeys to Italy. The doubtful one was in 1368 when he left the country long enough and with enough money to get to Italy; but there is no evidence where he went and no suggestion of Italian influence on his work. He would have been about twenty-five.[20] On December 1, 1372, he did go to Italy—we have documentary evidence of this—returning on May 23, 1373; he was then about twenty-nine. He spent a bit more than three months there, at Genoa (where his business was probably to negotiate the use of an English port by the Genoese) and at Florence. His reason for going to Florence is not known, but—for whatever reason he went—he would have returned with literary rewards and, very likely, an armload of books: there was an active cult of Dantisti there even then, it was the native town of Boccaccio,

20. *LR*, pp. 29–30. On the date of Chaucer's birth, see *LR*, pp. 370–374.

and it was a great cultural center.[21] From this trip scholars have always dated an Italian influence upon Chaucer's writings and so an "Italian period." The influence shows up first in *The House of Fame*; the "period" fades into the larger scope of his later works. In 1378 he went abroad from May to September, this time to Lombardy for perhaps a month's stay, probably on matters touching the war with France.[22] He was then about thirty-five.

Italy did make its mark on the young poet. There are indisputable influences and borrowings from Dante. And he was much taken with Boccaccio and Petrarch. True, he altered what he found in the great Tuscans. The *Troilus* and the Knight's Tale are brought within French traditions—are "medievalized," in C. S. Lewis's phrase, and have as much in common with the *Roman de la Rose* as with the *Filostrato* or the *Teseida*. That he knew, or knew about, the *Decameron* is more probable than was once thought, and its similarity to *The Canterbury Tales* has not escaped notice—though there are differences too. Where Chaucer imitated (rather than revised) Boccaccio was in the "collections"—in the Monk's Tale, an English counterpart to *De casibus virorum illustrum*, and in *The Legend of Good Women*, an English counterpart to *De claris mulieribus*.[23] In these he was imitating the grave, the scholarly Boccaccio—that later, reformed Boccaccio who was to be praised in the next century as a man learned in divine and humane letters who had "also written one hundred stories in the vulgar tongue."[24] And even toward them we find an ironic and humorous skepticism. In *The Legend of Good Women* we hear the poet's voice groaning under the

21. *LR*, pp. 32–40.
22. *LR*, pp. 53–61.
23. *De casibus* was written 1355–1374; Chaucer used it only slightly as a source (see *SA*, p. 616) but obviously knew about it. He may have thought it was by Petrarch (see MkT 2325). But the idea of writing such a work was distinctly Italian. *De claris mulieribus*, written 1360–1374, is the source of the story of Zenobia in the Monk's Tale (see *SA*, p. 632). The *Decameron* was completed in 1358 and cannot be disqualified as a possible source; Chaucer could easily have known about it and could have seen a copy on any of his trips to Italy.
24. Johannes Tritheim (Johannes Trithemius), *Catalogus scriptorum ecclesiasticorum. . . .* (Cologne: Petrum Quentell, 1531).

burden of condensing the "legends";[25] the hapless Monk has to be stopped in his "tragedies" and charged with dullness.

To talk about this Italian influence on Chaucer we must remove from our minds our own enthusiasms—for the Renaissance, for humanism, for the bawdy younger Boccaccio, for the "dawning" and the vivacity we are accustomed to see there—and try to imagine Chaucer's actual experience of Italy. If we had even a single letter, even a sentence or two of explicit comment from him, it might offer us a clue. The best we have are these lines, which the Clerk speaks in his Prologue:

> I wol you tell a tale which that I
> Lerned at Padwe of a worthy clerk,
> As preved by his wordes and his werk.
> He is now deed and nailed in his cheste,
> I pray to God so yeve his soule reste!
> Fraunceys Petrak, the lauriat poete,
> Highte this clerk, whose rhetorike sweete
> Enlumined all Itaille of poetrie,
> As Linian dide of philosophie,
> Or law, or other art particuler;
> But deeth, that wol nat suffre us dwellen heer,
> But as it were a twinkling of an eye,
> Hem both hath slain, and alle shul we die.
>
>   (IV:26–38)

In the General Prologue Chaucer presented the Clerk as an admirable young man, and it is reasonable to assume that he shared the feeling expressed here. If so, what this scrap points to is an admiration for the learning, the scholarship, the bookishness of the Italians, for the names of the great men themselves, for their poetry and rhetoric, for science, and for law. He shared the spirit of early humanism in its

25. I have in mind passages like 702–705, 2456–2457, or 2559–2561. It is a tradition going back to Lounsbury, and preserved by Robert Kilburn Root, *The Poetry of Chaucer* (Boston and New York: Houghton, Mifflin, 1906), pp. 145–146, that such passages of humor or exaggeration show that Chaucer grew bored with the task. It can as easily be explained as characteristic self-scrutinizing irony, or as courtly wit, directed at himself and at the task assigned. See E. T. Donaldson, *Chaucer's Poetry*, pp. 956–959. On Chaucer's purported boredom see Robert Worth Frank, Jr., *Chaucer and* The Legend of Good Women (Cambridge, Mass.: Harvard Univ. Press, 1972), esp. pp. 189–210.

essential form, which was an enthusiasm for books. The most important Italian influence on Chaucer was upon his reading: beginning with his "Italian period" we discover in him an interest in classical literature. He likes to mention the works and names of classical authors, and it is clear he read them. The humanists parted company with him, though, when they edited ancient texts or imitated Cicero's Latin; by way of such scholarship he chose works to translate or adapt, and chose medieval ones. Still, in other ways the Italian humanists were more medieval than he—they wrote in Latin, they were dreadfully bookish, and they were (as the Italians say) *molto della chiesa*. What marks them as humanists is their fads—vernacular poetry, the love of learning, the discovery and preservation of ancient texts, accurate hand-writing. All this we do find in Chaucer: he wrote *only* in the vernacular; translated what he thought were important Latin works; was steeped in book learning; scolded his scribe for copying badly and begged copyists to take care.

Beyond this scholarly bent, the Italian humanists were given to notions of idealized love and to aspirations for fame. In this they were emulating the fashions of aristocrats, for they were, like Chaucer, from the "middle class"—Petrarch the illegitimate son of a notary, Boccaccio a moneylender's son. Courtly love and the writing of love poems had been an aristocratic accomplishment for two centuries; and the love of fame, the "glory" of a good name which conferred an earthly immortality, had been a major preoccupation of knights since early feudal times. The humanists claimed a right to these aristocratic interests for their nobility of mind, their *virtù*, rather than for inherited family ties, and it is hard to escape a suspicion of class consciousness among their motives. In Chaucer, we find an interest in idealized love—he was indeed the poet of love in his youth—but he views it with irony, with self-humor about his own "unlikeliness," and, in the *Troilus*, with the noble dubiety of a religious and philosophical perspective. So with fame: in *The House of Fame* we see him preoccupied with the idea of reputation, but he views fame in medieval fashion as a thing made of hot air, bestowed capriciously. At the end of the *Troilus* he hopes modestly for fame, but nowhere in his works claims to have made a monument more perdurable than bronze or to have bestowed fame on others. He always dons the mask of a modest, useful fellow quite without pretensions—a humorous exaggeration, of course. We never find him, though, proclaiming a noble passion for a highborn lady as Boccaccio and Petrarch did,[26] or hoping for fame except with conventional medieval modesty.

Chaucer caught the spirit of incipient Italian humanism, liked it, and shared many of its interests; but he was conservative in following its fads, viewed them with ironic disinterestedness, humor, and tolerant skepticism. He was never really interested in Italian literary *forms* like the sonnet or the "renaissance epic"; where he used them he made them palatable to English or French ears. The matter is important because Italian literary circles of the fourteenth century, the circles in which we find the beginnings of Renaissance humanism, doted upon Dante. Can it be that Chaucer viewed Dante as he did the other enthusiasms of the Italian *literati*, with irony, with skeptical good will, with amused English detachment?

It is not a palatable notion. We, if we read Dante at all, can never read him without astonishment and reverence, and an earlier generation of scholars projected this fact upon Chaucer, very reasonably. Surely he would have admired the magnificent conception of Dante's *Commedia*, its vast learning, and its poetic excellence. We catch in his work enough echoes of Dante to know he read the *Commedia* with care, whether or not he read Italian well. But we forget that he would not have come to the *Commedia*, as we do, with a running directory of medieval Florentines at the bottom of the page. The contemporary and parochial references in the *Commedia* are something every reader has to come to grips with, and I have heard respected Dantisti recommend they be ignored. But they are easier to ignore when we know we *can* identify names if we choose to. For Chaucer, it would

26. Despite the contention of Margaret Galway, "Chaucer's Hopeless Love," *MLN* 60 (1945):431–439, that Joan of Kent was his poetical lady; the references are covert and the evidence tenuous.

have been a puzzle to find names of the poet's enemies mixed in Hell among the ancients, and one can imagine his curiosity turning to amusement as he saw what Dante was doing. He might well have fancied similar treatment for a few Londoners. Exactly such an interest in one's surroundings, in one's contemporaries and in one's own city, was an interest Chaucer shared with Dante. But Chaucer had a different temperament and a different experience of life. Dante was a disillusioned idealist; he was bitter, and an exile. Chaucer, though not without idealism, adopted an ironic view of the world; and, far from being an exile, he was a dutiful member of the establishment. Dante in exile looked at his contemporaries and saw the meaning of their lives from the viewpoint of eternity; Chaucer looked at his contemporaries close at hand with a certain even-tempered detachment. Dante's *Commedia* and Chaucer's "comedy" are miles apart in this respect, and almost the moment in Chaucer's early poetry where that parting took place, and the way it took place, have been isolated by Professor Fisher in a passage which I can do no better than to quote in full:

> Dante had responded to . . . artistic dissatisfaction with his early lyrics by spiritualizing courtly love in the *Vita Nuova* and *Divine Comedy*. Chaucer acknowledged this solution [in *The House of Fame*] by having Geffrey rescued from his wasteland in perhaps the noblest and most genuinely sympathetic echoes of Dante in all his poetry. "O Christ!" he prays, "Fro fantome and illusion / Me save" (492). Suddenly above him appears the eagle that had carried Dante's body to the first terrace of Purgatory: "In dream I seemed to see an eagle with feathers of gold poised in the sky, with its wings spread, and intent to stoop. And I seemed to be there where his own people were abandoned by Ganymede, when he was rapt to the supreme consistory" (*Purgatorio* IX:18). This image is fused with that of Beatrice gazing at the sun: "I saw Beatrice turned to her left side and gazing upon the sun: never did an eagle so fix himself upon it. [Inspired by her example] I fixed my eyes upon the sun beyond our wont. . . . Not long did I endure it, nor so little that I did not see it sparkle round about, like iron that issues boiling from the fire. And on a sudden, day seemed added to day, as if He who has the power had adorned the

heaven with another sun" (*Paradiso* I:45). In this context,
Chaucer's dreamer becomes aware:

> That faste be the sonne, as hye
> As kenne myghte I with my yë,
> Me thoughte I saugh an eagle sore,
> But that hit semed moche more
> Then I had any egle seyn.
> But this is sooth as deth, certeyn,
> Hyt was of gold, and shon so bryghte
> That never sawe men such a syghte,
> But yf the heven had ywonne
> Al newe of gold another sonne.
>
> (497)

Had Chaucer been able to sustain this note, he would have
been a different poet. But we prefer to have him Chaucer,
as he evidently preferred to be, for in the first ten lines of
Book II, he rejected the mystical way out of the wasteland,
employing the homely touches and incongruities of sound and
situation of which he was already such a master to reduce
Dante's divine bird to the slightly ridiculous, very human mentor who spoke, "In mannes vois, and seyde, 'Awak!' "[27]

There we see Chaucer's withdrawal from Dante. True,
The House of Fame shows the influence of the *Commedia*; but
the eagle borrowed from it is a funny eagle, the visit to a
world beyond is a comic visit, and that world is an absurd
world. It is not meant to discredit Dante—the highest praise
one can give an author is to parody him, so the maxim goes.
But it reflects one side of Chaucer's response to Dante. The
other side, which we encounter only at the end of the *Troilus*,
is serious: in its noble ending there are unmistakable echoes
of the *Commedia*. But that is almost the only place in Chaucer

27. Fisher, *John Gower*, pp. 210–211. For a quite similar view indepen-
dently arrived at and using a different passage from *The House of Fame*, see
Gabriel Josipovici, *The World and the Book: A Study of Modern Fiction*
(Stanford, Calif.: Stanford Univ. Press, 1971), pp. 52–55. See also Paul G.
Ruggiers, "The Italian Influence on Chaucer," in *Companion to Chaucer
Studies*, ed. Beryl Rowland (Toronto, New York, London: Oxford Univ.
Press, 1968), pp. 139–161, a detailed account with abundant references
and an emphasis different from the one presented here. And see Kean,
Chaucer and the Making of English Poetry, I:88–92.

where eschatological matters are raised.[28] Chaucer mentions Dante in five places,[29] never without reverence and twice in the same breath with Vergil. It may amuse us that the Wife of Bath has the hag in her tale quote Dante's *Convivio*,[30] but the incongruity strikes us this way precisely because Dante's sentiments are so elevated. When we call Dante the poet of the secular world, we mean that he saw that world bound in the *saeculum*, an historical age which would end and be subsumed in eternity—"an earthly reality preserved in transcendence, in a perfection decreed by divine judgment."[31] Chaucer was no less a poet of the secular world, but he fastened attention on the *saeculum* as it is known to us in this life; what lies beyond it, its ultimate reality, he does not explore. Between man's life in the secular world and the vast hierarchical design of eternity lie those acts of the human will which determine whether a man be saved or damned. In the secular world, the way to the eternal one is penance, and Chaucer fastens upon penance as the subject of the Parson's address at the end; a pilgrimage itself was, officially, a penitential act.[32] Beyond

28. See Robinson's notes on *TC* V: 1807–1827 and 1863–1865. *The House of Fame* (perhaps) and the death of Arcite in the Knight's Tale are eschatological matters, but these are both humorous passages. In KnT 2809–2814 Chaucer specifically, and I think comically, denies any knowledge of what happens to a soul after death. It may be allowed that *An ABC*, which Chaucer translated from Deguilleville in the 1360s, treats eschatology.

29. *HF* 450; *LGW* F Pro 360; MkT 2461; WBT 1126–1127; FrT 1520.

30. WBT 1125ff.; see Robinson's note.

31. Erich Auerbach, *Dante, Poet of the Secular World*, trans. Ralph Manheim (Chicago: Univ. of Chicago Press, 1961), p. 63; the notion is developed esp. in chap. 3. A similar insight made from a quite different frame of reference is Charles Singleton's characterization of the poem itself: "A human poem is thus by analogy participating in a divine poem, can be seen to be made in its image. In so doing, a poem does what all created things do in a Christian universe, a poem participates in true existence, in Being." See *Dante Studies* I: "Commedia: Elements of Structure" (Cambridge, Mass.: Harvard Univ. Press, 1954), p. 59, and pp. 77–78 for some remarks on the reality and importance of history in the poem.

32. See Sidney H. Heath, *Pilgrim Life in the Middle Ages* (London, 1911), rpt. and enlarged as *In the Steps of the Pilgrims* (London: Rich and Dowan, 1950), pp. 22, 251–262. On penance and indulgences see Donald J. Hall,

penance, this worldly means to eternal grace, Chaucer does not venture. Dante saw the secular world approaching its ultimate perfect state when it would be ordered for all eternity. Purgatory and Earth are transient, Heaven and Hell eternal. Chaucer limited his view to Earth, to the world of disorder, temporality, memory, and story.

When Chaucer announced that he would write a comedy, he meant, then, a work notably different from the tragedy of *Troilus*, one which would deal with ordinary men, with everyday cares, and with story rather than history. It would treat a life to be espoused and so treat the problem of living aright in the world. With Dante's poem it had in common a concern with the secular world and a movement from turbulence to tranquillity. He arrested the idea of his work upon that element in *The Divine Comedy* which looks backward to the experience of secular life; if we could extrapolate from Dante the characters who were his contemporaries, the stories people told him, his memories, his observations, his concern for politics and ethics, we would have the stuff of *The Canterbury Tales*—but it would certainly not be *The Divine Comedy*. When Chaucer announced "some comedye," he must have had in mind this limitation to the experienced world of memory and story. There is not a scrap of evidence that he had any notion of treating things eschatological or arranging things in a symmetrical design; there is abundant evidence that his interests and gifts narrowed upon the experienced world. There is evidence, too, that he had among his drafts during the years he worked on *The Canterbury Tales* serious Christian works which focused not on eschatology or spirituality, but on the world itself, on the way a Christian must come to terms with the world—works like Pope Innocent III's "Wrecched Engendring of Mankind,"[33] the life of St. Cecilia (which was to become the Second Nun's Tale),

English *Mediaeval Pilgrimage* (London: Routledge T. K. Paul, 1965), pp. 12–15. Tisdale, *The Medieval Pilgrimage*, puts emphasis exclusively on penance.

33. See Robert Enzer Lewis, "What Did Chaucer Mean by 'Of the Wrecched Engendrynge of Mankynde'?" *ChauR* 2 (1968): 139–158, and "Chaucer's Artistic Use of Pope Innocent III's *De miseria humane conditionis* in the Man of Law's Prologue and Tale," *PMLA* 81 (1966):485–492.

"Origines upon the Maudelayne,"[34] Guillaume Peraldus's
Summa de viciis, Raymond of Pennaforte's *Summa Casuum
Penitentiae* or Frère Lorens's *Somme des Vices et des Vertus*
(these last were to become the Parson's Tale). Chaucer, like
Dante, was a Christian poet, but he was a poet of the secular
world in a narrower sense—possibly a stricter sense—than
Dante was; his comedy leaves out the eschatological side of
Christianity which makes all life a comedy and which makes
all that happens happen for the best. From this larger point of
view we might say Chaucer showed things more nearly at
their worst, that he was a gloomier poet than Dante. That
greater eschatological vision which Dante wrote about must
be implied or understood in *The Canterbury Tales*, for it was
prominent enough in people's thoughts; but it is not expressed.

MORALITY AND IRONY

About the same time Chaucer was planning *The Canterbury Tales* his friend Gower began working on the *Confessio
Amantis*, a "frame narrative" like *The Canterbury Tales*, in
English, comprising a prologue and a series of tales. Chaucer and Gower evidently discussed their plans for these two
similar works, but it is not necessary to suppose that Gower
was Chaucer's "mentor." Gower was a dozen or more years
older than Chaucer and had finished two long poems, one in
Latin and one in French; but Chaucer had written all his
works in English, and by now had finished *Troilus and
Criseyde*. Chaucer had more experience writing English
poetry, and he had more talent. Whichever of them (if
either) got the idea of such a work first, it is instructive to see
how differently they conceived it. To Gower the work
seemed a kind of *summa*, a collection of tales illustrating the
seven deadly sins, its prologue introducing the idea of the
Three Estates, and the whole a dialogue between a penitent

34. See John P. McCall, "Chaucer and the Pseudo Origen *De Maria
Magdalena*: A Preliminary Study," *Speculum* 46 (1971): 491–509.

and his confessor. To Chaucer such a conception evidently
seemed unsatisfactory.

Chaucer twice mentions Gower in his works. First, he
dedicated the *Troilus* to him:

O moral Gower, this book I directe
To thee and to thee, philosophical Strode,
To vouchen sauf, ther need is, to correcte,
Of your benignites and zeles goode.

(V:1856–1859)

Second, in the Man of Law's Prologue, he had the stuffy
Sergeant-at-Law scorn two tales, both told in Gower's *Confessio*, because he thought them immoral. Speaking of Chaucer himself, the lawyer says,

But certainly no word ne writeth he
Of thilke wikke ensample of Canacee,
That loved hir owene brother sinfully;
(Of swiche cursed stories I say fy!)
Or ellis of Tyro Appollonius,
How that the cursed king Antiochus
Birafte his doghter of hir maidenhede,
That is so horrible a tale for to rede,
Whan he hir threw upon the pavement.
And therefore he, of full avisement,
Nolde nevere write in none of his sermons
Of swich unkinde abhominacions,
Ne I wol none reherce, if that I may.

(II:77–89)

What this joke meant is not certain. Moralists, like movie
censors, often object to vice depicted in a work without
considering the artist's intention in depicting it, so perhaps it
is the old joke between writers: "They won't understand
your book." Otherwise it is Chaucer's amusing response to
Gower's urging that he return from fabliaux to more moral
matters: "if I've told fornication, you've told incest."[35] It is

_____

35. Fisher, *John Gower*, p. 289. Fisher shows (pp. 6–7) how the six-
teenth-century tradition that Gower was Chaucer's self-proclaimed mentor is based on a misreading of *Confessio Amantis* VIII:2940ff.; in chap. 5
he shows in detail how the older poet might have urged and advised, and

not disrespectful to Gower's morality, but it is still a joke at the expense of it.

Both these places where Chaucer mentions Gower point to morality, and that is the area of real difference between the *Confessio Amantis* and *The Canterbury Tales*. Morality is all in the foreground of Gower's poem—explicit in the prologue and embodied schematically in its plan and structure; Chaucer had a different idea about the morality of his work. Morality is not central to the General Prologue—we learn the tales are to be told as an entertainment and judged either for "sentence" or "solaas" (798). Morality is not a part of the plan or the structure—those to tell tales are chosen by lot in the Prologue, and tales are arranged in what seems a haphazard way, surely not under headings as in Gower. Where Gower made the whole explicitly penitential by using a lover's confession for his frame, Chaucer used the pilgrimage, which was penitential in its goal but involved "wandering by the way." In Gower morality is uppermost in mind and comes to the forefront everywhere; in Chaucer good morality seems all mixed with bad—he must make an apologia for plain speaking.

This does not mean Chaucer considered his work less moral than Gower's or was chaffing Gower for being a moralist; their difference had to do with the quality and tone of morality in such a work, with the *method* of making such a work moral. In *The Canterbury Tales* moral questions are more subtly and tentatively raised than in Gower; but explicit moralizing is more straightforward—in the two most notable instances it is even prose. Chaucer's morality is both more direct and less direct. Perhaps this is just a way of saying that Chaucer was an ironist and Gower was not; if so, it was doubtless a matter of temperament, and of differences in their careers and lives, and would have been plain enough to either by the mid-1380s. Their styles of life were as different as the styles of their poems. Gower was at work in his priory at St. Mary Overeys on the *Vox Clamantis* and the *Mirour de l'omme*, both very somber works; Chaucer was with his family in the gate-

how the younger poet might sometimes have responded and sometimes not.

house at Aldgate writing the *Parliament of Fowls, The House of Fame*, and the *Troilus*. Gower wrote characteristic medieval "complaint," using the universal voice of reason and gravity which was conventional in such writings; Chaucer wrote satire, using the ironic voice which gives to his works their personal and direct quality.[36] In Gower we get ideology; in Chaucer, a thinking presence.

But Chaucer was a moralist after his fashion, as his early works reveal. To hear some critics talk, one would think him fanatically so. But one need not read all his works as allegories to see his profound concern with moral questions. He had, by the time he got *The Canterbury Tales* under way, translated Boethius, "Origen," and Pope Innocent III. He had brought the *Troilus* to its sobering, philosophical, and profoundly religious close. Most of his other works in the early period show moral concerns—explicitly in some of the shorter lyrics, implicitly in *The Book of the Duchess* and *The House of Fame*. For that matter, three of the Canterbury tales are generally thought to have been first written in his early years—an early version of the Knight's Tale, the "life of Saint Cecilia" (the Second Nun's Tale), and the Monk's "tragedies." Of course we do not know what other tales may have been written early and revised later—the Prioress's and Physician's tales are possible candidates, and perhaps others. But it is interesting that those tales most often considered early are chiefly sober ones.

It may be pertinent that the years during which Chaucer planned and began *The Canterbury Tales* were likely the somberest of his life. His job was unsteady: he left the Customs during this period, probably in a political shake-up, moved from London, was Justice of the Peace in Kent (1385–1389) and a member of the Parliament (1386), and was sent on a mission abroad. Gloucester's party was gaining control over the young king, so that the king's appointees must have been in a parlous circumstance. John of Gaunt, whose influence

36. Fisher makes much of the distinction between complaint and satire, for which he expresses a debt to John D. Peter, *Complaint and Satire in Early English Literature* (Oxford: Clarendon Press, 1956).

he could count on, was chiefly out of the country, waging wars in Scotland (1386) and Castile (1386–1388). During these years Chaucer fell into debt, and, at about this time, his wife died.[37] I do not mean to imply that cheerless years lead a writer to sober topics, or that morality and sobriety are akin. The case is as easily reversed: bad circumstances can bring out the humorist and ironist in a man (Mark Twain is an example), but they don't make him merry. And after all, humor, irony, and comedy, at their best, touch profoundly serious questions of morality. Anyone who thinks *The Canterbury Tales* is a light entertainment must skip half of it. Nor did Chaucer think of literature as entertainment alone: as critics constantly remind us, he never mentions "mirth" or "solace" without coupling "doctrine" or "sentence."

Chaucer believed then that the end of literature was to teach and delight. Everyone believed it[38]—who can believe otherwise? The problem is the proportions of the mixture. Chaucer goes much farther toward delight than Gower does, as any reader will agree, and not just because he was a better poet: he had convictions in the matter. If you read through his early poems, you find emerging elements of humor, realism, and dialogue; by the time he began *The Canterbury Tales* these had become his habit, that is, part of his style. It has been studied scores of times. As early as *The Book of the Duchess* we discover the obtuse narrator, the familiar Chaucerian persona with his wit and literal-mindedness— the humorous self-portrait which gives to all his works their ironic stamp. In *The House of Fame* and *The Parliament of Fowls* we find comic incidents and characters depicted with notable realism. To a large extent this realism is achieved

---

37. *LR*, pp. 61–62, 84, 247–269, 285–293, 348–369, 384–401. Fisher, p. 63, reminds us that Gower and Chaucer no longer lived in proximity during these years, that their friend Strode died in 1387 and that Usk was executed in 1388. On John of Gaunt's doings during the period see Sydney Armitage-Smith, *John of Gaunt* (London: Constable, 1904, rpt. 1964), chaps. 12 and 13.

38. De Bruyne, *The Esthetics of the Middle Ages*, p. 162, remarks, "A literary work is beautiful by virtue of the direct or indirect radiance of the emotionally experienced physical or moral truths it contains. This, in our opinion, is the fundamental principle of the medieval esthetics of art."

through dialogue; the chatty birds of the *Parliament* speak like real people, revealing their attitudes and characters, and their social positions, through the way they talk—it is a real departure from conventional "class satire." In the *Troilus* we can see these skills in relief by comparing the poem with its original, Boccaccio's *Filostrato*—critics have heaped up mountains of differences, and the lesson is now clear: Chaucer made his version more moral, more philosophical, and, in the end, more religious. He also made it more conventional, adding to the Italianate eroticism of his predecessor the "courtly" mannerisms of French poetry. But while he turned his poem toward gravity and tradition on the one side, he turned it toward realism and irony on the other. His additions to his sources include extensive dialogue and monologue, the comic Pandarus and the no less comic narrator, the psychological exploration of Criseyde's mental content, the "historical" background, erotic feeling and details, the controlled and ironic distancing. The result is a work more grave and thoughtful than Boccaccio's which is still more dramatic, more "realistic," and more frequently funny.

Obviously Chaucer had found something which made his poems and his ideas about them different from Gower's. He had found a way to make lustrous theatricality serve moral concerns. He had discovered that one makes a narrative poem more profoundly moral by fully engaging the audience's attention and its feelings—that mirth serves doctrine as doctrine never can serve mirth. If one's audience or readers laugh and cry, if they come to know the characters as though they were alive, if they are *moved*, then they learn morality from the story in the only way anyone ever learns morality anyway, by experience.

It is just this theatricality, this element of experienced feeling and this extravagance which have kept Chaucer alive for six hundred years. Kill them and he dies. Those critics who see in Chaucer only the doctrine of *caritas* preached over and over in a hundred allegories work hard to get around this, but they have to resort to nonsense. Medieval men, they have to claim, did not have personalities, did not feel emotions as we do, saw everything with unruffled rationality in hierarchies and signs; whence, they insist, the feelings Chaucer raises in us are our "sentimentality," his humanity our "psychologism," the turbulence and multi-valence in his works our "Hegelianism." It is all very dreary. If they were right, who would have read Chaucer after the sixteenth century? But the facts are otherwise. Chaucer's irony is the literary quality which generations of readers have most valued in his work. It was this, even, which made poor Matthew Arnold find him lacking in high seriousness. That "high" is the problem. Gower wanted to have "high" seriousness and it ended in drabness. Chaucer found in his ironic style a way to approach seriousness and avoid preten-tiousness and solemnity. And in the end it made his works more deeply and more searchingly moral than Gower's.

If we are to understand the differences between Gower and Chaucer, then, we have to read both for tone, not content. The difficulty comes when we try to understand their similarities. We think about "moral Gower" but have trouble thinking about "moral Chaucer." Yet the two poets shared a moral view which embraced religion, politics, eco-nomics, and ethics. They lived through the same time and reacted to the same events and circumstances, often in the same way. They belonged more or less to the same social class. They were professional associates—tradition has it they met at the Inns of Court—and were both attached to the royal household. They shared poetical careers:[39] after 1376 both turned from visions of courtly love to social criti-cism, and around 1385 both began love-visions which framed collections of tales—the *Confessio* and *The Legend of Good Women*. Both these poems were written on a royal command, and both used an ecclesiastical model (confession, saints' legends) as the framing device. As Chaucer was beginning *The Canterbury Tales* he left for Kent, and his work moved in a different direction. Even so, they still shared a number of themes: the three estates, "class satire," the

39. Fisher has given a full account of what they shared, which I here summarize (*John Gower*, pp. 207–302). Cf. D. W. Robertson, Jr., *Chaucer's London* (New York: John Wiley, 1968), esp. chap. 5.

virtues and vices, the "common profit," ideals of kingship and knighthood, clerical reform. And they shared *ideas*. Both seem to have been taken up with an idea of universal harmony based on individual virtue, law, and social order. Both evidently had legal training and a connection with the king's court, but their conception of law was philosophical— they thought about a common good based on love, on natural and human law, on reasonable ("natural") behavior. They saw marriage as having a natural place in this consti- tuted social order. Their conception of man and the uni- verse can be traced to Chartrean "naturalism" or platonism, which they apparently got from Alain de Lille and Jean de Meun, and from the climate of opinion. With such ideals in mind, both complained about an upside-down world, in- voked the conventions of medieval complaint literature, often used the same pat phrases; there are scores of parallel passages. They shared materials, too. Both translated inde- pendently nine of the same tales from Ovid, plus that of Virginia (from Livy and the *Roman de la Rose*).[40] Both made versions of the tale of the Loathly Lady. And Chaucer bor- rowed from Gower's version of the story of Constance in the Man of Law's Tale, whose prologue teases Gower.

So Gower and Chaucer, though they parted company on matters of technique and style, belonged to a literary "school" and had compatible philosophic opinions. We can see "moral Chaucer" just as clearly as "moral Gower" if we open both eyes—the other eye got closed in the nineteenth century when people used to say that *The Canterbury Tales* is notable for its bawdy and humorous presentation of human conduct. Professor Payne has demolished this estimate of the tales by tabulating the amount of seriousness in their content—there is more than four times as much (by sheer bulk) as there is of humorous content.[41] Only a few of the

40. Fisher, p. 285.

41. Robert O. Payne, *The Key of Remembrance: A Study of Chaucer's Poetics* (New Haven and London: Yale Univ. Press, 1963), pp. 155–160. Classify- ing the tales is a frequent enterprise; see, for example, S. S. Hussey, *Chaucer: An Introduction* (London: Methuen, 1971), pp. 125ff., who classi- fies the tales as the narrator does (I:3178–3180) but adds the sermon. The

tales—the most popular ones, it happens—can really be called bawdy or earthy. Less than half are humorous. Their morality hangs upon a number of variables: the reader's interpretation of each and his own moral values, the personality and morality of the individual pilgrim, the narrator's values and, whatever they were, Chaucer's own. No one could ever arrange them on a scale of morality which would satisfy all readers. But we can agree that the tales do have various degrees of morality and that the morality of a tale does not nec   arily correspond to the morality or motives of its teller.

The spectrum of morality in the tales is broad. On one end there are explicitly moral tales—the two which come at once to mind, the Parson's Tale and the *Melibee*, are both in prose, the language of explicit statement. Of the two, the *Melibee* is the more literary, having a negligible fable which gets if off to an allegorical start. On the other end of the spectrum are amoral tales. One example is the fantastical romance which the Squire embarks on, though it might have had a moral tacked on if it had ever ended. Still another example is the Monk's Tale: *de casibus* tragedies of the kind he tells presented a picture of the haphazard way things are, of an amoral world; a moral could be drawn from them, but the Monk does not do so. It is significant that these tales on the amoral end of the spectrum are all unfinished. If they had been finished it is possible that an ending would have implied a moral of some kind or at least would have tempted readers to seek one. But it is in the nature of amorality to be inconclusive, as it is in the nature of "concluded" works to have, or seem to have, a moral or a "theme." Between these

---

narrator is more flexible: he promises "storial thing that toucheth gentilesse," "moralitee and holinesse," and "harlotrie." This means we are going to hear romances, moral or religious stories, and fabliaux. The classification is hard to make work without considering some tales antitypes: *Sir Thopas* and the Wife's tale might be thought anti-romances, the Pardoner's tale an anti-sermon, and some tales like the Physician's false "moralitee." The Nun's Priest's tale could be reckoned an antitype of "harlotrie"—it is a funny story with a serious lesson. The classification still seems more workable than simple binal categories like mirth and doctrine; and it is presented by the narrator, whereas the binal categories are presented by the Host.

extremes is a panoply of tales every one of which involves some kind of morality, good or bad. The Second Nun's Tale is a saint's legend; the Clerk's and Man of Law's tales are, to adapt J. V. Cunningham's term,[42] ideal narratives, intended to teach a moral lesson by example. The Physician's and Prioress's Tales are moral tales whose morality seems questionable. The Shipman's Tale is downright immoral: in it the most sacred relationships of medieval society (the monk's vows, marriage, "brotherhood") are purposefully violated, and the one character who is not a scoundrel, the merchant, is himself venal, stuffy, and credulous—a gull.

We can assess the morality of other tales as we can of these; but how we do so depends on our own moral standards or on those we attribute to Chaucer's age or to Chaucer himself. About 90 percent of Chaucer criticism deals with this problem, and it is an unrewarding venture since Chaucer effaced himself, making us intuit or guess what his "ethos," if he had one, might have been. The two tales which Chaucer himself tells fall at opposite ends of this moral spectrum. He offers first a very bad metrical romance of the "bourgeois" or "popular" variety, thus making fun of himself as a bad poet and a hopeless specimen of the bourgeois mentality. It has no moral beyond an admonition against bad writing or mindlessness. We are given to understand that this is not the true Chaucer, the Chaucer we know. Then we get, in the *Melibee*, a serious prose work; some have tried to find it a joke too—I will make my case for its seriousness later.[43] It is explicit moralizing addressed to feudal barons; it is translated from a popular treatise of great interest to such an audience. If there is any conclusion to be drawn from Chaucer's two tales, it has to do with his audience more than with himself. They are, he suggests, sophisticated enough to think the bourgeois mentality absurd and to know bad poetry when they hear it. And they can profit from an idealistic discourse on proper behavior for the ruling class. This audience of high social standing

42. "Ideal Fiction: *The Clerk's Tale*," *Shenandoah*, 19, no. 2 (Winter, 1968): 38–41.
43. Chap. 5, pp. 309–316.

and advanced literary taste is given a collection of tales some moral and some not, told by figures some of whom are perfection itself and the rest imperfect by degrees. The author leaves such judgments in the audience's hands, adopting for his own part an impartial or "distanced" stance. This stance is part of what we perceive as Chaucer's irony. And it is the biggest difference between him and Gower.

Just how sure Chaucer was of himself in adopting this ironic stance we can never know. It is enticing to see the poet at the prime of life secure in his vision of a new style and a new narrative art. But the facts will not support it. He has to ask the reader's indulgence in the General Prologue (725–736); the disclaimer, being ironic, does not necessarily reveal *real* hesitancy on his part. Still, just before the Miller's Tale he again begs indulgence on the grounds of being a mere reporter (3167–3186). Similarly, in the Merchant's Tale, he has the Merchant beg pardon before the central bawdy episode:

> Ladies, I pray you that ye be nat wrooth;
> I can nat glose, I am a rude man—
>
> (IV:2350–2351)

And, at the end of his life he revokes in the Retraction such of the Canterbury tales as "sownen into sin." There is that much evidence that he was hesitant about the ironic stance. He is sometimes at pains to remind the reader that he *has* written works of sound morality.[44] Probably like any writer he had moments when he felt traditional Gower was doing the proper thing and he himself was floundering. This hint of uncertainty and compunction would not be there if he had meant each piece he wrote to have a "fruyt" of morality all by itself. But that does not make him amoral. When he

---

44. The passage in the Man of Law's Pro could be so interpreted, as could the passage from the Miller's Pro and the Retraction. See too *LGW* GPro 412–416. *The House of Fame* 614–640 can be interpreted as a resolve on the poet's part to turn from dream visions to more serious matter—see J. A. W. Bennett, *Chaucer's Book of Fame* (Oxford: Clarendon Press, 1968), esp. p. 185; Robert J. Allen, "A Recurring Motif in Chaucer's *House of Fame*," *JEGP* 55 (1956):393–405; and J. L. Simmons, "The Place of the Poet in Chaucer's *House of Fame*," *MLQ* 27 (1966):125–135.

said "moral Gower" he said it with respect, though the feeling behind it could be ambivalent and the tone ironic— with Chaucer we are never sure. To him morality was to be found in the totality of the work: it required that sense of the artist's overall intention which the Man of Law, speaking of Chaucer himself and alluding to Gower, ridiculously lacks.

THE CANTERBURY TALES AS A BOOK

In the Retraction at the end of *The Canterbury Tales* Chaucer named the "translaciouns and enditings of worldly vanities" which he meant to revoke.[45] He gives every title in the form *the book of*—he refers to "the book of Troilus," "the book also of Fame," "the book of XXV Ladies," "the book of the Duchess," "the book of Saint Valentine's day of the Parlement of Briddes," "the book of the Leoun," "and many another book, if they were in my remembrance, and many a song and many a lecherous lay." Before "The Book of the Lion," he names "the tales of Caunterbury, thilke that sownen into sin," but does not refer to it as a book. This must be either because he did not think of it as a book but merely as a collection of tales, or because he intended *not* to revoke it as a book but only to revoke those tales that "sownen into sin." The other possibility is that it is rhetorical variation or "just a slip"—but if it is that, it is a meaningful, a suggestive variation or slip. The rubric before the Retraction reads "Here Taketh the Makere of this book his leve," and the *explicit* after it reads "here is ended the book of the tales of Canterbury." Of course these are scribal and likely did not come from Chaucer's pen; the scribes who copied the work might have thought it a book though its author did not. But again, if it is a gloss, it is a meaningful one.

When Chaucer heard the word "book," he would have thought of the word as we do in either of two senses: a single

---

45. See James D. Gordon, "Chaucer's Retraction: A Review of Opinion," in *Studies in Medieval Literature in Honor of Professor Albert Croll Baugh*, ed. MacEdward Leach (Philadelphia: Univ. of Pennsylvania Press, 1961), pp. 81–96, and Lumiansky, "Chaucer's Retraction," 5–13.

piece of writing produced by an author, or a bound volume which a reader might hold in his hands.[46] Medieval bound volumes often contained miscellaneous works, so that a number of books (in the sense of "works") might comprise a helter-skelter collection of writings which could be called a book (in the sense of a bound volume). In the Retraction Chaucer uses the word to mean "works." The words which we use were not available in his time; "work" was scarcely ever used to mean a literary production, and "poem" was not in use till the sixteenth century. When Chaucer talks about his poems, he calls the longer ones "books" and distinguishes these from "lays" or specific forms of lyric like the "balade." We find this in the Man of Law's Prologue (II:52) and in *The Legend of Good Women* (F Pro 417−441). He refers once to *The Legend of Good Women* as a "large volume" (ML Pro 60) and uses for shorter poems once the word "ympne" (*LGW* F Pro 422) and once the rather pleasant word "thing" (*Ibid.* 430). Elsewhere he does use "book" to mean a bound volume of miscellaneous items, as when he speaks of Jankyn's "book of wicked wives," but in the Retraction he has in mind not bound volumes but his individual "translations and end-itings."

Yet it seems to me out of the question that Chaucer did not think of *The Canterbury Tales* as a "book." He doesn't hesitate to use the word of *The House of Fame* though it seems to be unfinished, and he uses it of *The Legend of Good Women* though it was, like *The Canterbury Tales*, an unfinished collection of tales introduced by a prologue. It was not unusual to use the word "book" in the title of a work, but there was just as small a tendency toward standard titles in

46. The place of the book in the culture of the fourteenth century has enjoyed a flurry of interest in recent years prompted by Marshall McLuhan, *The Gutenberg Galaxy: The Making of Typographic Man* (Toronto: Univ. of Toronto Press, 1962). A more sophisticated view, to my mind, is that of Josipovici, *The World and the Book*, esp. chap. 2. Some useful considerations are raised in Warren Chappell, *A Short History of the Printed Word* (New York: Alfred A. Knopf, 1970), chap. I; in vol. I of George Haven Putnam, *Books and Their Makers During the Middle Ages* (1896−1897; rpt. New York: Hillary House, 1962); and in H. J. Chaytor, *From Script to Print: An Introduction to Medieval Literature* (Cambridge: Cambridge Univ. Press, 1945).

the late Middle Ages as there was toward standard texts. The standard title is the child of the printing press. While Chaucer calls his elegy to the Duchess Blanche "The Book of the Duchess" in the Retraction, he calls it "The Deeth of Blaunche the Duchesse" in *The Legend of Good Women* (FPro 418), and refers to it obliquely as "Ceys and Alcione" in the Man of Law's Prologue (57). Since in the Retraction he gave *all* the works titles in the form "The Book of ———" he made an exception in the case of "the tales of Caunterbury." Yet there is no other indication anywhere in Chaucer that he regarded *The Canterbury Tales* as a mere collection. He promised "some comedy" at the end of *Troilus* and there is every reason to think that he meant *The Canterbury Tales* to be a work as integrated at least as *The Legend of Good Women*, which he did call a "book." The presence of the General Prologue, the links between tales, the grouping of tales together, and the Parson's Prologue and Tale at the end— which critics point to as unifying features of the work— argue that he considered *The Canterbury Tales* a "book" too.

In the Retraction, then, Chaucer did not mean to revoke *The Canterbury Tales* as a whole. He revokes only those tales "that sownen into sin." It is not hard to imagine which he had in mind, but it is important to notice that he does not name any. He seems to leave the matter to the reader; and this reliance on the reader's judgment is a characteristic of the work.

But then why did he explicitly revoke the *Troilus*, *The House of Fame*, *The Legend of Good Women*, *The Book of the Duchess*, and *The Parliament of Fowls?* In recent years some critics have found such a wealth of religious meaning in these works that one would hardly expect to find them revoked here, and no one who thinks them primarily religious has successfully answered this objection. Of course the Retraction may be a deathbed utterance, perfunctory and ritual in character. One might regret many things on one's deathbed about which one could have subtler thoughts under less pressing circumstances. Evidently Chaucer meant to name those works which were *about* secular subjects, which were not explicitly religious in content. It makes sense to play it safe when confronting eternity. No one who has read the end of Chaucer's *Troilus* can think it a positively un-Christian work. Still, the *Troilus* is a great story of human passion, and even at its end, though we are properly instructed in the full implications of that story, we cannot help but look back with pity and regret on the highest moments of the lovers' bliss. That must be the reason why Chaucer includes it among these works that he means to retract. And it is undoubtedly why he includes some of the Canterbury tales. So it is the more significant that he does not include the work as a whole. Evidently he did think it had sound "doctrine."

Chaucer addresses the Retraction to "all that herkne this litel tretise or rede." It is often thought that "treatise" here refers to *The Canterbury Tales*, though some think it refers to the Parson's Tale which has immediately preceded. The latter is surely true. Chaucer never uses the word "treatise" to refer to a literary work—a "book" or song—but always to writings in prose. He applies "treatise" to the *Melibee* (VII: 957, 963), the Parson's Tale (X:955−960), and the *Treatise on the Astrolabe*. Elsewhere he uses it to mean a written contract (Clerk's Tale 331) or an agreement with legal status (*Troilus* IV:64). It appears that Chaucer begins the Retraction saying that if there is anything in the Parson's Tale which pleases his readers they should thank Christ for it, "of whom proceedeth all wit and all goodness." But what he goes on to say seems to have a broader reference. "And if there be anything that displese hem" may refer to the Parson's Tale— it may be another way of saying what the Parson himself says, that its doctrinal content is "under correction" (X:56). If so, why does he go on to quote St. Paul, "All that is written is written for our doctrine," and to add the flat statement "that is myn intente"? It would be inappropriate to say that he means all he has written, including possible errors of doctrine, for the reader's learning! It looks as though he began referring to the Parson's Tale but slipped unawares into a general reference to the whole of *The Canterbury Tales*. The association is a natural one—talk about the end of a work and your mind goes to the whole of it.

What he says is true. There is some "doctrine" to be learned from everything in *The Canterbury Tales* if everything is seen in relation to the total conception of the work. Individual tales may themselves "sownen" into sin. But they are told by individuals, those individuals belong to a social order, and the work as a whole depicts that social order under the traditional figure of a pilgrimage to the heavenly Jerusalem. Chaucer revokes whatever in the work might be abused, but reminds us that we can learn something from everything we read. Unlike his friend Gower, he leaves the moral benefit up to the reader's participation in the work. It was an effective, but a daring, concession, and it has not always succeeded. But he says he meant it to.

In recent years a number of critics have noticed that we expect things of books which the medievals did not.[47] We expect "tightness" of structure and "organic" unity—we labor under the clichés of the book trade and the opinions of Coleridge. To the medieval or "gothic" mentality, we are told, a literary work might be disjunctive, digressive, inorganic, architectonic. Malory, we are reminded, would not have understood what we mean by a "book" or a "work." Surely a literary work was experienced differently in the fourteenth and fifteenth centuries from the way one is experienced now. And it is hard for us to imagine what the old experience was. But it was not wholly unlike ours and I do not believe it is inaccessible to us. We have developed new literary forms and therefore new literary responses; the drama and the novel dominate our thoughts when we think of narrative. But we can still find in our own experience of literature something comparable to the medieval experience. The word "book" has still the ambiguity it had then: we still use it to mean a bound volume containing hetero-

47. E.g., Jordan, *Chaucer and the Shape of Creation*, and Eugène Vinaver in such a discussion as *Form and Meaning in Medieval Romance* (Presidential Address, Modern Humanities Research Assoc., 1966), or *The Rise of Romance* (New York and Oxford: Oxford Univ. Press, 1971). And see *Essays on Malory*, ed. J. A. W. Bennett (Oxford: Clarendon Press, 1963), pp. 7–63.

geneous materials, and we still use it of a single literary work even if that work is contained with others in a bound volume. Nor do our books often have the organic unity which our critics prescribe. Take Tennyson's "In Memoriam." We know it is a collection of poems inspired by the death of the poet's friend; the poems have a common occasion and something like a common theme. But digressive themes are often introduced—there are sub-themes, side issues. The work is sometimes faulted for diffuseness, and I am sure no one ever wished it longer. We find in it a structure and development, concede that it is of a piece, then regret that it is loosely put together. If we regard it as a collection of poems which have more to do with each other than most collections, we fret less and take the work more willingly for what it is. We continue to read it and find value in it, and to the extent that we do so without measuring it against a construct of poetic unity not fairly applicable to it we may be in the position of a medieval reader approaching a work like *The Canterbury Tales* or the *Morte Darthur*.

In the twentieth century people have developed more of a feeling for such unstructured, digressive works. We have acquired a taste for the exploratory, decorative, and open-ended. It is always anachronistic, and sometimes ridiculous, to use a recent work as a model for an older one. But if we can find recent works which call for a kind of taste or response that older works would have called for, the anachronism becomes a useful tool. If we approach *The Canterbury Tales* with, say, Dickens in mind, we see it as unfinished, diverse, unstructured. But suppose we approach it with another kind of work in mind—with the novels of Robbe-Grillet, or a collection of discrete narratives having a common theme, setting, or characters, like Hemingway's "Nick Adams" stories (D. H. Lawrence called them "a fragmentary novel"), or a poem like Crane's *The Bridge*. The right anachronism makes us see the qualities of the work, not find shortcomings in it. The book of the tales of Canterbury, as the scribes called it, is what it is, and since it can never be otherwise we have to read it as it is. Its author thought it a book and meant it to be read as one. An enthusiasm for the book characterized the humanism of Italy with which he had come into contact, and his last book embodies that enthusiasm.

So the burden is upon us to perform an exercise in historical imagination, to guess what a book was in Chaucer's day. Pick up a fourteenth-century codex, leaf through it, read a little, touch the pages, scrutinize the illumination and handwriting. There is a ghostly "feel" about it—you live just a little in that world, even though you are sitting in the courteous hush and permanent chill of the British Museum. And if you pick up not one but hundreds of fourteenth-century manuscript books—some from Italy in round Roman hands or early humanistic script; some from France with glorious illuminations and miniatures shiny with gold leaf and bright colors; some plain and practical, on paper, in "charter hands" peppered with abbreviations; some in noble "book hands" done up with decorations on delicate vellum—you begin to get a sense of what *bookishness* was then. This experience is worth a thousand times more than theorizing about "print culture" or trying to obliterate from our thoughts what was to come later; instead we need to understand what went before and was going on then—which produced the *need* for the printing press. We get this only in a backhanded way by reading something like Caxton's prefaces. We get it first hand if we read something like Richard de Bury's *Philobiblon*, or browse in reference books like Johannes Tritheim's *De scriptoribus ecclesiasticis*, or read the less popular works of Petrarch and Boccaccio. Yet, what we get is puzzling—we get a sense of something old and reverential, but a sense too of something new, exciting, even faddish.

Books preserved writings from old times—"authorities." Chaucer says that books preserved "the doctrine of these olde wise" and are "of remembraunce the keye" (*LGW* F Pro 17ff.). Hence they were meant to be durable—they were copied on vellum, bound between stout boards—so that a great many *were* old. Their language, too, was a venerable formal one, whether in Latin or the vernacular—a written or literary language. Anything new in thought or knowledge was dependent on them: "out of olde bookes," Chaucer says, comes "all this newe science that men lere" (*PF* 24–25). That was the medieval tradition. Until the twelfth century a man, even a learned man, might in a lifetime hold in his hands only a few such books, reading from them with care—aloud or moving his lips. Such books were scarcely ever "private"— they were as often read *from*, out loud, to groups. The result is that the book had two opposing qualities, which I will (if the reader will excuse me) call *bookness* and *voiceness*. From one point of view the book was an object of veneration, an *objet d'art*, a relic, a collector's item, a thing with dignity, magic, the power to inspire awe. The Bible was "the book," and both memory and nature were sometimes figured as a book.[48] To *own* a book, a good book on vellum with pictures and colors, was to own something expensive and gorgeous, the work of many skilled hands. People sometimes estimate that it took a herd of sheep to produce the vellum for one good-sized book (three hundred sheep, they say, would have been needed to print the Gutenberg Bible on vellum), and it all had to be soaked in lime water nine days, stretched on a harrow, scraped, dried, treated, cut, and sewn into quires before anyone even put ruled lines to it. All vellum books were "rare books." Is it any wonder the voracious book collector Richard de Bury was accused of avarice by his detractors? That is *bookness*: to almost everyone the book was not a quotidian household object but a rarity. And just for that reason almost everyone's experience of a book was chiefly the experience of seeing the precious object at a distance on a lectern and hearing someone read aloud from it. The book recorded the language of a spoken voice so that it could be spoken again, "rehearsed." This quality, *voiceness*, is what people want to illustrate when they reproduce the famous frontispiece from an early fifteenth-century manuscript of *Troilus* (Cambridge, Corpus Christi 61) showing Chaucer reading aloud to the court. To have the author

48. On the book as a symbol, to be distinguished from my treatment of the book as a thing or phenomenon, see Curtius, *European Literature*, pp. 302–347.

himself read his own work aloud is always interesting, even now; but voiceness means that the voice is infinitely reproduceable—a book can generate untold readings or performances.

So there was something grand, antique, and authoritative about the book, but something temporal about it too. Like a musical score or the script of a play it was the indispensable product of the *auctor*—but by itself incomplete: one had to bring something to it, use it well, render it. If they had not been so rare, if the materials had not been so expensive, books wouldn't have had this "public" quality. Of course the rich always had some books they could read by themselves (if they could read), and the monasteries and schools had libraries; but all would have been different if only books could have been cheaper. That is why the introduction of paper into Europe in the twelfth century is one of the most important events in European intellectual history[49]—compared to it, the printing press was only gadgetry. Paper was imported into Arabic Spain from the Near East in the tenth century and into Sicily early in the twelfth century. It was first made in the West at Xátiva in Spain in 1150, and was being used in Italy by 1154. It was milled in Italy first in the 1270s, and there are paper manuscripts in England dating from 1307–1308. By that time another advance in the technology of reading had occurred: eyeglasses had been invented.

Paper was not as strong or durable as vellum. Johannes Tritheim in 1492 warned that a book copied on vellum would last a thousand years but one printed on paper could barely last 200 years. It was by no means as cheap as the pulp stuff we have today, but comparatively speaking it was within the means of ordinary people. Think what it meant—

49. I am here indebted to an unpublished paper by A. G. Rigg, "The Most Significant Date in the Middle Ages," of which the author kindly furnished me a copy; he gives the following references: to G. S. Ivy, "The Bibliography of the Manuscript-Book," in Francis Wormald and C. E. Wright, *The English Library before 1700* (London: Athlone Press, 1958), pp. 32–38; James Westfall Thompson, *The Medieval Library* (Chicago: Univ. of Chicago Press, 1939), pp. 630–646; and Chappell, *History of the Printed Word*, pp. 12–16.

before paper, any ephemeral kind of writing (letters, drafts, memoranda) had to be put on stray scraps of vellum from which sometimes previous writing had been scratched or washed, or on wax tablets, or just in one's head. Paper meant that a scholar could make his own book by copying it himself, or could purchase or rent a copied book; that cheap working copy or "drafts" could be farmed out to scribes; that a student, or a man with a taste for reading, could own a book of his own; that books could be objects of practical use or amusement. The long-term result everyone knows: paper made the printing press feasible (though early printers still used vellum for their choicest products), made books domestic items, made silent reading a possible entertainment for the literate, and so altered the "reading public" if it did not create it. Paper freed vellum for more important writings, made revision easier. Ultimately it made memory less important. And it made loss and destruction of books more common—even in the fifteenth century the better part of *extant* manuscripts are on vellum, but evidence of *lost* manuscripts is abundant. Probably at least three-quarters of the manuscripts produced are now lost, and it stands to reason that the better part of these were on paper, because it was less durable and less esteemed. Ultimately the process has made books into consumer items, even disposable or self-destruct items—the "paperback" is the end of the process.

The beginning of this process can be seen in the fourteenth century. A man like Chaucer could possess his own books, pick and choose what to read, stay up late with a candle, skip, select, compare, turn back, and reread. He had more power over the book—could stop his reading to think, could write notes in the margin. But, too, he became a slave to books—even then, there were so many books to read. All of this lies behind the development of humanism and later of skepticism. It is the heart or backbone of the "Renaissance." We can call it *paperness*: the book is available, controllable, instrumental, in part disposable. The solitary reader can, more than ever before, choose books, select passages, bring his private thoughts to the book, pick thoughts from it, and neglect what he wishes.

It will be seen that *The Canterbury Tales*, considered as a book, has these qualities. It has bookness because it contains "doctrine" and "authorities" and is intended for the reader's edification. It has voiceness because the author addresses us directly and himself rehearses tales told aloud by others: we seem to hear his and the pilgrims' voices, we presume oral delivery. The work has the "linear" organization appropriate to oral delivery, but has too the junctures, the beginnings and ends, incipits and explicits, appropriate to bookness.[50] But it has paperness too: we can select, "turn over the leaf and choose another tale," find different *kinds* of tales. Just as inside the work the Host orders things and the audience sometimes interrupts an unpromising tale, the author orders things and gives us leave to interrupt. The book is within our reach, in part disposable or dispensable: we are its owners. There is a new kind of reading public and a new reason for the traditional humility of the author.

So there is a new kind of reading experience. Reading a book becomes an adventure, a voyage or quest. It was traditional to equate a book with travel, with a pilgrimage of life or of the mind (Dante and the *Roman* do this); but it was not traditional to equate a book with the questionable side of travel—with *curiositas*, with sightseeing or exploration, with the festiveness, awe, danger, loose talk, and false tale-telling imputed to pilgrims and travelers. Chaucer in the *Troilus* (II:1−7) equates his task of writing with a boat struggling against heavy seas—and the struggle is, at that, with the hero's emotions and circumstances, his *disespeir*. Reading becomes now a voyage of exploration, writing a creation of worlds, often interior worlds, in which the reader travels. It is the real heart of humanism, this new attitude toward reading; Petrarch acknowledged it when he spoke of making "many brief visits with maps, and books, and imagination."[51] To settle down with a book becomes an experience comparable to taking ship; but the voyage is into an interior world, a

---

50. Cf. J. A. Burrow, *Ricardian Poetry: Chaucer, Gower, Langland and the Gawain Poet* (New Haven: Yale Univ. Press, 1971), pp. 57−69.

51. Quoted from *Letters from Petrarch*, trans. Morris Bishop (Bloomington, Ind.: Indiana Univ. Press, 1966), p. 261.

world drawn from other books, memory, and imagination, which can only exist as it takes shape in memory. When Chaucer called books the *key* of remembrance he must have had in mind a secret world to be unlocked, like an enclosed garden. It had always been a commonplace to say that you can read the world, nature, memory, or experience like a book, but this is something else: the notion is that you can read a book as you experience the world.

THE WAY OF THE WORLD

From the discussion so far we can see that Chaucer approached *The Canterbury Tales* with the idea that it would be a "comedy" as opposed to a tragedy—a work diffuse and inclusive like Dante's but without the grandeur and solemnity, the eschatological perspective, or the symmetrical structure of Dante's comedy. He saw it rather as a satiric and ironic work without the character of "complaint" literature which his friend Gower espoused. He regarded it as a "book" rather than a collection, a book about the world to be read in a new way.

We must consider one further bit of evidence which comes from outside the poem. Everyone agrees that *The Canterbury Tales* differs from other "frame narratives" like the *Decameron* by having for its setting a pilgrimage. Until very recently this was considered a realistic touch. Now, many consider it a metaphor representing human life as a one-way journey. The metaphor was a medieval commonplace: Chaucer knew it because everybody knew it. Some critics think this reason enough to call *The Canterbury Tales* an allegory. It would be a great convenience if we knew exactly what the metaphor meant to Chaucer himself, what specific associations it had for him. And it happens that in one of his short poems, the one called "Truth," he makes this plain in the second stanza:

That thee is sent, receive in buxomnesse.
The wrastling for this world axeth a fall.
Here is non home, here nis but wildernesse.
Forth, pilgrim, forth! forth, beest, out of thy stall!

> Know thy countree, look up, thank God of all,
> Hold the high way, and lat thy ghost thee lede—
> And trouth thee shall deliver, it is no dreede.

The poem counsels an attitude of renunciation, obedience, and patience; it argues against "wrestling for this world" because it can bring about a fall on Fortune's wheel as it brought about Adam's fall. The "truth" or "troth" it recommends is the keeping of all bonds required of man in a hierarchical universe. The poem represents man as a beastlike creature whose true home is not in this world: the world is not a home but a wilderness, and a man must leave it as a beast his stall. He must know his "country"—what his true home is—and must, knowing this, venture forth on a spiritual pilgrimage, upon the "high way."

This conception of *the way* is expressed at the end of *The Canterbury Tales* when the Host proposes that they "knit up well a greet mattere" outside their destination, probably at their first sight of Canterbury from afar.[52] The Parson says,

> And Jhesu, for his grace, wit me sende
> To shewe you the way, in this viage,
> Of thilke parfit glorious pilgrimage
> That highte Jerusalem celestial.

(X:48–51)

This speech, which has had a lion's share of attention in Chaucer criticism, and the text of the Parson's "meditation" (from Jer. 6:16), both contain the phrase which gives the unidirectional pilgrimage a name: *the Way*. A pilgrimage was figured as a highway passing from one's home to the destination. This was easily associated with the course of human life, and man was visualized as a traveler or pilgrim who must choose and then follow the right road.[53] The topos is

---

52. H. Snowdon Ward, *The Canterbury Pilgrimage* (Philadelphia and London, 1905), pp. 280–281, reports that pilgrims first saw Canterbury from a stretch of road at Harbledown; there they dismounted and made the rest of the journey on foot. Those under penance would remove their shoes and even put on a hairshirt.

53. On the background of this idea, see Erwin Panofsky, *Hercules am Scheidewege und andere antike Bildstoffe in der neueren Kunst*, Studien der Bibliothek Warburg, vol. 18 (Leipzig & Berlin: B. G. Teubner, 1930),

still familiar to any English-speaker in metaphors like "the road of life" or in dead metaphors like "the way of the world"; we still talk about crossroads and milestones. The conception receives a most explicit expression in the text of *The Canterbury Tales*, toward the end of the Knight's Tale:

> This world nis but a thurghfare full of wo,
> And we been pilgrims, passing to and fro.
> Deeth is an end of every worldly soore.

(2847–2849)

It is something of a pity that these lines from Egeus's speech, so often quoted in discussions of *The Canterbury Tales*, come immediately after he has spoken his famous platitude, that no one ever died who did not live "in some degree" and no one ever lived who did not die. But we are not trying to demonstrate the profundity of the idea—its presence in Egeus's speech in fact displays it as a commonplace, which is what a topos is. The lines link pilgrimage with the motif of a thoroughfare, make it a one-way voyage, and equate that voyage with human life. "Passing to and fro" reflects the ambiguity inherent in the notion of pilgrimage itself; it is a two-way journey, but it is figured as a one-way journey. That it is a thoroughfare full of woe, and death its end, is a predictable echo of *contemptus mundi*. It is a splendid example of the topos in most of its implications; and there are dozens of instances of its currency in late medieval England.[54] Such a journey is not a movement away from a stable domestic state into the unknown; on the contrary, the movement is toward man's proper home in the order of things. From this point of

---

chap. 1; Bernhard Kötting, *Peregrinatio Religiosa: Wallfahrten in der Antike und das Pilgerwesen in der alten Kirche* (Regensberg-Münster, 1950), pp. 302–307; Bruno Snell, *Die Entdeckung des Geistes: Studien zur Entstehung des europäischen Denkens bei den Greichen*, 3rd ed. (Hamburg, 1955), pp. 320–332; and Samuel C. Chew, *The Pilgrimage of Life* (New Haven and London: Yale Univ. Press, 1962), pp. 174—181. Tisdale, *Medieval Pilgrimage*, pp. 130–133, shows how the idea was applied to interpretations of Vergil.

54. See Bartlett Jere Whiting, *Proverbs, Sentences, and Proverbial Phrases from English Writings mainly before 1500* (Cambridge, Mass.: Belknap Press of Harvard Univ. Press, 1968), P200–201, and Roland M. Smith, "Three Obscure English Proverbs," *MLN* 65 (1950):443–447.

view, "we dwell here als aliens," and the world itself is "the way and passage, Thurgh whilk lies our pilgrimage."[55] The return home is therefore not "missing" from any account of a pilgrimage; it is present in the implication that such a journey reverses one's estimate of what his true home is.

The movement of *The Canterbury Tales* from one city to another can be seen, on this account, in an Augustinian way as a movement from the city of the world to the city of God; Augustine himself used the metaphor of the pilgrimage to describe this progress, and it was said that St. Thomas à Becket's last sermon, preached when he anticipated his death, was on Hebrews 13:14, "we have not here a lasting city, but we seek one that is to come."[56] True order being a quality of the eternal city, the earthly city by contrast was disordered, mutable, and hence comparable to a wilderness; it was sometimes associated with confusion.[57] The implication is present in a common motif of late medieval art where a background landscape is symbolically divided into two halves, one a wilderness and the other a civilized place such as a cultivated garden or walled town. In such landscapes a path is often to be seen. Depending on the context, this symbolical landscape may suggest the progress of civilization from a primitive state or its decline from a golden age, or it may suggest a life of pleasure as opposed to one of virtue. The wilderness suggests "the world," whether as a primeval state or as the "misery of the human condition" which tests virtue.[58] The "Way" is then a passage through a wilderness (the world) to a city (eternal life).

55. *The Pricke of Conscience*, 38:1377; 39:1394−1395, cited by Whiting, P201.

56. *City of God*, e.g. XV. 1 and XIX. 17. *Peregrinus* may have meant "resident alien" to Augustine; but readers of Chaucer's time would have thought it meant pilgrim. On St. Thomas's sermon see James Craigie Robertson, ed., *Materials for the History of Thomas Becket, Archbishop of Canterbury*, Rolls Series VII (London: Longman, 1875−1885), III:128.

57. Tisdale, *Medieval Pilgrimage*, p. 126, cites Bernard Silvestris, *Commentum Bernardi Silvestris super sex libros Eneidos Virgilii*, ed. Guilielmus Riedel (Abel, 1924), p. 12: "dicitur mundus Babylonis civitas i.e. confusionis."

58. See Erwin Panofsky, *Studies in Iconology: Humanistic Themes in the Art*

This is not, however, a reason for saying with Ralph
Baldwin that it was "in the nature of the construct that the
Parson conclude the tales of a journey whose destination
becomes thereby neither Southwerk nor Canterbury, but the
Holy City of Jerusalem."[59] Baldwin saw this aspect of the
unity of *The Canterbury Tales* as a *sovrasenso* by which the work
"becomes . . . the pilgrimage of the life of man" and which
makes the diversity of the tales and the waywardness of the
characters part of the metaphor, as when the innkeeper is
"supplanted" by the Parson.[60] Baldwin's term *sovrasenso* is
based on a comparison with Dante's *Divine Comedy*, though
he seems to argue not so much for the direct influence of
Dante on Chaucer as for a medieval esthetic which they held
in common. This esthetic, judging from what Dante says in
the letter to Can Grande, is based upon the four-level
interpretation of Scripture. Baldwin argued that medieval
rhetoric would have recommended the kind of treatment he
described; beyond this he offered no theory of medieval
esthetics in support of his thesis. Since Baldwin's time
Professor Robertson and others have done so in spades. In
Scripture, it is true, the conception of a "pilgrimage of
human life" had ample precedent. The Christian was a
"stranger and pilgrim" (Hebrews 11:13; 1 Pet. 2:11). The
Israelites in Egypt and the disciples at Emmaus were exiles.
And the life of man was a thoroughfare (Jer. 6:16). This last
is the text of the Parson's meditation:

"Stondeth upon the ways, and seeth and axeth of old paths
(that is to sayn, of old sentences) which is the good way, and
walketh in that way, and ye shall find refreshing of your
souls," etc. Many been the ways espirituels that leden folk to
our Lord Jhesu Christ, and to the regne of glory. Of which
ways, there is a full noble way and a full convenable, which
may nat fail to man ne to woman that thurgh sin hath misgoon

of the Renaissance (1939; rpt. New York and Evanston: Harper Torchbooks, 1962), pp. 40–42, 64–65.
59. Baldwin, *The Unity of the Canterbury Tales*, quoted from S&T, p. 29.
60. *Ibid.*, p. 35–37. Baldwin then went on to describe the Parson
preaching a "sermon" and the pilgrims listening intently without any
"modern unrest," each taking to heart that part of the discourse which
applied to him. But this is not in *The Canterbury Tales*.

fro the right way of Jerusalem celestial; and this way is cleped
Penitence, of which man shold gladly herknen and enquere
with all his herte. . . .

(X:76–80)

But this unilinear journey is not solely a matter of
literary convention or "scriptural tradition." It was endemic
to the idea of a pilgrimage; the institution itself made the
return a mere contingency, conceiving the destination Jerusalem, at the center of the world, as the primary goal. The
city Jerusalem itself symbolized the Heavenly City, and every
local pilgrimage was an imitation of the Jerusalem pilgrimage. The symbolism of "Scriptural tradition" promulgated
this idea, but that does not make the idea a "Scriptural" or a
literary one. On the contrary, as Professor Robertson reminds us, "Any pilgrimage during the Middle Ages, whether
it was made on the knees in a labyrinth set in a cathedral
floor, or, more strenuously, to the Holy Land, was ideally a
figure for the pilgrimage of the Christian soul through the
world's wilderness toward the celestial Jerusalem."[61] This
fact about the institution of the pilgrimage is borne out in
the pilgrimage narratives and in works of voyage literature
like Marco Polo's or Mandeville's. The homecoming, not
relevant until the late fifteenth century, was a tendency
toward "secularization," possibly an influence from the romance. The end of the Jerusalem pilgrimage was the contemplation of the great events of the Judaeo-Christian past
which gave meaning to all of human life; and the end of the
"pilgrimage of life" was eternity. A pilgrimage was, in the
traditional topos and in practice, a one-way passage *through
the world*. In that passage through the world curiosity might
lure the pilgrim—it could become, in Chaucer's phrase,
a "wandering by the way."[62]

61. *Preface to Chaucer*, p. 373.

62. Chaucer uses the word "way" in prominent places, but of course it
was an ordinary word for a road or a trip and did not by itself suggest a
metaphor. At the beginning of the General Prologue we are told that we
will "take our way," and at the end in line 856 that "with that word we
riden forth our way." In the Pardoner's Tale the revellers are told they

This curiosity and wandering drew Chaucer's attention: he saw possibilities for exploring the way of the world which no one had seen before. These possibilities were precisely the elements of visual and psychological realism, dialogue, and dramatic interplay which succeeding generations imitated, which illustrators of fifteenth-century manuscripts fastened upon, and which modern critics have admired. But it is essential to see this accomplishment in its full context. When the Parson is called upon at the end and says "Thou getest fable noon ytold for me" (X:31) we have, as so often elsewhere, an authentic bit of dialogue. One can hear in the utterance the stern tone which some parish priests of the fourteenth century no doubt took on many occasions (as clergymen do still); he has "snybbed" the Host as we are told in the General Prologue he "snybbed" his wayward parishioners. He is a real presence, this Parson—despite all the "idealized" details applied to him in the General Prologue, which make him seem an allegorical or iconographic figure, he really acts and talks in this moment like a living man. "*Benedicite!*" he cries earlier, on being addressed by the Host (II:1170ff), "What aileth the man, so sinfully to swere?" It should strain no one's credulity that there were in fourteenth-century England such stern parish priests. It is a touch of almost photographic realism that the Parson is a bit of a scold; that he can take a tone which some, like the Host, think priggish; that there is an astringent, peremptory edge to his response which provokes personal hostility or anticlericalism. In these brief moments one could justly consider the Parson a character as lively and authentic as the Wife or

---

will find Death "up this crooked way," and at the end of the Pardoner's Tale after the reconciliation between the Host and the Pardoner, we are told "Anon they kist and riden forth hir way." The forward progress of the pilgrimage is often referred to with the phrase "by the way": e.g., "goon by the way," "riden by the way" (GP 771, 780). Thus the Host suggests (774) the pilgrims do not mean to "ride by the way dumb as a ston." "By" is not the only preposition which could be used about a journey along a way; elsewhere we find "forth," "on," "in," but "by" occurs with unusual frequency in the General Prologue. People assume that "wandering by the way" means "wandering off the straight-and-narrow," but often it simply means "along the way." The emphasis falls on "wandering."

Monk or Pardoner. But it is just this bit of authenticity which entices critics into imagining that the prose piece at the end of *The Canterbury Tales* is a "sermon" and that the pilgrims listen to it. We are told that the Parson will preach what he calls a meditation. But at that point we have to give over our expectations of realism—have to suspend our belief. "The Host," says Professor Donaldson, "speaks to the Parson as if he had never seen him before, recognizing only the priest and knowing nothing of the man. In this suddenly alien and lonely world we must hurry to get in the last, virtuous tale."[63] What we get is not a tale and not a sermon either; that it shares some organizational and rhetorical features with the medieval sermon[64] does not make it a sermon. Its sources were not sermons or homilies, and it has all the trappings of a prose tract—explicits and incipits, Latin subheadings, numbered points; Chaucer could have made it look and sound like a sermon by removing these and shortening it. Instead he provided something for us to read silently, to study, to ingest and keep with us as a guide—in short, a book. At the end of *The Canterbury Tales* we are given a book to read. We are no longer addressed as an audience at a performance; we become readers. The pretending is over. "Voiceness" disappears—the Parson's voice, and the narrator's voice, are not to be heard again. "Bookness" is invoked. The book we have been enjoying, struggling with, and participating in, is quietly taken away from us, and an instructional treatise about the Way is somberly, and without comment, laid before us.

63. *Chaucer's Poetry*, p. 949.
64. See Coolidge Otis Chapman, "The Parson's Tale: A Medieval Sermon," *MLN* 43 (1928):229–234, and Alfred L. Kellogg, "St. Augustine and the Parson's Tale," *Traditio* 8 (1952):424–430, rpt. *Chaucer, Langland, Arthur: Essays in Middle English Literature* (New Brunswick, N.J.: Rutgers Univ. Press, 1972), pp. 343–352.

STYLE

WE HAVE been discussing for the most part what Chaucer said or suggested about the genre, tone, morality, and unity of his book; what he *did* is more important. If you piece together some potsherds into a vase, the next thing you want to do is compare it with other vases. You want to know which it is like and in what ways it is different from them, and you want to know this because you want to know what the artist had in mind as he worked. It's interesting to know what he said he had in mind, but his word is not the final appeal—he may have misunderstood or misrepresented the idea he executed. But the critic's "method" is suspect too: in the process of trying to understand through comparisons what was in the artist's mind that made him do as he did, the critic's preconceptions play a part in his choice of what to compare.

With Chaucer, however, there is one obvious choice of a comparison on which artist and critic can agree: the work which Chaucer himself suggested as the antithesis of his "comedy," the "tragedy" he had just finished, *Troilus and Criseyde*. The comparison will reveal more than the obvious difference of genre: it will reveal that in *The Canterbury Tales* Chaucer adopted a new style suitable to a new idea.

Most critics who discuss the style of *The Canterbury Tales* treat it as a mixture of preexisting styles—the high and the low, the French and the Italian, the conventional or courtly and the realistic or bourgeois.[1] We can only guess how that mixture came to be; we know the ingredients and the product but not the recipe. Using medieval notions of rhetoric may help us know the counsels and models medieval writers respected, but good writers, like good cooks, never follow such recipes slavishly.[2] What we need to know is the style itself, how it is different from other styles and what experience it gives us. Two styles set side by side can be shown different, and one specimen can be shown to share qualities of several styles.[3] These styles exist in a social milieu prepared to respond to them, and an artist is able to manipulate stylistic traits so as to affect his audience or reader in a more or less predictable way. Because writing is a solitary occupation during which the audience can only be imagined or supposed, it makes more sense to say that a writer writes for an imagined or supposed audience. We can often grasp something about this interiorized audience from the work itself—it isn't mere shorthand to talk about the

1. See Muscatine, *Chaucer and the French Tradition*, pp. 1–10 and chap. 6, and his restatement "*The Canterbury Tales:* Style of the Man and Style of the Work," in *Chaucer and Chaucerians*, ed. D. S. Brewer (London: Nelson, 1966), pp. 88–113. Brewer argues for the "Englishness" of Chaucer's style in "The Relationship of Chaucer to the English and European Traditions," *Chaucer and Chaucerians*, pp. 1–38. Norman E. Eliason, in *The Language of Chaucer's Poetry, Anglistica*, vol. 17 (Copenhagen: Rosenkilde and Bagger, 1972), pp. 60–136, taking an altogether linguistic view of style, argues convincingly against French influence; but on pp. 113–120 he isolates three styles in Chaucer, the artificial, simple, and colloquial, very like the styles Muscatine isolated.

2. On Chaucer's use of rhetorical precept and practice, see Payne, *The Key to Remembrance*, esp. pp. 188–201. In his restatement, "Chaucer and the Art of Rhetoric" (*Companion to Chaucer Studies*, ed. Rowland, pp. 38–57), he says that "medieval rhetorical doctrine and Chaucer's poetry should *both* be taken as expressions of the medieval idea of poetry, and we should interest ourselves in the ways in which they do and do not correspond" (p. 50). Chaucer knew, he observes, that "what one thinks he is doing is never quite exactly what he is doing" (p. 53).

3. Any specific analysis of style is always comparative in one way or another; critics talk about national and period styles, styles belonging to schools or groups of writers, styles appropriate to literary genres, types of publication, occasions, and so on, and styles of individual works. I am concerned with the last of these, and know of no previous effort to compare the styles of Chaucer's two long poems.

reader "in" the work.[4] The concept of style is probably the most useful way of getting at this circumstance of communication between writer and reader if we take style in its broadest sense as the whole range of forms, effects, and qualities which characterize a work: but seen this way, style in art reflects style in behavior and culture, brings form and content with it.[5]

This is not (some will say) what people normally mean by style. They think of style as a set of choices made from linguistic variants. It is a matter of style whether one says "cheap" or "inexpensive," "I shall" or "I will," "relations with people" or "interpersonal relationships." But a style is more than the sum total of such variants, so the analysis of a style must be more than an atomistic scrutiny of such items. What the student of style is looking for is a set of principles or codes, a way of seeing things, which directed and accounts for the author's stylistic choices. When we describe such principles we seem to be describing something metalinguistic—an ethos or "world." The individual item or variant may be what draws our attention to the dominant character-

4. Cf. Stanley Fish, *Surprised by Sin: The Reader in Paradise Lost* (1967; rpt. Berkeley and Los Angeles: Univ. of California Press, 1971), and *Self-Consuming Artifacts: The Experience of Seventeenth-Century Literature* (Berkeley and Los Angeles: Univ. of California Press, 1972), esp. pp. 383–427, originally published in *NLH* 2 (1970):123–162.

5. I have argued previously that *Troilus, Piers Plowman,* and *Sir Gawain* share characteristics of one "basic style" of fourteenth-century English literature; see *The Three Temptations: Medieval Man in Search of the World* (Princeton, N. J.: Princeton Univ. Press, 1966), pp. 5–6 and chap. 6. I am arguing here that the style of *The Canterbury Tales* is uniquely different from this basic style; the present chapter can therefore be read as a development of my earlier hypothesis. Subsequent treatments of fourteenth-century style, sometimes using the same three authors I used, have dealt chiefly with period and national style: e.g. Muscatine, *Poetry and Crisis in the Age of Chaucer* (Notre Dame and London: Univ. of Notre Dame Press, 1972), which concentrates chiefly on differences among the three poets in their response to the temper of the age; Burrow, *Ricardian Poetry,* which concentrates on the poets' relationship to their medium; Kean, *Chaucer and the Making of English Poetry,* and Robinson, *Chaucer and the English Tradition,* which concentrate on tradition. Pamela Gradon, in *Form and Style in Early English Literature* (London: Methuen, 1971) treats styles as they are appropriate to modes and genres and concludes, alas, that the time is not ripe for a definitive treatment of style.

istics of a style: I think it must be true that those critics most sensitive to style have a way of grasping significant exceptional items on instinct, of getting an inner "click" and following it up.[6] I may have done this after a fashion in *thinking* about the styles of the *Troilus* and *The Canterbury Tales*, but I am going to describe the results, not the process—am going to describe the larger principles which make the style of *The Canterbury Tales* part of its idea.

THE NARRATIVE NOW

In the *Troilus*, as in *The Canterbury Tales*, time moves forward from Creation to Doomsday and the past is a sequence of unique events. But in the *Troilus* these events are selected because of their historical and moral meaning. The story of Troilus is told because Troy's fall brought the founding of the West and because Troilus reveals a type of earthly striving in which the reader is able to divine a moral meaning. In addition the story of such a hero, who died honorably in a decisive battle, is told to preserve his name and reputation, to establish in the successive stream of human lives the "glory" which medieval knights deemed a just reward for noble deeds. Thus everything specific and historical in this style gets its profoundest meaning from what it shares with other unique events; the events of the *Troilus* happen in a span of three years, but their meaning is the same as that of any passing love or any fallen city. Troilus sees this meaning at the end when he is removed from time. From such a point of view the unique historical event is one in a series of endless repetitions. This repetitive quality in human experience invites the author to associate

6. Leo Spitzer, *Linguistics and Literary History: Essays in Stylistics* (1948; rpt. Princeton, N. J.: Princeton Univ. Press, 1967), pp. 7–29; the inner click refers to the starting point at which a critic notes a discrete stylistic item and associates it with larger stylistic traits which in turn draw his attention to other discrete items. Spitzer called this process the "philological circle" and characterized it as "mentalistic." Cf. Karl D. Uitti, "Philology: Factualness and History," in *Literary Style: A Symposium*, ed. Seymour Chatman (London and New York: Oxford Univ. Press, 1971), pp. 111–132.

events with the repetitions of seasonal change: Troilus's experience of three years is equated in the poem's imagery with a single revolution of the seasons and with the turning of Fortune's wheel.[7]

The Canterbury Tales has no such pattern. It depicts a one-way journey. There is no suggestion in the Parson's Prologue that a new day will dawn, or that the pilgrims will turn about and go home. We part from them at a "thropes ende" beyond Harbledown on the Canterbury Way, probably the place where pilgrims first caught sight of the cathedral and dismounted to praise God. The journey is allegorized as the "parfit glorious pilgrimage / That highte Jerusalem celestial." Nothing happens here which has happened before. In the last fragments there are no repeated lines or backward references. The unexpected arrival of the Canon's Yeoman suggests rather the random and unpredictable quality of events as they follow in sequence, and his tale introduces a new kind of subject. Everything moves on, nothing is finished. The sun casts long shadows; the moon rises into Libra, a symbol of justice.[8] The Host's ordinance is "almost fulfilled"; he says all tales have been told but one. It is 4 P.M., the "eleventh hour."[9] Nor in the tales themselves do we ever go over the same ground twice—each tale is a new beginning. Often, it is true, the tales look back to previous tales in a parodic or ironic or disputatious spirit, but this looking back always adds something new, makes a reply, sees

7. On this cyclical view of time and its influence on medieval style, see Howard, *The Three Temptations*, pp. 260–272, and esp. pp. 265–266, n. 10. To the influence of annual taxation and the invention of the mechanical clock which exhibited the pattern of the cosmos, I might have added the idea of circumnavigating the globe proposed in Mandeville's *Travels*, and the controversies about astrology and astronomy. On the latter see Chauncey Wood, *Chaucer and the Country of the Stars: Poetic Uses of Astrological Imagery* (Princeton, N. J.: Princeton Univ. Press, 1970), pp. 12–69, and Hamilton M. Smyser, "A View of Chaucer's Astronomy," *Speculum* 45 (1970):359–373. And see Sue Ellen Holbrook, *Medieval Notions of Time in Literature and Art with a Special Emphasis on Malory's* Le Morte Darthur, Diss. Univ. of California (Los Angeles), 1971.

8. See Wood, chap. 7, and Rodney Delasanta, "The Theme of Judgment in *The Canterbury Tales*," *MLQ* 31 (1970):298–307.

9. Wood, p. 297 and n. 35.

things in a different light. We never get the feeling, as we do at the end of the *Troilus*, that we are back where we started, that *plus ça change plus c'est la même chose*.

As we pass along in the linear sequence of *The Canterbury Tales*, each experience of the pilgrimage—each person, each interchange, each tale—has a momentary interest which makes it *seem* to happen in the present. If we imagine the present moment—"now"—as a moving dot between the remembered past and the unknown future, this "now" in *The Canterbury Tales* is simply our continued experience of reading or hearing the work; the dot moves along the span of time during which the narrator describes the pilgrimage incident by incident and tale by tale. Into this linear performance the tales introduce events of various past times and various places[10]—a "then" which was once "now," and which becomes "now" again in the telling. This is altogether different from *Troilus and Criseyde*, in which Chaucer portrayed a *distant* past: acknowledging that "in sundry ages,/ In sundry londes, sundry been usages" (II:27-28), he deliberately dwelt upon the strangeness and distance of ancient Troy. As he drew close to the most intimate scenes (in Book II) he invoked the muse of history. He depicted an ancient, doomed city in the last days before its fall, represented its pagan rites and philosophies, showed its people moving haplessly in intellectual and spiritual darkness. He described that world with scenes and language of fourteenth-century England, but he used this anachronism intentionally to create an impression of immediacy and reality.[11] He was

10. If we try to put the settings of the tales on a map we discover that the romances and moral tales are set in distant lands, the realistic ones closer to home. The Knight's Tale is set in Athens and Thebes in the age of Theseus; the Squire, outdoing his father, sets his tale in Tartary in the age of the great Khan. The tales told by the Man of Law, Clerk, Second Nun, and Physician are all set or at least begin in Italy during the earlier part of the Christian era; the Prioress's tale takes place in Asia. The remaining tales are set in England, France, Flanders, or Lombardy. The geographical placement helps make the romances and ideal narratives seem more exotic than the realistic tales; but all seem equally to happen before our eyes.

11. See Howard, *The Three Temptations*, pp. 112–122, and Bloomfield, "Distance and Predestination in *Troilus and Criseyde*," rpt. in *Essays and Explorations*, pp. 201–216.

aware that "in form of speche is chaunge / Within a thousand yeer," and that words which then meant something "now wonder nice and straunge / Us thinketh hem" (II:22-24), so he translated their words and actions into modern equivalents. There is nothing "naive" about this—it does not betray a defective "sense of the past": it is used for artistic effect, to make vivid and understandable a pre-Christian culture. When the poet wanted he could make Trojan life appear so familiar that it seemed to be happening before our eyes; but no less often he put that world at a historical distance, playing up its strangeness.

In *The Canterbury Tales* Chaucer abandoned this technique. He brings the past momentarily into the present, flattens out foreignness and distance in time. All the scenes of the actual pilgrimage, in the General Prologue and the various prologues and links, are recounted in the simple past: "At night *was come* into that hostelrye. . . ." "A knight there *was*. . . ." "With him there *was* his son, a young Squier. . . ." Whatever else we need to know is related as anterior: "thereto *hadde he riden* . . ."; "he *hadde been* sometime in chyvachie." The "historical present"[12] is never used for the events of the pilgrimage itself. "Greet chiere *made* our Host," we learn. "Our conseil *was* nat longe for to seche"; "This thing *was* graunted"; "Amorrowe . . . up *rose* oure Host"; the Knight "*bigan* . . . His tale anon. . . ." These events, when done, pass into anterior time:

Whan that the Knight *had* thus his tale *ytold*,
In all the route *nas* there young ne old
That he ne said it *was* a noble storie.

(I:3109-3111)

Chaucer does not say "it had been" a noble story; the stories themselves are not placed in anterior time once told, but are permitted to come up into the present and remain there, preserved in memory, tradition, or writing, able to be told again. Events are bound to time (and telling or hearing a tale is an event), but a tale has a life of its own—it lives in the

12. See Larry D. Benson, "Chaucer's Historical Present: Its Meaning and Uses," *ES* 42 (1961):65–77.

pseudoeternity of tradition and reputation, in the house of Fame.[13] The present tense is thus used for the immediate moment in tale-telling, the moment of direct communication between teller and listener. For example, we learn of the Friar,

> He *was* an esy man to yeve penaunce
> Ther as he *wiste* to have a good pitaunce.
> For unto a povre ordre for to yive
> *Is* signe that a man is well yshrive.
>
> (223-226)

The narrator reports the Friar's words or thoughts in the present tense, as if the Friar were saying it himself or Chaucer the pilgrim repeating it and expecting us to agree. The present tense is the moment of participation, the moment when a thing that *was* is passed from one brain to another in the mutual act of communication. Thus the narrator says, speaking of the Monk, "And I *said* his opinion was good": his agreement with the Monk is presented as an event which took place on the pilgrimage. But then he lapses into the present: "What sholde he study . . .? How shall the world be served?" We get a little monologue—a thought, as it actually is—which has passed from the Monk's mind to the narrator's and now passes from the narrator's to ours. Then we return to past events: "Therefore he *was* a prika-sour. . . ." In the same way Chaucer says of the Summoner's Latin "No wonder *is,* he herd it all the day," and goes on

> And eek ye *knowen* well how that a jay
> Can clepen "Watte". . . .
>
> (642-643)

In a moment he will lapse from the present tense back to the past:

> But now *is* time to you for to telle
> How that we *baren* us that ilke night,
> Whan we *were* in that hostelry alight;
> And after *wol I tell* of our viage. . . .
>
> (720-723)

13. On the relationship between Chaucer's idea of a house of Fame and the idea of *The Canterbury Tales,* see below, pp. 330–332.

This "now" has for its future the narrator's stated intentions and expectations. He includes us, the audience, in the ongoing action, lets us know what we can expect.

This circumstance—that we are present *in the work* as hearers or readers—is expressed in a passage whose temporal relationships are remarkable:

> The Miller *is* a cherl, ye know well this;
> So *was* the Reeve eek and othere mo,
> And harlotrie they tolden bothe two.
> Aviseth you, and put me out of blame;
> And eek men *shall* nat make ernest of game.
>
> (1:3182-3186)

Why in these lines is the past tense used of the Reeve, the present tense of the Miller?—because the Miller is there at hand about to tell his tale. It is as if the narrator were watching with us. What he remembers from the past he can promise for the future—both "tolden" harlotry. But he states this in the past tense as a fact, not in the future tense as an expectation. Addressing us parenthetically, he removes (so to speak) the mask of the Miller, which he is about to put on again—holds the mask at arm's length as he pauses to comment. It is one of the most extraordinary moments in medieval literature: "Aviseth you," he tells us—think it over, make up your minds. And then he makes up our minds for us: "Men *shall* nat make ernest of game." Like the Host, who had the company hold up their hands in assent before they knew what they were assenting to, he tells us to respond freely and then tells us how to respond!

All the double truths we must accept are present in this passage: the voice addressing us is at once the poet who writes and the narrator who rehearses; the narrator is at once teller and performer; the pilgrims are at once being performed and performing; we the audience are at once hearers and readers; and we are free to choose but told how to react. The present moment in the General Prologue and in the links between tales is precisely the moment when all these paradoxes are held in balance—the moment when we are paying attention and are successfully in communication with the narrator as he tells or "rehearses." Hence the

pilgrims' voices have the same ring of vivid direct communication as the narrator's. This is most evident in the prologues
to tales: what personal presence in all literature is more
immediate than the Wife or the Pardoner in their prologues? But it is notable in most of the tales as well. The
pilgrims address us directly in the here and now: "This
duke," says the Knight, "of whom I make mencioun, / Whan
he was comen almost to the town. . . ." And the duke is thus
recreated in the present by the Knight's "mencioun."

The narrator's voice helps create this sense of immediacy. Rarely does it emerge through the voice of the performing pilgrim, and at that in the most innocuous way—for
example, in the Prioress's apostrophe: "Now maystow sin-
gen, follwing ever in oon / The white Lamb celestial—*quod
she* . . ." (VII:580-581). At the end of the Pardoner's Tale, it
is true, the narrator's voice recounts the squabble and the
peacemaking that follows; but the voice is so gentle, and so
solemn, that it is hard not to hear in it Chaucer's own.
Chaucer's *own* voice intervenes constantly; it is one of the
striking, and original, marks of the style. In the Knight's
Tale we get many overtones of the poet's presence. The
precedent is set there. But as often as not it is ambiguous: we
have to decide for ourselves whether, say, at the end of the
Nun's Priest's Tale the simple ironic moral is the priest's
words or Chaucer's own, or both. One characteristic of the
style is that we are often not able to tell what voice we hear
and are not meant to.

This intervention of the poet's voice is comparable to
the narrator's "interruptions" in the *Troilus*; but in the *Troilus*
the narrator's direct address to the audience created distance, reminding us that he and we exist in the here and
now, centuries later than the time of the story. In *The
Canterbury Tales* there is no such contrast. Direct address by
the poet or narrator never "distances" the story; it always
achieves immediacy. The narrative present—the "now" we
listen in—gives contemporaneity to the "then" of the story,
never pushes it into the long ago or the far away.

If we could find any exception to this we would find it in
the Knight's Tale. Like the *Troilus* it is adapted from a work

by Boccaccio, is set in the ancient world, and is a tale of knightly deeds and courtly love. Like the *Troilus* it has a narrator (the Knight) who addresses us about the difficulty of his task: "I have, God wot, a large feeld to ere, / And wayke been the oxen in my plough" (886-887). But unlike the *Troilus,* this narrator is not explicitly identified with the author. Instead there emerges a voice who talks about writing (1201); for example, it asks about Palamon's imprisonment "Who coude rime in English proprely / His martyrdom?"—and then answers "for sooth it am nat I" (1459f). How or why this voice gets into the tale is a problem we will put aside for a later chapter. No one denies it is there. No one, I think, is any longer so bent on realism in *The Canterbury Tales* as to suppose that such a passage is the Knight's own words. Assuming then that it is an intrusive voice (Chaucer's own), what is its effect? Does it "distance" the story, remind us of its pastness and remoteness by bringing us momentarily back into the present? Can it for example be reckoned comparable in its effect to the following interruption in the *Troilus*, which occurs as the lovers embrace for the first time?

> What might or may the sely larke saye,
> Whan that the sperhauk hath it in his foot?
> I kan namore but of thise ilke twaye—
> To whom this tale sucre be or soot,
> Though that I tarry a yeer, somtime I moot,
> After myn auctour, tellen hir gladnesse,
> As well as I have told hir hevinesse.
>
> (III:1191-1197)

I think that it cannot. The interruption in the *Troilus* just quoted has a dramatic value. In a moment of heightened intensity it draws the reader away, puts esthetic and historical distance between us and the lovers; to the extent that it is funny it can be compared with "comic relief." Its purpose is to draw us back, let us get our breath. The passage in the Knight's Tale is different. It is not an interruption; it comes at a moment of transition. The poet has just told how Arcite returned to Athens in disguise. "And in this blisse," he says, "let I now Arcite, / And speke I wol of Palamon a lite"

(1449-1450). Then follow eight woeful lines about Palamon's long imprisonment, ending with the statement (in the present tense) that

> . . . he is a prisoner
> Perpetuelly, noght only for a yeer.

No sooner has this lame rime hobbled past than we get the question,

> Who coude rime in English proprely
> His martyrdom? for sooth it am nat I.
> Therefore I pass as lightly as I may.

Then the teller continues:

> It fell that in the seventh yeer, of May
> The thridde night (as olde bookes seyn,
> That all this story tellen more pleyn). . . .

This fleeting glimpse of a narrator searching old books clearer than his own and hurrying on does not at all create a momentary "distance" or "relief." On the contrary, it renders dramatically the very act which gives the Knight's Tale its immediacy and excitement—the act of drawing events from the recorded past into the narrative now.

How intensely this effect works in the Knight's Tale is best illustrated in its major scenes—the descriptions of the temples in Part III, the prayers, the battle, and the death of Arcite. Throughout there is constantly present an "I" who hovers over the story, representing himself as having been an eyewitness to the events:

> There saugh I Dane, yturned til a tree,
> I mene nat the goddesse Diane,
> But Penneus doghter, which that highte Dane.
> There saugh I Attheon an hert ymaked,
> For vengeaunce that he saugh Diane al naked;
> I saugh how that his houndes have him caught
> And freeten him, for that they knew him naught.
> Yet peinted was a litel further moor
> How Atthalante hunted the wild boor,
> And Meleagre, and many another mo,
> For which Diane wroght him care and wo.

STYLE 87

There saugh I many another wonder storie,
The which me list nat drawen to memorie.

(2062-2074)

This "I" has actually *seen* the stories painted on the temple's
wall, seen them with the kind of understanding which
permits him to warn us like a schoolmaster against confusing
Dane and Diane. He claims, then, to be producing the stories
out of memory, out of personal experience. From any representational point of view it is preposterous—neither Knight,
narrator, or poet has been in ancient Athens. It is rhetoric.
But it will not do to dismiss it as a conventional "device" of
rhetoric: no rhetorical device ever existed without a purpose, and no poet worth the name ever used any device just
because it was conventional. The purpose here is to achieve
immediacy through a deliberate anachronism: the pastness
of the events is obliterated, "then" drawn up into "now."
Pagan temples and prayers are modernized by association
with planets and their influences. The teller becomes an eyewitness, represents the recorded past as the remembered
past. It is akin to the deliberate anachronism of the *Troilus*,
but the "I" in the Knight's Tale is a more spectral presence
than the bookish narrator of the *Troilus*, and no book is
involved; the preposterous truth-claim is that the teller was
there.

As we approach the climactic scene, a medieval tournament, the events of the story come less and less to be
reported in the past tense: we get the "historical present," a
familiar bit of rhetoric which draws the past into the narrative
"now" and makes it happen before our eyes. This is the case
in the famous description of the battle, where Chaucer
astonishingly lapses into an approximation of alliterative
verse:

The heraudes left hir pricking up and down;
Now ringen trumpes loud and clarioun.
There is namore to sayn, but west and est
In goon the speres full sadly in arrest;
In gooth the sharpe spore into the side.
There seen men who can joust and who can ride;

There shiveren shaftes upon sheeldes thicke.
He feeleth thurgh the herte-spoon the pricke.
Up springen speres twenty foot on highte;
Out goon the swerdes as the silver brighte;
The helmes they tohewen and toshrede;
Out brest the blood with stierne stremes rede;
With mighty maces the bones they tobreste.
He thurgh the thickest of the throng gan threste.
There stomblen steedes strong, and down gooth all.

                                            (2599-2613)

In what follows, the teller of the tale hovers over events, scrutinizing them in the present tense as if they were happening in the palms of his hands. Of Arcite's victory: "Who sorrweth now but woeful Palamon" (2652). Of the moment of triumph: "Anon there is a noise of peple bigunne" (2660); Arcite "pricketh endelong the large place" (2678). Of Arcite's wound: "Swelleth the brest of Arcite" (2743). Of his death: "Arcite is cold" (2815). Of the aftermath: ". . . by length of certein yeres, / All stinted is the moorning and the teeres / Of Greekes" (2967-2969). These uses of the present tense are taken at random—there are scores of others. The tale never abandons the past tense, which is used for events that advance the main lines of the story; but toward the end it uses the present tense more and more often. The very opposite technique was used in the *Troilus*: the ending actually stretched distance in time and space. Criseyde was removed to the Greeks, Troilus to the eighth sphere; we and the narrator were removed into the Christian present and, from it, into contemplation of the Christian mysteries. But in the Knight's Tale the ending collapses temporal distance. The closing sentence even couples the final outcome and the final blessing on the audience, as if the speaker had his eye at once upon the characters of the story and the company of his listeners or readers:

Thus endeth Palamon and Emelye;
And God save all this faire compaignye!

The Knight's Tale sets this "narrative now" in the reader's mind and establishes it as a stylistic feature of the

work. The appropriation of the distant and past to the here
and now does not give us, as the *Troilus* did, a picture of a
civilization long dead to which we draw up and then away,
part of a cyclical process of rises and falls. The Knight's Tale,
and *The Canterbury Tales* generally, give us instead a picture
of time ticking away, one event following another, the
recorded and the remembered past coming alive randomly
in the narrative now, where we perceive them, and passing
again into the storehouse of memory.

OBSOLESCENCE AND THE SOCIAL FABRIC

Yet there is a difference between the way we perceive time
and the way we experience it. We perceive time by concep-
tualizing in periods or ages or tenses; but we experience time
in little things. Dust on a tabletop, cracked plates, and piles
of unread books give us messages which clocks and calen-
dars do not. We experience time in newness and oldness,
sameness and difference, unpredictability, repetitions, gaps.
In various works Chaucer rendered time by various such
experiences. If time in *The Canterbury Tales* is perceived as a
passing "now" which moves in a passing age and that age is
the last of a series, we have a very intellectual (and medieval)
perception of time.[14] But this moving "now" is rendered
dramatically by the experience of *obsolescence*.

14. This medieval idea of successive ages and a world growing old is,
I believe, implicit in *The Canterbury Tales* and the *Troilus*, but the point is
not important to my argument. The "whilom" we look back upon in the
tales is an indeterminate span in which we can only distinguish former
times from recent times, time before Christ from time after Christ. The
Middle Ages visualized time as divided into "ages"—according to Joachim
of Flora there were three such ages, according to Abelard five, and
according to most other writers seven (six ages corresponding to the days
of creation, plus a seventh in which, as on the day God rested and creation
ceased, time was to end). Because at the end of this "age of ages" time
stops and all is eternity, "linear" Christian time was really part of a cycle:
the end of time was the "eleventh hour," after which beginning and end
become one. This conception is present in *The Canterbury Tales* in the
Canon's Yeoman's appearance and in the Parson's Prologue; see Wood,
p. 297, and Bruce A. Rosenberg, "Swindling Alchemist, Antichrist,"

By obsolescence I mean the experience of things not yet obsolete about which it is feasible to predict an end. Chaucer distinguishes it from "newfangleness" and from "old things." Obsolescence bears the marks of past and future, for in it we see the boundary of each. Chaucer says of the Monk that he "let olde thinges passe, / And held after the newe world the space": the Monk chooses between new and old. Obsolescence has the Janus-like quality of encapsulating past and future; it is for that reason the most intense manifestation of the present. To grasp obsolescence requires an immersion in one's own time and place, a sensitivity not just to fads and fashions but to all fluctuations of ideas, hopes, customs, perceptions, habits, usages, structures and relationships, people and things. A sense of obsolescence calls for the most delicate response to the changes and movements of these, and so requires an eye for detail and a gift of precise expression: obsolescence lurks in subtleties—in the uses and textures of things, in nuances of languages, in gestures, in attitudes. It is based on memory. In our own time (and our own country) we grasp obsolescence unerringly—it is something we have a sense of, as one is said to have a sense of humor, of direction, or of the past. Once out of our own culture or milieu our sense of obsolescence fails us, as our sense of humor may do.

Let me offer an example. In America, at least on the east coast of America at the time I write, railroad travel is obsolescent. It is still part of life and for many a necessity; new trains go on being manufactured and improvements go on being made. It is in no way obsolete—train travel is still taken for granted. But trains have lost all newfangledness; there is no more glamor in them—there is perhaps romance and nostalgia. A sure sign of obsolescence is the emergence of enthusiasts who want to preserve what is passing, study what is past, and forestall what is to come. Whenever a train

---

CentR 6 (1962):566–580. On the ages of the world see George Boas, *Essays on Primitivism and Related Ideas in the Middle Ages* (1948; rpt. New York: Octagon Books, 1966), pp. 177–185 and passim. The fullest treatment is James Dean, *The World Grows Old: The Significance of a Medieval Idea*, Diss. Johns Hopkins, 1971.

makes its last run, it is filled with writers and cultists, cheered at every stop by well-wishers and sentimentalists. And this is because the *idea* of train travel is obsolescent; the reality exists as much as ever in some places, but people experience that reality differently. All the appurtenances which once seemed luxurious—the chair cars, the dining cars, the lounges and bars, the little rooms and "parlours" with their stuffed chairs and chrome and mirrors—came to seem worn and démodé. The conductors, once grand dignitaries with waistcoats and precise gold watches, became surly officials of a dispirited bureaucracy. The waiters and porters who once practiced their arts with proud grace became grubby, fumbling, and annoyed. Compare the crisp affability of airline stewardesses, all Cheshire smiles and golden voices. In fact trains travel faster and are better and safer than they were ten years ago; but they have lost their dignity and wonder.

There are really no obsolescent things, only obsolescent ideas, attitudes, and values. The obsolescence is in us. It is our notions and our feelings about a thing which make it obsolescent and finally obsolete. There are obsolescent heroes (the cowboy), institutions (the church), locales ("downtown"), social ranks (servant), jobs (shoeshine boy), manners (tipping one's hat); and of course obsolescent styles, ideals, and words. Obsolescence is not to be found in fads or fashions, things by nature short-lived which owe their very existence to newfangledness and timeliness. The garment which is already "out" by the time it is bought, the automobile designed to look old (and fall apart) next year, this season's fashionable tag-words, songs, plays, dances, theories of literature—all these are just the flotsam and jetsam of culture; their changing is itself part of a culture. Nothing can be obsolescent until it has been institutionalized, has enjoyed some measure of stability in the life of a society. A newspaper, a bibliography, or a dictionary may be *obsolete* the day it is published, but that does not make newspapers, bibliographies, or dictionaries obsolescent. As a part of culture they will only be obsolescent if there emerges—as some think there has—a real possibility that they will be replaced by electronic devices.

One sign of obsolescence is nostalgia; another is renewal. Nostalgia produces all kinds of efforts to force renewal upon obsolescent things. The "Metroliner," the fast train which now speeds between New York and Washington, seems a model of train travel—comfortable, clean, frequently on time. Its attendants adopt a cheerful manner—all politeness and efficiency. Of course the meals in one's seat, the solicitous voice over the loudspeaker, the forced cheer, the display of efficiency, reveal how the new train is modelled on the airplane—and this makes some nostalgic for the way trains used to be. But such renewals are a part of obsolescence. And for that reason, another feature of obsolescence is uncertainty. We are never sure whether the renewal will succeed. It is unpredictable. If we *knew* that trains would disappear we would begin to call them obsolete. But as I write, a new company is formed to take over passenger trains; an official proclaims a "new era."

Obsolescence is probably one of the most important ways we experience time: it is entwined with the particularities of daily life, with what we esteem, think, and do. Yet in the *Troilus*, for all its focus on the domestic realm, we do not find obsolescence. We are thrown back into a former age which we know *is going to* pass away. We are reminded of a fallen civilization which went before (Thebes). We get a vivid picture of the life of noblemen in the ancient city (very like that of medieval knights and ladies), are made to understand their customs and values. But we never get a sense of their customs and values passing away or of new ones taking their place. We sense that a catastrophe is to happen. We know from hindsight it *will* happen. But we observe no changes subtly taking place in people's minds or in their culture or society. Their world is doomed, but their way of life is stable and secure.

In *The Canterbury Tales*, as we are made to feel the immediacy, the contemporaneity of its setting, we do observe changes in thought, culture, and society; our sense of obsolescence is invoked. The opening lines of the General Prologue, with their high-flown literary conventions modelled on French poetry, embody an obsolescent style—

or so it would have seemed to Chaucer, who had turned to
other models. This style is abandoned at once, and except
here and there within the tales we do not encounter it again.
The theme of springtime in these lines suggests time passing, and people turn in this season to old customs and traditions; but precisely at the moment when the poet abandons
the obsolescent style—"Bifell that in that seson on a day, / In
Southwerk at the Tabard"—he reminds us that the pilgrimage is the familiar national one, that it begins in a tavern and
in the disreputable suburb Southwark. Everyone agreed the
institution of the pilgrimage was not what it had been in old
times, and Chaucer, though he represents the pilgrimage in
its ideal and symbolical form at the end, shows the pilgrims
at the outset and along the way following an obsolescent
custom "after the newe way." We see too, in the General
Prologue, that their stations in life are changing, that the
social structure and the culture itself are changing.

This difference between the *Troilus* and *The Canterbury
Tales* occurs because the poems deal with different social
classes.[15] In the *Troilus* all the characters are (to adopt a
modern British distinction) "royals" or "nobles." The only
social-class difference to be found is that between the ranks
of princes (to which Troilus belongs) and the lesser ranks of
nobles (to which Criseyde belongs). We never see anyone
below this class. Imagine how altered the work would be if
there were scenes where the servants gossiped, as in the
novels of Ivy Compton-Burnett, about secrets happening
"below stairs." Suppose we saw the "commons" reacting to
events or participating in the affairs of the doomed city; suppose a duenna like the nurse in *Romeo and Juliet* were present, some character like the Wife of Bath; or suppose
characters like the Miller or even the Physician or Man of
Law had a part in the *Troilus*. In the Trojan "Parlement" a
wrong decision is made because of the "noyse of peple"
(IV:183), the "folk" (202); these are presumably the lower

15. In what follows I have had in mind D. S. Brewer, "Class Distinction
in Chaucer," *Speculum* 43 (1968):290–305, and a paper by John F.
Benton, "Class, Audience, and Meaning," presented at Ohio State University, February 1971, of which the author kindly sent me a copy.

classes. But we do not hear them talk. They only make noise, and they are wrong. If we saw more than one social group we might see changes in the social fabric, but the limitation to the upper classes obscures obsolescence. At the seat of power life seems stable—even private life. A story set exclusively in Buckingham Palace or the White House might—like the *Troilus*—give us a sense of a nation about to collapse, but it would probably leave us in the dark about specific social and cultural developments. For this reason clothes (which reveal status and social roles) figure much less prominently in the *Troilus* than in *The Canterbury Tales*.

In this respect *The Canterbury Tales* was a departure in Chaucer's style. None of his earlier poems, except for the last scene in the *Parliament of Fowls*, had anything to do with differences in social class. Not that there weren't precedents— there was "class satire" of the kind Gower was writing, and the lower classes get into the Italian frame-narratives. But in *The Canterbury Tales* Chaucer presented social-class distinctions in such a way as to point up the disparity between what people thought and what they did—between the obsolescent idea of social class which his society held and the more complicated actuality of its gradations. In the General Prologue he suggests the Three Estates (Gower *named* them in his prologue); but he describes a variegated and mobile set of social distinctions or "degrees." And he sets the idea of their obsolescence in our minds with the Knight.

The Knight, of the lesser nobility, is an obsolescent hero, a "knight of the Cross." The battles in which he has participated stretch back forty years. The three lists in which he has engaged at Tramissene would have seemed old-fashioned in the 1380s, for proper wartime lists became less frequent as warfare and weaponry became more elaborate.[16]

16. That Chaucer's "model and the ideals which it embodied were already doomed," that "Gunpowder and cannon had come to take away the occupation and the prestige of the knight" was pointed out long ago by John Matthews Manly, "A Knight Ther Was," *Transactions and Proceedings of the American Philological Association* 38 (1907):89–107. The lists described by Froissart, whom Manly quotes at length, had taken place within living memory; but Froissart describes them with nostalgia. See also Muriel

During the period he has been on these crusading expeditions, the English kings were at war with France, and this makes him seem the more an idealist.[17] His values are the old chivalric ones—"trouth," "honour," "freedom," "courteisie," the unwillingness to say "villeinye." That he is meant to be viewed as an obsolescent figure is underscored by the portrait of his son the Squire. While the father is a warrior for old causes, the son exemplifies the fads of courtly life—he is elaborately dressed, accomplished in various skills, full of stylish joy, "curteis," "lowly," "serviceable," a "lover." As a fledgling warrior he has "borne him well" on

Bowden, *A Commentary on the General Prologue to the Canterbury Tales*, 2nd ed. (1948; rpt. New York and London: Macmillan, 1967), pp. 44–69, and Thomas J. Hatton, "Chaucer's Crusading Knight, A Slanted Ideal," *ChauR* 3 (1968): 77–87.

17. Ward, *The Canterbury Pilgrimage*, p. 159. It was once suggested that the Knight is a composite figure modeled on Henry of Lancaster (John of Gaunt's father-in-law, father of the Duchess Blanche) and Henry Bolingbroke (Gaunt's son); see A. S. Cook, "The Historical Background of Chaucer's Knight," *Transactions of the Connecticut Academy of Arts and Sciences* 20 (1916):161–240. The suggestion is very unlikely—Lancaster was one of the most powerful barons of the realm, whereas the Knight appears to be of a lower echelon. He *is* imbued with the kind of ideals which apparently moved Henry of Lancaster. Henry was known as "the Good Duke." He built churches, endowed monasteries, helped the poor and the oppressed; during an illness he wrote a book of devotions called *Mercy, Grant Mercy* in which he recalled his sins and blessings. And he went on crusades, in Lithuania, Algeciras, Rhodes, and Cyprus; at least the first two were campaigns which the Knight himself might have been on. When the plague struck Henry of Lancaster down in 1361, his daughter Matilda in 1362, and Blanche in 1369, John of Gaunt inherited the greatest estate in England; on the background of these events see Armitage-Smith, *John of Gaunt*, pp. 19–23, 75–93. The contrast between Gaunt, Chaucer's "patron," and the old Duke of Lancaster (of whom Chaucer would have had some knowledge or acquaintance) could not have escaped the poet's eyes. Gaunt was turbulent, irascible, arrogant, and self-indulgent. As a warrior he was no crusader—his ruling passion in later years was the conquest of Spain: he had married Costanza, the exiled heiress to the throne of Castile, and the conquest would have made him king. Costanza herself, a pious, withdrawn creature, made a startling contrast with Gaunt, who had a mistress (Chaucer's sister-in-law), an elaborate palace, and no ascetical streak that I have noticed. Compared with his predecessor Henry "the Good Duke," Chaucer's patron must have represented something of a falling-off. It isn't necessary to argue for any specific identification of the Knight or Squire, but the presentation of them should be read with these historical circumstances in mind.

one campaign, the disreputable "crusade" waged in 1382-1383 against the French in Flanders, a scandal, as it actually was, on which unruly captains plundered the land.[18] The Squire must not be thought foppish or degenerate; but the knighthood and chivalry to which he has been bred is shown in decline.[19]

There is reason to say that chivalry was always in decline, because its ideals, which originated in the twelfth century, bore at first a religious stamp.[20] The old ideal of a chaste, monklike knighthood devoted to the protection of Jerusalem pilgrims, and the ideal of a united Christian commonwealth in which European knighthood might join forces, conquer the Holy Land, and Christianize the Mohammedans, was pretty much tarnished by the fourteenth century. Chivalry was a wordly institution based on otherworldly ideals: it was inevitable that the ideals should be compromised, mingled with a feudal and courtly ideology inimical to the ascetic tenor of Christian morality.[21] If we ask what were the motives of knights, we come up with conflicting

18. See Alan Gaylord, "A85–88: Chaucer's Squire and the Glorious Campaign," *Papers of the Michigan Academy of Science, Arts, and Letters* 45 (1960):341–361, and Stanley J. Karhl, "Chaucer's *Squire's Tale* and the Decline of Chivalry," *ChauR* 7 (1973):194–209.

19. Ruth Nevo, "Chaucer: Motive and Mask in the 'General Prologue,'" *MLR* 58 (1963):6, points to the ambiguity of his position as a youth: he may become like his father, or may be "the ancestor of the Elizabethan and Restoration fop."

20. The religious side of the chivalric ideal was no doubt shaped by the Knights Templar; they were praised by St. Bernard of Clairvaux (*De laude novae militae ad milites templi*, *PL* 182:921–940), who had a hand in formulating their rule. But by the early fourteenth century they had fallen notoriously into decay; the order was broken up by the church and its leaders executed. While the specific charges against them may have been trumped up, there is little doubt that they became worldly and degenerate. The Teutonic Knights, with whom Chaucer's Knight has fought, maintained respectability more successfully.

21. On the decline of chivalry see F. J. C. Hearnshaw, "Chivalry and Its Place in History," in *Chivalry: A Series of Studies to Illustrate Its Historical Significance and Civilizing Influence*, ed. Edgar Prestage (New York: Alfred A. Knopf, 1928), pp. 25–27; on chivalric and Christian ideals, see A. B. Taylor, *An Introduction to Medieval Romance* (1930; rpt. New York: Barnes & Noble, 1969), pp. 195–200, and Henry Osborn Taylor, *The Mediaeval Mind: A History of the Development of Thought and Emotion in the Middle Ages*, 2 vols. (London: Macmillan, 1930), I:545–547.

ones. To do good, to do justice, to punish the wicked—that is one side of it. Conquest and booty were the other. And in some respects these were legitimate motives—St. Thomas allowed that the wicked do not have the right to own property. Their other motive was "glory." It is said that by the fifteenth century this had replaced the profit motive. St. Thomas tells us that glory is the just reward for virtuous deeds, but he warns against the love of glory for its own sake, which is "vainglory."[22] If we may judge from Theseus's stirring speech on Arcite's death at the end of the Knight's Tale, the Knight himself is motivated by glory. How easily it turned to vanity, arrogance, and pride may be seen in any history or biography of the period (John of Gaunt's would not be an exception). Froissart's *Chronicles* furnish nostalgic pictures of contemporary knights who were noble and chivalric; but Froissart shows us, too, the vain, arrogant ones. Later, the idea of knightly glory became centered in the king and the nation—it became the *gloire* of Louis XIV's time and the "national pride" (now obsolescent) which keeps us at war to this day.

The Knight's ideals are directly related to pilgrimage: the crusades were meant *au fond* to secure Jerusalem for Christian pilgrims. And a pilgrim's purpose was to do penance and adore relics. By Chaucer's time any thoughtful man would have seen this complex of goals with a jaundiced eye. There was already a fearful dichotomy between Church and State, symbolized by the martyrdom of Becket (very much in the background of *The Canterbury Tales*). Pilgrimages were discredited, relics scandalously abused. In depicting the Squire whose first campaign was a national disgrace, in revealing the unruly mirth and spite of the pilgrims, in placing at the end of the General Prologue the startling figure of the Pardoner with his pigs' bones for relics, Chaucer was depicting cultural ideals and practices which had lost their luster.

22. Sidney Painter, *French Chivalry: Chivalric Ideas and Practices in Mediaeval France* (Baltimore: Johns Hopkins Univ. Press, 1940), pp. 36–37, 85–94, 149–172.

Of the clerical group described in the General Prologue—
the Prioress and her entourage, the Monk, and the Friar—
Chaucer makes much the same observation that he makes of
the Knight and Squire. They exemplify obsolescent styles of
life based on obsolescent ideas and practices. All three reveal
what was throughout the Middle Ages the fundamental flaw
in the practice of the religious life, that its values and ideals
were contaminated by secular—and chiefly aristocratic—
ones. Laymen put a high value upon social status, upon the
acquisition of property and wealth, upon sexual relations,
love, and family. Members of religious orders were, by
ancient tradition, expected to renounce these preoccupations—to renounce "the world"—in vows of obedience,
poverty, and chastity.[23] Yet the Prioress Monk, and Friar are
all class conscious. The Prioress "peyned hir to countrefete
cheer / Of court"; the Monk is handsomely dressed, loves
horses and "venerie"; the Friar is "curteis" and "lowly of
service." Some amount of wealth was required for the indulgences of which they are guilty, so it is apparent that none
follows anything remotely like voluntary poverty. In addition the Monk and Friar, it is broadly hinted, indulge their
sexual appetites; the Prioress, "digne of reverence," directs
her maternal feelings to little dogs, mice in traps, little children in stories. The abuses of the three mount in intensity—
the Prioress's are peccadillos which have a certain charm, the
Monk's are bold offenses against the heart of the tradition
(he apparently violates all three of his vows), and the Friar's
make a veritable compendium of the wrongs ascribed to
friars in fourteenth-century attacks.[24] For the most part

23. The process by which initial fervor was replaced by laxity and laxity
remedied by reform is too familiar to need documentation. Gerhart B.
Ladner, in *The Idea of Reform* (1959; rpt. New York, Evanston, and
London: Harper Torchbooks, 1967), shows how the ideas of decline and
reform were endemic to Christian thought from earliest times. The
imperfection of the worldly order made reform a perpetual necessity.
Ladner argues that monasticism "was the principal practical vehicle
through which the Augustinian idea of reform was carried into effect"
(p. 377).

24. Arnold Williams, "Chaucer and the Friars," *Speculum* 28 (1953):
499–513, rpt. S&T, pp. 63–83.

their offenses are the traditional ones of reformist and complaint literature.

We see each of the three religious against a past implied or stated in the portrait itself. It is not clear whether the Prioress is the daughter of a noble house or, as seems more likely, from the *haute bourgeoisie* or the "gentry": one rather assumes that in the circles where high social rank was taken for granted such manners and bearing were second nature—a lady of such a background wouldn't need to "countrefete" them. Madame Eglentine, when she took up the religious life, brought with her the values and mannerisms of her "degree." Her facial features are stereotyped aristocratic ones; the rosary of coral with green gauds which she wears about her arm is a ladylike adornment; the last detail—the brooch of shining gold inscribed with a crowned "A" and the motto *Amor vincit omnia*—similarly expresses her compromise between religion and "gentilesse." The brooch could be a pilgrim's badge, or a medal of St. Mary, or a medallion struck at the marriage or coronation of Queen Anne.[25] The ambiguity of its religious and secular significance is not an unusual aspect of medieval art and artifacts. It is gold, it is ornamental, and its ambiguity is carried out in its Latin motto. What is striking is that she *has* it, for it is in all probability a memento, and an elegant one, of some past occasion.

The past associated with the Monk and Friar is institutional and historical, that of the Benedictine and Franciscan traditions. Speaking of the Monk, Chaucer explicitly describes this obsolescence of "old things" and speaks of the

25. It is impossible to know what the brooch is, and I suspect Chaucer meant it so. A crowned "A" is extant in the Guildhall Museum, London (No. 8731); it is shown in Loomis, *A Mirror of Chaucer's World*, no. 106. The design combines the letters "M" and "A," thought to stand for MAria or for St. Mary and St. Ann; the Guildhall Museum identifies it as a pilgrim's badge. But the piece is of lead and combines two letters whereas the Prioress's ornament is of gold and shows the letter A alone. Crowned letters were worn as royal ornaments, and are found as decoration in manuscripts; see Haldeen Braddy, *Geoffrey Chaucer: Literary and Historical Studies* (Port Washington, N. Y. and London: Kennikat Press, 1971), pp. 97–98. Such medallions, of whatever meaning, were very often given as gifts on specific occasions.

emergence of a "new world" (173-188). The famous passage refers to the chief characteristics of the Benedictine rule—the cloistered life of prayer, manual labor, and study—and compares the Monk's bare-faced scorn for the restrictions of monastic regimen. His class-consciousness is emphasized: he is capable of being an abbot, is a "lord" (172, 200), a "prelate" (204). His interests are the perquisites of nobility: hunting, fine horses and dogs, rich clothing, fur, ornaments. The "fat swan" mentioned at the end of the portrait (his favorite roast), like the palfrey he rides, is suitable to a nobleman. His ostentatious manliness is the nobleman's demeanor. And of course it is implied that he has not left behind him the nobleman's adventuresome sexuality—the hunting, the "pricking," the hare, possibly the "swink" he will reserve for St. Augustine and the "lust" mentioned in line 192, the "love knot" of his elaborate pin, bear down heavily on this implication. Later, taunted by the Host as a "tredefowl aright," he is to adopt the stance of a scholar and reveal his taste for reading stories about the falls of famous and powerful men, a "humanistic" interest. Not only old and new ideas are put in juxtaposition here, but monastic and aristocratic cultures, religious and secular values, the solitary and worldly lives, and divine and humane letters.

The Friar similarly holds after the new world. His abuses suggest the ideals of the Franciscan order—poverty, begging, good works—and Chaucer underscores this with ironic thrusts: "Unto his ordre he was a noble post" (214); "He was the beste begger in his hous" (252), and so on. As one who is supposed to be at large in the world and do acts of charity, he elects to do only what is pleasure or "profit." And yet it is part of Chaucer's style to make us empathize with his way of life even while we recognize it as a prototype of abuses. One imagines him to be handsome and young: his white neck is said to be a sign of sensuality,[26] but if it is like the fleur-de-lys it is smooth and soft (and aristocratic), and he is physically strong (239) and undeniably energetic. He

26. Baugh's note on line 238; source not stated.

too has an aristocratic air: he is "vertuous" (251).[27] The Friar is to the Monk and Prioress somewhat as the Squire was to the Knight: emphasis is thrown upon superficial traits, upon his fashionableness and stylishness. It is no accident that Chaucer uses the same phrase of him that he used of the Squire: "Curteis he was and lowly of servis."

Of the "commons"—those who are not knights or clerks—we get a social hierarchy going as high as the prominent Sergeant at Law and as low as the five "rogues" described last in the General Prologue. The Yeoman and Plowman represent the old ideal: the Yeoman, a forester dressed in green, is the Knight's servant and wears a warlike costume; the Plowman is the Parson's brother. The two idealized figures they are attached to represent the two dominant groups of medieval society, the nobles and the clergy. It is to be assumed that the Yeoman has accompanied the Knight on his crusading expeditions; but, as is often pointed out, the reference to his arrows and "mighty bow" reminds one of the yeoman archers' successful performance at Crécy (1346) and Poitiers (1356)—battles fought a generation before. The Plowman is not merely an idealized but a symbolical figure, drawn ultimately from commentaries on Ecclus. 6:19 and 2 Tim. 2:6. That he is the brother of the idealized Parson suggests the twelfth-century ideal of clergy and laity laboring in accord. There is a kind of primitivism in the conception: his hard manual labor symbolizes the possibility that honest toil and charitable works can restore human dignity lost in the Fall. And plowing itself symbolized the good works a Christian might do; the frequent references in Scripture to plowing and sowing were so interpreted, as the references to reaping and harvesting were understood to signify judgment.[28]

---

27. The word is splendidly ambiguous; it could refer to moral virtue or to the *virtù* of the nobleman (as when Aurelius in the Franklin's Tale is called "Yong, strong, right vertuous, and riche, and wys," 933).

28. Langland's figure Piers the Plowman is the most fully developed treatment in literature; several paintings of the elder Breughel, e.g. "The Fall of Icarus," illustrate its currency in art. Wyclif remarked "What lif that plesith more to God, is betere preiere to God . . . as lif of a trewe

A trewe swinker and a good was he,
Living in pees and parfit charitee.
God loved he best with all his hoole herte
At alle times, though him gamed or smerte,
And than his neighebor right as himselve.
He wolde threshe, and therto dyke and delve,
For Christes sake, for every povre wight,
Withouten hire, if it lay in his might.
His tithes payde he full fair and well,
Both of his propre swink and his catel.

(531-540)

Any reader of Chaucer who has looked down at the footnotes knows that agricultural laborers were at a premium in
the late fourteenth century because the Black Death and subsequent plagues had wiped out over a third of the work
force. Serfs demanded freedom and agricultural small-
holders chafed against the old manorial impositions. Their
discontent was constant, the Peasant's Revolt of 1381 being
the most violent expression of it. In such a period it is not
surprising that the "churls" behave in a cheeky way, as they
do in *The Canterbury Tales*. So it is the more surprising to find
a small tenant farmer like the Plowman living in peace and
perfect charity without a trace of discontent. To the extent
that he can be thought a reality rather than an ideal, he
would indeed have seemed an anachronism.

These two obsolescent figures from the lower end of the
social scale contrast with other commons who are in a
dependent or servile state; the Reeve and Manciple, for

---

plowman" (quoted in *General Prologue*, ed. Phyllis Hodgson [London:
Athlone Press, 1969], p. 21). The relevant passages of Scripture are
Prov. 22:8, Eccl. 11:4, Isa. 37:30, Os. 8:7 and 10:1, Mich. 6:15, Matt. 7:16
and 21:34–36, Mark 12.2, Luke 20:10, 1 Cor. 9:11, 2 Cor. 9:6. Possibly
most significant was Gal. 6:8, "For what things a man shall sow, those also
shall he reap. For he that soweth in his flesh, of the flesh also shall reap
corruption. But he that soweth in the spirit, of the spirit shall reap life
everlasting." Also important in the tradition was Prov. 20:4, "Because of
the cold the sluggard would not plough; he shall beg therefore in the
summer, and it shall not be given him." On this scriptural idea, see D. W.
Robertson, Jr. and Bernard F. Huppé, *Piers Plowman and Scriptural
Tradition* (Princeton, N. J.: Princeton Univ. Press, 1951), pp. 17–21,
79–91, and passim.

example, live by their wits and attain a stealthy independence. The Cook, temporarily in the employ of the Guildsmen, is a revolting figure with his "mormal" caused by uncleanliness, heavy drinking, and lechery.[29] He is not really a servant but a small businessman with his own shop (it is full of flies, the Host remarks). Where the Yeoman and Plowman are from a rural, agrarian society, the Cook and Manciple are from London, a mercantile center. But the Miller and Reeve, who come from the country and have agricultural occupations, are no less venal. In the background are social and cultural changes subtly taking place in Chaucer's time—the shift from an agrarian to a mercantile society, from a simple barter and money economy to a complex commercial and credit economy, from a feudal and baronial government to a centralized monarchy.

When Chaucer turns to the burghers in the General Prologue he puts the Merchant first, perhaps to typify the mercantile basis for the "rise" of this social group.[30] The others are presented in a more or less descending order of rank: the Man of Law, the Franklin, the Guildsmen, the Shipman, the Physician, and the Wife. They share (again, the Shipman is an exception) a certain pretentiousness about their social status. With most of them this is tied to money, for money or property or professional competence, not inherited titles or land, was the basis of their newly won standing. The notion is introduced with the picture of the Merchant, "Sowning alway th' encrees of his winning" (274-275). We learn that his winning comes in part from profiting illegally on rates of exchange, and we learn "There wiste no wight that he was in dette." This line means just what it says: no one knew that he was in debt. The next line makes clear the thrust of the statement—"So estatly was he of his governaunce." It is not implied that he was or wasn't in debt but that

29. Walter Clyde Curry, *Chaucer and the Mediaeval Sciences*, rev. ed. (New York: Barnes & Noble, 1960), pp. 50–52.

30. Harold F. Brooks, *Chaucer's Prilgrims: The Artistic Order of the Portraits in the Prologue* (London: Methuen, 1962), pp. 21–22. One might add that Chaucer ends the description of him "sooth to sayn, I noot how men him calle," perhaps using this namelessness to make him the more paradigmatic.

he managed prudently to keep his financial state to himself; he puts up a good front. Five of the seven portraits which follow repeat the Merchant's concern for wealth and appearances. The ways the pilgrims express their interest in rank and wealth run down the social scale in a fugue of pretensions. The Man of Law is a "greet . . . purchasour" (318) of land; the Franklin is a "householdere, and that a greet" (339); the Guildsmen have "catel . . . ynogh and rente" (373); the Physician loves gold "in special," is slow to spend money, has saved what he earned in plague times (441-442); the Wife spends her money on clothes and travel. Money is after all something different to everyone. The Man of Law wants landed property, the Franklin a great house, the Guildsmen silver knives rather than brass, the Physician savings. As each has a ruling passion, each has a special way he or she wants to *seem*. The Man of Law is "war and wise," "discreet," "of greet reverence"—"he seemed swich," adds the narrator, "his wordes weren so wise"; a busy man, "he seemed bisier than he was." The Franklin wants to seem rich, hospitable, "gentle." He is "Epicurus owene son," a gourmet with a penchant for lavish and ostentatious entertainment. Later (V:673-694) we find that he is disappointed with his son, who has failed to learn the aristocratic "virtue" and "gentilesse" for which he overpraises the Squire. The five Guildsmen, lower in status, are more modest in their expectations. Each of them "seemed," we learn, "a fair burgeys / To sitten in a yeldehall on a deys" (369-370). Their silver knives, it is said, reveal their status;[31] they are well dressed and equipped, and have sufficient property and income—a matter of importance to their wives, who like to be called "Madame" and walk at the head of a procession.

31. See Skeat's note on line 366; he thought the knives indicated they were of higher status than tradesmen and the like who were not supposed to wear silver. Donaldson, *Chaucer's Poetry*, p. 891, reports silver was appropriate only to people of superior birth; Hodgson, p. 109, that decorated knives were forbidden to those who did not own at least £500 in goods and chattels. But we do not know they are obeying these sumptuary laws, which were hard to enforce. J. Wilson McCutchan, "A Solempne and a Greet Fraternitee," *PMLA* 74 (1959):313–317, argues they are members of a craft guild and men of eminence.

The Physician is remote and conservative—learned, skillful, cautious in his diet, thrifty, well dressed, and acquisitive. Of all the "middle-class" members, the Wife, a cloth-maker, ranks lowest; where the wives of the Guildsmen aspire to walk at the head of a procession in a "mantel royalliche ybore," she is content with (but insistent on) going up first to the offering in her parish church. But "seeming" is no less important to her than to the others—her dress is elaborate and of excellent quality, though possibly bizarre, overdone, and rather old-fashioned. Her hat is appropriate to the lower classes and her wimple appropriate to a married woman.[32]

It is curious that these worldly and faddish burghers show themselves bound to the past in their choice of tales. Only the Shipman tells a tale that seems to happen in the present day. The Man of Law and the Physician, sententious figures who display their learning, tell idealized, moralistic tales set in the long ago and far away. The Wife and Franklin turn to old romances—theirs are the only tales which begin with the formula "in th'olde days" or "in hir dayes." Of course each selects or adapts the romance to his or her own viewpoint and purpose: it is in keeping with the Franklin's awe of "gentilesse" that he has committed a Breton lay to memory,[33] in keeping with the Wife's roots in southwest England that she knows an Arthurian tale. Then, too, the

32. Manly, *Some New Light on Chaucer*, pp. 230–231, thought the cover-chiefs out of fashion. Dale E. Wretlind, "The Wife of Bath's Hat," *MLN* 63 (1948):381–382 argued that large hats, introduced by Queen Anne, were in fashion; but a broad-brimmed hat comparable to the Wife's was worn by the wives of small farmers—see Herbert Norris, *Costume and Fashion*, 2 vols. (London: Dent, 1927), II:264–265. The description is not detailed enough for one to be sure whether she is wearing typical native garb or emulating the styles of the court. The wimple worn under the chin and the coverchief tied over it were hard to distinguish; these throat coverings and headdresses were symbols of wifehood. The Wife does not wear the "widow's barbe," but this was perhaps an upper-class custom. See Blanche Payne, *History of Costume* (New York: Harper and Row, 1965), pp. 194–195. The red hose is not characterizing—it was the predominant medieval color for shoes and hose; see R. Turner Wilcox, *The Mode in Footwear* (New York: Scribner, 1948), p. 68.

33. Kathryn Hume, "Why Chaucer Calls the Franklin's Tale a Breton Lai," *PQ* 51 (1972):365–379.

Wife and Merchant are obsessed with their *own* pasts—the Merchant cannot shake out of his mind his disastrous marriage and dashed hopes; the Wife's thoughts trail back over her husbands, her youth, her "gossib," her mother, her childhood.

Why are these upwardly mobile pilgrims, the ones most taken up with "newfangleness," so taken up with the past? They share a desire to make a future for themselves—the Man of Law is building up landed estates, the Franklin has great expectations for his son, the Guildsmen's wives anticipate higher honors, the Wife of five husbands' schooling cries "Welcome the sixth." Their immersion in their own time leads them toward its deepest values, and these are rooted in the past. Their thoughts go to the counsels of the Church and the traditions of the nobles. In their society status came from what the hag in the Wife's tale calls "swich gentilesse / As is descended out of old richesse." They might all like to believe with the hag that "genterye / Is nat annexed to possessioun," that wisdom and moral probity confer status, but they all know that for them money does so. Each uses the past to express his own self-image or hopes or anxieties.

All this emphasis on class distinctions and class consciousness gives us a feel for the contemporaneity of the setting and a sense of social changes and individual conflicts, but does it make any difference in diction or usage, in style as it is normally conceived? We might—in sheer bulk—find more passages of high-flown rhetoric, more of the "high style," in the *Troilus*, but we could find a fair amount of this in *The Canterbury Tales*. The difference is that in the *Troilus* whatever there is of high style and epic pretentions is under control: it all comes from the narrator. In *The Canterbury Tales*, except for the opening sentence, high style turns up only in the tales, where it has a way of *losing* control: the Knight's high style is parodied, the Squire's does a pratfall, the Nun's Priest mocks the thing itself. The *Troilus*, though, is a domestic story. Battles and heroic deeds are pushed into the background; chitchat, dinner parties, and a love affair are kept in the foreground, so there is plenty of colloquial

speech. When Pandarus enters Criseyde's chamber she cries
"What! which way be ye comen, *benedicite?* (III:757). That is
not the way Dido and Beatrice talk; it has more in common
with the Host's "Abide, Robin, leeve brother." It is an imitation of the way people speak familiarly to each other. In the
Troilus there are long scenes of dialogue in this colloquial
style. And the narrator, too, as often as he speaks a poetic or
rhetorical diction, can buttonhole the reader and lapse into
the familiar style:

> I passe all that which chargeth nought to seye.
> What! God foryaf his deth, and she also
> Foryaf, and with her uncle gan to pleye,
> For other cause was there none than so.
>
> (1576-1579)

Still, all the characters in the *Troilus* are from the upper
classes and the narrator is a scholar, so their colloquial language is upper-class or educated speech. We never hear
rude folk talking "low" speech.

The Canterbury Tales does give us "rude folk"—pulls us
right into their little worlds. Their speech may sound like
lower-class dialect, but Chaucer only makes a token effort to
reproduce this. He has the Reeve speak a few words in an
East Anglian dialect, and has the Reeve's clerks speak a
broad Northern. He lets the Wife babble in her back-fence
manner ("But now, sire, lat me see, what I shall seyn? / A ha!
by God, I have my tale again . . ."), but she certainly doesn't
speak the dialect of Bath; and the Manciple really speaks
rather like an educated person (unless perhaps he has
picked up his masters' speech patterns, like the lowly butler
with the dandy accent). Though the Cook, Host, and Miller
sound as if they are speaking like ordinary folk, there is little
linguistic realism in their speech. The Cook would have
spoken gutter-talk, but what does he say to the Host when he
is falling-down drunk? he says,

> So God my soule blesse,
> As there is fall on me swich hevinesse,
> Noot I nat why, that me were levere sleepe
> Than the beste gallon wine in Chepe.
>
> (IX:21-24)

There, for sure, is a well-formed sentence; it is no less grammatical and no less toney than the Franklin's remark,

> . . . by the Trinitee,
> I hadde lever than twenty pound worth lond,
> Though it right now were fallen in myn hond,
> He were a man of swich discrecioun
> As that ye ben!
>
> (V:682-686)

True, Chaucer gives the Man of Law a few legal phrases and has the Host swear often. But that is about as far as it goes. Count up dialect variants and vocabulary items and you have to conclude that the characters all speak in much the same way. And all speak in verse. But we *perceive* them as speaking differently: the Lawyer's or Franklin's discourse seems more elevated than the Host's or Cook's because the minute scrutiny of social degrees and social mobility makes us anticipate this and presume it. The author doesn't need to imitate differences in their speech but only to suggest it.

The matter is important because it is sometimes argued that the tales themselves are all in the same style. To an extent this is true: any passage from any tale shares characteristics which could be distinguished from the styles of other fourteenth-century writers. But isn't it true, too, that the Wife's discourse can be distinguished, at least in some characteristic particulars, from the Knight's or the Reeve's? If style cannot be separated from content, each pilgrim's choice of a tale already recommends a certain style appropriate to that choice. As we have tales within a tale, we have styles within a style. It is another instance in which Chaucer contrives to have it both ways. The Cook is the lowest in degree, but he is capable of saying,

> For sikerly a prentise revelour
> That haunteth dice, riot, or paramour,
> His maister shall it in his shoppe abye,
> Al have he no part of the minstralcye.
>
> (I:4391-4394)

The Knight is the highest in degree, and he has his kingly hero say,

And whoso gruccheth ought, he dooth follye,
And rebel is to Him that all may gye.
And certeinly a man hath most honour
To dien in his excellence and flour,
Whan he is siker of his goode name.

(3045-3049)

Where is the stylistic difference between these utterances?
not in the lexicon or syntax or dialect. Both *are* in the same
style. But because the sense of obsolescence and the attention
to social degrees has been pressed upon us, we *suppose* these
utterances to be different. The difference is a matter of content and of social milieu. It would not suit the Cook's "style"
to observe, like Theseus,

. . . gladder ought his freend been of his deeth,
Whan with honour up yolden is his breeth,
Than whan his name apalled is for age.

(3051-3053)

It would certainly not suit the Knight's style to say that his
hero

. . . had a wife that held for contenance
A shop, and swyved for hir sustenance.

(4421-4422)

But only the word "honour" in the one passage and the word
"swyved" in the other are stylistic clues in the narrower
linguistic sense; and it is the choice of subject—the content—
which prompts the choice of those words. The tellers choose
their tales from the grab-bag of memory; the styles of all are a
standard literary style, but we get such a vivid sense of their
society and their individual lives, of subtle changes taking
place in the social fabric, that content alone and a few
touches of individual traits are enough to make us supply
differing styles within this style—to make us believe or
imagine that *le style c'est l'homme même.*

THE IDEAL AND THE ACTUAL

To medieval men obsolescence, like all change, illustrated

the mutability of the world and hence the vanity of human wishes. But Chaucer treated these standard medieval themes in a new way: he gave a vivid experience of temporality by drawing attention to the Prioress's golden keepsake, the Cook's warmed-over pies, the Merchant's regret, the Wife's nostalgia. He set these against a fragmented and largely forgotten past—the "old days," the days of the Bretons, the days when there were "fairie," when beasts and birds could talk and sing, when Phoebus dwelt here. And the "vivid" details are memorable but fleeting experiences—the Friar's sparkling eyes, the Pardoner's voice singing "the murierly and loude," the Miller's bagpipe that "brought us out of towne." Remembered time and recorded time are the stuff of narrative, and narrative creates a microcosmic eternity which outlasts the present day. We know that the Friar's name was Huberd and the Shipman's barge was called the Maudelayne, that the Host is named Harry Bailly and the Cook named Roger of Ware, not because their names were more important than anyone else's but because the poet snatched them, as if at random, from oblivion. But the random quality of these particularities puts us in mind of how much more has passed beyond our knowing.

This articulation of the passing of time is uniquely Chaucer's, but the picture it provides is a fundamental medieval conception, that of a world in decline from the "former age" or the Golden Age, growing old, becoming physically and morally weak. Chaucer gives explicit expression to this idea only once in *The Canterbury Tales*, in the ironic passage spoken by the Clerk at the end of his tale, which he had from Petrarch:

> This world is nat so strong, it is no nay,
> As it hath been in olde times yoore. . . .

> (1139-1140)

But the idea is implied in the General Prologue and throughout *The Canterbury Tales* by the pervasive sense of obsolescence. Chaucer shared this theme with Gower, who in the prologue of the *Confessio Amantis* announced his subject as the world which declines and renews itself daily:

Thus I, which am a burel clerk
Purpose for to write a book
After the world that whilom took
Long time in olde dayes passed:
But for men sayn it is now lassed,
In worse plit than it was tho,
I thenke for to touch also
The world which neweth every day. . . .

(52-59)

Characteristically Chaucer shows in minute and accurate detail what "moral Gower" stated as a generality. But both poets agreed that the senescent world of medieval thought was not an emblem of despair. While the world is winding down from its first Golden Age, it also "neweth every day," and men can follow ideals of conduct which would impose upon the world a corrective and civilizing influence. It was not the Church alone which was to accomplish this but the state and the individual. So much the worse, then, if men and institutions flouted those ideals which might counter the world's decline.

The *Troilus* does not represent such a set of ideals in the past from which actualities have fallen off, and does not suggest that human effort can exert a corrective or civilizing influence; instead it shows a former civilization which did not have the advantage of Christian ideals. We see the men of this pre-Christian age groping blindly for ideals of conduct, worshipping false gods, caught up in an endless war whose purpose is all but forgotten. Their ideals are not forsaken but ill-formed. And the ideals singled out for scrutiny are identified with the chivalric and courtly ones which were the fashion of medieval aristocrats, valor and love. Troilus, the hero, is the idealist: his story is that of a failed, an inadequate ideal. From this point of view the *Troilus* is a critique of idealism itself. The great ideal of a love which ennobles is always immediate and before us, never a thing of the past, never tarnished. We see Troilus first cynical about love, then "converted." Pandarus cannot persuade him to reveal the reason for his sorrow until he happens upon that appeal which is to Troilus irresistible, the appeal to his idealism:

What! many a man hath love full deer ybought
Twenty winter that his lady wiste,
That nevere yet his lady mouth he kiste.

What! shold he therefore fallen in dispair,
Or be recreant for his owne tene,
Or sleen himself, al be his lady fair?
Nay, nay, but ever in oon be fresh and greene
To serve and love his deere hertes queene,
And think it is a guerdon, hir to serve,
A thousand fold more than he can deserve.

(I:810-819)

In these words Pandarus reminds Troilus of the noblest
ideal of long-suffering love, and we learn at once "of that
word took heede Troilus" (820). Troilus's high-mindedness is
contrasted with the intelligent skepticism of Pandarus and
the cautious pragmatism of Criseyde, but this is not such a
violent contrast as some have thought. When Troilus in an
unwonted moment of pragmatism suggests that the lovers
steal away (IV:1503) Criseyde is able to present not only the
practical reasons against such a move but the idealistic ones.
She ends reminding Troilus just how high-minded a love
they have and how important it is that this be maintained
(1667-1687). Nor is Pandarus without ideals. He is steeped
in the philosophy of the ancient world; we ought to understand that his wise saws and proverbs are part of his
learning, the possession of one whose views have been
formed by reading and thinking as much as—perhaps more
than—by experience. And what Pandarus knows is true:
times change, circumstances alter cases, everything has its
time. It would be sensible for Troilus to follow his advice,
forget Criseyde, eschew regret, start a new life. But it is just
because of his idealism that he does not follow the pragmatic
course which is the best Pandarus can recommend. The
ideal which awed us at its poetical height turns into a false
hope. We see this happen before our eyes. At the very end,
when the narrator sadly draws his moral about "This world,
that passeth soon as flowres faire," he implies that the
audience still follows these hopeless "pagan" ideals and still
needs to learn the lesson which the poem teaches. That

lesson has never been more succinctly phrased than by
Professor Donaldson: "The poem states, what much of
Chaucer's poetry states, the necessity under which men lie of
living in, making the best of, enjoying, and loving a world
from which they must remain detached and which they must
ultimately hate."[34]

In *The Canterbury Tales* ideals are presented differently.
If one could abstract from the *Troilus* that aspect which
reveals love manqué, which views the ideal regretfully,
which sees it far in the past and losing its luster, one would
have the quality with which idealism is shown throughout
The Canterbury Tales. But to abstract this would mean turning
only to the ending, forgetting the immediacy and vibrancy
with which ideals are treated throughout the poem. In *The
Canterbury Tales* the narrative "now" focuses upon actualities
and puts ideals back into the blur of history. The ideals
which stand immediately before us are false and unappeal-
ing—the burghers' ambitions, the Pardoner's avarice, the
class-conscious and money-grubbing motives which energize
most of the pilgrims. The true ideals of the "ideal" pilgrims—
the Knight's crusading spirit, the brotherhood of Parson and
Plowman, perhaps the Clerk's selfless dedication—seem obsolescent. And the tales told by these ideal pilgrims do not
reflect the luster which the ideal is presumed to have had in
better days. In the Knight's tale an undercurrent of comic
irony and a certain number of ridiculous circumstances or
anticlimaxes undercut the romance idealism. The Clerk's
tale ends with the Clerk's ironic admission that the ideal is no
longer followed. And the Parson's tale, like the *Melibee*,
represents not so much an ideal as the application of an
ideal. The two prose treatises are practical, "how-to" works:
the one tells members of the ruling class how to choose
counselors, when to wage war, how to do justice, and so on;
the other tells the Christian listener how to avoid sin and do
penance. Both the prose works concentrate upon the effort
men must make to carry out an ideal, not upon the ideal
itself; and neither gives to its subject the luster and magnifi-
cence which the poetry of the *Troilus* gives to the ideal of

34. *Speaking of Chaucer*, p. 100.

love. The "ideal narratives" (like the Man of Law's, the Prioress's, or the Clerk's tales) are moral tales, but in the mouths of their tellers they become, as we shall see later, "misguided moralism"—moralism which fails to instruct the moralist himself. The single narrative which presents an ideal without discrediting it is the Second Nun's tale; but like all saints' legends it calls attention to ideals of perfection so high as to be reserved for those especially called, and so reminds us of our imperfection.

Ideals are false but lustrous in the *Troilus*, true but tarnished in *The Canterbury Tales*. So with actualities: in the *Troilus* they call for compromise with ideals, in *The Canterbury Tales* for new ideals or renewed ones. In the *Troilus* actuality is the everyday domestic life of the Trojan upper classes. We observe a style of life, customs and preoccupations wholly familiar to aristocrats of the fourteenth century—a day-to-day world of personal machinations, of polite conversations, of singing songs and reading aloud, attending religious ceremonies, following wars, worrying about love. It is a style of life for which medieval aristocrats themselves felt an enthusiasm and which the bourgeois took as a model. It is not a falling-off or decline from an imagined worthier past. What makes things go wrong, what decimates the idealized love, is the circumstantial or conditional actuality which accompanies every style of life. An exchange of prisoners is arranged, political decisions—wrong-headed ones—are arrived at in a parliament, and appropriate conduct dictates that the principals resign themselves to Criseyde's departure. In the background, blind chance, the goddess Fortune, presides over this circumstantial or conditional aspect of affairs. The pragmatism of everyday life calls for adjustment to altered cases. Criseyde among the Greeks must resign herself: it is unfeasible to return. Troilus must resign himself: she will not come back. And compromise is a condition of pragmatism—Troilus, outside the bedroom, must hold his tongue while he hears Pandarus lie, and the deception, without which the ideal would never come to fruition, tarnishes his conduct but not the ideal itself. There is a tension between ideals and those actualities of daily life which make ideals impracticable.

In *The Canterbury Tales* there is no such tension. Ideals are in the past, actuality in the narrative "now." This is forced upon us in the General Prologue by the way the portraits end. The ideal portraits end with a sententia, a general statement: the Knight "was late ycome from his viage / And wente for to don his pilgrimage"; the Clerk would "gladly . . . lerne and gladly teche"; the Parson taught Christ's lore "but first he follwed it himselve." The other portraits end with a particular detail or a piquant phrase. The Squire carves before his father at the table, the Prioress wears her crowned A with its motto, the Wife knows of the "old dance," the Miller pipes the company out of town with a bagpipe, the Reeve rides at the rear of the procession, the Summoner bears with him a cake, the Pardoner sings merrily and loud. Names are sometimes used to end the portraits—the Friar is named Huberd, the Shipman's barge is the Maudelayne. The Franklin's portrait ends describing him with the obsolescent word "vavasour." Twice the narrator begs off, leaving details for us to surmise: he does not know the Merchant's name, will not say more of the Man of Law's array. He ends the portrait of the Guildsmen and their wives with the striking detail "a mantel royallich ybore," the portrait of the Manciple with the statement that he "set hir aller cappe." The portraits conclude by encapsulating the pilgrim, making him vivid and memorable. These details suggest an inner reality, the reality of each pilgrim's character, frame of mind, place in society—the very realities which will dictate their choice and treatment of tales.

The *Troilus*, then, gives us a picture of an ordered social unit in a society which existed before the age of grace and is about to be swallowed up in the process of history; we know where it is headed. *The Canterbury Tales* gives us a picture of a disordered Christian society in a state of obsolescence, decline, and uncertainty; we do not know where it is headed. The *Troilus* shows us noble if inadequate ideals and a glittery actuality whose fate is sealed; *The Canterbury Tales* shows us ideals no longer followed and an evanescent actuality whose fate is unknown. Both works teach contempt of the world, but the *Troilus* teaches that lesson by fastening chiefly upon the themes of mutability and vanity.[35] *The Canterbury Tales* fastens upon the other themes of *contemptus mundi* writings— upon the corruptness of human nature and society and the world's decline. Both works are ambivalent about the vanity of human wishes, pursuits, and efforts; so were the treatises on contempt of the world. Pope Innocent III in his classic treatise (which Chaucer says he translated) inveighed against the vanity of curiosity and learning, but when he fastened upon actualities—the corrupt judge, the avaricious lawyer, the lecherous priest—he implied that reform was needed. That is the seed of satire, perhaps the real origin of medieval satire: Bernard of Morval actually called his *De contemptu mundi* a satire. And the implication that things should be reformed is present in *The Canterbury Tales*—present in the minute actualities of its un-ideal characters and present in the author's irony. The great ideas of the Middle Ages—the mutability, vanity, and corruption of the world, the decline of the world from a Golden Age, the need of the individual to transcend in his thoughts the mundane order, the need for charity and reform—all get into *The Canterbury Tales*. But it is not enough to find them spread here and there in explicit statements or suggested in emblems and allegories. They are there in actualities, in the way events and people are presented—or, I should have said, in the way we are made to see them.

35. On contempt of the world as a phase of Christian doctrine, see Robert Bultot, *Christianisme et valeurs humaines: La doctrine du mépris du monde* . . . (Louvain and Paris: Nauwelaerts, 1963—). Some articles on the subject are collected in *Revue d'ascétique et de mystique*, 41 (1965), No. 3. About contempt of the world and its associated themes see my introduction to *Lothario dei Segni (Pope Innocent III), On the Misery of the Human Condition*, trans. M. Dietz (Indianapolis and New York: Bobbs-Merrill, 1969), esp. pp. xxiv–xxxiii; also *The Three Temptations*, pp. 65–75, and, for the presence of the idea in the *Troilus*, pp. 155–160. On the theme in Chaucer, see Joseph J. Mogan, Jr., *Chaucer and the Theme of Mutability* (The Hague and Paris: Mouton, 1969), esp. chap. 6 which deals with *The Canterbury Tales* chiefly by reporting explicit references to the theme.

IRONY AND THE SOCIAL FABRIC

Chaucer's irony, the most famous feature of his style and the most discussed,[36] is the most elusive. In much of what I have said about his treatment of time, and of the ideal and the actual, I know I have been describing effects which could be reckoned ironical. The slippery word irony, according to the *OED*, means a figure of speech in which the intended meaning is different from the one which seems to be expressed: it usually takes the form of "sarcasm or ridicule in which laudatory expressions are used to imply condemnation or contempt." Because it is this, it requires a role or stance on the part of the speaker—as when Socrates pretended ignorance or when Chaucer says he agreed with the Monk. But irony expressed by such a stance often describes straightforwardly the way things are, which is often ironic in itself. The *OED* provides a felicitous phrase when it mentions "a contradictory outcome of events as if in mockery of the promise and fitness of things." We say it is ironic when it rains at a picnic, but the irony depends upon a community of understanding. One can imagine picnickers (in England, say) who would find nothing contradictory about the rain, put up umbrellas and pour more wine. Irony is a shared attitude which falls between outrage and indifference. The Monk's thoughts seem ironic because we know what he *ought* to think; if we view the Monk as puritans or cynics would, the irony is gone. The ironist must gamble on the wave length of his audience: if I say I will take a paragraph to define irony, I have a right to hope the reader will note my wry wit, but someone is bound to miss the tone and think me naive. Then, too, it is hard to talk about irony, as it is hard to explain humor, without violating the spirit of the thing itself. Every discussion of irony must be ironic by intention or be ironic because the writer's somber tone jangles with the tone he describes. It is probably true of irony, as it is said to be true of Zen, that one understands best by saying nothing.

36. For a good survey and a full bibliography, see Vance Ramsey, "Modes of Irony in The Canterbury Tales," in *Companion to Chaucer Studies*, ed. Rowland, pp. 291–312.

Irony seems to rely upon a disparity between what we expect or hope and what we get or observe. If this is true, irony depends on a disparity between the ideal and the actual, between what should be and what is. Expectations, hopes, and ideals, once violated or fulfilled, are always in the past. For this reason irony always involves a disparity between past and present. The qualities of style we have been discussing, which proceed from the treatment of time, actuality, and ideality in *The Canterbury Tales*, therefore seem inherently ironic. I am not sure if obsolescence isn't inherently ironic. To me it is ironic that new trains imitate airlines, as it is ironic when men like Chaucer's Monk take ancient vows and don't observe them. But this depends upon a taste or sensibility in me. There are those who would react with indignation, or who would not react at all. Irony, like obsolescence, is not in the thing or in the word but in ourselves, a way of perceiving life and expressing what we perceive.

In the *Troilus* the greatest irony is the tragic irony of its ending, which springs from the turning of a cycle, from things happening as before. It is ironic that Criseyde, after all her scruples and indecisions about accepting Troilus, repeats among the Greeks the timorous and indecisive selection of another lover. It is ironic that Troilus waits, expects, hopes, even thinks he sees her (V:1158); it is ironic that what he sees is only a "fare-carte." It is ironic that Troilus will not believe Cassandra's correct interpretation of his dream, and ironic that Chaucer at this point uses the same line with which he ended Book I, "And thus he drieth forth his aventure" (1540). There is "dramatic irony" because we know things the hero does not know, "tragic irony" because things turn out other than as we had hoped. It is ironic that Criseyde gives Troilus's brooch to Diomede, that at the end Troilus still loves the one who causes his woe, that in death he laughs again. But the ironies of *The Canterbury Tales* do not ever rely upon a cycle or repetition of events. There are repeated phrases in *The Canterbury Tales*, but their ironic effect depends on a difference in context (as when the Miller repeats phrases from the Knight's tale); in the *Troilus* repeated phrases are ironic because they occur in a similar context but under changed circumstances. Irony in *The Canterbury Tales* is static: the ironies hover over the whole conception of the work, but they do not unroll or happen (except within individual tales) in an historical process. It is ironic that the setting, and the metaphoric structure of the whole, is a pilgrimage begun in "full devout corage" but that mirth and "harlotry" are what stand out. It is ironic that many of the pilgrims represent social institutions based on the society's noblest ideals but that the individuals flout those ideals. But none of these ironies develop or come to a head at the end as they do in the *Troilus*; they are données.

Irony in *The Canterbury Tales* shares some features with irony in the *Troilus*, but these features operate differently and have a different effect:

1. In both poems the poet addresses us directly, adopting the ironic mask of a naif; in both there is a "double vision," an ironic contrast between what we see through the narrator's eyes and what we see through our own. In the *Troilus* the narrator is an outsider observing an elaborate courtly game. He observes it through an "old book"—like us, he is a reader, and he belongs to his readers' time. His truth-claim is "I have read it." Hence much of the irony proceeds from his removal and distance. He can be enraptured over the lovemaking, sorrowful over the outcome; it is ironic when he comments on the action as if he did not know its outcome or understand its import. But in *The Canterbury Tales* the narrator was a participant in the pilgrimage who now remembers and records. His truth-claim is "I was there." Hence the irony proceeds from his presence. He reports from direct observation and without comment. He shows himself telling the worst tale. Where the narrator of the *Troilus* hovering over his old book comes at last to a philosophical understanding—sees through a glass darkly and then face to face—the narrator of *The Canterbury Tales* sees everything as a participant and understands almost nothing.

2. Both poems contain a manipulator inside the poem who presides over the action as the narrator presides over the story. In the *Troilus*, the manipulator, Pandarus, seems

eminently successful, almost a magician who can put the weather to work for him. Ironically, Pandarus understands all along that while the moment must be seized, Fortune can as easily snatch the moment away; he knows perfectly well that Criseyde will not return. In *The Canterbury Tales* the Host is the manipulator, but he manipulates with little success. He gets the pilgrims to agree to his plan, but ironically the plan goes awry—as often as he directs the action he fails to do so: the Miller foils his intention to have tales told by rank, an unexpected pilgrim joins the group, no one tells two tales. It is not Fortune or chance that disturbs his manipulations, but the characters of people and their interaction. Nor does the Host understand what is going on. He plays everything by ear and never knows what will happen next.

3. Both poems contain verbal irony—ironic lines or phrases—but the reasons for the irony differ. In the *Troilus* most of the verbal irony reflects the irony of life itself, the irony of events, particularly those associated with the game of love. It is ironic when the narrator exclaims "Why nad I swich oon with my soul ybought, / Ye or the leeste joie that was there?" (III:1321). We the audience know that the joy is bought at a price, and being Christians know one's soul is not to be used in such a bargain. Most of the ironic lines which we remember from the *Troilus* reflect the ironies of the dramatic situation. When Troilus speaks of himself as being in heaven's bliss, or when Criseyde says "To Diomede algate I wol be true," the irony is created by our understanding of the circumstances. But in *The Canterbury Tales* verbal irony rarely depends upon plot or situation, and that only in particular tales; it depends upon our understanding of medieval society. The narrator's enthusiasm for the pilgrims in the General Prologue is comparable to the enthusiasm of the narrator in the *Troilus* as he beholds the love affair consummated. But where in the *Troilus* irony depends upon our foreknowledge of the outcome, in *The Canterbury Tales* the irony depends upon our knowledge of the social background. The famous ironic thrusts of the General Prologue are precise statements of fact. When the narrator says the Prioress takes pains to "countrefete cheere / Of court" or

that the Monk is "a lord full fat and in good point" the irony is not in any misstatement or distortion but in our sense of something questionable which is lost on the narrator. Thus the Friar really is "worthy" (269) from one point of view; it is our awareness of another point of view that makes the adjective ironic. It is a fact that the physician "loved gold in special" (444)—the statement is ironical because the narrator thinks this has to do with the use of gold as a cordial in medicine and because we know an ethical question is involved. In the *Troilus* much of the verbal irony in the speeches of characters rises from the fact that we know they do not mean what they say. They may protest, like Pandarus, "I mente naught but well," yet they do not always say what they think—Pandarus lies, Criseyde hedges, even Troilus can talk to Pandarus about his "need" (III:417) with an urgency which he would conceal from the lady. In *The Canterbury Tales* such ironic hypocrisies occur sometimes within the tales, but the pilgrims' discourse is not merely hypocritical. The misguided moralism of the Man of Law, Physician, or Prioress is ironic because the pilgrim speaks it unawares. The irony springs more often from straightforwardness. The rich irony of the Wife's Prologue or the Pardoner's Prologue and Tale is owing to their surprising candor—we expect people under such circumstances to dissimulate.

4. In both poems events are concluded but not quite resolved. In the *Troilus* the author makes a noble statement of Christian principles at the end, seeming to draw a moral which gives philosophical meaning to the sad events which have gone before. But the tone of this final passage is not wholly consistent, is not without its ironies: the pagan gods are written off as "rascaille" and are lumped with "olde clerkes speche / In poetrie"—yet not a moment ago the author had spoken reverentially of five "old clerks," the pagan poets Vergil, Ovid, Homer, Lucan, and Statius (1792). Our attention is diverted to literary tradition, to the copying of this text in English, to the "younge, freshe folkes" of the present day, to the poet's colleagues Gower and Strode. If the great images of the ending are Troilus on the eighth

sphere and the Blessed Virgin addressed at the end, the poet's attention is still scattered, the reality of the story fragmented. It is hard not to look back upon the story with regret: we remember a fleeting moment of earthly joy, of noble love. In *The Canterbury Tales* the ending is similarly ambiguous: we learn that the Parson will "knit up well a greet mattere." Yet the Parson's Tale is so different from anything before it that generations of readers have regarded *The Canterbury Tales* as unfinished. The work ends with the pilgrims in sight of the shrine but not quite there. The action is not complete as it was in the *Troilus*; the ending forces our attention not back to a moment which has passed, but back to the whole action of the pilgrimage and forward to the future of man's pilgrimage—to each man's death and to the heavenly city.

There are other ironic features in *The Canterbury Tales,* which are perhaps the most notable source of its irony, yet spring from circumstances that do not obtain in the *Troilus.* One of these features is the kind of "double truth" which we must accept as part of the work's fictive premise. The voice which addresses us is both the poet who writes and the narrator who rehearses; the pilgrims, while being performed by this narrator, are themselves performers; we the audience are both hearers and readers. When the Nun's Priest performs the roles of barnyard fowls it is comic irony of the highest kind that we catch Chaucer's voice ridiculing literary conventions; and in the sensible moral which the Priest draws it is hard not to catch an echo of the poet himself. It is an irony of the same order that the performer of the tales performs his own performance in *Sir Thopas*; again we catch the poet himself in a literary parody. It is probably a further ironic turnabout that he then tells a "little thing in prose" meant to be taken in earnest. The circumstance is simpler in the *Troilus*: the narrator never drops his mask, even at the end. He plays the role of a love-poet who learns and states at the end the harsh lesson which love poetry and love itself almost always teach. But in *The Canterbury Tales* he must drop the mask of the naive observer all the time in order to adopt the masks of the pilgrims

whose tales he repeats. We the audience are cast in the role
of listeners at a protracted performance, but the performer
ironically acknowledges that he is an author, that we are
readers with the power to turn over a leaf, to select,
assimilate, supply, and interpret. In the *Troilus* the book is in
the narrator's hand: he draws his material from it, and
directs us. In *The Canterbury Tales* the book is put in our
hands to make of it what we will.

Another kind of irony not to be found in the *Troilus*
hangs upon the appropriateness of the tales to the pilgrims
who tell them. In the *Troilus* the characters speak like
themselves, each having a characteristic "style," favorite
phrases, or mannerisms of speech. The storytelling in *The
Canterbury Tales* would be like this if all the characters gave as
dramatic and forthright a self-presentation as, say, the Wife
or the Pardoner. Even at that it is ironic that the Wife in her
tale reveals her fantasies and wishes with unwitting vividness
and at the end fails to grasp the full implication of what she
has revealed. The germ of this dramatic self-presentation
might be found in Criseyde's dream of a white eagle, or
Troilus's dream of a boar, or in the soliloquies. In the *Troilus*
the characters speak as we expect them to speak, and this is
often true in *The Canterbury Tales*: it is appropriate that the
Knight tells a romance, the Prioress a miracle of the Virgin,
the Miller a fabliau. The irony is that the tales reveal
something about the teller—they tell a tale of their own
which the teller doesn't intend. This circumstance is like that
of a fabliau: the paradigm of the "trickster tricked" is
applied to the storyteller—he tells a deliberate falsehood and
it tells a truth about himself. The problem comes in those
instances where Chaucer assigned to a pilgrim a tale that one
would not expect him to tell. We cannot be sure there is an
intended irony, for example, in the fact that the money-
grubbing Physician tells a moral tale. Yet the principle that
the tale reflects its teller is firmly established in *The Canterbury
Tales*: for example it *is* intentionally ironic that the avaricious
Pardoner preaches against avarice. Since Chaucer had a
reason for the assignment of some tales to their tellers, we
ought to look for a reason even when we find the assignment

puzzling or unaccountable. The workroom critic says "Well, Chaucer was running out of material." Where does that get us? If we allow that the artist had a reason, conscious or instinctive, for what he did, the "unaccountable" assignments are ironic; they are instances of misguided moralism (as with the Physician or Prioress) or of pomposity or dullness (as with the Monk) or ineptitude (as with the Squire). That doesn't mean the tales are necessarily profound comments upon the characters of their tellers, or that they are intended as satire. And it doesn't take away their mirth or doctrine. It is just among the ironies of life that immoral people love to talk morality, that people don't know when silence says more than talk, that every one of us is his own most attentive listener.

Finally there is throughout *The Canterbury Tales* the irony which springs from the conflict between religious and secular ideals. In the *Troilus* there is the conflict between a pagan past in which the action takes place and a Christian present in which it is viewed, but the motives of the characters are never mixed; the characters may be in inner conflict, but the conflicts do not spring from a conflict of values in their society. Where they try to decide whether to do what is honorable or to do what they want, their ideals of conduct are all secular and courtly; they have no religious prohibitions to grapple with. Criseyde even supposes the gods are a projection of our fears (IV:1408). But a major theme in *The Canterbury Tales* is that members of a Christian society gathered on a pilgrimage are largely prompted by class-conscious or hostile or selfish motives. The General Prologue ends with the description of the Summoner and Pardoner, the one a corrupt official of the archdeacon's court, the other an outrageous exploiter of religion. Justice and Crime ride together, both preying upon the church. The disparity between what should be and what is must be thought a bitter irony in *The Canterbury Tales* when it is this gross. But there are some secular and even selfish motives which seem inoffensive—the Squire's fashionableness or the Franklin's cheery affability. Even so, these motives are ironic when put beside the old ideals: neither the Squire nor the

Franklin is like the Knight, and none of the lower-class pilgrims is anything like the Plowman.

Times were changing, the good old days passing away. That *The Canterbury Tales* represents medieval institutions in a state of obsolescence is not itself ironic unless social change is ironic. Irony is a frame of mind which lets us accommodate to disappointment and change, which lets us view with equanimity the gap between expectation and actuality, between "old things" and "the new world." If irony is a sensibility which we can cultivate, one of its uses is to make us adapt to change even when it is for the worse. Hence revolutionaries never use irony. Students of Chaucer argue whether his irony is harsh and moralistic, or tolerant and disinterested. I believe it was the latter—not because Chaucer was amoral or "genial" but because he practiced in his style the spirit of charity as it was conceived in Christian times. In the wide-eyed, observant narrator we have a figure who is nothing if not charitable: he practices in the extreme what the church taught, that it is not for us to judge our fellow men, that he who is without sin should cast the first stone. Much of the spirit of Chaucer which we admire as ironic, and consider part of his style, springs from the open-minded, dispassionate attitude which charity requires. That Christianity taught believers to "love the man but hate his vice," to love those we do not like, might be thought irony of the highest order. Loving one's neighbor, or doing to others as we would have them do to us, calls for an ironic frame of mind unless—like the narrator—we do not see anything wrong with our neighbor and cannot guess what others would do to us.

THE SEARCH FOR THE WORLD

Every reader of Chaucer criticism must be struck by the contradictory pictures of Chaucer which critics give. One man's Chaucer is an impish fellow with a taste for bawdry, another's a humorist and ironist, another's a satirist with the satirist's reforming spirit and an edge of *saeva indignatio*, another's a moralist. Probably all these Chaucers can be extrapolated from his works, depending on which works one selects. It is true of writers, as of people, that one man can wear many masks, and it could be thought a successful feature of Chaucer's style that he reveals himself in so many guises. We know he could be raucously funny in one place, high sorrowful in another—in various places enraptured, detached, witty, sardonic, snobbish, gloomy, even bitter. So it shouldn't be a contradiction to find a side of him which was socially conscious, thoughtful, and serious-minded. We can find this in both the *Troilus* and *The Canterbury Tales*, but again we find a difference.

Chaucer wrote, probably during the years he was working on *The Canterbury Tales*, a short poem about the world's decline, "The Former Age." In it he presents both the "soft" and the "hard" primitivism which historians of our own day have distinguished.[37] Men of the Golden Age were happy in their pristine, simple life:

> A blissful life, a paisible and a sweete,
> Ledden the peples in the former age.
> They held him paid of the fruites that they ete,
> Which that the feldes yave hem by usage.
> They ne were nat forpampred with outrage.
> Unknowen was the quern and eek the melle:
> They eten mast, hawes, and swich pounage,
> And dronken water of the colde welle.

At the same time they lacked the skills of civilized man, which they did not need:

37. See Boas, *Essays on Primitivism and Related Ideas in the Middle Ages*, passim; for a definition see Arthur O. Lovejoy and George Boas, *Primitivism and Related Ideas in Antiquity* (1935; rpt. New York: Octagon Books, 1965), pp. 9–11. This primitivism is related in medieval thought to the idea of an earthly paradise in a distant place, a golden age at the beginning of time, a normative concept of nature against which corruption and decline are measured, the vanity of arts and sciences, and the preference for wilderness over civilization, simplicity over diversity or complexity. See A. Bartlett Giamatti, *The Earthly Paradise and the Renaissance Epic* (Princeton, N. J.: Princeton Univ. Press, 1966), pp. 3–93; George H. Williams, *Wilderness and Paradise in Christian Thought* (New York: Harper, 1962), pp. 28–64; and Charles S. Singleton, *Journey to Beatrice* (Cambridge, Mass.: Harvard Univ. Press, 1958), pp. 141–158.

Yit nas the ground nat wounded with the plough,
But corn up-sprong, unsowe of mannes hond,
The which they gnodded, and eet nat half ynough.
No man yit knew the forrwes of his lond;
No man the fire out of the flint yit fond;
Uncorven and ungrobbed lay the vine;
No man yit in the morter spices grond
To clarre, ne to sauce of galantine.

No mader, welde, or wood no litestere
Ne knew; the fleece was of his former hewe;
No flesh ne wiste offence of edge or spere;
No coin ne knew man which was false or trewe;
No ship yit carf the waves greene and blewe;
No marchaunt yit ne fette outlandish ware;
No trumpes for the werres folk ne knewe,
Ne towres heye and walles rounde or square.

The tone of these lines is nostalgic; the poet looks back with
regret upon the untrammeled early state when plows, tools,
weapons, coinage, ships, commerce, and war were unneces-
sary. Yet the passage implies the hardness of such a life—
primitive man "eet nat half ynough," did not know fire, lived
in caves and woods, ate "pounage." The lines suggest that
civilized arts were necessary to compensate for decaying
nature. The ironic process of history is that man in the
Golden Age led a life of natural simplicity, but in his
subsequent decline needed arts which, of themselves necessary and good, provoked in him evil desires and furthered
his decline:

But cursed was the time, I dare well saye,
That men first did hir swety bisynesse
To grobbe up metal, lurking in derknesse,
And in the riveres first gemmes soughte.
Allas! than sprong up all the cursednesse
Of coveitise, that first our sorrwe broughte!

Civilized arts became the tools of the tyrant; in the ancient
world they provoked Jupiter "that first was fader of deli-
cacye" and Nimrod "desirous to regne." The poem singles
out the "three temptations" (riches, pleasure, and power)

and puts images of civilized advance and luxury—gems, palaces, towers, armor, and the like—against an image of man not cursed with profit, sleeping "in caves and in woodes soft and sweete" with "parfit quiet" and "seurtee." Their hearts "were all oon," each "his faith to other kept," and there was no pride, envy or avarice. The poem ends with a stark description of the present day—a sentence so dolorous that some have thought it prompted by the rise of Gloucester, or other political events which touched the poet deeply in a personal way:

> Allas, allas! now may men weep and crye!
> For in our dayes nis but coveitise,
> Doubleness, and tresoun, and envye,
> Poison, manslaughtre, and murdre in sundry wise.

The sentiment, whatever may have inspired it, is characteristic of medieval "complaint." It is a mistake to see in it a gloomy mood on Chaucer's part during a few bad years, or some inveterate gloom of his time. The gloom which characterizes medieval complaints of the world's mutability and senescence was balanced by idealism and hope. In three other short poems written during the Canterbury-tales period Chaucer gives clear expression to this idealistic side of medieval thought. One of these is the "moral balade" (so called in manuscripts) titled "Gentilesse" by modern editors:

> The firste stock, fader of gentilesse—
> What man that claimeth gentil for to be
> Must follow his trace, and all his wittes dresse
> Vertu to sewe, and vices for to flee.
> For unto vertu longeth dignitee,
> And noght the revers. . . .

The opening phrase, "The firste stock, fader of gentilesse," usually thought to mean Christ, could refer to Adam.[38]

---

38. See Robinson's note on line 1 (p. 862). The Golden Age of medieval thought was sometimes equated with the earthly paradise, so it would be reasonable for a poet to recommend that we follow the state of man in his first innocence, seeking virtue and fleeing vice, in order to attain true "gentilesse," The virtues listed in lines 8–11 sound to me somewhat too quotidian to be applied to Christ—wouldn't it be jejune to say that Christ, who was God made man, "loved bisyness, / Ayeinst the vice of sloth"? But it

Whichever it means, the point is that no one can bequeath
his own "vertuous noblesse" to his heir, yet everyone can
choose virtue. True nobility is a moral quality independent
of riches and inheritance: "unto vertu longeth dignitee /
And noght the revers" means "dignity (worth) belongs to
virtue (morality)." The "reverse" would be taken in the
courtly sense, "virtue (knightly quality) belongs to dignity
(inherited status)." We are, the poem says, all the heirs of
Adam and of Christ, however high our status, and are all
capable of virtue however low.[39] The same sentiment,
spoken by the Franklin and the Wife probably in a rational-
izing spirit, sounds like a platitude. But if Chaucer
addressed the poem to the royal court, or to himself, its
sentiment cannot be written off as mere convention or
cliché.

   The balade "Lack of Steadfastness," which *was*
addressed to King Richard II, expresses in its final envoy a
sentiment equally stern:

   O prince, desire to be honourable,
   Cherish thy folk and hate extorcioun!
   Suffre nothing that may be repravable
   To thyn estate don in thy regioun.
   Shew forth thy swerd of castigacioun,
   Dred God, do law, love trouthe and worthinesse,
   And wed thy folk again to stedfastnesse.

The poet's hope for social justice done by the monarch's
hand is added to a poem about the world's decline: it begins
"Sometime the world was so stedfast and stable / That
mannes word was obligacioun. . . ." Again one is reminded
of the Franklin's Tale with its high value placed on keeping
one's word. Whether or not Chaucer viewed ironically the
spirit in which the Franklin expressed these sentiments, he

---

is possible to think of man as the heir of both Adam and Christ—the two
were called by the Fathers the "first man" and the "second man"—so that
possibly the "fader of gentilesse" is Adam before the Fall and the "first
fader in magestee" (19) is Christ after the Resurrection; or perhaps the
phrase is intentionally ambiguous, referring to both.

   39. On this moral view of social class, see Brewer, "Class Distinction in
Chaucer," 299–302.

obviously takes them seriously here. "The world," he cries, "hath made a permutacioun / Fro right to wrong, fro trouth to ficklenesse, / That all is lost for lack of stedfastnesse."

Chaucer's time, like ours, was a period of social unrest, violence, and accelerated change. In such an historical period there are some who view obsolescence without enthusiasm or terror and simply say "Let us stop and think." I believe Chaucer did this. It is what one would expect (or hope to expect) in a man of great learning who had travelled widely and known the great men of his time. D. S. Brewer thinks Chaucer was among the "new men" of the age, a member of a social group which was outside the established groups of the society—not a noble, not "gentry," not like his father from the guilds or trades—and therefore saw his society more objectively, saw it from an alienated viewpoint and so saw it more clearly.[40] Then, too, he was a genius—itself, one imagines, an alienating circumstance. And if we perceive his temperament correctly from his works, he had a certain withdrawn skepticism. But he was not without convictions. In these short poems written during the period when he was working on *The Canterbury Tales* we get a clear notion of the kind of convictions he had. He evidently believed in a mercantile nation headed by a powerful and just monarch who would enforce law, and believed that the success of this ideal depended upon moral virtues—"steadfastness," "truth," and the dignity which belongs to virtue. These were the ideals he shared with Gower. He addresses himself earnestly to moral issues, addresses directly the seat of power, urges ethical and moral acts for the sake of society and the nation; he espouses the civilized arts as a way to improve man's fallen state. Emphasis is on the present and the future; the past is a guide.

There is almost nothing of the ironic Chaucer in these poems. Yet they refer to a circumstance which might be viewed ironically, for they refer to the gap between old ideals and present practices. When we see a "new world"

40. Brewer, "Class Distinction in Chaucer," 304, and "Love and Marriage in Chaucer's Poetry," *MLR* 49 (1954):461–464.

taking shape which controverts our expectations, we often see this as an irony of life. The son whose values fly in the face of his father's is an ironic figure; so is the father. Irony is promoted by changing times, and our ability to see the irony of change, or to view it ironically, is one of the ways change is permitted to take place. In seeing the cultural changes of his age from an ironic perspective, Chaucer was in part accommodating to or accepting those changes. We cannot say that he espoused them all—there is reason to believe he deplored many. But the Chaucer we know, unlike his friend Gower, scarcely ever (except in these short poems) deplores out loud. He is an idealist and an ironist. And to the extent that he is able to accept changing times and think about ways to make them right, he is "in search of the world," is seeking moral and ethical norms for the world—is asking "How shall the world be served?" Those norms must be based upon premises of man's dignity and of a positive value in secular pursuits. Not that the church had no such norms to supply by "authority," and not that Chaucer does not sometimes appeal to authority. But in *The Canterbury Tales* he approaches the question in an experimental, a pragmatic spirit. If we are to know how the world is to be served, we must first know the world.

In the *Troilus* there is such a search for the world, but it is not central to the poem and hasn't the character of the search embodied in *The Canterbury Tales*. We leave the poem instructed about the vanity of earthly life and human loves and strivings. Many think that this is the whole point of the poem, its one meaning. But it is hard to get away from the fact that some positive human values are espoused in the *Troilus,* though we see them only in retrospect. At the end we look back upon the completed work and see regretfully a time-bound world which has passed into history. Nevertheless, we see in this world a love which, however fleeting, was at its best civilized and idealistic, a union of two people won, maintained, and lost at great pain. The *Troilus* does not suggest that anyone can expect more, but it does not deny that at least so much is possible, and for a time beautiful. Then too we look back upon the hero as a man justly famous as a warrior and prince—a man of high ideals and principles whose deeds won him a place in history. And we look back upon the value of the work itself: the poet ends his poem wishing that it might kiss the steps in which the great poets of antiquity walk. The transitory love which the poem describes is thus realized and given meaning in the work of art: the work implies a positive value placed upon books and poetry.[41]

In *The Canterbury Tales* this search for the world is as positive and idealistic as what we find in the *Troilus* or the short poems Chaucer wrote in his last fifteen years; but the style is different. The ending of the work, the Parson's tract, puts secular values in perspective, but the perspective is other than the eschatological one introduced at the end of the *Troilus*; much of the Parson's Tale recommends moral values which would be productive in making a better world. And the ending of *The Canterbury Tales* draws a line short of the end of human life. We know that ultimately all is to be understood from an eschatological perspective, that things of the world have meaning or being, arrive at their perfection or fulfillment, only in eternity. But this consideration is symbolically "distanced," for the destination is not reached. At the end of the *Troilus* we are outside time; in *The Canterbury Tales* we remain inside time, and moral values introduced are appropriate to this secular realm. Even the Parson's Tale, for all its religiosity, fastens upon penance, an act done in and because of "the world."

This search for the world in *The Canterbury Tales* suggests what the short poems written during the Canterbury tales period suggest, that during that period Chaucer experi-

41. Cf. Rosemary Woolf's remark, in "Chaucer as a Satirist in the General Prologue to the *Canterbury Tales*," *Critical Quarterly* 1 (1959):156, that Chaucer was "the first English medieval poet explicitly to accept the permanent value of his work, and hence to care about the unsettled state of the language and its dialectal variety, the first to see himself as of the same kind as the classical poets. . . . [B]ehind this disguise, and sometimes heard openly, is the truly personal tone of the satirist, which is quite un-medieval." The three values which I point to as implicit in the *Troilus* correspond to the "three temptations" of medieval thought. I suggested in *The Three Temptations*, pp. 74, 275–276, 291–292, that these in turn correspond to the major enthusiasms of the Renaissance humanists—love, fame, and letters.

enced such distressing events in the English court, such enormous changes in the society, and such insecurity about the future, that it affected the idea of his work. The idea was a sufficiently moral and religious one, but the style appropriate to that idea made it impossible to scold or to despair. His response was secular and pragmatic within the limits of a Christian ethic: the work was a book about the world—its values and manner, its style, had to be "worldly." In "Lack of Steadfastness" and "Truth" he made it plain that he believed man in this world could follow reason, "do law," and serve social justice. This would be man's bulwark against the world's decline. And he expressed that belief with the metaphor which gave to *The Canterbury Tales* its distinctive form: "Here is non home, here nis but wildernesse: / Forth pilgrim forth! . . . / Hold the high way."

IV

MEMORY AND FORM

ONE phase of the idea of *The Canterbury Tales*, then, is a "search for the world" carried out on a pilgrimage through the world. The object of the pilgrimage, the Heavenly Jerusalem, is our ultimate concern. But the object of the search is reason, law, and social justice: our immediate concerns are of the world. The style of the work gives expression to this search. It makes the present moment pass vividly before us and represents the past as a storehouse of ideals and authorities to guide us into the future. In this passing "now" we experience obsolescence, and obsolescence relies upon memory: it evokes ideals forsaken and a past in which we imagine them embodied. "Now" is never more intimidating than when it is thus set in isolation from what was and what is to come. This feature of the style gives the search immediacy, even urgency: we are prisoners of the present, must move with it. Yet the one-way pilgrimage into the myth of the future draws us into the myth of the past, precisely as real pilgrimages to Jerusalem or Canterbury drew the pilgrim into the contemplation of the Heavenly Jerusalem to come but brought him factually among *relics*, tangible and visible objects mythologized by Christian lore. Such a pilgrimage, if we understand its fullest implications, explains the form of *The Canterbury Tales*.

We would understand that form better if we knew how Chaucer himself conceived of literary form. He did not use the word itself as we do; when he talks in the *Troilus* about "the form of olde clerkis speche / In poetrie" (V:1854–1855) he has literary tradition in mind but is thinking about "speche"—he probably means what we would call style or manner. But he does afford us in the *Troilus* one small hint of his attitude toward form in our sense:

> For every wight that hath an house to founde
> Ne renneth naught the werk for to biginne
> With rakel hond, but he wol bide a stounde,
> And send his hertes line out fro withinne
> Aldirfirst his purpose for to winne.
>
> (I:1065–1069)

Chaucer translated this sentence from the opening lines of Geoffrey of Vinsauf's *Poetria nova*, representing it as a thought which crosses Pandarus's mind as he ponders how to arrange a love affair between Troilus and Criseyde. Geoffrey's Latin reads as follows:

> Si quis habet fundare domum, non currit ad actum
> Impetuosa manus: intrinseca linea cordis
> Praemetitur opus, seriemque sub ordine certo
> Interior praescribit homo. . . .
>
> (43–46)[1]

The passage is a great favorite of Chaucer critics, for it shows Chaucer's familiarity with an important work of medieval rhetoric. Robert Jordan argues that it shows Chaucer subscribing to a disjunctive or architectonic conception of poetic unity unlike the "organic" conception of modern times.[2] The rhetorician Geoffrey starts his discourse by telling us that "if one sets out to build a house he does not rush to work helter-skelter; instead the heart's inner plumb-line first measures out the work and the inner man plans the steps in a particular order." Chaucer adds the

---

1. Edmond Faral, *Les arts poétiques du XIIe et du XIIIe siècle* (Paris: Edouard Champion, 1924), p. 198; trans. mine. J. J. Murphy, "A New Look at Chaucer and the Rhetoricians," *RES*, n.s. 15 (1964):1–20 raises doubts about Chaucer's familiarity with rhetorical writings, but the point is not important to my argument; clearly he knew the passage he translated.
2. *Chaucer and the Shape of Creation*, pp. 42–43.

phrase "but he wol bide a stounde," and substitutes "send out" for "measure," probably because his manuscript read *praemittitur* (or *praemittetur*) for *praemetitur*.[3] The reading, or misreading, results in an interesting switch of metaphor. Geoffrey wrote that he measures his work with the heart's plumb-line; Chaucer wrote that he sends out his heart's line to "win" his purpose, an image less appropriate to the builder's line than to a fisherman's.[4] He appears to have formed, through a misreading in his Latin text, an image of the artist first catching his "purpose" like a fish.

I say "artist" in full consciousness that the thought is Pandarus's. Pandarus *is* an artist—a plotter and manipulator of the action who hovers over the two lovers and responds to them vicariously in quite the same way as the narrator; Pandarus is a counterpart within the poem of the narrator outside it, both of them stage managing and emoting, the one in the lovers' world and the other in ours. And Pandarus has no more control over the outcome than the narrator has. He takes thought, conceives a plan, and follows it by steps, pretty much as Geoffrey recommended.

The form of a work is planned, as Geoffrey puts it, *sub ordine certo*, and the artist's "inner man" is limited by that form as the builder is limited by the form of a house; "its state," Geoffrey says in the next line, "is an archetype before it is a reality."[5] Hence he counsels the artist to "construct the whole work within the heart's citadel; let it be in the heart before it is on the lips."[6] The initial act of poetic creation, this winning of a "purpose," does resemble the fisherman's casting his line into the waters: the artist wants a purpose and he has to take his chance on finding it in his heart or mind.[7] What he catches there—though Geoffrey thinks it an

3. See Robinson's note on I:1065.
4. On "line" see *OED*, use 3; the word was used only in the plural when referring to catching birds. I find no use of "win" which suggests builders.
5. "Status ejus / Est prius archetypus quam sensilis" (47–48).
6. "Opus totum prudens in pectoris arcem / Contrahe, sitque prius in pectore quam sit in ore" (58–59).
7. Lat. *pectus* does not suggest emotion in quite the way modern "heart" does, but the heart was the seat of the affections; if Geoffrey had meant a purely cerebral function he might have used *mens* or *ratio*. What he is

"archetype"—evidently squares with experience, as does the builder's plan. Chaucer's image introduces a suggestion of chance, as Geoffrey's does not, but neither author suggests anywhere that there are platonic ideas of poems or plenary inspiration for poets; both see the art of writing poetry as a craft learned by experience, which is what rhetoric is. And both think the artist needs an idea before he sets to work.

If I am right that Chaucer adopted such an attitude toward poetic form (he based it, after all, on the most influential rhetoric text of his age), it helps account for the kind of form which *The Canterbury Tales* possesses. The work is planned and measured as Geoffrey recommended, and we see, almost, the plan unfold before us. The General Prologue is the initial step: the season, the pilgrimage, and the pilgrims are described in that order, and Chaucer acknowledges his debt to rhetoric when he says that the description is "accordaunt to resoun," for he then proposes to adopt rhetorical categories.[8] So reasonable is this plan that it makes everything seem inevitable, even what is random and *un*-planned. It introduces into the work itself the tension between form and formlessness. The narrator will recount all from memory, and memory is nothing if not "within the heart's citadel." But it is inescapably bound to one's experience—is, as the medievals would have said, a storehouse of images and intentions—so that memories, however distorted, must retain in some measure the form of the things remembered. A work ordered on principles of memory must therefore be bound in part to the *dis*ordered way things happen, to "aventure, or sort, or cas."

What we stumble against here is the relation between form and reality. Recent critics—Erich Auerbach, for example, and E. H. Gombrich—have made us see how style, in its broader sense, shapes and reflects the artist's experience of

---

speaking of here is *inventio*, that part of rhetoric concerned with conceiving an argument; on its place in medieval theory, see Payne, *The Key of Remembrance*, pp. 42–51.

8. I have this suggestion from Phyllis Hodgson, ed., *General Prologue*, p. 74.

reality.[9] We customarily think about "objective reality" and "subjective responses," but in recent years we have come to see reality more as the dynamic relation of subject and object. The literary work is the "object" before us, its reality expressed in it; the artist's idea is behind this expression of reality, and the work's form and style are inherent in that idea. When we grasp the one we grasp the other. We do not grasp any of it if we are not equipped with appropriate responses, ideas, or *Gestalten*. But critics do go on talking about "the text itself" and "an objective examination of the text" as if they had moon rocks or a cadaver before them. Hence the confusion about literary form. If you set out a sonnet for examination, its form seems immensely palpable: fourteen pentameter lines in a specific rhyme scheme, an octave and sestet, and so on. One can observe it "objectively." But this view of the sonnet as "a form" really describes rules or norms pertinent to a genre. Such an estimate of form must represent as "variations" those features which make each sonnet unique. When we *read* a sonnet, our attention is caught by the "variations"; we want to know what makes the sonnet itself, want to know how it represents and shapes reality, how it reveals a perception on the author's part different from other perceptions. Seen this way, every sonnet has a form of its own—form is intrinsic, immanent in the idea of a work and perceptible only through our experience of it. Form, like style, is the result of choices the poet has made, but we experience it as an identifiable phenomenon—it is not the mere sum of the artist's choices, it has the "inner man" and his "heart's line" behind it.[10]

9.   Erich Auerbach, *Mimesis: The Representation of Reality in Western Literature*, trans. Willard Trask (1953; rpt. Garden City, N. Y.: Doubleday Anchor Books, 1957), chap. I and passim; E. H. Gombrich, *Art and Illusion: A Study in the Psychology of Pictorial Representation*, Bollingen Series 35.5, 2nd ed., rev. (Princeton: Princeton Univ. Press, 1961), pp. 1–30 and passim. A suggestive recent book is the three essays by Gombrich, Julian Hochberg, and Max Black, collected as *Art, Perception, and Reality*, ed. Maurice Mandelbaum (Baltimore and London: Johns Hopkins Univ. Press, 1972).

10.   Cf. the discussion by various critics of "Form and Its Alternatives" in *NLH* 2 (1971), no. 2, pp. 199–356.

The difficulty is to perceive form across a chasm of six centuries. We cannot be sure that what we take as the form of the poem is not a projection of our own, that history and "the background" are not projections of our own. We look at medieval buildings or artifacts in a museum and say "If only they could speak." Yet their poems, which are made of words, *do* speak to us, and whatever direct response we get from them puts us so much the more intimately into their world.[11] The author set out to instruct, or entertain, or move his readers. If we are instructed or entertained or moved, we have received something authentic from him for which "historical scholarship" can never provide a substitute. That *The Canterbury Tales* still has the power to give us such a direct reponse, even in a world alien to its own, is a demonstrable fact—not just a fact about us but a fact about the poem. Yet by scholarship we seek to validate this direct response, to claim that the response squares with myths, or complexes, or most often with "the background." If we are to see the poem against its historical background, we must as best we can see the whole of the poem against the whole of the background. But we must be prepared to find that the poet, conceiving a form after the manner of one building a house, selected some materials from that background and omitted others.

THE GENERAL PROLOGUE

Memory, central to the experience of reading *The Canterbury Tales,* is embodied in it as its central fiction and becomes the controlling principle of its form. The expressed idea of the work is that the pilgrim Chaucer, like the pilgrim Dante of the *Commedia,* reports an experience of his own which includes stories told by others. Both are returned

---

11. C. S. Lewis, in "The Anthropological Approach," in *English and Medieval Studies Presented to J. R. R. Tolkien on the Occasion of His Seventieth Birthday,* ed. Norman Davis and C. L. Wrenn (London: Allen and Unwin, 1962), pp. 219–230, has argued for a direct response of the kind I mention here.

travellers, both rely on memory. Frances Yates has even suggested that Dante relied for his structuring principles upon the artificial memory systems prevalent in the Middle Ages.[12] This fictional premise, probably Chaucer's greatest debt to Dante, is hardly ever noted. Simple and natural as it seems to us who read novels, it was unusual for a medieval work explicitly to take the form of an imagined feat of memory: we find it in romances, but only a simple version of it. And it was unusual for a work to have as the subject of that memory an imagined experience of the author's own.

It is not surprising that this fundamental fiction of *The Canterbury Tales* has been overlooked. Chaucer the "observer" and "persona" have been fixed in people's minds since Kittredge's day, and these conceptions mitigate the element of personal experience in favor of distance, irony, and control. Chaucer used to be admired as an open-eyed observer of contemporary life (which he was) and so reckoned a naif; it seems astonishing now to find Kittredge in 1914 arguing that "a naif Collector of Customs would be a paradoxical monster."[13] Since then, the sophisticated and ironical Chaucer, adopting for satiric purposes the persona of a naif, has been the going thing in Chaucer criticism. Forty years after Kittredge's lecture, Professor Donaldson in a famous article[14] described this persona, emphasizing the

12. Frances A. Yates, *The Art of Memory* (Chicago: Univ. of Chicago Press, 1966), pp. 95–96.

13. George Lyman Kittredge, *Chaucer and His Poetry* (Cambridge, Mass.: Harvard Univ. Press, 1915), p. 45.

14. "Chaucer the Pilgrim," *PMLA* 69 (1954):928–936 rpt. in *Speaking of Chaucer*, pp. 1–12 and in S&T pp. 1–13. My own response to this much-discussed aspect of Chaucer's art was an article called "Chaucer the Man," *PMLA* 80 (1965):337–343 (rpt. *Chaucer's Mind and Art*, ed. Cawley, pp. 31–45), perhaps the first step in the direction of the present book. It was a meditation—by no means a rebuttal—on Donaldson's article. It raised matters like oral delivery and silent reading, Chaucer's relation to his court audience, the transition in the nature of authorship and the character of the reading public taking place in Chaucer's time. It had footnotes to Marshall McLuhan, Wayne Booth, and so on—it was, like everything, a product of its time. Some years later my attention was drawn to W. Nelson Francis's "Chaucer Shortens a Tale," *PMLA* 68 (1953):1126–1141, and there on pp. 1136–1141 was a formulation about oral delivery and Chaucer's relation to his audience *remarkably* like my own—in

disparity between Chaucer the pilgrim, Chaucer the poet, and Chaucer the man. In a climate of formalism the fictional pilgrim was, and perhaps still is, often viewed as a kind of puppet; but in fact, Donaldson closed his article by pointing to the relatedness of pilgrim and man, doubting that one can tell which has the last word. Among those interested in the rhetoric of fiction or the "dynamics" of literature, this inter-relation of man and persona has captured some amount of interest; where it was once possible to talk seriously about the "finiteness of the narrator-role," such a phrase now seems all gesture and bluster. Not that role-playing isn't involved; but in all role-playing, masquerade, or disguise, the art and excitement come from the living presence of the performer behind the role or mask.

The remarkable aspect of this performer's mind, as he presents it to us, is not just a power of observation but a prodigious memory. Memory is endemic to all story-telling and all literary composition; Mnemosyne, we recall, was the mother of the Muses. St. Augustine in an amazing passage showed how memory is endemic to understanding itself:

> I carry . . . facts in my memory, and I also remember how I learned them. I have also heard, and remember, many false arguments put forward to dispute them. Even if the arguments are false, the fact that I remember them is not false. I also remember distinguishing between the true facts and the false theories advanced against them, and there is a difference between seeing myself make this distinction now and remembering that I have made it often in the past, every time that I have given the matter any thought. So I not only remember that I have often understood these facts in the past, but I also commit to memory the fact that I understand them and distinguish the truth from the falsehood at the present moment. By this means I ensure that later on I shall remember that

different words, of course, with a different frame of reference—yet published a dozen years before my article and a year before Donaldson's. I had no record or memory of reading it and had never met the author; I had read books he had read and probably talked with people who had talked with him or read his article or heard of it. Tracing the course of such trends—the provenience of an insight—has something in common with the study of folk motifs, and I hope it is not necessary for a critic to cite each instance of such a *déja vu* experienced after self-flattery.

I understood them at this time. And I remember that I have remembered, just as later on, if I remember that I have been able to remember these facts now, it will be by the power of my memory that I shall remember doing so.[15]

Augustine recognized that memory contains all experience, even the experience of forgetting. For all that happens to us in time there must be memory. Every writer, as he composes, must remember what he has set out to write and what he has already written—the action is divided, as Augustine says of recitations, between memory and expectation until all has "passed into the province of memory." Durations themselves cannot be known without memory, so even language depends on memory, requiring the recollection of syllables spoken in sequence and the measurement of long and short vowels.[16] But this reliance of story-telling and composition on memory rarely used to be brought into literary works themselves. Medieval writers were more apt to write as if authority resided in them, so that the "I" in medieval works is frequently impersonal. At other times they wrote as recorders or copyists—Chaucer adopts this pose in the *Troilus*—putting into their books what they found in others. Dante in the *Vita Nuova* does claim to be writing of personal experience from memory, but he depicts memory as a "book" and himself as a copyist and glossator of that book. Even bards, minstrels, or scops, among whom prodigious feats of memory *were* performed, rarely alluded to memory itself. The fashionable premise of fictions in Chaucer's time was the dream, and Chaucer's early poems all employ that convention; but little was ever made of the fact that the dream is remembered, and little notice given to the act of writing it down. When Chaucer ended *The Book of the Duchess* with a specific reference to the act of writing the dream in verse, he was doing something unusual, and even here he made nothing of memory as the step between dreaming and writing: he saw that step as a matter of time moving on in "process." The dreamer hears a clock strike twelve, wakes,

15. *Confessions* X:13, trans. R. S. Pine-Coffin (Baltimore: Penguin Classics, 1961).
16. *Ibid.*, XI:27–28.

finds the book he had been reading when he dropped off, and says,

> Thought I, "This is so queint a sweven
> That I wol, by process of time,
> Fonde to put this sweven in ryme
> As I can best, and that anon."
> This was my sweven; now hit is don.

(1330–1334)

The narrator of *The Canterbury Tales*, like the narrator of *The Book of the Duchess*, remembers a past experience well enough to write it down in detail—to describe some twenty-nine pilgrims and repeat in their own words the tales they told. His memory becomes a wellspring of narrative, like the "old book" in the *Troilus*. This fictional *tour de force* of memory makes *The Canterbury Tales* different from other frame narratives. It was how Chaucer bestowed upon his work the ironic and equivocal stamp which no such work had had before: every pilgrim and every tale stands out as an independent reality but all is mediated by the author-narrator. If he got the hint anywhere, he got it from Dante, or the dream-vision, or some actual account of a pilgrimage. No writer of a frame narrative had done anything like it. Boccaccio, in neither the *Filocolo*, the *Ameto*, or the *Decameron*, used the first person and never claimed directly to have participated in the framing action; one has to know the code-name "Filostrato" to get the implication that the author was present among the company and even at that his point of view does not color what he reports. Sercambi, though present on the journey, told all the tales himself and referred to himself in the third person. In Gower's *Confessio Amantis*, most like *The Canterbury Tales* in subject matter, themes, conventions, and motifs, we get the faceless "I" of medieval complaint who identifies himself as the writer, and the conventional love-vision (not explicitly a dream); the tales are told in Boethian fashion by the Lover and his confessor Genius; the organizing principle is that of the "tree of vices." In Chaucer we find a form, simple and natural though it seems six centuries later, which was then new: the voice of the poet himself recalls and recreates the voices of others, the form and matter seeming to take shape as they come into mind.

This last remark will delay us a moment, for the way things come into mind has changed since Chaucer's time. The physiology of memory is no doubt basically the same in each individual, but things remembered vary with the importance placed upon them by individuals or cultures, and the character of memory itself varies with our notions of what memory is and does. Because Freud or Wordsworth placed more importance on childhood memories, they likely had more childhood memories (though of very different kinds). Preconceptions about history, or causality, or human nature doubtless affect the selection, association, and structuring of memory. If we are to see *The Canterbury Tales* as a fictional feat of memory, then, we have to ask whether memory itself did not have a different character in the fourteenth century from what it has now.

As with most other things, the medievals had two contradictory notions of memory and believed in both. From one point of view they saw memory as a "faculty" of the soul and forgetfulness as its failure to function well. Memory played a minor role in the life of the mind. It was one of the five "inner senses" or "inward wits" (with common sense, fantasy, imagination, and the "estimative" sense) which resided in the sensitive soul. Among the powers of the soul this sensitive power was higher than the vegetative but inferior to the locomotive and the intellectual.[17] That memory contained all experience, a fact Augustine marvelled at, did not raise its status much; Augustine was arguing, after all, that we must seek God beyond memory or through the total experience of memory, but not in particular memories.[18] Memory was supplied by imagination, the image-making faculty of the mind, which extrapolated "phan-

17. St. Thomas Aquinas, *Summa theologica* I, q. 78, especially art. 4.
18. St. Augustine, *Confessions* X:8−26. On Augustine's rejection of platonic innatism and his transformation of Plato's idea that the mind remembers truth and therefore God, see Etienne Gilson, *The Christian Philosophy of St. Augustine*, trans. L. E. M. Lynch (New York: Vintage, 1967), pp. 64−65, 74−76, 82, 100−105, 219−223.

tasms" from the evidence of the senses and could make combinations of these phantasms. Because memory was a storehouse of such images, it was bound to the intense particularities of the sensible world, which made it the less reliable as a means of knowing truth. Memory was "an organ, a cerebral ventricle," and "what is described in it must be something sensible, which has all the limitations of individuality and particular nature."[19] Such an estimate of memory, fostered by the old faculty psychology, lingered into the seventeenth century.[20] Modern conceptions of associative process, of a form-giving or structuring power inherent in memory itself, were foreign to the medievals. They saw memory as a storehouse on which one must *impose* form. Thus Augustine refers to the "compartments" of memory. St. Thomas adds that memory stores intentions as well as images.[21] When Chaucer the pilgrim claims to remember the particularities of a past experience he is not therefore boasting of mental powers which were admired or thought reliable. He is limiting his scope to the experience of the temporal or secular world.

19. Elisabeth Ruth Harvey, *The Inward Wits: An Enquiry into the Aristotelian Tradition of Faculty Psychology in its Literary Relations During the Later Middle Ages and the Renaissance* Diss. Univ. of London 1970, p. 144; on memory in St. Thomas Aquinas, see pp. 143–147. Part of this dissertation, the best treatment of faculty psychology I have seen, is to be published by the Warburg Institute; I am extremely grateful to the author for lending me a copy of her typescript.

20. See Georges Poulet, *Studies in Human Time*, trans. Elliott Coleman (1956; rpt. New York: Harper Torchbooks, 1959) pp. 23–24. In the nineteenth century the classic treatment is Henri Bergson's *Matière et mémoire*. On the transition from eighteenth-century ideas see Christopher Salvesen, *The Landscape of Memory: A Study of Wordsworth's Poetry* (London: Edward Arnold, 1965), pp. 1–45.

21. "But for the retention and preservation of these forms, the *phantasy* or *imagination* is appointed, being as it were a storehouse of forms received through the senses. Furthermore, for the apprehension of intentions which are not received through the senses, the *estimative* power is appointed: and for their preservation, the *memorative* power, which is a storehouse of such intentions. A sign of which we have in the fact that the principle of memory in animals is found in some such intention, for instance, that something is harmful or otherwise. And the very character of something as past, which memory observes, is to be reckoned among these intentions." *Summa theologica* I, q. 78, art. 4, trans. A. C. Pegis (Modern Library, 1948).

But while medieval thinkers put a low value on memory when they saw it as a faculty of the soul, they valued it highly as a necessity of everyday life. St. Augustine, with his customary verbal felicity, called it the "stomach of the mind." From this practical view they imagined memory had to be supplied with shelves, so to speak, and kept in order. They could hardly do otherwise in an age before the printing press when books were scarce and paper dear, and when devices used to write memoranda on, like wax tablets, were cumbersome. One always supposed men had better memories in those days; but it was not until Frances Yates published her remarkable book, *The Art of Memory*, that most of us realized how fully men *trained* their memories.[22] The memory systems of the ancient world, Miss Yates shows, survived into the Middle Ages; there is even a short treatise *De arte memorativa* by Chaucer's contemporary Bishop Bradwardine.[23] This "artificial" memory was understood as a corrective to human ignorance, a way of supplying capacities the mind had lost because of the Fall. Its moral utility was comparable to the fact that a remembered image carries with it an "intention" (for example, that the wolf is dangerous); but associating intelligible ideas with images was an art which had to be learned. It was useful as a means of remembering moral truths—the "trees of virtues and vices" familiar to any student of the Middle Ages were almost certainly memory devices; Miss Yates even argues with some conviction that the sculptures in Gothic cathedrals were influenced by and even intended as memory devices.[24] But apart from this moralizing use of artificial memory, it was a practical necessity; it was, we know, taught as a phase of rhetoric, and beyond a doubt it was used for quotidian purposes in place of the maps, directories, and lists which have become second nature in the modern world.

Artificial memory worked on the principles of order and association.[25] It was by nature spatial and visual. It

22. See esp. pp. 50–104.
23. Yates, p. 105.
24. *Ibid.*, pp. 79–81.
25. *Ibid.*, p. 71.

required, first, a mental store of "places"—mental pictures of actual buildings or interiors. To these one associated mnemonic images or sometimes words, "placing" one upon a column, another on an altar, another in an alcove; visual images were thought more useful than words.[26] Meditate for a moment on this habit of mind and one becomes aware of the most startling difference between our medieval ancestors and ourselves. We memorize a few things—grammatical forms, or the presidents of the United States, or the English kings—almost always in lists and with words; otherwise the memory of modern man is an intellectual rabbit's warren made from slips of paper. But the medievals made of their memories vast storehouses of visual images, disposed upon structured "places," systematized and concrete.

That Chaucer knew an artificial memory system there can be no doubt. If, as most people now believe, he was educated at the Inns of Court, he would have been required to get by memory vast amounts of legal information. We learn in the General Prologue about the Man of Law that "every statute koude he plein by rote" and that he had "in termes" all the cases and judgments since King William's time.[27] Anyone holding the kind of posts Chaucer held would

26. *Ibid.*, p. 81.
27. The meaning of "in terms" is disputed. Some think it refers to the "terms," i.e. Year-Books, compiled annually from notes of trials, which served lawyers as a record of precedents; but they went back only to the reign of Edward I. Most editors think it refers to the Lawyer's specific knowledge of cases and judgments, meaning "in technical expressions" (see *OED* under "term," use 13) or "in express words," "in so many words" (*OED*, 14b). Chaucer almost always uses "terms" this way in the plural, though nowhere else does he use the phrase "in terms." The phrase seems to suggest what is plainly stated four lines later (327), that the Lawyer knew English law "by rote," that is, by memory. It stands to reason a memory system would have been used. There is a record of the plundering of the Inner Temple during the Peasants' Revolt which mentions how the rebels seized and burned "all the books and remembrances that were in the hatches of the prentices of the law" (Stow, *Chronicles*, cited in Robert R. Pearce, *A History of the Inns of Court and Chancery* . . . [London, 1848], pp. 213–218). These "remembrances" were evidently notes used by students as an aid to memory. An alternate meaning of "in terms" could be the terms appointed for the sitting of courts (as opposed to vacations, *OED* use 5). It has this sense (of annual terms) when applied to the Year-Books. It would mean that the Lawyer had (by memory) all the

have needed to remember laws and names and people and a myriad of facts. Besides, he *thought* of memory as a storehouse: while he uses the reflexive form ("remember me") or the impersonal one ("it remembereth me"), he often uses such idioms as "to have in memory" or "have remembrance," "to draw to memory," "to clepe agein unto memory" to "fall, be, or put" in remembrance. These usages suggest control over a disciplined memory and represent memory as a *place* supplied at will by a storehouse; implicit in them are the habits of "artificial" memory—order, association, and visualization.

Memory is, moreover, central to the reading experience which *The Canterbury Tales* affords: as we come to each new tale we must call to mind from the General Prologue the description of the pilgrim telling it; if we do not, a whole level of meaning drops away. This is, everyone knows, one of the notably original elements of *The Canterbury Tales*: the tales themselves characterize the tellers and so contribute to the narrative of the pilgrimage itself. If it is true that Chaucer read the work aloud at court, his audience could not have kept the left index finger stuck in the General Prologue, as we do, at the beginning of each tale. They would have had to recall "the condicioun / Of each of hem. . . . And which they weren, and of what degree, / And eek in what array that they were inne." If they could not do this, their memories would have had to be refreshed from time to time, or they would have had to miss an exciting feature of the work. Sometimes the headlinks, prologues, and tales themselves remind us of the pilgrim's traits as set forth in the General Prologue, but this is not always so. True, the tales fascinate in themselves. But the unity of conception which distinguishes *The Canterbury Tales* in its fullest complexity relies on memory or the refreshing of memory: it presup-

---

cases and judgments since King William's time and had remembered them according to terms—i.e. by years. This would be a likely way of remembering legal precedents since precedents by nature follow in chronological sequence; the "terms" would serve as places in a memory system.

poses a listener who can remember the pilgrims or a reader
who can turn over the leaves.

The narrator claims to be remembering the pilgrims,
and seems to be describing them as he first encountered
them at the inn; that is the setting, at the moment when he
launches into the description—"ere that I ferther in this tale
pace." Yet as he describes them he includes details about
their appearance on the road and even details about their
private lives at home. Though he claims to be an objective
reporter, he turns out strangely omniscient—a fact sometimes put forth as evidence against the "realism" of the
General Prologue, which it is. If we ask "where we are" as we
read the General Prologue, the answer must be neither on
the road nor in the inn, but in the realm of mental images, of
memory, of hearsay and surmise, of empathy, even of
fantasy. And Chaucer draws attention to himself fictional-
ized as observer and recorder; we relate to him, and his
participation in the pilgrimage becomes part of the fictional
reality. We pass through the looking-glass of the narrator's
mind into the remembered world of the pilgrimage; from it
into the remembered worlds of the various pilgrims; and
from these sometimes even into the remembered worlds of
their characters.

This controlled lapse from one remembered world to
another, this regression by successive steps into the past and
the unreal, is the essential principle of form in *The Canterbury
Tales*. The General Prologue which introduces it is structured upon principles of memory as memory was then
experienced; and it introduces principles of form and structure which are to operate in the work as a whole. Its memory
structure is comprised of several components superimposed,
and these we shall see best by separating them into the
features of association and order which they owe to the habit
of artificial memory.

The characters are arranged in associations easiest to
remember, associations of class, alliance, and dependency
endemic to medieval society. First, they are arranged according to the conception of the Three Estates. There is the
aristocracy (Knight and Squire, with their Yeoman); then the

clergy (the Prioress and her entourage, the Monk and the Friar); all the rest, from the Merchant on, belong to the "commons," except for the Clerk and Parson whom I shall mention in a moment, and except for the Summoner and Pardoner, two classless pariahs who are put at the end.[28] This perfectly natural order is then subdivided—Chaucer might well have had in mind Geoffrey of Vinsauf's advice, that one should divide a thing to be remembered into small parts.[29] He arranges the pilgrims in associations so natural that because of them the people themselves in such relationships would have fallen into groups in the inn or on the road, and we are told they did so. There is the Knight, his son, and their yeoman; the Prioress, her companion and "preestes three"; the Man of Law and the Franklin; the five Guildsmen and their cook; the Parson and his brother the Plowman; the Summoner and Pardoner. Call to mind any of these and their companions come to mind automatically. Others are described together, though we are not told they travelled together: the Monk and Friar (two kinds of religious); the Shipman, Physician, and Wife (three "bourgeois"); the Miller, Manciple, and Reeve (three small-fry functionaries).

The well-known "idealized" portraits seem thrown into this order at random. Three of them (Knight, Parson, and Plowman) correspond to the Three Estates. The portrait of the Clerk is idealized too, and perhaps he represents a style of life (that of the universities, or of humanism) which Chaucer considered separate from the usual three. But the Clerk comes for no apparent reason between the Merchant and the Man of Law, the Parson and Plowman for no apparent reason between the Wife and Miller. I should like

28. Cf. the divisions and subdivisions suggested by Kemp Malone, *Chapters on Chaucer* (Baltimore: Johns Hopkins Press, 1951), pp. 149–157, and by Hodgson, *General Prologue*, pp. 31–34. What I suggest here about the arrangement of portraits is not necessarily inconsistent with the theory of a "socio-economic ranking based upon an analysis of the origins of income" advanced by Ruth Nevo, "Chaucer: Motive and Mask in the 'General Prologue,'" *MLR* 58 (1963):1–9; nor with the divisions by social class proposed by Brooks, *Chaucer's Pilgrims*.

29. *Poetria Nova* V:1990–1991: "sit secta minutis / Particulis, pluresque simul ne sume. . . ."

to offer a possible explanation for this seemingly haphazard arrangement. If we take the description of the Prioress and her followers and that of the Guildsmen and their cook as single descriptions (which they are), and if we count the description of the Host, the portraits of the General Prologue can then be seen arranged symmetrically into three groups of seven, each headed by an ideal portrait:

Knight:	Squire, Yeoman, Prioress, Monk, Friar, Merchant
Clerk:	Man of Law, Franklin, Guildsmen, Shipman, Physician, Wife
Parson, Plowman:	Miller, Manciple, Reeve, Summoner, Pardoner, Host

I do not mean to suggest that this arrangement is like statues in niches or an allegorical painting, but it is interesting that the "images" in artificial memory *were* emblematic or symbolical, that is, were meant to call abstractions to mind. To the medievals, as Frances Yates points out, memory's highest function was to remember moral precepts.[30] The "ideal" portraits undeniably have an emblematic quality, and the other portraits, for all their warts and red stockings—which make them memorable—suggest, in the old phrase, "types of society." Yet one of the principles of artificial memory was that one remembered best the image which startled one's feelings. Hence the mixture of particularities and abstractions which we admire in the General Prologue was itself a phase of artificial memory; as Geoffrey of Vinsauf said, "delight alone makes the faculty of memory strong."[31] Then, too, the symmetry of the arrangement is characteristically medieval; some might suspect numerical composition or number symbolism clicking away in the background. Such efforts at proportionableness were a habit of mind in the Middle Ages, and the ordered "places" of artificial memory gave powerful support to such a habit if they did not create

30. Yates, pp. 50–57.
31. *Poetria Nova* V:2021–2022: "delectatio sola / Vim memorativam validam facit." The *vis memorativa* was one of the five inner "wits" or senses in faculty psychology.

it. I think Chaucer apportioned the ideal portraits in this architectonic way more by habit than design; it is not really an effective *aide-mémoire*. But it results in an arbitrary shape or placement which resembles the artificial order imposed as an aid to memory upon words or things by "placing" them upon the doors or columns or windows which one had imprinted in one's mind for such a purpose.

What is the idea behind such an arrangement? What purpose does it serve? Chaucer was straining at many purposes—to group the pilgrims in associations reflecting fourteenth-century society which would be easily remembered; to marshal them according to the prized concept of the Three Estates which his friend Gower had used with such brittle certainty; to include ideals of conduct among his satirical vignettes; to get order into the series, an order based on what mattered most to most of the pilgrims, status and money. The kinds of order we perceive in this complex arrangement leave some loose ends, but each detail has a rightness of its own. The Parson and Plowman are put together because they are "brothers"—which suggests an ideal relationship between clergy and commons. The idealized Clerk represents an estate other than the traditional three, but by Chaucer's time the universities *were* a world unto themselves. The Host, being the leader, is appropriately described apart from the series and last. And the Merchant is, lonely man, between the Friar and the Clerk where no one in the world would expect him to be.[32]

So much else is accomplished in this arrangement that it is remarkable it all hangs together as perfectly as it does. The "voice" is introduced first as the poet's (lines 1–18), then as the pilgrim's or returned traveller's. There is a kind of

---

32. The placement, though, is suggestive. The Merchant introduces a group of bourgeois, i.e. members of the "merchant class." The Clerk comes next, then the Man of Law and Franklin. A series of contrasts is involved—the Friar's and Merchant's kinds of venality, the Merchant's venality and the Clerk's unworldliness, the Clerk's use of his learning and the Lawyer's use of his, and so on. See Brooks, esp. pp. 21ff. It is notable that the Merchant's tale follows the Clerk's, answering its idealism with disillusionment.

progression in the gravity of the pilgrims' shortcomings: we get first the pleasant self-indulgence of the Squire, then the minor peccadillos of the Prioress and the abuses of the Monk, the various swindling of the burghers and churls, and at length the monstrous exploitations of the Summoner and Pardoner. Because the narrator's wide-eyed delight in all these sorts and conditions of men and women is so unswerving, the irony becomes greater as their vices become more serious. After the aristocracy and clergy are introduced, a bevy of "commons" is paraded in what seems no particular order; it is perhaps true that the pilgrims are introduced in a socioeconomic schema based on the degree of respectability with which they earn their livings[33] (but I can see no socioeconomic reason why the Merchant precedes the eminent Man of Law, and no explanation for the sequence Guildsmen-Shipman-Physician-Wife). In a general way, the "commons" are all independent entrepreneurs; those in a servile or dependent state (Yeoman, Cook, Plowman) are introduced with those on whom they depend; and the last group (Miller, Manciple, Reeve, Summoner, Pardoner) are lower in status, more given to swindling, and fonder of fabliaux.[34]

This arrangement in all its ramifications neatly mirrors the conditions of fourteenth-century society which, like all societies, was stratified. Knights and clerks were easily distinguished by their titles and tonsures. There were serfs still, though there are none on this pilgrimage.[35] The "commons" were more subtly stratified—they were not really disposed into a class or even classes but into numerous gradations. The "class structure" in the fourteenth century was conceived of as a hierarchy, and like all social structures *was* a hierarchy; but it was changing and mobile. "Middle" classes existed, though the *conception* "middle class" did not. The "Three Estates" was an established authoritative idea, but it did not interfere with practical distinctions of prestige,

33. Nevo, "Chaucer: Motive and Mask."
34. Baum, *Chaucer*, p. 66, proposes that this last group was added as an afterthought. See the discussion in Fisher, *John Gower*, pp. 284–286.
35. Neither the Yeoman nor the Plowman is a serf. See Hodgson, *General Prologue*, pp. 80, 124.

which had many minute degrees.[36] A man of the fourteenth
century might in his mind have lumped into one "estate" the
Franklin, the Physician, and the Miller, but he would readily
have known which should go through a door first.

The General Prologue, then, as everyone always says,
introduces a cross-section of fourteenth-century English
society. It used to be styled a "portrait gallery," but if it is like
that at all it is like a remembered portrait gallery, the figures
themselves marshalled in convenient mnemonic groups
which correspond to actualities and probabilities of fourteenth-century life, symmetrically disposed as if on mnemonic "places." We will understand the General Prologue
best if we discard all notions of a serial description. If
descriptions *seriatim* were all he wanted, Chaucer would have
been well advised to parcel out the portraits among the tales.
He described instead a *group*. Like any group it is made of
individuals, but it has a dynamics of its own based on
interpersonal and social relationships. Like any group, it is a
society in little. The group behaves in a predictable way: they
gather into subgroups based on social degrees and small-
group solidarity—those of a household or a retinue or guild,
those with similar professions or trades, stick together. A
leader emerges, and the group becomes a "flock." A game-
like aura pervades the arrangements: those superior in class
to the Host assent to his leadership, but the Host is exceedingly deferential to them and makes an effort to observe
accepted social proprieties. As in any group those who
violate the norms are made pariahs: this is so of the
Summoner and especially of the Pardoner. As the pilgrimage progresses, hostilities break out which are based on
cultural or temperamental conflicts. Opinion leaders

36. See D. W. Robertson, Jr., *Chaucer's London*, pp. 4–8. Robertson's
remarks on small-group solidarity and hierarchy in social class distinctions
during Chaucer's time are very good; "class" and "personality," it is true,
are modern constructs. It does not follow that we should not use these
terms about medieval society or medieval people; Robertson distinguishes
personality from character (which it so happens was not a medieval
concept either) and concludes that men of Chaucer's time had character
but not personality. Similarly he refers to medieval society as "classless."
But these are matters of definition, not historical facts.

emerge—the Host because he has charisma, the Knight because he has status. The group gangs up on some, takes sides with others: the Pardoner is made a scapegoat in part with his own collaboration, the drunken Cook becomes the butt of a cruel joke. Disagreements and discussions arise, and a spirit of competitiveness emerges—in telling tales the pilgrims are often moved to "quit" one another.[37]

I hope no one will suppose that in saying the General Prologue reflects a contemporary society and group dynamics I am suggesting that Chaucer broke with literary conventions and went "direct to life." It is quite the contrary; he used literary conventions as a means of interpreting life. For the conception of a journey remembered by a returned traveller he was indebted to Dante and to accounts of journeys and pilgrimages like Mandeville's *Travels*. For its "mentalistic" form, its quality of inner, remembered experience, the design of the General Prologue and of *The Canterbury Tales* was indebted to the French dream-vision. The correspondence between *The Canterbury Tales*, the *Roman*, Gower's *Confessio Amantis*, and Chaucer's four early dream-visions is palpable: each begins with a description of a particular season, introduces a narrator, describes a place, introduces a company of personages depicted in panel fashion, singles out a leader or guide, and proposes a device which orders the remainder of the poem.[38] Let me add that Chaucer had already tried out in his dream-visions those individual variations on the pattern which taken together make *The Canterbury Tales* unique: in *The Book of the Duchess* he depicted a real memory, the haunting memory of the Duchess Blanche; in *The Legend of Good Women* he introduced a series of narratives; and in *The Parliament of Fowls* he represented spirited dialogue among characters from different social strata.

37. On group behavior see George C. Homans, *The Human Group* (New York: Harcourt, Brace and World, 1950); Howard S. Becker, *Outsiders: Studies in the Sociology of Deviance* (New York: Free Press, 1963); Philip E. Slater, *Microcosm: Structural, Psychological and Religious Evolution in Groups* (New York, London, Sydney: John Wiley, 1966).

38. Cunningham, "Convention as Structure," in *Tradition and Poetic Structure*, pp. 59–75.

The General Prologue is then a natural evolution from the dream-vision with memory replacing dream. It is like a *vade mecum* which we must carry with us as we proceed into the tales. It informs the whole; it centers attention upon the artist-narrator's consciousness as essential to the conception of the whole, and makes us aware that in consciousness things remembered are by nature things of this world. The General Prologue is therefore above all what gives unity to the whole. In constructing his work this way Chaucer followed Geoffrey of Vinsauf's advice perfectly: "Let the mind's inner compass," said Geoffrey, "first circumscribe the entire area of the subject matter."[39] The General Prologue in a number of ways reveals and imposes principles of unity upon the tales that follow:

> The General Prologue *seems* to have a random lack of organization, but is artfully structured to reveal a typifying group. The tales *seem* to follow spontaneously, but many are artfully ordered into thematic or dramatic clusters.

> The General Prologue includes ideal figures at fixed though seemingly random intervals. The tales include ideal narratives—the tales of Constance, Griselda, Virginia, Cecilia—dispersed among the tales or clusters of tales.

> In the General Prologue, the Host dominates the group and is the leader. In the tales he directs their order when he can.

> In the General Prologue we get elements of class conflict, conflict of interest, and temperamental differences. In the tales these produce moments of competition and aggression which account for the order of most other tales.

> In the General Prologue, the very first thing mentioned after the season is the pilgrimage to Jerusalem (in the allusion to "palmers" and "straunge strondes"). In the

---

39. *Poetria nova* I:55−56: "Circinus interior mentis praecircinet omne / Materiae spatium."

Parson's Prologue we are reminded of the glorious pilgrimage to Jerusalem celestial.

In the General Prologue the narrator's feat of memory is announced and begun. In the tales it opens to us a world of remembered fictions, the irrepressible world of story, passed by books or traditions to the pilgrims, by them to the author-narrator, and by him to us.

In the General Prologue the narrator thus brings the pilgrims into the present through memory, and the Host invites them to tell "Of aventures that whilom have bifalle"; in their tales each, recaptured from the past, recaptures some part of the past. Literary tradition, notable to the point of exaggeration in the opening lines of the General Prologue, becomes the substance of the work: things remembered, known to the mind and spirit, and preserved in language, are the world of *The Canterbury Tales*—a world more real, more articulate, and more perdurable than the day-to-day world, the pilgrimage of human life, which purports to be its subject. At the end we get a prose meditation about the way to deal with that day-to-day world, and after it a terse statement in which the author rejects that world, and with it his books about that world, and "many another book, if they were in my remembrance," to embrace the world he believed existed beyond memory.

Where in all of literature is there any comparable conception? There are other medieval prologues which introduce the form and themes of the work to follow—those of *Piers Plowman* or Gower's *Confessio*, for example, or the *Decameron*—but none is so rich or complex, so totally unified a conception. The opening of *Paradise Lost* or the first book of *The Ring and the Book* may be comparable, but the most instructive comparison is the "Overture" with which Proust began *À la recherche du temps perdu*. In it the characters, the circumstances, the social structure of the day, the character of the narrator's mind, the form of the whole and its major themes are introduced. Everything that is to follow harkens back to this passage—the whole cannot be read without it, because it imposes unity; like *The Canterbury Tales* it even permits us to read sections out of order, to "choose another tale," without losing our awareness of its formal integrity. Proust said the opening of the first novel was written on the same day as the ending of the last, that the whole was a unified idea; who can doubt it? And memory is the principle of form in Proust's work as in Chaucer's.

The differences are even more instructive than the similarities. Proust used an associationist conception of memory, and so centered remembrance wholly upon his own experience. Chaucer used the medieval conceptions of memory as a faculty which stores images and intentions and as an artificial skill by which one stores intelligible ideas; and so he centered remembrance on the structure of a game played along a road and called upon the memories of others, upon tradition. In Proust, memory is involuntary: try as he will "Marcel" cannot bring back a forgotten world until he gives up trying, then as if by accident a taste and smell bring to mind a structure of associated percepts—a remembered world opens before him. In Chaucer, memory is voluntary: the narrator will do his best to recall "everich a word" and will set out the cast of characters not as they spring from his own inner experience but as they exist in the social world which he shares with his audience. And in the end that memory of a pilgrimage must be allowed to pass out of mind, to take its place among all past things and all forgotten books in the ordered rightness of a transcendent realm. For Proust, writing at the end of the nineteenth and the beginning of the twentieth century, no such ending was possible. He must turn to the world of art itself, must ruminate upon his own accomplishment as part of the human enterprise which creates an order higher than that of things past: a past recaptured and made meaningful by language, by art. Proust gives full and articulate expression to an idea of which Chaucer, living in the dawn of literary humanism, could scarcely have had more than a glimmer. Boccaccio's storytellers in the *Decameron*, in their elegant, temporary retreat, come closer to it. Yet it is not wholly absent from *The Canterbury Tales*, for we sense the importance which Chaucer, like Proust, attached to the great enterprise of making a book.

THE OUTER FORM: THE "FRAME"

If *The Canterbury Tales* is, as the foregoing argument suggests, more literary and more "formal" than some analogous works, it attains this character in part by being more
circumstantial, more familiarly true to life. There would
have been nothing surprising in the very literary opening
lines which describe the spring—it was the kind of poetry
read at court most of the time. The Tabard, Harry Bailly, or
the Miller would have been more surprising, but only
because they violate our literary expectations, and their
familiarity in everyday life is what seems out of context.
Once this familiarity is established, however, the reader's
expectations are violated again. We are led to believe that we
will hear not the wonders and curiosities of the pilgrimage
abroad, conventional in works like Mandeville's *Travels*, but
the familiar experiences of the popular pilgrimage at home;
yet we get almost none of this. If you tell a reader you will
describe something he knows, you set up expectations in his
mind; how you satisfy those expectations is part of your
effect. We know that behind the Canterbury pilgrimage was
a national cult of the martyr Saint Thomas and behind that a
whole ideology of shrines, relics, pilgrimages, indulgences.
But the "blissful martyr" is scarcely mentioned in the work—
when he is, he is presented only as he existed in people's
thoughts, the one who helped them when sick or who might
"quit" them their "meed." You would never know from *The
Canterbury Tales* that Becket's martyrdom symbolized the
struggle between Church and State. Along the road to
Canterbury were a number of shrines to Becket; but they are
never mentioned. The saint was depicted on the leaden
ampules containing his holy water or on badges and medallions which pilgrims bought;[40] his shrine was one of the
sights of the day and remained so until the Reformation,

40. On the cult of Becket see Paul Alonzo Brown, *The Development of the
Legend of Thomas Becket* (Philadelphia: Univ. of Pennsylvania, 1930),
pp. 154–224.

and of course the shrine drew its importance from the presence of his remains there, for "relics" were the object of this, as of every pilgrimage. But none of this is even hinted at. None of the artifacts or shrines of his cult are mentioned. Canterbury Cathedral is never reached. One saint's legend and a few pious tales are told, none about Englishmen.[41] Relics and indulgences come into the picture once—with the Pardoner's sordid collection of fraudulent bones and bits of cloth. The relics of the saint's hair shirt and breech, which pilgrims kissed (to Erasmus's disgust) is once alluded to in a backhanded way when the Host hurls at the Pardoner his famous taunt, "Thou woldest make me kiss thyn olde breech, / And swere it were a relic of a saint" (VI:948–950).[42]

Much that is left out throws attention away from the pilgrimage and upon the individuals. We know, for example, that pilgrims sang songs on the way,[43] but there are no songs, only tales—for tales characterize the teller far better than a song the singer. The clothes of the pilgrims are described in such detail that the reader visualizes and remembers most of them, yet these details characterize them as individuals and types, never as pilgrims.[44] There were badges, medallions, and the like which pilgrims wore, but the only suggestions along these lines are the Yeoman's "Christopher," the Prioress's crowned A, and the Pardoner's vernicle, none of them associated with the Canterbury pilgrimage. There is no way of knowing whether the bells on the Monk's horse are the familiar "Canterbury bells." Similarly, the pilgrims' horses only characterize the pilgrims individually.[45] The Knight has good but not handsomely

41. The Prioress mentions Hugh of Lincoln in an afterthought, but the young English martyr was not a saint. In my opinion, Chaucer intended the allusion to be ironic.

42. Knapp, "The Relik of a Seint," *ELH* 39 (1972):1–26.

43. Bowden, *A Commentary on the General Prologue*, p. 29.

44. Francis Watt, *Canterbury Pilgrims and their Ways* (London: Methuen, 1917), pp. 51–52. By the fourteenth century the traditional pilgrims' "weeds" had probably been abandoned on the Canterbury pilgrimage, but the staff and scrip were still used by those who traveled afoot. Chaucer's pilgrims ride, whether with scrips we do not learn.

45. See John H. Fisher, "Chaucer's Horses," *South Atlantic Quarterly* 60

appointed horses, the Monk rides a palfrey, the Wife an ambler, the Plowman a mare (an inferior mount), and so on. Pilgrims to Canterbury very often rented horses in relays, and there were by Chaucer's time livery stables along the way where horses were exchanged,[46] but none of this is brought into the account. Chaucer does mention the Squire's horsemanship and the Shipman's lack of it, and notes sometimes, as with the Wife and Merchant, how the pilgrims sat their horses. Otherwise horses are scarcely mentioned. When the drunken Cook falls off his horse (IX:48) the horse's behavior is ignored. The pilgrims do not *seem* to be travelling on horseback, and for this reason it is easy to ignore the improbable circumstance of their telling and hearing tales, all thirty of them, as they ride.

Pilgrimages had, too, a certain ritual of prayers and blessings.[47] Certainly a blessing would have been imparted at the outset; but although we are given a detailed description of the Host's proposal, the pilgrims' assent, and their departure, not a word is said of any religious observation. There were shrines along the way where pilgrims stopped to worship, but such stops are never mentioned. When pilgrims arrived in sight of their destination they stopped to praise God,[48] but we only see a "thrope's end" at which no ritual observance is made: instead we get the Parson's "meditation." For the rest, the only suggestions of ritual are the conventional blessings with which the pilgrims conclude their tales, and the kiss of peace exchanged by the Host and Pardoner.

Chaucer *chose*, then, to overlook some kinds of "historical" or "realistic" detail in his account of the pilgrimage in order to focus on the behavior, interaction, motives, characters, and discourse of people, their lore and thoughts and

---

(1961):71–79, and Rodney Delasanta, "The Horsemen of the *Canterbury Tales*," *ChauR* 3 (1968):29–36. And see Beryl Rowland, *Blind Beasts: Chaucer's Animal World* (Kent State Univ. Press, 1971), pp. 112–140.

46. J. J. Jusserand, *English Wayfaring Life in the Middle Ages (XIVth Century)*, trans. Lucy Toulmin Smith (London: T. Fisher Unwin, 1891), p. 348; cf. Ward, *The Canterbury Pilgrimage*, p. 165.

47. Ward, pp. 111–114.

48. Watt, p. 128; Ward, pp. 280–281.

feelings, their beliefs and opinions, their stories. Chaucer put this exploration of people's inner worlds into a framework which is ultimately metaphoric and Christian, but this framework does not transform or even affect what it frames until the end. *The Canterbury Tales* can be regarded on this account as an anti-pilgrimage in which things traditionally peripheral are brought to the fore and things traditionally central allowed to lapse into the background. The medieval notion was that what one had in his mind, what choices he made in his will, determined the character of every act. Hence the deepest reality of the pilgrimage was not at all a matter of horses or sights or places, but was in the heart of the individual pilgrim; this made the pilgrimage by proxy and the substitute or vicarious pilgrimage possible. Seen this way, what the narrator of *The Canterbury Tales* remembers *is* central. He remembers the group itself, what each said, what tales each selected from the storehouse of his own memory; remembers the essential character of each, the inner reality of each one's little world of thoughts which is to determine the character of the pilgrimage for each; and in the end records the official fact about any pilgrimage, that it is an act of penance.

Because *The Canterbury Tales* is focussed this way upon an inner reality, we must understand that its unfinished quality is largely a feature of its form, not a fact about its author's career. We have already seen that the topos of the Way implied an act unfinished, that the style adumbrates the continuing obsolescence of a transient world. We will see that these tendencies are carried out in the form if we put out of mind our thoughts about what Chaucer meant to add, and ask what kind of pilgrimage the work *as it is* describes. If the poet embodied his idea as one builds a house, we want to ask about major, factual features—how he represents space and time; how he represents the world through which the pilgrimage passes; what view of people's behavior he affords; how his work ends. What we will see is that the medieval sense of plenitude[49] is precisely figured in the work—that the sense of something unfinished or imperfect does not depend on the absence of more tales but on the presence of specific literary effects.

The first of these effects is the way the pilgrimage progresses at a remove, as if displaced from geographical locations. The actual pilgrims to Saint Thomas's shrine, who came from all over England, tended to gather in London. The route from London to Canterbury passed through towns, where pilgrims stopped for food or a night's lodging or a change of horses. But in *The Canterbury Tales* the pilgrimage gathers outside London, in Southwark, and the tales begin "a litel more than pas" at the Watering of Saint Thomas. Both these places had a questionable or sinister implication. Southwark, not then a part of London, was famous for its taverns and brothels; Saint Thomas à Watering was the place of execution for the county of Surrey— pilgrims passing it might well have seen bodies hanging from the gibbet.[50] Major towns are seen in the distance— "Lo Depeford! And it is half-way prime.—Lo Greenwich" cries the Host (I:3906f.), Deptford and Greenwich being about two miles apart on the left as the pilgrims passed along the Old Kent Road. Later, "Loo, Rouchestre stand here faste by" (VII:1926). The Canon's Yeoman joins the party "at" (not necessarily *in*) Boghtown under Blee (VIII:556), a little village probably considered a suburb of a regular stopping place on the pilgrimage, Ospring. "Bob-up-and-down" (probably Harbledown) was also a small town along the Canterbury Road:

> Wot ye nat where there stant a litel town
> Which that ycleped is Bobbe-up-and-down,
> Under the Blee, in Caunterbury Waye?
>
> (IX:1–3)

Finally we see the pilgrims "at a thrope's end" (X:12) outside

---

49. For the term and the principle see Lovejoy, *The Great Chain of Being*, pp. 45–86 passim.

50. Robertson, *Chaucer's London*, p. 58; Watt, pp. 68–69.

Canterbury (a thrope was a small agricultural village, and they are, one should note, at its "end").

This displaced quality of the pilgrimage, departing and arriving in the outskirts of its origin and destination and passing *by* major towns or through their suburbs, gives the journey a spectral, removed quality. That the pilgrims stopped to eat and drink, and to stay the night, we assume; but the Pardoner's "alestake" is the only indication of this, its locale not even hinted at.[51] Because the Way was a journey through a wilderness, there is perhaps a kind of iconographic meaning to this placelessness, this tendency of the pilgrimage to weave about the edges of civilization. But it is not the less realistic. In our imaginations, and often in reality, things unpleasant, unwanted, and menacing lurk at the edges of civilized places. In the late Middle Ages suburbs were where one found junkheaps and dunghills, and where outcasts and outlaws gathered. This sinister character, which suburbs and outskirts actually had in Chaucer's day, is revealed in a speech of the Canon's Yeoman:

> "In the suburbs of a town," quod he,
> "Lurking in hernes and in landes blinde,
> Whereas thise robbours and thise theves by kinde
> Holden hir pryvee fereful residence,
> As they that dare nat shewen hir presence. . . ."
> (VIII:657—661)

So, in the Pardoner's Tale, the revelers encounter the old man going toward a village (VI:706), hence outside it, as they are about to pass over a stile (712), and are directed up a "crooked way" (761) to find Death. In the Nun's Priest's Tale, Chauntecleer's anecdote depicts a man murdered as he went out of town, his body found at its west gate (VII:

---

51. I reject the notion, which seems widely accepted, of Gordon Hall Gerould, *Chaucerian Essays* (Princeton, N. J.: Princeton Univ. Press, 1952), pp. 57—59, that the alestake is really the Summoner's garland (GP 667f.), said to be as great "as it were for an alestake." He thought the Pardoner took a piece of the Summoner's cake (GP 668) and drank the ale from a flask; hence no tavern is suggested. But no flask is mentioned in the text, and it was not the Pardoner but Chaucer who compared the Summoner's garland with an alestake.

3030–3036) in a dungcart going "as it were to dunge londe."
In the Friar's Tale, the Summoner meets the Devil "under a
forest side" (III:1380) fast by a town (1389) and meets his
damnation coming "somewhat out of towne" (1571). Lepers
were to be found at a "town's end."⁵² This feeling for the
sinister aspect of outskirts and suburbs was a strong one in
the late Middle Ages, for larger towns were usually walled. It
is perhaps pertinent that at the time he planned and began
The Canterbury Tales Chaucer lived in the gatehouse at
Aldgate where he could have observed people's activities
within and without the city wall. One could control who
entered a walled town, lock the gates at night, and police the
inside, so that outcasts and outlaws flourished outside the
walls, as the Canon's Yeoman puts it, "by kinde."

Duration in *The Canterbury Tales* is similarly at a remove:
it corresponds very little to the actual duration of a pilgrimage, normally a three- or four-day journey. Students of the
poem have divided tales and links into conjectural days,
using references to time and place as clues to the order of
the manuscript fragments. In fact there is no mention of
passing days or of stopping for the night. In the Man of
Law's Introduction the date April 18 is given (II:5–6), but
there is no convincing reason to suppose this the second day
of the pilgrimage.⁵³ There is nothing in the least "realistic"
which can be applied, here or elsewhere. For example, the
Knight's Tale is begun at the Watering of Saint Thomas
(I:826) and the Miller's Tale is ended near Deptford (3906),
a passage of about three miles: the Knight's Tale would in
fact take more than two hours to tell—little wonder the Host
is distressed at their slow progress. But at the end, the
Manciple's Tale is told in the morning (IX:16) and the
Parson's Tale, which is said to follow immediately (X:1), is

52. See Henryson, *Testament of Cresseid*, line 382 and the note in Denton
Fox's edition (London and Edinburgh: Nelson, 1968), p. 116.
53. See the discussion in Chauncey Wood, *Chaucer and the Country of the
Stars*, pp. 161–172; Wood agrees that only tradition preserves the realistic
apportioning of tales among days, but he is convinced that it is the second
day because April 17 was the date on which Noah began his "pilgrimage"
in the ark.

told in the late afternoon. If any realism were involved, the Parson's Tale would then keep the pilgrims occupied until about 7:30 P.M., an inconvenient time to be arriving in a crowded town.[54]

Perhaps the major references to time reveal not facts about the journey but a poetical image, that of a day's passing. There is the beginning of a new day in the General Prologue:

Amorrwe, whan that day bigan to springe,
Up rose oure Hoost, and was our aller cock.

(I:822—823)

In the Reeve's Prologue we learn it is "half-way prime," about 7:30 A.M. (I:3906) and in the Man of Law's Introduction 10:00 A.M. (II:14). There are no other specific references to time until the Parson's Prologue, when it is 4:00 P.M. (X:5). Chaucer may have meant to employ, as he did in the *Troilus*, a dual time-scheme—one reckoning of time realistic and factual, another artistic and symbolical.[55] In the *Troilus* the artistic time-scheme is the passage of a year, a revolution of the seasons; in *The Canterbury Tales* it is the passage of an "artificial day," measured in twelve hours from sunrise to sunset (which vary in length according to the time of the year) as opposed to the "natural" day (in which the hours have equal length). Only one of these references to the time of day is to canonical hours ("half-way prime" I:3906); three are to the position of the sun. Sunrise is mentioned in the General Prologue (822); two other passages, one early in the work and one at its end, give detailed accounts of the sun's position in the heavens and the lengths of the shadows on earth, and these two passages contain the only two references to time by the clock:

Oure Hoste saugh well that the brighte sunne
The ark of his artificial day hath runne

54. The contrast with Dante is instructive; in the *Commedia* the year of the journey, the dates, and even the times of day are precisely indicated and symbolically meaningful.

55. Henry W. Sams, "The Dual Time-Scheme in Chaucer's *Troilus*," *MLN* 56 (1941):94—100.

The ferthe part, and half an hour and more,
And though he were nat deep ystert in lore,
He wiste it was the eightetethe day
Of April, that is messager to May;
And saugh well that the shadwe of every tree
Was as in length the same quantitee
That was the body erect that caused it.
And therefore by the shadwe he took his wit
That Phebus, which that shoon so clere and brighte,
Degrees was five and forty clombe on highte;
And for that day, as in that latitude,
It was ten of the clock, he gan conclude. . . .

(II:1–14)

By that the Manciple had his tale all ended,
The sunne fro the south line was descended
So lowe that he nas nat, to my sighte,
Degrees nine and twenty as in highte.
Four of the clock it was, so as I guesse,
For eleven foot, or litel more or lesse,
My shadwe was at thilke time, as there,
Of swich feet as my lengthe parted were
In six feet equal of proporcioun.
Therewith the moones exaltacioun,
I meene Libra, alway gan ascende,
As we were entring at the thropes ende. . . .

(X:1–12)

Such a presentation of time, in which the revolutions of
heavenly bodies (and of clocks) and the day's shifting of
shadows are singled out, suggests the cyclical, self-renewing
time of external nature and the universe. The reference to
sunrise at the beginning and sunset at the end depicts a
delimited segment of this cyclical time. The image of a day's
passing is a natural metaphor for the life of man—the idea is
expressed in Psalms 89:6: "In the morning man shall grow
up like grass . . . in the evening he shall fall, grow dry, and
wither." This symbolic day is consistent with the linear
ongoing quality of time which we observed in chapter 3, and
with the pervasive sense of obsolescence. The movement and
the duration of the pilgrimage are indefinite and seem
unfinished: they are a segment of time whose past and

future are obscured. Chaucer ended the *Troilus* reminding his audience that the world "passeth soon as flowres faire," and this symbol of the evanescence of worldly things, the flower, was so common a motif in medieval writings—and in Scripture—that a medieval reader might have caught the implication as he read in the opening clause of the General Prologue "Of which vertu engendred is the flowr." The last image in the work, the lengthening of shadows of the Parson's Prologue, is in this respect consistent with the first image of the work: flower and shadow were images of mutability no less than ashes, dust, wax, and the like. The Scriptures said man's life "cometh forth like a flower, and is destroyed, and fleeth as a shadow."[56]

When Chaucer chose the pilgrimage as the setting of his work, and chose to represent it thus disoriented in space and time, insubstantial and transient, he was adopting and representing "the world" as his subject. He chose to represent the stuff of memory grounded in the particularities of the sensible world, the characters and intentions of people, and their tales. He omitted the substantial, old, monumental things of the world—London, "New Troy" as they called it, with its ancient heritage, and the cathedral with its shrine two hundred years old—limiting himself to wisps of experience en route and to stories, some old, some not. He presented this reality everywhere in relief against cultural ideals, chiefly religious ones, of his time—in the General Prologue the ideal portraits, in the tales the ideal narratives, at the end the Parson's *summa*. But within this overriding form he placed what was unmistakably the forbidden underside of pilgrimage, *curiositas*—the delight men took in divertisements, in "wandering by the way."[57] He put at the center

---

56. Job 14:2. Cf. Isa. 40:6−8 and Ps. 102:15. On this conception of dark and light and its relationship with ideas of the world and the ordered universe, see De Bruyne, *The Esthetics of the Middle Ages*, pp. 55−61.

57. This secular aspect of the pilgrimage was symbolized by the pilgrim's staff and scrip, so notably phallic that Jean de Meun in his part of the *Roman de la Rose* made it explicitly a figure for genital sexuality. Chaucer managed to include such a detail, though pilgrims on horseback carried no staffs, by substituting the Miller's bagpipe. The usual bagpipe of the day was unmistakably phallic, having but one pipe (Robertson,

ll!ЁЁ

precisely those matters for which the pilgrim authors like Mandeville vouched least of all, what others *say* to the pilgrim as he travels.

In making this choice of emphasis, Chaucer afforded his readers perennial delight. The characters and their tales have never ceased to please, though tastes have changed many times over since the work was written. They engross us, and we do not ask how or why the tales are told; we pass it off as a "device" that they follow one another because of "dramatic interplay." Yet in this interplay Chaucer singled out the most pessimistic view of people's behavior, and it was not necessary for him to do so. The Middle Ages had many optimistic and idealistic estimates of human endeavor—it believed in the noble life, in "trouthe," in duty, in saintliness, in love. It held the individual man incomplete if he did not embrace another—God, or his lady, or a cause; its conception of human motives was in many ways more hopeful than ours. Chaucer had been known as the poet of love, and ideals of chivalry and virtue and faith pervade his work. But in the pilgrims' behavior he selects on the whole men's meaner motives. It is not in the least an appealing picture of human conduct; it is made entertaining and pleasurable because it is familiar, because the narrator sees it in a generous spirit, and because it makes us laugh. A few tales begin without links and so without motivation, and a few begin in a spirit of great courtesy. There are idealists and moralists in the company and a handful of honest men. But in the larger part we find an all too characteristic picture of group conduct, governed by patterns of dominance and submission, by motives of aggression and defense. We get the darker side of group dynamics. At the outset the Host asserts himself as leader and the pilgrims agree to his leadership before they have even heard his proposal: with the instinct of the politician he has them assent to nothing— "Hold up your honds, withouten more speeche," and they submit. He then proposes the tales and has lots drawn; it is often suspected that he manipulates these in order to get the

Preface to Chaucer, 128–133). With this extraordinary instrument the Miller, leading the procession, "broght us out of towne."

Knight in first place. He addresses those pilgrims having social status—the Knight, the Man of Law, the Prioress, the Squire—with utmost courtesy. But when he calls on Chaucer he does so with spirited mockery—"What man artow?"—then interrupts his tale to scorn it. He completely misunderstands Chaucer's second and more impressive effort. He taunts the Cook for a cheat, mocks the Monk cruelly as a lecher, denounces the Parson for a Loller, ridicules the Nun's Priest's horse, addresses the Pardoner "thou bel ami," and joins the Manciple in publicly humiliating the drunken Cook.

The other pilgrims do not present a more attractive picture. They are moved largely by hostility and by the spirit of "quitting." The Miller, drunk, proposes to "quit" the Knight's Tale which he parodies in his own story, and taunts the Reeve into the bargain. The Reeve in extreme spite turns upon the Miller—"I pray to God his necke mot to-breke" (3918). The Cook, goaded by the Host, promises to tell a tale of a hosteller (4360). The Friar restrainedly advises the Wife that she has stumbled into matters beyond her competency, then turns invidiously upon the Summoner, who responds in kind; the Clerk rebuts the Wife with the scholar's weapon, irony. The Canon's Yeoman betrays his master, who withdraws in shame, the Yeoman in his absence adding "all that I kan anon now wol I telle" (704) and consigning his master to "the foule feend." The Knight does not conceal his boredom with the Monk's "tragedies" and the Host calls them a "pain," says some of the pilgrims should by now have "fallen down for sleepe." The Parson scolds the Host for swearing and the Host and Shipman conspire to silence him.[58] The Pardoner attempts a final mockery of himself and his audience, and the Host reacts by delivering what may be the most vicious personal insult in all of English literature. As in all groups, this one produces its scapegoats and losers—the Monk's tale is rejected, the Cook's drunkenness mocked openly, the Pardoner's eunuchry held up to public ridicule, the Canon exposed, and Chaucer himself, or his "drasty riming," deemed not worth a turd. Peoples' less generous impulses

---

58. II:1163−1190. The reading "Shipman" in line 1179 is disputable.

and emotions thus dominate the interplay which makes tale follow tale. As a picture of group conduct it is like what Chaucer had described in the *Parliament of Fowls* or the *House of Fame* or in the Trojan parliament depicted in *Troilus*, IV:141−217; as a customs official, an official of the court and onetime member of Parliament during a turbulent period he must have seen plenty of such behavior. It is "realistic" in its details, "universal" in revealing a constant tendency of groups, "medieval" in its pessimistic expectations of human behavior. It presents men's conduct not just as it was and is but as the medievals thought it had to be in a fallen world.

A work so conceived could end with a sense of finality only if it ended in apocalypse.[59] For this there was precedent in works like Dante's *Commedia* or *Pearl* or the *De contemptu mundi* by Bernard of Morval. But Chaucer chose not to follow that precedent. He chose instead to end the work with that experience of the world which men really have—its imperfect, ongoing, and insubstantial quality. The work is by nature effulgent and self-generating: memory being almost inexhaustible, the narrator's recitation might go on indefinitely, producing more people and from them more tales. The General Prologue arbitrarily sets a limit upon the number of people and the number of stories each would tell, but the unanticipated appearance of the Canon's Yeoman gives the lie to this limitation. To represent the pilgrimage of human life—the "world"—is to represent something almost without bound or form. I say "almost" because Christianity held that time itself, and the world, had a definite beginning and were to have an end. All existence in time was to break off at an unpredictable moment and be subsumed in eternity. Life in the world had therefore an ongoing, sequential quality whose limits and form were by nature arbitrary. The form of *The Canterbury Tales* reflects such a conception of ongoing experience. Its principal metrical form, the heroic

59. In what follows I am indebted to Frank Kermode, *The Sense of an Ending: Studies in the Theory of Fiction* (New York: Oxford Univ. Press, 1967), and to Barbara Herrnstein Smith, *Poetic Closure: A Study of How Poems End* (Chicago and London: Univ. of Chicago Press, 1968).

couplet—which Chaucer introduced into English literary tradition—sets up an expectation of infinite continuity, for each couplet, complete in itself, can call for nothing more than another couplet. Hence the poet, if he wishes to set up in the reader's mind the expectation of an end, must introduce other kinds of formal units. Chaucer does this with the tales, each of which is to have an end and whose number is to have a limit. He does it also with the pilgrimage "frame," which has a stated destination and return. But he violates all these expectations. The tales do not all have an end. The limit set on their number is never attained. The return journey is not represented. The destination is not reached. We are left with the characteristic medieval feeling that the effulgence of the possible has been cut unpredictably short.

Yet the ending of *The Canterbury Tales* does produce a sense of closure. By various devices it signals its end while remaining open-ended in a manner which is poetically effective. The ongoing flow of couplets is abandoned in favor of prose discourse. This discourse is a straightforward statement of morality—a customary medieval way of ending narratives. The statement relates specifically to the setting and controlling metaphor of the work, for it purports to tell of the "parfit glorious pilgrimage" to the Heavenly Jerusalem, taking as its text a passage from Jeremiah on the choice of the good "Way." The Host states explicitly that the tale will knit up "a greet mattere" (X:28), and the Parson echoes him, promising to "knit up all this feest, and make an ende" (47). The subject of the discourse, penitence, suggests Judgment and the imminence of death. Its last sentence is about life in the world: the Parson, comparing eternity with the world, leaves us to contemplate the ongoing toils of life's pilgrimage. His final topic is *contempt of the world*.

Finally, the author adds his own act of penance. In the Retraction, Chaucer prepares for and embraces death after the manner of his age. He is practicing "the art of dying." The treatises *De arte moriendi* urged the dying man to contemplate all the reasons why he should fear death, and then through penance and prayers attain that state in which he might embrace and *choose* his death with equanimity. This meant rejecting all the wrong choices of one's life as best one knew what they were. It was not a time for cavils and distinctions. Hence the ring of extravagance, even of falsity, which some hear in this passage. The art of dying was the ultimate art—before it all arts of life, even the "art of holy living," paled into emptiness. Chaucer rejected therefore not only his secular works by name and such of the Canterbury tales as "sownen" into sin, but "many another book, if they were in my remembraunce, and many a song and many a lecherous lay." This phrase is always taken to suggest, as it may, a body of his writings which has not survived; but the passage says that he revokes other books and secular lyrics, *even those he cannot remember.* He could have had in mind not a drawerful of minor pieces and false starts but books and poems themselves, those he had read, even the memory of them and even those forgotten. In the Retraction he rejects art itself, the very province of art and the province of memory, which is the temporal world, to embrace the world beyond memory and time. His death, which made the work complete, made it a vanity. The Retraction makes the poet's death a part of the world he contemplates in the work. The work, like all the things of this world, is imperfect, not yet come to its true end in time. And its only use is that use which St. Paul assigned to all the foolish things of the world, *to confound the wise.* That is why Chaucer quotes St. Paul, "All that is written is written for our doctrine," adding "and that is myn entent." We are to use the work as best we can to know the truth even if that truth discredit the practice of writing books, or of reading, or of remembering them.

THE INNER FORM: THE TALES

Within this "outer" form is the seemingly haphazard "inner" form, the series of pilgrims' tales. People on a pilgrimage took an idea with them when they took up staff and scrip and set upon the Way; the staff, the scrip, and the way were tangible realities, but they were signs or symbols too and were part of the idea. *The Canterbury Tales,* I have tried to show, expresses this idea at the expense of familiar actualities: its treatment of time, of space, and of the relations among characters depicts the wilderness of the world as a transient and fallen state whose inhabitants will never reach their perfect state until the Day of Judgment when their world will be destroyed. As part of such an idea the tales are "curiosities" of the kind pilgrims were warned against, an entertainment or pastime. Because they are things remembered, they are things of the temporal realm, an unuseful and untrustworthy kind of knowledge. Because they are "Canterbury tales," they are expected to be lies.

And the work, because of this idea, discourages us from assenting to the tales, from giving them credence. Almost every tale is presented in circumstances which discredit it. Even the Knight's Tale, a high-minded story told by an ideal figure, gives us reason to approach it skeptically. In it, as we said earlier, Chaucer permits his own voice to intrude upon the Knight's. These ironic intrusions may discredit the tale itself, or the Knight, or the style and manner of its telling, or the cultural and literary tradition it represents. However explained, this ironic element raises questions in the reader's mind which the tale never settles. In other instances what we know about the pilgrim raises such questions. The Miller's Tale parodies the Knight's and holds some of its values up to ridicule; but the Miller does not get the last word and there is no reason to think Chaucer sided with him more than another—he is, we are told, a drunk and a churl. Besides, the Reeve's tale "quits" the Miller and his tale, discrediting both with another churlish viewpoint. Tales discredit each other, as with the Friar and Summoner. The Nun's Priest subtly discredits the Monk's tale and other tales which have preceded it. Whole groups of tales discredit one another by presenting various viewpoints in conflict—the sequence Knight-Miller-Reeve is an example, as is the "marriage group."

Certain tales, it is true, are to be understood as reliable "sentence" or "doctrine," but these are set apart and some still provoke skepticism. The *Melibee* and the Parson's Tale, because they are in prose, seem the most didactic. Yet the prose puts them in a different order of reality—they lack the excitement and literary quality of the other tales. And neither is appropriate to the "personality" of its teller or to the situation in which it is told. The *Melibee* doesn't suit Chaucer the pilgrim at all; unless we presume it is a joke or parody, we have to say that the poet removes his mask as pilgrim and presents some high-minded "doctrine." In the same way, the Parson's "meditation" is not appropriate to the simple Parson of the General Prologue or the peremptory one who appears twice in the tales, and does not suit the situation in which he is supposed to speak it. From any realistic view, one can only imagine the pilgrims fidgeting and clearing their throats; the Host has already denounced the Parson as a Loller, and two tales have been stopped because they bored the pilgrims. The two prose pieces are *not* two pecks of clichés and do *not* present mere tedious ideology. They are philosophical, expository, and moral. Standing apart with a straightforward nonliterary merit of their own, they throw into relief the literary, theatrical, and "storial" quality of the poetical prologue, frame, and tales.

With the tales in verse, even the moral ones, we are less sure of having sound "doctrine." The tales of the Man of Law, the Monk, the Prioress, the Physician, the Clerk, and the Second Nun all sound like solid morality. They are the only tales (the Physician's is an exception) written in stanzas: like the prose pieces, they are set apart in form as in content. But the pilgrims who tell them are by no means all idealized figures, so we are left asking questions about their motives. We suspect them of *misguided moralism*. The Prioress lauds an excess of medieval antisemitism explicitly forbidden by papal decrees; the Physician lauds a father who slays his daughter to preserve her virginity, a deed against which there were imposing theological arguments. The Man of Law offers a prologue on poverty which makes us wonder whether he does not miss the point of his own tale. The Monk offers a definition of tragedy which makes us wonder whether he does not misunderstand *de casibus* tragedy or understand it in the wrong spirit. What we already know about the pilgrim makes us ask questions about his or her tale, and the tale leaves us asking more questions about the pilgrim. These questions have furnished an occasion for scores of articles proposing answers. But the intended effect, I am convinced, is the ambiguous one produced by the questions themselves.

Two of these moral tales might be taken in full earnest, the Clerk's and the Second Nun's. The Clerk is an idealized figure, his tale an ideal narrative. There is nothing about him to make us doubt his motives. The tale, "figural" in the extreme, is a far fling from real life: its heroine's patience and her husband's malevolence seem exaggerated, almost abstract. The Clerk himself concludes that the story is told as an exemplum "that every wight, in his degree, / Sholde be constant in adversitee" (IV:1145–1146), and acknowledges the unreality of such idealized behavior with an ironical utterance about the world's decline, capping these words with an ironical song:

> Grisilde is deed, and eek hir pacience,
> And both atones buried in Itaille. . . .

He thus discredits his own tale and his own idealism, but in such a way as to validate the ideal itself: his irony works like a modesty topos, gaining our sympathy and indulgence. Like all irony it puts us at a distance from the subject, so that the picture he gives at the end—a characteristic medieval one of the world grown old and in decline—engenders regret.[60] It is a superb bit of rhetoric. But no sooner does the Clerk conclude, ironically, that wives *should* be shrews and husbands "weep, and wring, and waille" than the Merchant breaks in without any irony at all: "Weeping and wailing, care and other sorrwe, / I know ynogh. . . ." His tale fastens upon the actualities of the Clerk's song with such bitterness as to make ideals seem futile. We are left again asking questions.

The one moral tale not discredited at all is the Second Nun's. Because the nun is not described in the General Prologue, we know nothing about her which can make us question her motives. Her tale is a genuine bit of hagiography, the only saint's legend offered on the pilgrimage. Its heroine, St. Cecilia, is not merely an idealized figure like Constance, Griselda, or Virginia, but an historical saint of Christian times. The tale is therefore unique among the Canterbury tales. I think it is more interesting and more important than it is normally reckoned. As with all saints' legends the heroine is real in the historical sense—there is an implicit claim that she walked the earth. Of course storytellers like to authenticate their characters with historical claims—the Physician appeals to the authority of Livy—but saints' legends possess, behind such claims, the authority of the Church itself. And like all saints Cecilia stands apart from ordinary mortals by virtue of her special vocation. The Second Nun's Tale thus discredits *all* the foregoing tales by reminding us of the highest ideal, beneath which lesser virtues pale. But by discrediting them this way it also throws attention back, from a widened perspective, upon the foregoing tales, which conflict with and discredit one another.

In describing this reciprocal discrediting of tales I know I have described what sounds like a matching game in which everything cancels everything else. Was it Chaucer's idea to leave everything up in the air? Not at all. The work has form, and to the extent that it has form it has a degree of finality.

Finality or "poetic closure" is a convention of literature and changes from age to age. Its character in medieval literature has, as far as I know, never been investigated. If a critic were to lay before his readers the full range of endings in medieval narrative, I imagine he would need to arrange them on a spectrum. At one extreme would be those works which end with a final explicit moral addressed directly to the reader, at the other extreme those which seem to trail off or peter out. The final explicit moral retrospectively dilutes the narrative by skimming off its "true meaning." The allegorical *moralitates* of the *Gesta Romanorum* are an example of this tendency: the stories themselves retain their interest as narratives—they can be read, probably sometimes were, without the appended allegories—but they are told in a barebones manner which betrays the writer's intention to abstract and isolate "inner" meanings. Many conventional medieval endings are similar to the *moralitas*—the formulaic blessing or prayer, the author's address to his book or his farewell to the reader, and the envoy. Any of these, unless used ironically, writes a strong *finis* to its work. With the palinode we enter a middle category of endings which recall attention to the story itself and thus tend to leave its meaning open. The palinode *seems* to reject the work or the values implicit in it, to turn its back and look toward higher things. But if the palinode is, as C. S. Lewis once suggested, comparable to the truant returning to his master, it promotes nostalgia and regret.[61] We are, in the famous medieval palinodes, left to savor the fleeting joy of Troilus's love or the faded grandeur of Arthur's court. Beyond the palinode lie those endings which leave the poem's concerns open to review and reflection. Some medieval poems end with a change in the level of perception—a dreamer wakes and returns to everyday reality (as in the *Roman*), or sleeps again and dreams another dream (as in *Piers Plowman*), or is waked by an appropriate noise (as in *The Parliament of Fowls* and *The Book of the Duchess*). Some poems end by suggesting a cycle in human experience—we are (as in the *Troilus*) reminded of the way things started out, of rises and falls, of Fortune's wheel. Some end with ending itself—with the teller saying "here I shall make an end" or with the end of time, the apocalypse or the beatific vision. Such apocalyptic endings do not have the finality one might suppose, for they remind us of the continuity of experience—remind us that a narrative goes on until its narrator chooses to end it, life until death ends it, the world until time ends it. Some poems end by posing a question (as in the Franklin's *demande d'amour*). Some, like *Sir Gawain*, end with an ambiguity. Beyond this kind of underplayed finality, at the end of the spectrum—if they deserve a place—are the large number of medieval poems, including some of the best, which were not finished at all.

61. C. S. Lewis, *The Allegory of Love: A Study in Medieval Tradition* (New York: Oxford Univ. Press, 1936, rpt. 1958), p. 43.

Viewed against these kinds of poetic closure in medieval literature, *The Canterbury Tales* seems another instance where, as Professor Donaldson likes to say, Chaucer has it both ways. We saw earlier how the ending of *The Canterbury Tales* at once concludes the work and leaves it open-ended. At the end we seem abruptly to enter another order of reality. In the Retraction the author appears *in propria persona* without irony. One feels as if the play is over and an actor, tired and downcast, has come forth to bow. We are satisfied and not satisfied. Like all the works of this world, it is imperfect; if we seek perfection in the world we must turn to its Maker, and so Chaucer does in the end. Within this imperfect and inconclusive pilgrimage we have an inner world of stories, three of them (the Cook's, the Squire's, and *Sir Thopas*) unfinished. Are these only "chaff" which we are to forget? Or does the ending of the whole, to the extent that it is *in*conclusive, throw our attention back to the unfinished body of tales, make us try to find something positive in it? And do the nineteen tales which are complete[62] have an effect of closure? The first four completed tales (the Knight's, Miller's, Reeve's, and Man of Law's) end with great finality, but this has to be called not poetic but narrative closure. Each ends with a summary statement which unravels the plot by telling how things turned out for each character, by stating the outcome. The four pilgrims add other devices. All four pronounce a blessing on their listeners; the Knight and Man of Law end with a prayer. The Miller and Man of Law state explicitly that they are done. The Knight, Reeve, and Man of Law in addition point a moral, and each of these reflects the teller's point of view: the Knight's moral is courtly and idealistic, the Reeve's vengeful, the Man of Law's hopeful; the Miller's last words— "God save all the route"—bubble over with his lusty ebullience.

62. I do not count the Monk's Tale. It is a collection within a collection, and it is interrupted. But the tales the Monk tells come to their stark conclusions with awesome regularity and finality, illustrating their stock moral.

All the tales, like the first four, end with the teller's stating the outcome, but that is the only feature of narrative closure which all share. Other pilgrims use other signals: Six pilgrims state explicitly that their tale is done;[63] the Pardoner, having done so when he says "thus I preche," goes on to add his famous gambit which produces the angry exchange between himself and the Host. Two pilgrims, the Merchant and the Pardoner, follow the formula of pronouncing a blessing upon the company, but each blessing is ambiguous in its conclusiveness: it is ironical that the Merchant ends his antifeminist tale by invoking the blessing of the Virgin Mary, and the Pardoner's blessing, "Jesu Crist . . . graunte you his pardon to receive," is an about-face from which he quickly retreats. Five pilgrims point a moral, but in each case something arouses our skepticism. The Canon's Yeoman has an ax to grind. The Nun's Priest's common-sense moral, that one should keep one's eyes open and one's mouth shut, is offered with affable irony. The Clerk wipes his Petrarchan moral away with an ironical envoy in which he cheers on the shrewish wives of the present. The Physician, in the manner of his profession, ends giving advice which sounds a little pat: "Forsaketh sin, ere sinne you forsake." The Pardoner's conclusion, that God's pardon is best, is apparently a heartfelt truth from which he then backtracks in terror. Four pilgrims who do not end with an explicit moral end with a prayer; but they are all tendentious prayers, each reflecting the pilgrim's ruling passion. The Wife prays for husbands who are "meeke, young, and fresh abedde, / And grace t'overbide hem that we wedde." The Friar prays that "this somonour him repente / Of his misdeeds, ere that the feend him hente!" The Shipman prays that God send us "Taillyng ynough unto our lives ende." The Prioress prays to "younge Hugh of Lincoln, slain also / With cursed Jewes."

---

63. Summoner: "My tale is done; we been almost at towne."
Merchant: "Thus endeth here my tale of Januarie."
Franklin: "I can namore, my tale is at an ende."
Shipman: "Thus endeth now my tale. . . ."
Canon's Yeoman: "And there a point, for ended is my tale."
Pardoner: ". . . And lo, sires, thus I preche."

The pattern in these endings is evident: the pilgrims all end by stating the outcome of their tales, and so seem to wrap them up and make an end. Of those who *say* they are through, only the Pardoner belies his own statement. But the other devices they use—the final blessing, prayer, or moral—all reflect an individual bias, character trait, or ruling passion. This throws attention back on the pilgrim himself, makes the story contingent upon its teller. Chaucer returns us at the end of each tale to the pilgrims moving along the way, and so to the inexhaustible store of tales from which is to be drawn "another tale," "the nexte tale," "a tale . . . as forward is," "a tale next." "Tell forth," they say, or "tell on." At the ends of tales we are reminded that each is *another* tale, able to be followed or "quit" by still another. These come from the bottomless world of story and of the past: the tales are preserved in words and traditions, in memory, or in books, but selected and slanted by individual tellers.

Six endings, each unique, do not leave us in this "storial" realm:

1. The Franklin's Tale ends with a question, a *demande d'amour* that calls for a discussion of the kind aristocrats evidently enjoyed.

2. The Second Nun's Tale ends without a direct address to the audience. Her saint's legend contains a moral explicitly stated, but she speaks as if *ex cathedra*. Her tale leaves us in the "authoritative" realm of saints' legends, contemplating the church consecrated to the saint and the continuous tradition of worship since her martyrdom.

3. The Pardoner's Tale is the only tale in which the narrator's voice intervenes at the end. After the Host's insult, the poet-narrator says "This pardoner answered nat a word; / So wroth he was, no word ne wolde he saye," and after the speeches of the Host and Knight reports "Anon they kiste, and riden forth hir waye." His tale leaves us contemplating a simple symbolical action, the "kiss of peace," and the great symbol of the Way.

4. The Nun's Priest's Tale is the only tale whose ending includes a quotation from Scripture, "all that written is, / To our doctrine it is ywrite, ywis."

5. The Manciple's Tale ends with a speech which is a collection of proverbs.

6. The *Melibee* ends with a speech by a character in the tale, Melibee himself, who makes a resolve and so points a moral.

These six endings draw our attention away from the matter of the tale itself, as the others do. But where the others fasten our attention upon the pilgrim and the pilgrimage, these draw us outside the work into extraliterary realms— courtly conversation, ecclesiastical tradition, symbolical action, "doctrine," proverbs, moral choices. These endings are especially important because they come in key positions: the Franklin's (or the Second Nun's) at the end of the "marriage group," the Nun's Priest's at the end of the tales which make up Fragment VII, the Pardoner's at the end of the "floating fragment," the Manciple's at the end of all the tales before the Parson's Prologue, and the *Melibee* at the end of the author-narrator's contribution.

So the tales, when finished, point us to the larger form of the work as a whole, or to areas of thought which fall outside the work. Everything seems to lead to something else. The smaller parts point us to the larger whole, the larger whole to the smaller parts. And everything seems open to question. This questioning spirit challenges our powers of discrimination, requires that we make choices.[64]

64. It may be relevant that choice is a theme throughout. In the General Prologue the pilgrims appear to have chosen each other as companions; the Host chooses the entertainment to follow and calls upon them to choose him as leader. They agree "we *wol* reuled been" (two mss. read *wolde*, but the switch of tense is effective; cf. *PF* 588, where the Turtledove seems to lapse into the future rather than the conditional as if carried away by enthusiasm). The Host's "flock" choose the first tale by "drawing cut," and the cut falls appropriately to the Knight who agrees "by his free assent." After this the Host chooses tellers or they choose themselves without interference; all must choose a tale. In the tales, too, choice is a major theme: some half center on the choice of a mate, the moral tales on moral choices. The Franklin's characters each make a proper choice, the Shipman's an improper one; the *Melibee* is about the choice of advisers, occasions for warfare, and the like, the Parson's about choosing the good way. One could single out a substratum of chance occurrence in the tales, as when Arcite is thrown from his horse or when

The author anticipates free choice on the reader's part. He
knows we read or cease to read as we choose, and so enlists
our indulgence, "Ere that I ferther in this tale pace" (I:36),
with the claim that what he says is "accordant to resoun" and,
later, with modest excuses for plain speaking (725–746).
At a key point—the first link between tales—he acknowledges the reader's freedom:

> . . . whoso list it nat yheere,
> Turn over the leef and chese another tale;
> For he shall find ynoghe, greete and smalle,
> Of storial thing that toucheth gentillesse,
> And eek moralitee and holinesse.
> Blameth nat me if that ye chese amiss.
>
> (I:3176–3181)

Implicit in this license is his assumption that we *can* tell good
from bad, great from small, "storial thing" from "moralitee
and holiness." "Taketh the moralitee, goode men," says the
Nun's Priest, quoting St. Paul. In the less colorful statement
with which Chaucer ended the whole work, he quoted the
same text.

But again, while we play the game of making choices,
the game is in part manipulated. We are subtly pointed
toward the right choices. And who points us? The narrator.
With something like the ironic permissiveness of the Old
Man in the Pardoner's Tale, who directs the revellers
seeking Death "up this crooked way," the narrator points us
toward three kinds of reality in the work, leaving it for us to
see in focus what he sees in a haze.

First, the narrator points us toward the pilgrims, so
seemingly real that some have thought them photographs.
Their tales are "true" in so far as each reflects its teller's
character and so lends veracity to the account of the pilgrim-

---

January's sight returns, but then these are choices of gods. Chance has,
too, a role in the pilgrims' lives—they were born to a social status, or under
stars which shape their characters; the Pardoner was presumably born
deformed. But in the tales chance has less of a role than choice; and
indeed it was characteristic of the medievals to suppose, after Boethius,
that what seemed like chance to humans was a choice made by powers
beyond their ken.

age. Yet the pilgrims are believable not for their warts and lisps and red faces but because they are types. We see them as individual, private persons, but we learn what group or institution each belongs to. To the extent that we play those roles which society assigns us we are familiar and understandable to other members of that society. Think how much we can surmise once we know the stranger we meet is a used-car dealer, a professor, a psychiatrist. The pilgrims, we learn, all have such roles. There are no mavericks among them. In the Pardoner we get a grotesque, in the Wife a detailed character study—we attain something like an interpersonal acquaintance with each; but both can be placed in categories known and familiar in medieval life.[65] They are not just "literary" conventions, even if they do resemble Faux Semblant and the Duenna; they *behave* in conventional ways, and are therefore subject to conventional judgments. The circumstantial detail convinces us that the narrator observed them well, but what reveals them to us is their work, their talk, and their stories. We get an idea of each because such an idea exists in the society. We need to know about "real" people not whether they have warts or lisps or wear red stockings, but whether they fit a type familiar enough to let us "place" them and ask the right questions about them. Part of what makes the pilgrims seem real is that we can put and answer such questions. We are made to share with them a social and national milieu.

Then, too, the narrator points us toward the author. He is of course real—not just a historical personage we know from life-records but a living presence in and behind the work. And the narrator leads us to the author because he *is* the author. That Chaucer indulges in a delightful feat of ironic role-playing puts him all the more squarely in the work, for as often as we doubt the narrator's view we are required to intuit Chaucer's own. Chaucer thus sets up the unique device by which, as he plays the narrator's role, he makes us play his. We have to put ourselves in his frame of

---

65. Fisher, *John Gower*, pp. 255–283 offers a valuable comparison of Chaucer's characters with those Gower used in his class satires.

mind, see things as he sees them, become one with him. There is a conspiratorial accord between reader and author: we share with him the knowledge that the pilgrimage, the pilgrims, and the narrator are a fiction. We share with him moral reservations about the pilgrims which are lost on the narrator, and we share these just because we share with him the familiar literary stereotypes of "complaint"—the outriding Monk, the venal Friar, the grasping Lawyer, the thieving Miller. We share with him an intellectual, theological, and literary world, a world of books and ideas.

Finally, the narrator points us toward the established morality and "auctoritee" which come into the pilgrimage not only in the two prose tracts and the ideal or moral tales, but in *every* tale—in Egeus's platitudes or Theseus's "Boethian" speeches, in the Nun's Priest's final "moralitee" or for that matter in Chauntecleer's *mulier est hominis confusio*, in the Reeve's "A guilour shall himself biguiled be" or the Wife's "No woman of no clerk is praised." The pilgrims and the characters in their tales are all full of wisdom—the Pardoner himself boasts he can tell a moral tale though a "full vicious man." They are engaged in a competition to tell "Tales of best sentence and most solaas" (I:798): the author promises those who do not relish a "cherles tale" that they will find enough, "grete and smalle" (I:3178) of "storial thing," morality, and holiness. The "great" storial, moral, and holy things, like the Knight's or Parson's tales, are not likely to escape attention, but the "small" are matters we must be on the lookout for. And it is understood that we can tell true from false. The old idea, part of the neoplatonic heritage of Christianity, was that the truth is one but the expession of it varies in various "sentences." When the Host demands of Chaucer that he tell "in prose somewhat, at the leeste / In which there be some mirthe or some doctrine" (VII:934–935), Chaucer drolly has himself state this idea in a pompous, circumlocutious, bumbling way. But what he says so ineptly was true all the same:

> . . . ye wot that every Evaungelist,
> That telleth us the pain of Jhesu Crist,
> Ne saith nat alle thing as his fellawe doth;

But nathelees hir sentence is all sooth,
And all accorden as in hir sentence,
Al be there in hir telling difference.
For some of hem sayn more, and some sayn lesse,
Whan they his pitous passioun expresse—
I meen of Mark, Matthew, Luke, and John—
But douteless hir sentence is all oon.
Therefore, lordings all, I you biseeche,
If that you think I vary as in my speeche,
As thus, though that I telle somewhat more
Of proverbes than ye han herd bifore
Comprehended in this litel tretise here,
To enforce with th'effect of my mattere,
And though I nat the same wordes saye
As ye han herd, yet to you all I praye
Blameth me nat; for, as in my sentence,
Shull ye nowhere finden difference
Fro the sentence of this tretise lite
After the which this murye tale I write.

                                    (943–964)

The gusto of the medievals for seeking "sentence" in varied expressions makes a difficulty for the modern reader. Fashions in wisdom change. Most proverbs had a luster in the fourteenth century which they have lost since, though not all. I am not convinced, as some are, that we have lost the taste for explicit moral precept; I think we have such a taste, but usually for moral precepts of a different kind from those which appealed to medieval tastes, about different matters, and couched in different styles. When we hear the *word* "proverb" we conjure up Poor Richard or the old saws of the puritan ethic—"Nothing ventured, nothing gained," "Early to bed, early to rise." But people still quote authors to lend their thoughts "authority"—Camus, Heidegger, and Sartre have been recent favorites. We still like wisdom of a pithy, epigrammatic kind; we have maxims of our own (*Power corrupts*), slogans (*Make love, not war*), and wise old saws (*The mass of men lead lives of quiet desperation*). We like our proverbs to have the sound of "insights," and we like it best if we can identify the author. We have a taste, as the medievals did, for homely truths which help us lead our lives, though our

truths sound less "moral." We like dire "existential" utterances with Significant Words in capital letters (*The Dreadful
has already happened*) or mental-health precepts which point
us away from the abyss (*Regret is based on the illusion that one
can relive the past*). We take a kind of esthetic pleasure in
weighing such utterances, retaining and quoting those which
seem "meaningful" and ignoring or disputing those which
do not. For us a good saying is probably more a matter of
personal preference than it was when the pervasive authority of the Church might settle a disputed "sentence." But
a medieval man could still say, like January, "Straw for thy
Senek, and for thy proverbes."

To the extent that we retain this taste for wisdom
expressed succinctly we can grasp the spirit in which proverbs are offered in *The Canterbury Tales* and indeed find a
good many worth possessing; but like the pilgrims we are
free to pick and choose. Proverbs are only *sayings*, after all:
some are true and some are not. Chaucer uses the word
"proverb" with a favorable connotation in the singular but
with an unfavorable one in the plural. People speak confi-
dently of a proverb—"the proverb saith," or "this proverb is
said full sooth," or "is full sooth and full commune"—but
when more than one at a time come into play, disputes arise.
"I sette noght an hawe," says the Wife, "Of his proverbes
n'of his olde sawe" (659–660). The great Chaucerian pur-
veyor of proverbs is Pandarus—his store of wise saws and
modern instances is almost always a subject of mirth among
commentators; but Chaucer depicts him as a genuinely
learned man, much of whose lore comes from books. Even
so, disconsolate Troilus protests that "thy proverbes may me
naught availe" (I:756). "Lat this proverb," says Pandarus to
Criseyde, "a lore unto you be" (II:397). "Lore" is anything
learned or known—it is often coupled with "reed," anything
advised.[66] Proverbs, like "ensamples," are offered as *lore* and
reed, but the test of either is the truth of its *sentence* (meaning)
or *doctrine* (teaching). And the test of that truth is its *auctoritee*—or common sense, the common experience of the

66. See *TC* V:22, 327; *CT* I:3527.

senses. We share with all the users and hearers of proverbs in *The Canterbury Tales*—from the Parson to Chauntecleer—the desire for lore, sentence, and doctrine, and share with them the grounds for judging and disputing *auctoritees*.

Look at it from this smaller perspective and the inner form of the tales is a microcosm embraced by the outer macrocosm of the pilgrimage. The author claims the tales are fables which are contingent upon their tellers, but he makes their meaning and veracity depend on us—on what we share with him and with the pilgrims, a culture and a tradition. Individual tales in their conclusions return us to the outer form, the ongoing pilgrimage, where another tale is produceable. At key points the tales end in such a way as to direct us outside the pilgrimage into other realms of discourse. The inner form of the tales thus shades into the larger realm of truth acknowledged by medieval culture—as does the outer form at the end of the work. Look at it from the perspective of this larger realm and the story of the pilgrimage which the narrator rehearses seems but another pilgrim's tale. The inner form, in its bulk and complexity, comes to dominate the work. The tales still need to be related to the General Prologue and the pilgrimage frame, but now they need to be related to each other too. They become a world unto themselves, and this world seems to have a structure of its own, unfolding like a flower from within the work, more encompassing, more variegated, and more complex than the pilgrimage which frames it.

THE ESTHETICS OF THIS FORM

I know the form I have described must seem like a puzzle whose parts cannot be made to fit, like a hall of mirrors reflecting everything from angles multiplied upon themselves, like a maze. The most attentive and patient reader in the world might well ask at this point, "the esthetics of *what* form?" I rush forward with a résumé. At base the form is that of a memory: in the General Prologue it is a memory as the Middle Ages conceived of memory, a set of "places" structured on principles of order and association. This memory is presented as the narrator's own, and the narrator is identified with the author. He remembers a group of pilgrims interrelated in such a way that they make up a society in little, remembers the game they planned, and remembers the tale each told. But the pilgrims did not follow the plan; their tales tumbled upon one another in an apparently random order dictated by group dynamics and interpersonal relations, by the characters and moods of the individuals. Hence a new form takes shape: the narrator's memory serves up the seemingly disordered quality of experience itself. Each tale becomes detachable, can be read for itself: each was in the pilgrim's memory before it was in the narrator's. We experience a memory of others' memories and thus lapse into a mentalistic realm, a world of story, of reality remembered, distorted, tendentious. This "mentalistic" quality shows in the pilgrimage frame. It is far from "realistic": the pilgrims progress at a remove from civilization, passing through a wilderness from the outskirts of one city to the outskirts of another within the arc of an artificial day. Such a figural representation of the pilgrimage would make the work seem unfinished, however many tales might have been added.

This "outer" form contains and hovers over the inner form, the series of tales. These consist chiefly of curiosities and fabrications, discredited by their tellers, their arrangement, or their tone and content. The endings of the tales tend to leave matters open, throwing attention back to the outer form of the pilgrimage, forward to the next tale, or at key points into realms of discourse beyond the literary realm of the work itself. These multiple viewpoints and multiple degrees of closure make the inner form of the tales seem a maze of contradictions in which the reader is left to find his own way, to participate as hearer and judge. But the guidelines for our participation are suggested in the work. The role-playing narrator points our attention to the pilgrims, with whom we share a social and national milieu; to the authorial self behind his role-playing, with whom we share a world of books and ideas; and to proverbial lore, for which we share a taste and a capacity to weigh and select.

Some will no doubt throw up their hands and say that such a form is impossibly abstract. But is it any the less abstract when we talk about dramatic or climactic or episodic form, about rises and falls, turnabouts, ironic twists? Is it less abstract when we choose a simile to describe form, when we say a form is like a circle or a spiral or the building of a house? If we talk about form at all we are talking about something imposed upon or abstracted from the particulars of a work, and the problem is that in modern times *we* like form to be simple, unadorned, pure. We want "clean lines" in our buildings, single colors, the simple majesty of aluminum and glass. If Chaucer believed with Geoffrey of Vinsauf that the form of a work is like the builder's *archetypus*, that it becomes a reality through a process of construction like that of building a house, must we not ask what kind of houses were admired in Chaucer's time? Must we not remind ourselves that their best and greatest houses were not quaint homes of wattle-and-daub but grand stone castles, walled and pinnacled and wondrously turreted? It has become a cliché to compare a medieval poem with a Gothic cathedral, yet the comparison is just: the Gothic cathedral was a complex structure with outer and inner forms that could be viewed from multiple perspectives, by its very nature unfinished in execution but complete in design. "Gothic" form was enormously abstract (the mysteries of number and light played a part in it) and endlessly complicated—worlds apart from the "clean lines" we admire. Yet the Gothic cathedral was the medieval idea of a house par excellence, for it was the house of God.

Some will say still that this is all very theoretical—that I have let my thesis ride me hard. But here I must protest with vehemence: what I am arguing is far *less* theoretical than other approaches. Those who find a simple form like the metaphor of the pilgrimage must fall back on elaborate theories about scriptural exegesis, esthetic response, medieval culture. Those who find simple realism "breaking with convention and going direct to life" must accept modern theories about "life" and representation. I do not offer a theory at all. I claim to have done my best to experience a work as it was written and meant to be read, and to have described that experience in a straightforward way. I have done with the poem what I did with the Ellesmere drawing of Chaucer—I have looked at it as sympathetically as I know how, resisting any attempt to explain it away, and have written down what I saw. If what I have written *sounds* theoretical, that is because what I have seen is itself abstract and complicated; but my "method" is inductive and descriptive, its spirit tentative and pragmatic.

"Yes, yes," the objector will reply, "but then wouldn't you be better off to talk about *ideas* instead of *the* idea, about *forms* instead of *a* form?" But—my answer is—if we resort to these plurals, would we not then be talking about *works* rather than *a* work? My thesis has to do with an idea which I take to be unique and inclusive, many faceted, an idea hard to grasp—yet an idea.

The real problem with such a thesis, when it comes to discussing form as part of an idea, is that we are discussing something definite and describable which is hard to *visualize*. That is generally true of form; hence we are always using visual images to clarify our notions—we say the General Prologue is like a portrait gallery or a cross-section, the pilgrimage like a frame, a poem like a house. I am going to call these comparisons "models."[67] In trying to grasp a complicated idea or a puzzling set of observations, we can of course use any model we please if it helps us. But we need to be aware that it can limit us too. The world we see around us prompts us to explain that world, but the models we use to explain it shape what we see. In literary study we often use historical models as a means of comparison: we compare *The Canterbury Tales* with a Gothic cathedral or *The Divine Comedy* with a

67. On the term see C. S. Lewis, *The Discarded Image* (Cambridge: Cambridge Univ. Press, 1964), pp. 11–21. The term is borrowed from the sciences; a model is a device used for its convenience in explaining evidence, in "saving appearances," and is judged not for its intrinsic or objective truth but for its usefulness—if it helps us it is a good model, and for that reason two or more models may be adopted if they help us better. As the medievals had a "model of the universe" which explained the appearance of the universe to them, medieval poets conceived models of their own poems—so I am arguing here—which explained the form of the poems.

summa. Isn't there some model which would illustrate the principle of an inner form so complex and variegated in its interrelations that it seems to overburgeon, to dominate and obscure the presumably dominant outer form? I will propose such a model, one much closer to the book: a characteristic initial capital from an early fourteenth-century English manuscript, the Tickhill Psalter.[68] If the reader will look at the full-page initial S of Psalm 68 (Figure 7) he will see a set of six medallions divided by the cross-stroke of the S into two sets of three, each framed in circles which interlock chain-fashion. These represent the story of 2 Sam. 6:2–7:3. Essentially the form is a capital S; it is clearly framed in a rectangular border whose corners are carefully interlocked so that they themselves are a chain. Yet our attention goes to the story depicted, to the decorations which surround the pictures, to the "channels" which lead from inside each drawing to the margin (where it was intended that captions and quotations be written). The outer form, the capital S, frames and seems to dominate, but the inner form, the narrative, draws our attention: we ask at once where it begins, what its episodes represent, how it is put together or "structured." We need rules or theories to perceive this structure—need to know where to begin, in what direction to proceed, how to relate the drawings in the frame to those at the bottom of the page. Look at the design one way and it is a decorated capital. Look at it another way and it is a world of story framed by a circular design which seems to have no beginning and no end, and yet which seems to have a remarkable unity. Like the Ellesmere portrait of Chaucer it may be seen in either of two ways.

I do not claim any expertise as an art historian, and I offer this "model" because it is suggestive and illustrative of an esthetic effect which seems abstract and exotic. In what follows I wish to offer three models for which I claim more

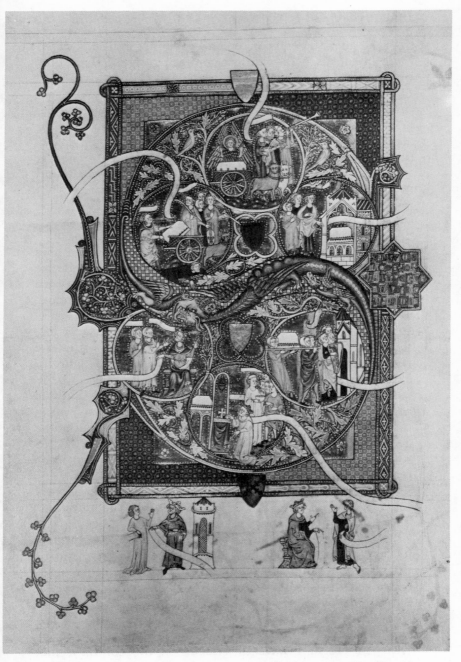

Figure 7. Outer and inner form. Full page initial S of Psalm 68, with drawings illustrating 2 Samuel 6:2–7:3. Tickhill Psalter, Spencer ms. 26, fol. 64ᵛ.

than the advantage of convenience: they are explicitly stated in *The Canterbury Tales* in its opening passage. I claim they were in the author's mind and were part of his idea. Hence I claim that what follows is descriptive and concrete, not theoretical. About structure, which will be the subject of the remaining chapters, I make no such claim. Form may be abstract but it can be stated in a work and kept palpably present in the reader's mind; structure involves the piecing together of parts, is experiential rather than abstract, and requires extrinsic rules and theories to be perceived. But *stated* models of a form provide an intrinsic key to perception.

That a literary work should state its own models of form is a convention of western literature which modern authors inherited from the Middle Ages. In late medieval literature the example which comes to mind is the dream-vision, which conventionally states its own form by introducing a dreamer who falls asleep. The opening passage of *Piers Plowman* states its own form, that of recurrent or cyclical dreams, in a startling image of swirling waters. Such statements often use visual images from traditional iconography. In *Troilus and Criseyde* Chaucer states the form of the work—"Fro woe to wele, and after out of joye"—and associates this rise and fall with the image of Fortune's Wheel. These are what I mean by stated models; they can be as straightforward as Dante's "book of memory" in the *Vita Nuova* or as subtly entwined with the texture and content of the poem as the image of the margarite in *Pearl* or that of "gomen" in *Sir Gawain*.

If Chaucer agreed with Geoffrey of Vinsauf that a work is an *archetypus* before it is a reality, found by the inner man who casts out his heart's line, this initial "purpose" (as Chaucer called it) is what I call form. There is every reason to suppose that an author would have been aware of such a purpose. And Chaucer might have found a purpose newly conceived: he is often praised for originality, and the praise is justified, as Egeus would say, "in some degree." Yet the three models he stated at the beginning of the work are familiar medieval images. These models are not different from the form I have described; on the contrary, they precisely visualize three aspects of that form. They are like emblematic directions telling us what we should look for as we read. And each had a heritage in medieval ideas about art.

The Performance

The narrator's monologue about his remembered experience is the most familiar of these models, and the others depend on it; the form of the work is tied to our sense of a personal relationship with him. It is often a help to imagine Chaucer reading *The Canterbury Tales* aloud at court, but the model of an extended performance is embodied *in the work*. We are drawn into a relationship with a monologuist, a performer. We perceive that he is playing a role and behind this role we sense a living man, the author himself, as we sense behind every Hamlet or Lear the actor playing Hamlet or Lear. At times we are so far convinced that we forget the author altogether; but during the tales we may forget the performer and catch the echo of the author's voice. Hence the identity of this "Chaucer" becomes a running joke. The Man of Law discourses on his works as if he were not there. The Host inquires of him "What man artow?" Called on to tell a tale, he reveals himself no teller of tales at all; on a second try he seems to doff his mask and offer a straightforward discourse in prose. For the rest, he places over his mask of the fool the masks of the pilgrims which he has displayed before us in the General Prologue. Yet each of these pilgrims whose roles he plays is himself a performer who plays the roles of various figures in his own tale. (In some instances the figures in a tale are performers too: Chauntecleer performs two tales, complete with characters, plot, and dialogue.) We have therefore a performer playing the parts of performers. And nothing could be more medieval. Telling tales really *was* a pastime on Canterbury pilgrimages, as telling or reading them was at court. In an age when originality was little prized, nearly all such tales had been told before by another author or teller: every performance *was* a performance of a performance. And Chaucer tells us this at the outset. The narrator is not going to "feine thing" or "finde wordes newe"; he is going to "tell a tale after a man," to "reherse."

Seen this way, the pilgrimage is a descent from one level of verisimilitude to another, an accumulation of fictions within a fiction. As with any performance, the work calls for our participation, for our suspension of disbelief: it relies upon us to distinguish essential truth from artistic pretense, and whatever is theatrical, fantastical, and unreal helps us do so. In medieval esthetics, though in general it supported a mimetic theory of art, the *accurate* portrayal of reality in art was the greater deception: art achieved its truth by deliberate falsity. The test of its truth was not in its correspondence with reality but in the intentions of the artist. And St. Augustine had stated this principle precisely with respect to a performance:

> On the stage [the actor] Roscius was a false Hecuba by choice, a true man by nature; but by that choice also a true tragic actor because he fulfilled his purpose, yet a false Priam because he imitated Priam but was not he. And now from this comes something amazing, which however no one doubts . . . that all these things are true in some respects for the very reason that they are false in some respects, and that only the fact that they are false in one sense helps them towards their truth. Hence they cannot in any way arrive where they would be or should be if they shrink from being false. For how could the actor I mentioned be a true tragic actor if he were not willing to be a false Hector, a false Andromache, a false Hercules . . . ? Or how could a picture of a horse be a true picture unless it were a false horse? or an image of a man in a mirror be a true image unless it were a false man? So if the fact that they are false in one respect helps certain things to be true in another respect, why do we fear falseness so much and seek truth as such a great good? . . . Will we not admit that these things make up truth itself, that truth is so to speak put together from them?[69]

The Pilgrimage in Retrospect

The narrator's performance, begun in the opening

---

69. St. Augustine, *Soliloquia* II:10 (*PL* 32:893), trans. mine with an assist from my colleague Georg Luck. See Singleton, *Dante Studies I*, pp. 62–65 and De Bruyne, pp. 40–41.

passage of the General Prologue, looks back upon a pilgrimage now completed and remembered. In some instances we must as we read look back upon previous tales or groups of tales to understand the performance we witness—we look back to the Knight's Tale during the Miller's performance, to the Wife's during the Clerk's. At the end of the work we are given a *summa* on penitence, and penance itself requires a retrospective examination of past deeds. At the end of that *summa* the author himself looks back upon the corpus of his writings. An actual pilgrimage, to be sure, looked forward to its destination, as the metaphorical "pilgrimage of human life" looked forward to the Heavenly Jerusalem. But every pilgrimage had to be viewed as a single action with an intention, so that the pilgrim at his destination had to look back through memory upon the journey itself. That is what the Parson sets out to do when he promises the pilgrims to "shewe you the way, in this viage, / Of thilke parfit glorious pilgrimage / That highte Jerusalem celestial." For this tendency to look back upon a past action and see it as a whole there is no dearth of precedents in medieval thought. St. Augustine perceived that linear experience has no meaning until lapsed time permits that experience to take form in memory. Charles Singleton[70] has pointed out that *The Divine Comedy* is meant to be read with this retrospective understanding, and that Dante provides a paradigm (*Paradiso* II:22–25) in the image of the arrow striking its target, then flying through the air, then springing from the bow—the hysteron-proteron is possible only through memory. A paradigm closer to our purpose is the image of Troilus looking back from the eighth sphere upon this "litel spot of erth, that with the sea embraced is" and despising "this wrecched world." To look back in this specific way is to look at things through memory, and the narrator in his performance, a feat of memory, embodies this principle of the retrospective image. In fact *The Canterbury Tales* ends with a hysteron-proteron, not as visual as Dante's but more embracing. The Parson's last sentence does not put things temporal first and things eternal last as one would expect; it reverses the order:

70. "The Vistas in Retrospect," *MLN* 81 (1966):55–80.

This blissful regne may men purchase by povertee espirituel, and the glory by lowness, the plentee of joy by hunger and thurst, and the rest by travail, and the life by deeth and mortificacioun of sin.

(X:1080)

The work thus directs us to look back upon tales and groups of tales, to perform our own feat of memory. But when we do so, what we remember is not necessarily a progression or an order. We remember the tales, as we remember the pilgrims, in groups and relationships. And we are at liberty to remember them in various combinations, not necessarily in "dramatic" sequences like that of the marriage group. For example, when we think of the Knight's Tale we associate it with the Miller's Tale which follows it and parodies it. But because the Knight and Squire are father and son and are introduced together in the General Prologue, the Knight's and Squire's tales invite comparison—it is for example sometimes remarked that the Squire tries to emulate his father's rhetorical art with unwieldy and less promising material and a youthful lack of skill. Because the Knight's Tale is about a "courtly" love which ends in a marriage, it may be, and has been, associated with the tales of the marriage group. And because it is aristocratic in its preoccupations, intended for an audience accustomed to the values implicit in it, and accustomed to romances, it could profitably be associated with Chaucer's two tales—Sir Thopas, which parodies romance conventions debased for bourgeois ears, and the Melibee, which addresses the ruling class about serious issues. Even its Boethian sentiments about bearing adversity with patience allow that it be associated with the de casibus tragedies of the Monk or the penitential discourse of the Parson. And its optimism, which expresses the Knight's predilection for "joy after woe," can be associated with the Man of Law's Tale, the Clerk's Tale, and the Knight's interruptions at the end of the Pardoner's and Monk's tales. Whenever we read any single literary work to the end we can see patterns and structures emerge in its linear progress, but a collection of tales does not necessarily admit patterns or structures. Yet few collections have inspired in critics so much thematic juxtaposition and contrast as *The Canterbury Tales*. Why? The answer lies in the General Prologue. It is the heart or backbone of the work; it provides a central point of reference which invites us to relate one tale to another because it relates their tellers to one another, to the society they share, and to their common presence in the narrator's consciousness. We can see this only in retrospect; but what we see is boundless. A finite number of tellers and tales gives us the possibility of an almost infinite number of associations, a plenitude of meanings.

The Flower

The relationship between the General Prologue and the tales, that of a central schema to which diverse parts are related in retrospect, and which encourages the reader to perceive relationships among those parts, is a characteristic medieval form. A visual counterpart of this form is stated at the beginning of the work in the image of the flower. Critics of *The Canterbury Tales* have most often seen the flower of the opening lines as a traditional springtime image; some, noting the flow of "licour" from April's showers into the roots and through them into the "veins," recognize in it the natural process of "engendering" by which all living things renew themselves in cycles. It isn't fantastical to find, as some have done, a covert phallic or sexual reference in the liquid flowing through the vein.[71] The renewal of life in spring suggests the primeval, cyclical conception of nature, the simplest and most natural way of viewing time and the world. Upon this cyclical conception Christianity imposed its linear view of time as an expanse of years passing from Creation to Doomsday; from this Christian vantage point the springtime image suggests the great rebirth of the Resurrection.[72] From either the natural or the Christian viewpoint

71. Arthur W. Hoffman, "Chaucer's Prologue to Pilgrimage: The Two Voices," *ELH* 21 (1954):1–16.

72. On the initial spring-song, see Bowden, pp. 19–21, and Baldwin, *Unity of the Canterbury Tales*, esp. pp. 24-27. Probably Baldwin was the first to allegorize the passage; its connections with Lent, Easter, pilgrimage, hence penance, the Resurrection, and travel are self-evident. For a characteristic allegorical reading see Bernard F. Huppé, *A Reading of the*

Figure 8. Flower-wheel design. Church of St. Zeno, Verona.

the image of the flower implies the transience of all things, the mutability of life itself. It appeared in Scripture with this meaning. We read that "All flesh is grass, and all the glory thereof as the flower of the field. The grass is withered, and the flower is fallen, because the spirit of the Lord hath blown upon it. Indeed the people is grass: the grass is withered, and the flower is fallen" (Isa. 40:6–8); that "man's days are as grass, as the flower of the field so shall he flourish" (Ps. 102:15); that man "cometh forth like a flower, and is

Canterbury Tales (Albany: State Univ. of New York Press, 1964), pp. 12–20. Trevor Whittock, in *A Reading of the Canterbury Tales* (Cambridge: Cambridge Univ. Press, 1968), pp. 44–47 argues that the passage emphasizes the affirmative and celebratory aspects of the Christian myth rather than its negative aspects.

Figure 9. Circles-in-circles design. Cathedral, Lausanne.

destroyed, and fleeth as a shadow" (Job 14:2). If the passage suggests Chaucer's "feeling for nature" it suggests such a feeling as his age *had* for nature—the feeling that the worldly and natural order, which is part of God's plan, "passeth soon as flowres faire."[73]

Yet this image of the passing flower was precisely the visual image which the medievals used to figure the order and reasonableness of created things: a circle in which various parts of the design relate symmetrically to the center. Of this there are—or so it seems to me—two prin-

73. See George D. Economou, *The Goddess Natura in Medieval Literature* (Cambridge, Mass.: Harvard Univ. Press, 1972), esp. pp. 50–67 and chap. 5, and Brian Stock, *Myth and Science in the Twelfth Century: A Study of Bernard Silvester* (Princeton, N. J.: Princeton Univ. Press, 1972), esp. pp. 63–87.

cipal variations. (1) The *flower-wheel* or *rota* design in which lines radiate from the center. The lines are often curved in such a way that they make a kind of "optical illusion," as in the window of the church of St. Zeno in Verona (Figure 8): look at it one way and you see a flower with petals like a daisy, look at it another way and you see a wheel. There can be no doubt that this was intended, for around the edge we see small carved figures of men climbing and falling on the wheel of Fortune. Windows with such carvings are an oddity, but they do show that the design was understood from one viewpoint as Fortune or mutability. It seems to represent the world; eternity seems to be in the still center. (2) The *circles-in-circles* design, which might be called wheels within wheels. The notion is immanent in the window of St. Zeno in Figure 8, for a single smaller wheel with its own circular axle can be seen at the center. But in some instances, for example the rose window at Lausanne (Figure 9), the wheel principle is obscured: within the larger circle we find not spokes or petals but an embracing square, in it a diamond. About these are arranged overlapping circles, in each of them four smaller circles arranged around a central circle. These smaller circles contain illustrations of cosmological figures—signs of the zodiac, the seasons, the months, the winds, the elements, and so on. The overlapping inner circles still have somewhat the quality of the rota, for the spaces between their smaller interior circles are carved out, making the sides of the circles suggest the spokes of a wheel. But the whole is meant to represent the unity of the cosmos. The original stained glass medallions at the center, it is thought, represented the year, sun, moon, night, and day. The most highly wrought rose windows, like those at Notre Dame in Paris, involve all these principles—radiating lines, concentric circles, and smaller circles within the concentric circles.

The complexities of this flower or "rose" design are infinite and lie very far beyond my competence. What lay behind these complexities, however, is clear: it was the medieval world picture. The Ptolemaic universe was depicted as a series of concentric circles with the Earth at its

Figure 10. Microcosm and macrocosm: man inscribed within the zodiac. Vienna Nationalbibliothek, ms. 2359, fol. 52r.

center. Since each planet was a globe and turned in epicycles, each was a circle on its concentric circle and made circles within that circle. Because man was thought to be influenced by the stars and planets, the image of man was sometimes represented as inscribed within such a heavenly circle, the zodiac (Figure 10). In such a microcosm-macrocosm design as this one the lines of zodiacal influence are emphasized: the design becomes a wheel-like one. I am not sure, but I think the germ of the one image was always present in the other. The eternal and cosmic had the time-bound world or man at its center; but the world had at its center Jerusalem which symbolized eternity—as man had within his earthly body his eternal soul. The center of one design becomes the periphery of the other—it is wheels within wheels indeed.

Pilgrimages might have been visualized by a rota design. A pilgrimage, though a linear journey, was made by many pilgrims to a central shrine; all roads led to Jerusalem in a wheel-like pattern. Chaucer has in mind such an image when he introduces the pilgrimage in the General Prologue:

And specially from every shires ende
Of Engelond to Caunterbury they wende. . . .

Figure 11. "T–O" map of the three continents surrounded by wind-
circle showing the twelve winds. Walters Gallery, ms. 73,
fol. 1ᵛ.

A map of the Jerusalem pilgrimage might show roads
leading to the central shrine (for it was understood there
were Christians east of the Holy Land): in the old "T-O"
maps Asia was placed at the top (east was placed where we
place north), Europe to the left below, and Africa to the
right, divided by the vertical base of the T, which represented the Mediterranean. Such a diagrammatic map showing the three continents of the terrestrial orb (in the image of
its triune Creator) can be seen inscribed in the center of
a late twelfth-century English wind circle (Figure 11). It

depicts the twelve winds of heaven blowing upon the world and has each wind saying what he does—readers of Chaucer will note that Zephirus, the west wind (shown at the bottom), says he decorates the earth with flowers: "*Tellurem floribus orno.*" In some maps of the period Jerusalem was represented (as it is in the famous *mappa mundi* at Hereford Cathedral) as a round walled town, and was always shown in the center of the world, a circle in a circle; in the "T-O" maps Jerusalem is at the cross of the T.[74] There, at the center of the *orbis terrarum*, stood the prototype of every pilgrim's destination. Some maps of the city Jerusalem repeat the pattern of the "T-O" map, as if it were a world in the center of the world.[75] Segments of time, too, were represented by such diagrams of concentric circles and radiating lines—the year was so represented,[76] and the life of a single man.[77]

74. See *Mappemondes, A.D. 1200–1500,* ed. Marcel Destombes, International Geographical Union, Commission on Early Maps (Amsterdam: N. Israel, 1964), plate VIb (Gautier de Chatillon, 13th cent., Paris: Bib. Nationale Ms Lat. 11334, f. 1) and plate XIV (Ranulf Higden, 14th cent., London: British Museum, Royal ms. 14.C.IX, fol. IV–2). Both maps make the location of Jerusalem very clear. This arrangement, with Jerusalem at the center of the land mass and east at the top, placed the earthly paradise (which was east) on the top of the world. For a general account see Leo Bagrow, *History of Cartography,* ed. R. A. Skelton (rpt. Cambridge, Mass.: Harvard Univ. Press, 1966), chaps. 3 and 6.

75. See M. W. Evans, *Medieval Drawings* (London, New York, Sydney, Toronto: Paul Hamlyn, 1969), plate 97 (Stuttgart: Württembergische Landesbibl. Cod. Bibl. fol.56, back endpaper, ca. 1150); Evans on p. 36 points out that the map is an abstract diagram representing important shrines and doctrinal features, not a map in the modern sense. He observes that it is arranged according to a preconceived plan, that of a Roman camp. It is interesting however that more elaborate "T-O" maps are laid out also in this "Roman camp" fashion; see the examples in Bagrow, pp. 42–43, and in Konrad Miller, *Mappaemundi: Die ältesten Weltkarten* (Stuttgart, 1895), III:62–63, figs. 14, 15, and 16.

76. See Evans, plate 79 (Stuttgart, Württembergische Landesbibl. Cod. his. fol. 415, fol. 17ᵛ, ca. 1180), which shows a personified Year surrounded by the circle of months, signs of the Zodiac, the seasons, the four times of day; he is holding the sun and moon and is flanked by night and day. As Evans remarks on p. 33 "a physical form is provided for every major unit of time."

77. Evans, plate 84 (Vatican Library: ms. Pal. lat. 1993, fol. 11ʳ, ca. 1334–1336). The remarkable diagram is identified as an autobiographical schema of the life of Opicinus de Canistris (Evans, p. 34). It shows forty

These circumscribed designs showing the unity of temporal things are clearly associated with the rose or flower design so common in medieval art and literature. The radiating petals and concentric figurations represented unity and perfection within multiplicity and variation. They were a flower with radiating petals or a garland made of flowers (*flos florum*) which was "one in all and all in one." Peter Dronke[78] has demonstrated how the topos, initially a figure of divine perfection, was used in the twelfth century in hymns to the Virgin, and how it was associated with the figure of the tree of Jesse (Isa. 11:1) which bore the Virgin who bore Christ. In medieval love lyrics the lady, the "flower of flowers," is thus earthly and heavenly, uniting the diverse beauty of the world and, for her lover, representing the source of all beauty. The rose windows of cathedrals in this same way attempted to depict the unity and perfection in the order of things. Professor Bober has collected a large number of schemata from medieval manuscripts which represent theological, moral, or scientific conceptions in precisely these circular and reticulated forms.[79] The great culmination of this tradition, its most sublime expression, is Dante's multifoliate rose in *Paradiso* 30–31, which expresses the ultimate unity and perfection of all creation bathed in eternal Light. The "flower" of medieval thought is therefore very far from the flower as moderns conceive it; we may share with our medieval ancestors the mandala design which

---

concentric circles standing for the years of the artist's life up to the time of the completion of the drawing. The years are divided radially into 366 days. Christ oversees the whole. The reproduction is too small for me to see in its minuscule inscriptions whether there is any reference to the pilgrimage of the life of man; but it is notable that in the center we see the Virgin and Child and a map of the Mediterranean, which of course suggests Jerusalem. There is every reason to suppose that Chaucer, with his interest in astrology, cosmology, and navigation, would have been familiar with such cosmological schemata.

78. *Medieval Latin and the Rise of European Love-Lyric*, 2 vols. (Oxford: Clarendon Press, 1968), I:181–192. Cf. De Bruyne, p. 70.

79. Bober presented some of his material in a paper which I heard at the meeting of the Mediaeval Academy of America, Chicago, 1969; and see his treatment of the ms. from which fig. 11 comes, "An Illustrated Medieval School-Book of Bede's 'De Natura Rerum,'" *Journal of the Walters Art Gallery* 19–20 (1956–1957):64–97.

Jung reckoned a universal archetype and may inherit from them certain stylized designs and even certain attitudes about the nature of unity or perfection or diversity. But when a nineteenth-century poet said he saw the universe in a blade of grass, he had in mind universal processes of nature embodied in a single instance; when the medievals saw the universe in a flower they had in mind the hierarchy, plenitude, and order which encompassed all that is diverse and mutable.

The passage on the adoration of the daisy, which sparkles so bright in the prologue to *The Legend of Good Women*, is an example of this medieval motif. As at the opening of *The Canterbury Tales*, the poet places in a key position the springing of flowers to life in springtime:

> . . . whan that the month of May
> Is comen, and that I heer the foules singe,
> And that the flowres ginnen for to springe,
> Farewell my book, and my devocioun!
>
> (F36–39)

At once he singles out the Daisy as his favorite, refers to it in the feminine gender, calls it "of alle flowres flowr, / Fulfilled of all vertu and honour" (53–54). The Daisy, which he tells us means "day's eye" (184), represents lightness: it is "the cleerness and the verray light / That in this derke world me wynt and ledeth" (84–85). Its whiteness was a sign of perfection and purity; its French name (*margarite*) also meant "pearl," and the pearl too was a symbol of purity and perfection. Chaucer's daisy is therefore a figure of ideal femininity, of perfection and unity in creation, comparable to the symbol of the rose and the topos of the *flos florum*. In the passage there is still a suggestion of the flower's transiency: the poet rises early "To seen this flowr ayein the sunne sprede, / Whan it upriseth erly by the morrwe" (48–49) and then returns at evening "to seen this flowr, how it wol go to reste, / For fere of night, so hateth she derkness" (62–63).[80]

---

80. It is probably pertinent to *The Canterbury Tales* that Stephen Langton, preaching at Rome on the fiftieth anniversary of the martyrdom of St. Thomas à Becket, compared Thomas to the rose and the lily in a

I suggested earlier that we need to see *The Canterbury Tales* in two ways at once—on the one hand as a series of tales within an encompassing tale, on the other hand as an inexhaustible world of stories among which the story of the pilgrimage is only another pilgrim's tale. Such a double perspective characterizes the topos of the flower: the "rose" design represents order, perfection, and permanence, yet it represents as a part of such order the facts of change, flux, and transience which were symbolized by the wheel. John Leyerle[81] has drawn attention to this combination of *rosa* and *rota*, and believes it was buttressed by the phonetic similarity of the Latin words. He has evidence, too, that the design was associated with the notion of the "eye of God."

These circular designs, which represent relationships and interrelationships within a larger unity, were often mnemonic devices. They arranged, on the principles of order and association, images to be held in memory, for memory's highest function was to retain not experience but "authorities," moral truths. In singling out the flower at the beginning of the work, though I expect he did so unconsciously, Chaucer suggested the great impulse of medieval thought to study the phenomena of the temporal world as segments of a universal and timeless plan, and to envisage those phenomena and that plan as a flowerlike circle in which all is one and one is all—in which all things are interrelated, held in memory by their relationships, and destined to pass from diversity and plenitude into an ultimate oneness.[82] But it was an original stroke of Chaucer's imagination that made him put at the center of this encom-

---

protracted passage of exegesis into which he drew the image of springtime and the passing year: *Beatus ergo martyr quasi flos rosarum fuit in temporibus vernis.* The phase echoes Eccles. 50:8. See Phyllis B. Roberts, "Langton on Becket: A New Look and a New Text," *MS* 35 (1973):38–48; the relevant passage is on pp. 44–45.

81. I heard Leyerle present his paper at the Mediaeval Academy of America, Chicago, 1969, on the same program with Bober (n. 79 above), but his photographic materials and text have not been available to me and remain unpublished; I do not know what evidence supports his claims.

82. On the background of this impulse in medieval esthetics and its important influence on medieval art, see De Bruyne, 62–67, 100–108, 125–130.

passing design a minutely accurate representation of his own age and nation. This stroke might be compared with the "creatural realism" of late medieval literature and manuscript drawings, and might be seen as reflecting the transition from "scientific" to "literary" humanism. The mysterious interrelationship of all things encompassed warts and bagpipes and draughts of corny ale, even stories people remember and tell; and this knowledge of the minute and disordered particulars of experience could be expressed in literary language and preserved in a book so as to render up something for our "doctrine," an idea meaningful because it reflected the idea of the constituted whole, the form of creation.

THE TALES:
A THEORY OF
THEIR STRUCTURE

FORM as I have described it implies structure. The two terms can barely be plucked apart in literary parlance; in modern times the notion of organic unity has done a lot to keep them together. But the two *words* have different meanings: historically, "form" has always tended to suggest an image, pattern, or fixed idea, "structure" to suggest a process by which parts have been put together. We may end up talking about the same thing if we discuss the form and structure of some object, but we approach the inquiry from different directions. Ask about the form of a pencil and you come up with requirements which, if not met, would disqualify a single specimen from being *called* a pencil—its purpose comes into the discussion; ask about its structure and you come up with its parts and the way of constructing these. At the extremes of the distinction one would have the Platonic ideas on the side of form, something like an outline or blueprint on the side of structure. Inquiries about the form or the structure of most literary works probably yield the same results in the end. And the creative process must involve an influence of one upon the other.

The difference and the relationship between them may devolve upon philosophical issues, but it is a real difference, not a word game.[1]

Readers of *The Canterbury Tales* have never come to any agreement about its form or structure. We see in an intellectual way some "big" features: a pilgrimage, a journey, a narrator, a series of tales, debate, discussion. But we sense in the totality of the parts something more complicated.[2] In approaching this problem about the way the tales are put together, I want to draw an analogy from structural linguistics. In structural linguistics it is necessary to isolate discrete units and describe syntactical or transformational rules: a stream of spoken discourse is a series of such units put together by such rules. One kind of unit is *juncture*—the "pauses" which divide one sentence, phrase, or word from another, but which join them too, and in such a way as to make relationships clear. The term is useful if we are to talk about a literary structure whose units are tales. We need to look for the kinds of junctures between the tales: they seem to be "pauses" or gaps or starting points, but if there is structure at all they are points where units are *related*. In *The Canterbury Tales* these junctures come where there is (1) a new teller or tale, (2) a new series of tales, or (3) a new theme.

1. The twenty-four junctures where we have a new teller or tale make a structure which is largely imposed by form, and the General Prologue imposes this form: it introduces the tellers and the rules of the tale-telling game, and so accounts for the tales' appropriateness to their tellers. In most cases this appropriateness in turn accounts for little structures like "quitting" or "discussions" or parodies of previous tales. And it accounts for those instances where a tale is "discredited" by its teller's character or by another tale

1. On the relation of form and structure, see Frye, *Anatomy of Criticism*, esp. pp. 85–87.

2. On structure among the tales see Payne, *Key of Remembrance*, chap. 5, who raises some of the problems dealt with here. Eliason, *The Language of Chaucer's Poetry*, pp. 143–149, and Jordan, *Chaucer and the Shape of Creation*, e.g. pp. 8, 117, acknowledge the problem of "gaps" or "exposed joints," i.e. the junctures which I take to be the crucial consideration.

offering another viewpoint. We see this kind of structure, however, in various ways. As we read from the General Prologue through the series of tales we see it as something which grows and develops, something "dynamic." As we see it in retrospect we see it as a complex of interacting viewpoints, related to its society and to human nature, something "schematic." We realize that the form and structure announced in the General Prologue are not fulfilled in the work, but this tension between what is announced and what is executed isn't "resolved" by the Parson's Tale. Among all these tensions—between form and structure, between announced and executed intentions, between dynamic and schematic perceptions—*The Canterbury Tales* introduces another, perhaps unique, tension: the end of the book (the Parson's Tale) is another kind of book.

This way of looking at the tales makes one see that the problem of sequential order has loomed larger than it deserves to. From the manuscripts we have ten fragments, some containing several tales, some only one. Narrational links in the text place some tales in a serial sequence; all but one of these links fall within the manuscript fragments (the remaining one, the opening line of Fragment X, links it with Fragment IX). The order of the fragments between the first and last varies in manuscripts, but one order has support from the prestigious Ellesmere manuscript and from eight others. In this order, the "Ellesmere order," Fragment VI presents a difficulty. Various manuscripts put it in various positions, and unlike other fragments it contains no internal evidence for its position. In the following scheme I enclose it in brackets:

I   General Prologue, Knight, Miller, Reeve, Cook
II   Man of Law
III   Wife, Friar, Summoner
IV   Clerk, Merchant
V   Squire, Franklin
[VI   Physician, Pardoner]
VII   Shipman, Prioress, *Sir Thopas, Melibee,* Monk, Nun's Priest
VIII   Second Nun, Canon's Yeoman
IX-X   Manciple, Parson

References to towns passed along the road do not jibe with this order, and at the end of Fragment II (line 1179) various manuscripts suggest the next pilgrim will be the Shipman, Squire, Summoner, or Wife. So the general supposition is that Chaucer meant a different order.

There are three ways to deal with this supposition. One is to rearrange the fragments in a "realistic" order by plotting in sequence the references to time and place, and to tales previously told.[3] A second is to rearrange tales or fragments by appealing to literary propriety, thematic juxtaposition, a presumed return journey, and so on.[4] A third is to ignore geographical realism and leave the fragments in the best manuscript order, as shown in the scheme above.[5] In what follows I mean to propose that form in the work does not require serial order except where it is self-evident, that tales are related to one another in more ways than the sequential or linear way, and that the more complex structure which emerges makes serial order a minor issue.

2. The five junctures where we have a new *series* of tales

3. Robert A. Pratt, "The Order of the *Canterbury Tales*," *PMLA* 66 (1951):1141–1167.

4. See above, chap. 2, n. 1, and see the remarks of Beryl Rowland, "Contemporary Chaucer Criticism," *English* 22(1973):3–10, esp. 6–7.

5. This involves rejecting the "Bradshaw shift," which puts Fragment VII after Fragment II and so gets the towns which are referred to in geographical order; the Summoner's remark (III:847) that he will tell two or three tales before he comes to Sittingbourne does not, however, necessarily mean that Sittingbourne is the next town. For the case against the Bradshaw shift, see Donald C. Baker, "The Bradshaw Order of *The Canterbury Tales*: A Dissent," *NM* 63 (1962):245–261; Lee Sheridan Cox, "A Question of Order in the *Canterbury Tales*," *ChauR* I (1967):228–252; and John Gardner, "The Case Against the 'Bradshaw Shift'; or, the Mystery of the Manuscript in the Trunk," *PLL*, 3 supplement (1967):80–106. Cox argues from conjectures about scribes and about artistic and thematic propriety, Gardner from conjectures about Chaucer's revisions of his plan; Gardner defends the Ellesmere order on grounds of thematic unity similar at least in their premises to those of my own argument in the present chapter. For the skeptical view of a good textual editor and critic, see E. T. Donaldson, "The Ordering of the *Canterbury Tales*," in *Medieval Literature and Folklore Studies: Essays in Honor of Francis Lee Utley*, ed. Jerome Mandel and Bruce A. Rosenberg (New Brunswick, N.J.: Rutgers Univ. Press, 1970), pp. 193–204; Donaldson defends the Ellesmere order on the grounds that it is the most economical way of taking all ms. evidence into account.

are the ones which create the problem of serial order. These do not begin with a "headlink" introducing the pilgrim; the Knight's Tale has such a link but it is in the General Prologue. If we take the other four "headless" junctures as marking the beginnings of units, those units turn out to be the "marriage group" tales, Fragment VI (the Physician-Pardoner fragment), Fragment VII, and Fragments VIII-IX-X. This gives us not ten manuscript fragments but five sequences. In the following scheme the dashes mark the "headless" junctures:

I	Knight, Miller, Reeve, Cook
III	—Wife, Friar, Summoner; IV Clerk, Merchant; V Squire, Franklin
[VI	—Physician, Pardoner]
VII	—Shipman, Prioress, *Sir Thopas*, *Melibee*, Monk, Nun's Priest
VIII	—Second Nun, Canon's Yeoman; IX-X Manciple, Parson

The four "headless" junctures are usually thought hiatuses where Chaucer meant to supply a link. It is assumed that he did not get around to writing a headlink or prologue for them, never that he intended to have them start off without fanfare as they do. Since Chaucer provided a headlink or prologue for other tales, it makes sense to suppose he meant to provide one for all. But it is not an obligatory conclusion. One possibility is that he meant to do exactly what he did: that he meant the Wife's, Physician's, Shipman's, and Second Nun's performances to start without any words from the narrator, as if *in medias res*. Out of nowhere comes the Wife's voice, unannounced, blustering: "Experience, though noon auctoritee. . . ." We have to rely on the bookish title, not the narrator's performance, to know the speaker's identity; "bookness" supplants "voiceness." And at least the Shipman's and Wife's tales do initiate groups of tales which are often thought to have dramatic and thematic unity. To say Chaucer planned it this way is to say a great deal. Yet some instinct, some pleasure he found in these abrupt beginnings, might have kept him from supplying the links. Couldn't their unmotivated, unsequential quality have struck a chord in his sensibilities? His sensibilities were after all shaped by the dream-vision; he, who had described the haunting appearance and disappearance of the little whelp in *The Book of the Duchess,* was no stranger to the artistic uses of unmotivated, dreamlike events. It is a conjecture, true; but so is anything else we say about what Chaucer *didn't* write. And all I am saying is that these headless junctures, which come at key positions, are effective as they are.

If we take these five sequences as structural units, the matter of serial order is reduced to two problems. We know that Fragment I comes at the beginning of the work and Fragments VIII-IX-X come at the end. One problem, then, is where to put Fragment VI, the so-called "floating fragment." The other problem is whether to put the "marriage group" tales (Fragments III-IV-V) before or after Fragment VII. Perhaps the solution is to say that you can read them in any order you please. In this and the last chapter, though, I will suggest a preference for reading the marriage group tales before the tales of Fragment VII, and for viewing the Physician-Pardoner fragment as "floating" or detached, as it is.

3. The one juncture where we have a new theme but no series is the Man of Law's Tale (Fragment II). The Man of Law is, after the Knight, the pilgrim of highest rank, and there is a relationship between their two tales: we get the Knight's tale of chivalry with its churlish addenda in Fragment I, then the Man of Law's tale of Christian virtue in Fragment II. The two tales treat the two dominant value-systems of medieval society, the chivalric and the Christian. Together they initiate in the work what I am going to call a *metastructure.* The Knight's Tale is the first of several romances interspersed throughout the work, the Man of Law's Tale the first of the ideal narratives. Hence we can see a generic and a thematic relationship between them. This relationship is repeated in the two recited "rimes" (which come one after the other in Fragment VII), *Sir Thopas* and the Prioress's Tale: these represent respectively chivalric and Christian ideals, and are a romance and an ideal narrative, but they are debased and mindless. The same relationship is carried out in the two prose pieces: the *Melibee* is addressed

to the knightly class, the Parson's Tale to the Christian reader. The two prose pieces can be seen in retrospect as two major structural elements which respond to or dispose of knightly and Christian matters raised earlier[6] in two idealistic narratives, two genres of tales, and two "drasty" rimes.

The problem of structure in the tales hangs upon the problem of content or meaning: we cannot find meaningful groups without finding themes, but the critic has to interpret tales before he can claim thematic links among them. And his interpretation of any single tale is open to debate. Still, we know there *are* thematic sequences because tales like the Miller's and Reeve's are paired. This pairing occurs among many of the tales and there are sometimes *concatenations* of pairs: the Knight's and Miller's tales are paired (one being a parody of the other), the Miller's and Reeve's are paired (one "quitting" the other), and so on. Seen this way the dominant structure of the tales is a system of *pairs within groups*. I was tempted to say "thematic pairs within thematic groups," but that would be begging the question.

This structure of pairs within groups is puzzling because it seems destructive or self-consuming. In what follows we will see that the structure consists of three thematic groups which do no more than raise questions and a fourth which seems to destroy the whole enterprise. The tales have been presented as a game, but in the end all the players seem to lose, all the rules seem to be violated. We have to start over or turn back. And if we see the structure of the work this way, there *is* something like a return journey: we are asked to read the Parson's Tale and then turn about and go over the tales again in memory, see them anew from a better perspective. One could say that the Parson's Tale imposes a retrospective structure comparable to what the General Prologue imposes sequentially. This retrospective way of perceiving the work makes it possible for us to see things in it

6. This is if we read them in the Ellesmere order. Even if we do not the matters would have been raised earlier in the Knight's Tale and the Man of Law's Tale, but one might advance this "metastructure" as an argument in favor of the Ellesmere order.

which we would not see "linearly"—from this viewpoint the old idea that the Seven Deadly Sins is a structural principle in the work may not be as far-fetched as it was once made to seem.[7] The work remembered makes us change our estimate of the work experienced. True, this always happens when we read a book; but *The Canterbury Tales* is different, perhaps unique. Its ultimate structure takes shape in the reader's mind when through the linear experience of reading he forms a retrospective image *which he must then restructure.* Viewed this way, the structure of *The Canterbury Tales* is like two mirrors set opposite one another with the "world" of the tales between them. The General Prologue is like a *speculum humanae vitae* reflecting the individuals and the society which produce the tales; the Parson's Tale is like a *speculum moralitatis* reflecting values which apply to the society and the individual. From either end we see the whole reflected from the viewpoint of the individual or the society and then see it reflected again in reverse, and we see the author and ourselves in the picture trying to see it clearly.

This is, I know, a very impressionistic way of talking about structure. But part of the problem is that structure itself can only *be* an impression. We are given models within the work for its form: it is a one-way journey which cannot be retraced except in memory, a performance which in the end will be over, a *florilegium* elaborately constructed with parts interrelated which like all flowers will fade and die. But we are given no models for structure; we have to experience the way units are pieced together and divided up, and we cannot experience this except cumulatively, in retrospect, with an understanding of the rules or theory behind it. The experience is like watching a game. If the watcher does not know the rules, he sees only random events or brute facts[8]— sees a man throw a ball, another hit it with a stick, others run around a diamond-shaped path. If he knows the rules he "sees" bases, innings, strikes. But he sees too that every game

7. See Francis Lee Utley, "The Seven Deadly Sins: Then and Now," *Indiana Social Studies Quarterly* 25 (1972):36–38.

8. My example is imitated from John Searle, *Speech Acts: An Essay in the Philosophy of Language* (Cambridge: Cambridge Univ. Press, 1969), p. 52.

has a structure of its own: because randomness is built into the rules, structure takes shape only as the events unfold and has meaning only when they are over. And, of course, there is always the chance that the rules will be violated, or the scores disputed, or the game "called."

As we read from tale to tale we therefore find themes overlapping, find structures within structures and "meta-structures" which seem to emerge from the smaller structures of pairs and groups. While these are based on "themes"—on content—the deepest structures may be based on dominant visual images which spring naturally from the surfaces of the narratives and lodge in the hearer's or reader's mind, which carry with them associations and meanings that accumulate in memory and make a structure sustained at the deepest level of consciousness. That is, if I understand it correctly, what V. A. Kolve will argue in a forthcoming book;[9] I believe his argument will go far to explain the structure of *The Canterbury Tales*. For we know— and we know it from experience—that reading *The Canterbury Tales* leaves us with something tangible, memorable, and visually lucid; and that for all its complexity the work as it exists in our remembrance is vivid, simple, and striking. All the dramatic or thematic pairing and grouping, all that is detailed, complex, discursive, all that can be seen diminishing into sub-themes or peripheral issues or burgeoning into thematic metastructures, has still a natural place in our experience of the work. Perhaps the visual images with which the work provides us make a frame, like the images associated on "places" in the old systems of artificial memory, so that we remember first these, then a multitude of details associated with each image. But how do we decide which images are "dominant"?

This eidetic structure may be the most important aspect of structure in *The Canterbury Tales* because it is most deeply rooted in our experience of the work, but it is still certain to be thematic. One would expect such images to correspond

9. I know of Kolve's work from his paper, "Aural Narrative and the Memorial Image: Notes toward a Theory of Literary Iconography," presented at the Modern Language Association, New York, 1972.

with major themes. The structure I describe below is not based on images or such formal principles as "dramatic interplay" or "discussion"; it is based on the way the content of one tale relates to the content of another. The work does not prepare us for this structure: when the Host sets up the tale-telling game at the beginning we would never guess that the tales are going to be interrelated in this way. We sense a "grammar"[10] in operation which goes beyond that imposed by the performance or the journey; indeed, the model of the flower-wheel design suggests something ordered and symmetrical, something interrelated and logical, which the structure does not appear to realize.

To understand this structure we need an analogue or model to compare it with. Much of what used to be said about structure in medieval narrative presumed, until a few years ago, dramatic or novelistic models which would have been foreign to medieval authors and readers. The same was true of "unity"; as Robert Jordan has shown,[11] we see unity in the Coleridgean way as something "organic," but the form and structure of medieval works—of literature, and of art and architecture too—is not "organic" but architectonic, disjunctive. Recently Eugène Vinaver has moved the discussion forward by showing how in the history of the romance a thematic mode emerged and a thematic structure evolved; the thematic (as opposed to the fictional) mode is "above all a questioning one," and the structure which emerged was the *interlace*. Vinaver credits Ferdinand Lot with the discovery of this narrative structure:

> In an endeavor to prove that the major part of the "Lancelot-Grail" Cycle was the work of one man (a point which he failed to establish), Lot made the all-important discovery that no single section of the Cycle is self-

10. I have in mind two recent approaches to medieval narrative, Tsvetan Todorov, *Grammaire du Décaméron* (The Hague: Mouton, 1969) and Eugene Dorfman, *The Narreme in the Medieval Romance Epic* (Toronto: Univ. of Toronto Press, 1969), but have been influenced by neither.

11. *Chaucer and the Shape of Creation*, esp. chaps. 1 and 2; see also A. K. Moore, "Medieval English Literature and the Question of Unity," *MP* 65 (1968):285–300.

contained: earlier or later adventures are recalled or
announced, as the case may be, in any given part of the
work. To achieve this the author, or authors, had recourse
to a narrative device known to earlier writers, including
Ovid, but never before used on so vast a scale, namely the
device of interweaving a number of separate themes. Far
from being a mosaic from which any one stone could be
removed without upsetting the rest, the Cycle turned out
to be remarkably like the fabric of matting or tapestry; a
single cut across it, made at any point, would unravel it all.
And yet it was clearly not a unified body of material: it
consisted of a variety of themes, all distinct and yet inseparable from one another. "Everything leads to everything
else, but by very intricate paths. At every point the question 'How did we get here?' arises, but there is always an
answer."[12]

The visual counterpart of this structure is a design we
find often in medieval art, the "ribbon" or floriated design
so common in illuminated manuscripts. Vinaver offers a
number of examples; the most common form of the design
appears to have been a vine with leaves or flowers inter-
twined in an endless knot. Such a design is used within the
initial capitals of the Ellesmere manuscript (see Figures 1
and 2 above). The interlace often has no beginning or end or
center, yet is coherent; it can be geometric and balanced, or
nongeometric and dynamic—it is not unusual to find the one
imposed upon the other.[13] Now of course no such visual
design can prove anything about literary structure; it can at
best illustrate a habit of mind, a way of organizing experience, furnish an image of the way the structure of things
"looked." But such analogies are very attractive: for
example, critics have shown how *Beowulf* is a geometric
"diptych" or bipartite structure, two symmetrical parts put
together back-to-back with a seemingly abrupt juncture
between them; but seen another way this two-part structure
can be a three-part one, and seen closely, it is an interlace.[14]

12. Vinaver, *The Rise of Romance*, pp. 71–72.
13. *Ibid.*, pp. 77–81.
14. John Leyerle, "The Interlace Structure of *Beowulf*," *UTQ* 37 (1967):

It is therefore a structure within a structure. Vinaver shows how this principle of the structure within a structure is illustrated by certain ornamented capital letters; the letter itself is a single, distinguishable form, but integrated with an interlaced ornamental structure. Following Vinaver's example, but using a different illustration, I ask the reader to contemplate the full-page initial D of Psalm 26 in the Tickhill Psalter (Figure 12). It illustrates all the component principles of structure involved—it illustrates much, much more than the inner and outer forms illustrated earlier in Figure 7. Here, as earlier, the dominant form is the letter itself but it contains a set of medallions which show the story of David and Jonathan. These are set in a flower-like circular pattern, their frames interlaced with chainlike links. The story is further illustrated in two drawings at the bottom of the page. We need to know rules—conventions—in order to understand what principles of selection and relation are involved. The outer form of the initial D seems almost to lose its meaning, to be inundated by this inner world of narrative. Yet here we see something which was not present in the earlier illustration: the text proceeds after the initial D in two frames below: "Dominus illuminacio mea et salus mea quem timebo. . . ." This opening verse is set in a diptych design matching the double columns of the succeeding pages. The two lines of lettered text in each column are separated by an interlace design. And these two interlace designs are themselves interlaced at the vertical juncture by two heads which seem to have grown out of the stalk, the faces benignly regarding one another. Wildly complex, needlessly convoluted, overdone—all these charges we may bring against such a design from the standpoint of modern tastes. Yet it is a great piece of medieval art: look at it laid before you by a patient curator on a felt-covered table in the New York Public Library, glorious with gold leaf and brilliant colors and the microscopic craftsmanship of its design, and you

---

1–17. The initial discovery of diptych structure was made by J. R. R. Tolkien in 1936 and independently in the same year by Kellerman and Curtius—see William W. Ryding, *Structure in Medieval Narrative* (The Hague and Paris: Mouton, 1971), pp. 25–27.

feel a shiver up your spine. It is indeed variegated and complicated, with a multiplicity of junctures and interlaces and structures; it is very "Gothic." Yet it is pleasing, and not at all incomprehensible: we can unravel its component principles and describe its form and structure, isolate its themes and meanings. It does have something to say to us. But we must learn its language.

When interlaced structure is executed in a long narrative, Vinaver remarks, "The assumption is not only that the reader's memory is infallible, but that the exercise of such memory is in itself a pleasurable pursuit which carries with it its own reward."[15] There, surely, is the model of structure which will serve us best when we approach *The Canterbury Tales*. There is a "dramatic" structure generated in a natural way by form—by the remembered pilgrimage and the tale-telling game; it has a beginning, middle, and end. Within this self-evident structure there is a series of interlaced, interrelated themes among which "everything leads to everything else"; it has no beginning, no end, and no center, but is all the same coherent.

It is convenient to visualize an interlace as the ribbon design or endless knot which interweaves and has no end; but it is extremely *in*convenient that this analogy leads us to imagine continuous "strands," for that is not what we get. We get instead abrupt transitions, unmotivated entrances and exits, interruptions. The interlaced story is a collection of units pieced together by different kinds of junctures which at once divide and join episodes or groups of episodes. In dream-visions this is particularly evident: we see one episode follow another but must intuit the connection. In *The Book of the Duchess* we see the hunt, then the whelp:

> Therewith the hunte wonder faste
> Blew a forloyn at the laste.
>   I was go walked fro my tree,
> And as I went, there came by me
> A whelp, that fauned me as I stood,
> That had yfollowed, and koude no good.
>
> (385-390)

15. Vinaver, p. 83.

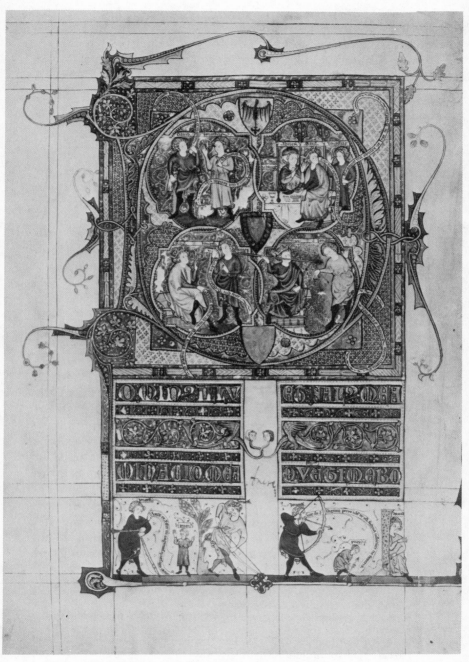

Figure 12. Full page initial D of Psalm 26, with interlace and diptych designs. Tickhill Psalter, Spencer ms. 26, fol. 26ᵛ.

There is no apparent reason for this sequence. The images are disjunctive, like the images of actual dreams as far as their "manifest content" is concerned. We assume there is a meaning to them ("latent content"), but we can only grasp that meaning by understanding *why* the images or episodes are associated and we can only do this by seeing the whole, by reconstructing it in memory and recognizing its correspondence to conscious thought. Hence if we are to see the structure of a narrative interlace we have to focus our attention on these associative points of juncture, these "exposed joints."[16] And when we look at a single specimen we find two narrative units paired in such a way that the first cannot realize its full potential of meaning unless we proceed to the second. The hunt does not mean anything until the whelp appears, and the whelp does not mean anything until he leads us to the hunter. Now it happens that this circumstance, taken in isolation, exactly defines a recognized kind of structure in medieval narrative, the binary or "diptych" structure which we find, for example, in *Beowulf,* the *Roland,* or Mandeville's *Travels.* The essential fact about this binary structure is that the second part adds to the first, asks that the reader see something new or different which changes his perspective on the first. The triumphs of the young Beowulf take on a different light and become part of a larger meaning after we have read of his later triumph-in-death; Mandeville's pilgrimage to the Holy Land takes on a different light and becomes part of a larger meaning after we have read of his travels into the "lands beyond" as far as the earthly paradise which none can enter.

If one takes such a binary structure and makes a concatenation, so that the second part of one pair becomes the first part of the next, and so on, one has the beginning of an interlaced narrative structure.[17] It opens the possibility of

16. The analogy is Jordan's, who speaks of "the exposed joints and seams, the unresolved contradictions, the clashes of perspective," etc., p. 8 and passim. See Ryding, pp. 82–86, on "the principle of free association."

17. Cf. Ryding, pp. 139–154. The frequency of repetition in medieval narrative, its connection with the rhetorical concept of *amplificatio,* and the

interrupting an episode with a new episode, then returning to the interrupted episode. It has a "grammar" of its own, and the morpheme of that grammar is not the "episode" but the diptych structure: narrative unit + juncture + narrative unit. This concatenated binary principle is evident in *The Canterbury Tales*. The General Prologue presents a picture which is altered when we have read the tales; and the story of the pilgrimage—the General Prologue and the world of tales it generates—presents a picture which is altered when we have read the Parson's Tale and Retraction. It is the same within the series of tales: the ideas we have in mind when we have finished the Knight's Tale are thrown into a different light by the Miller's Tale. When Chaucer says we can "turn over the leaf and choose another tale" I believe he has this effect in mind: we turn from one tale to another without forgetting the first, but the second adds something to our experience, and if the tales touch upon a common theme it alters something. If we choose to skip a tale we miss something. True, all—or most—narratives have an effect like this; the present recasts the past as the future will recast the present. But not all *collections* of tales have such an effect; the *Confessio Amantis*, for example, does not. However, the interlaced romances and many dream-visions, which are collections of tales, do have such an effect; and from them I believe Chaucer drew the idea of interlaced thematic structure.[18]

In the sections which follow I will try to describe this interlaced structure of *The Canterbury Tales*. The "themes" of the romance interlace were of course strands of narrative

principle of motif duplication are often mentioned in connection with medieval structures of this kind. Prof. Harry Sieber has suggested to me that an analogue exists in certain medieval verse forms like the zejel, virelay, balade, or rondel.

18. Cf. Ryding's analysis of the *roman à tiroirs*, pp. 43–52, 154 and passim. *The Canterbury Tales* may be described as Ryding describes two types of *roman à tiroirs*—that with a beginning and end, or that with a beginning which leads "only to an arbitrarily designated conclusion" (p. 50). The *groups* of tales I describe might be compared with the *tiroirs* or chest of drawers, but even the groups are thematically interrelated, or so I hope to show, in a way that makes the delightful metaphor of French criticism inapplicable.

events, not ideas; we can find in romances something like a content of ideas, but it is never as complicated or as intellectual as the multiple discussions and viewpoints of *The Canterbury Tales*. In this, Chaucer departed from, and enhanced, the interlace structure of medieval literary traditions. But it is not a surprising stroke of originality. If memory is the essential principle of form in the work, if it is memory that allows multiple viewpoints, multiple degrees of closure, and an open-ended form which admits randomness and unreality, what structure but the interlace could be more appropriate? Interlaced structure is fundamentally questioning and associative; in it—to borrow Lewis's phrase, as Vinaver does—everything leads to everything else, but when we ask at any point "how did we get here" there is always an answer. It strikes me that in our experience of our own memories, memory does seem a self-contained whole in which everything leads perplexingly to everything else. For that reason, one suspects, the ancients and the medievals felt it needed form—"artificial" form—imposed upon it. And for that reason too one suspects that the romance interlace is *au fond* a figure of raw memory, of remembered experience.

To trace such associations in *The Canterbury Tales* and demonstrate an interlaced structure means asking what each tale is about and how each relates to another. So I have to ask the reader's patience in what follows, not just because of its length and its detail but because in spite of that length and that detail it is too short and too simple. One can hardly ever *stop* showing how everything leads to everything else; one can only begin and let the ways and detours tangle suggestively. The trouble is that one has to begin by making it sound easy and has to end in a tangle. That tangle may look like an interlace design in the mind's eye, but I must remind the reader that the design is only an analogy. If it was part of Chaucer's idea it was in his unconscious, as were all such visual counterparts unless stated in the text. At the end of the chapter I will propose a visual counterpart which resembles an interlace, the *labyrinth*. And I will offer some reasons for believing that this labyrinth design lay much closer to the surface of consciousness in Chaucer's mind, that it is more demonstrably a part of the idea of *The Canterbury Tales*, and that it helps explain how structure and form are related in the work.

THE TALES OF CIVIL CONDUCT: FRAGMENT I

The Knight's Tale introduces three thematic strains related to three realms of human conduct: the civil, the domestic, and the private. These were the three areas in which worldly authority was called for—the state or nation, the family or home, and the individual will. The appropriate authority figures are the king or ruler, the husband or father, and the church or conscience.

The major theme of the Knight's Tale is the major theme of all medieval romance—chivalry. Whatever else it may be, the Knight's Tale is a projection about the noble life. It praises valor in warfare, courtesy and honor in interpersonal relationships, and the fame or "glory" which was thought the just reward of noble deeds. The two prisoners in the tale love the same lady; when one escapes and the other is exiled, they come upon each other accidentally in a forest and engage in furious battle. Arcite, in the chivalric spirit, will not fight Palamon until he gets food for him and armor. The battle is stopped by the duke Theseus, who imposes civil restrictions: it must be made a game, a tournament with rules, blunted weapons, and ritual. And the winner of the tournament, Arcite, when the gods take his prize away from him, resigns the lady to the rival in a self-sacrificing manner appropriate to (it is his own word) a "gentleman."

A part of this ethos is the idealized love for the distant and indifferent lady which sets the two young prisoners at odds; this love is in no way conceived as an adulterous relationship—its end, in the minds of the lovers and in fact, is marriage. Later we are to have a group of tales on marriage and domestic life.

The Knight's Tale introduces not only these civil and domestic realms of conduct, but the private realm of thought and moral choice. It is a philosophical romance into which its teller injects chivalric and religious conceptions. The principle of Fortune's Wheel, the principle of the Chain of Love, and the notion that we can make virtue of necessity by resignation are familiar medieval ideas drawn from Boethius. This "Boethian" element in the Knight's Tale has been endlessly remarked on and is its most evident intellectual feature.[19] But the Knight intellectualizes in other respects too: at the end of his first section, for example, he raises a courtly "demande d'amour" of the kind medieval aristocrats evidently liked to entertain: "You lovers axe I now this questioun: / Who hath the worse, Arcite or Palamon?" (1347-1348). And he includes details about the ancient world, the pagan gods, astrology, medicine, and so on. We can view these as his private thoughts and opinions, his mental content. But it should not surprise us that his mental content has much in common with what we might expect from any knight.

The Knight's learning comes not, as a clerk's learning would have, from books, but from a body of lore some of which was preserved in books but most of which was probably passed on orally. It is useful when we think of medieval oral traditions to suppose that there were separate traditions for separate groups—a "folklore" of the people, a "knightlore" of the aristocracy, a "clerklore" among churchmen. Since churchmen were the literate segment of the society, we can suppose that more clerklore was written down than knightlore and folklore. This fact has helped create the impression that all medieval art and thought is religious, but the impression is not true and the Knight's tale shows it is not: the things the Knight thinks about are in part

---

19. The most influential reading of the tale in recent years, that of Muscatine, *Chaucer and the French Tradition*, pp. 175–190, emphasizes the struggle between order and chaos in the tale. Without needing to mention Boethius he shows how the Boethian concept of an ordered universe is rendered in the tale through a conventional and symbolic literary style. Cf. his earlier article, "Form, Texture and Meaning in Chaucer's *Knight's Tale*," *PMLA* 65 (1950):911–929. See also William Frost, "An Interpretation of Chaucer's Knight's Tale," *RES* 25 (1949):289–304, who like Muscatine brushes aside the humor in the tale, and John Halverson, "Aspects of Order in the *Knight's Tale*," *SP* 57 (1960):606–621.

religious, but not exclusively so. He is interested in questions
of honor, courtesy, and valor; in lists, weapons, armor,
tactics—in what Othello called the "quality, pride, pomp, and
circumstance of glorious war." He is interested in the
pageantry of warfare, in the fame or glory due the individual warrior, "service" to a lady, and noble last words. He tells
a story set in a pagan world, and admires in his pagan
characters those qualities which make them chivalric and
philosophical. The forces of destiny in his tale impose order
on what would otherwise seem haphazard events; this is also
an intellectual construct, even a scientific one, for it involves
the stars. When Arcite has won the battle, a "fury infernal"
(2684) makes his horse leap aside and founder; this would
seem a trivial, even ridiculous incident if the fury were not
sent at the behest of Saturn. That such destinal order exists
in the universe is often taken as the theme of the tale. The
lore which the Knight possesses involves an epic and fatalis-
tic way of looking at things, which is probably the way
soldiers need to see life if they are to go on being soldiers.

Chaucer also introduced into the Knight's Tale the
limitation to the secular world which he imposed on the
work as a whole. In the *Troilus* we saw the hero translated
into a timeless realm from which he looks upon the world,[20]
but in *The Canterbury Tales* we never pass out of the world or
out of time. This limitation is introduced at the key scene of
the Knight's Tale, the death of Arcite. In a famous anticli-
max the author makes a point of omitting the soul journey
through the spheres which was in his source:

> Dusked his eyen two, and failed breeth.
> But on his lady yet cast he his eye;
> His laste word was, "Mercy, Emelye!"
> His spirit chaunged house and wente ther
> As I came never, I can nat tellen wher.
> Therefore I stinte, I nam no divinistre. . . .
>   (1806-1811)

Once Arcite is dead we must cast our eyes away from him

---

20. Now fully explored by John M. Steadman, *Disembodied Laughter*:
Troilus *and the Apotheosis Tradition* (Berkeley and Los Angeles: Univ. of
California Press, 1972).

and examine the survivors, for we are on the pilgrimage of human life and the span of our vision is limited to it.

In such speeches as this one Chaucer also introduced a jocular and exaggerated element that seems to call the Knight's convictions into question. For example, while the two heroes are fighting he says "in this wise I let hem fighting dwelle" and turns his attention to Theseus:

> The destinee, ministre general,
> That executeth in the world over all
> The purveiaunce that God hath seen biforn,
> So strong it is that, though the world had sworn
> The contrary of a thing by ye or nay,
> Yet sometime it shall fallen on a day
> That falleth nat eft within a thousand yeer.
> For certainly, our appetites here,
> Be it of wer, or pees, or hate, or love,
> All is this ruled by the sight above.
> This mene I now by mighty Theseus,
> That for to hunten is so desirous,
> And namely at the grete hert in May,
> That in his bed there daweth him no day
> That he nis clad, and redy for to ride
> With hunt and horn and houndes him biside.
> For in his hunting hath he swich delit
> That it is all his joy and appetit
> To been himself the grete hertes bane.
> For after Mars he serveth now Diane.

(1663-1682)

All this machinery is intended to let us know that on a certain day Theseus took it in mind to go hunting. It is impossible not to see a mock-epic quality in such a passage, and hard not to conclude that its purpose is ironic, that it is meant to put us at a distance from the Knight's grandiose ideas of destiny and make us think about them. This humorous element in the Knight's Tale is the most controversial aspect of the tale: where one critic writes it off as an "antidote" to tragedy another puts it at the center of things, but no one denies it is there.[21] It introduces a feature which

21. Muscatine, p. 187, warns the reader "not to convert a deftly admin-

we will experience in many a tale: we read the tale as a dramatic monologue spoken by its teller but understand that some of Chaucer's attitudes spill into it. This feature gives the tale an artistry which we cannot realistically attribute to the teller: I am going to call this *unimpersonated artistry*. In its simplest form it is the contingency that a tale not memorized but told impromptu is in verse. The artistry is the author's, though selected features of the pilgrim's dialect, argot, or manner may still be impersonated. In its more subtle uses it allows a gross or "low" character to use language, rhetoric, or wit above his capabilities. (Sometimes it is coupled with an impersonated *lack* of art, an artlessness or gaucherie which causes a character to tell a bad tale, as in *Sir Thopas,* or to violate literary conventions or proprieties, as in the Knight's Tale.) The effect is that of irony or parody, but this effect is Chaucer's accomplishment, not an impersonated skill for which the pilgrim who tells the tale deserves any compliments.

The "I" in the Knight's Tale who provides this unimpersonated artistry has always been a riddle. One kind of "I" occurs in the descriptions of the temples, where the Knight begins to speak as if he himself had been an eyewitness—

> There saugh I first the derk imagining
> Of Felony, and all the compassing. . . .
>
> (1995-1996)

---

istered antidote for tragedy into an actively satiric strain," but the strain has often been noted, perhaps first by H. B. Hinckley, *Notes on Chaucer* (Northampton, Mass., 1907), p. 113, who thought such passages "out of place." This comic strain is the subject of Paul T. Thurston, *Artistic Ambivalence in Chaucer's Knight's Tale* (Gainesville, Fla.: Univ. of Florida Press, 1968)—see my review in *MLQ* 31 (1970):112–115; and of Edward E. Foster, "Humor in the *Knight's Tale,*" *ChauR* 3 (1968):88–94. About an intrusive bawdry, as suggested passim in Thomas W. Ross, *Chaucer's Bawdy* (New York: Dutton, 1972), there are strong reasons to remain skeptical since this relies so largely on puns; in most cases it is hard to establish that a pun is intentional, harder still to demonstrate its artistic function, and hardest to be sure a medieval audience would have reacted to puns as moderns do. The "etymologies" which were taken so seriously in the Middle Ages as mystical significations were for the most part puns. Of course there are funny puns in Chaucer, but there are reasons why the medievals would not have been titillated by puns as moderns are and would have been awed by them as moderns are not.

Yet saugh I Woodness, laughinge in his rage. . . .
                                        (2011)

Saugh I Conquest, sitting in greet honour . . .
                                        (2028)

Now to the temple of Diane the chaste,
As shortly as I can, I wol me haste. . . .
                                        (2051-2052)

Chaucer had this from Boccaccio; it is a familiar rhetorical device of the Middle Ages—the nonpersonal "I" which Leo Spitzer described,[22] a kind of Everyman. But when Chaucer uses another rhetorical device (*occupatio*) to condense his original, we get an "I" who is not the Knight and not a faceless Everyman, but an author. The most famous example, if one can judge fame by measuring footnotes, is line 1201: "But of that story list me nat to write."

This "I" who writes is certainly Chaucer, not the Knight; the only question is, whether the line was included by mistake or for an artistic purpose. It is often argued that such passages are leftovers from an earlier version not intended for *The Canterbury Tales*. Thus Professor Williams reminds us that "We of the twentieth century . . . may not quite appreciate the difficulties of revision in an age when writers used various scraps of paper, vellum, parchment, and even wax tablets for their work, and scribbled with muddy ink, a feather quill, and no professionally fitted spectacles, in the dim candlelight of drafty closets."[23] Are we then to believe that Chaucer, who was not a stranger to revision, took from his files the first of the Canterbury tales and inserted it without even reading it? If his notion was that every line in every tale should sound like its teller in style and manner, if each tale was to be a dramatic monologue pure and simple, wouldn't he have struck out such passages of ironic self-humor? Any quill pen dipped in some muddy ink would have done it without any difficulty. Or are we to believe that in the dim candlelight and without proper spec-

22. "Note on the Poetic and the Empirical 'I' in Medieval Authors," *Traditio* 4 (1946):414–422.
23. Williams, *A New View of Chaucer*, p. 109.

tacles he didn't notice such a line? Suppose instead that at some level of consciousness Chaucer in this instance intended his *own* voice (not the naive narrator's) to intrude into the Knight's Tale. The effect is not so peculiar if he wrote for oral delivery and included the model of performance in the work: to listeners the author's presence was never forgotten—everyone knew the pilgrims were all roles being played by the poet. Even fourteenth-century *readers* (the Man of Law is an example put before us in the work itself) would have known the author's identity and felt his presence, as we still do.

But if we say this happens, what are we to say it accomplishes? The "I" who writes is bored with writing: after describing Arcite's suffering, for example, he asks "What shold I all day of his woe endite?" (1380) Sometimes he appears to be making fun of the narrative, as when he describes Palamon's imprisonment (1454-1468). He permits moving and dramatic speeches to end abruptly with a curious anticlimactic ring—for example, Arcite's beautiful lament (1563-1571), a moving and courtly utterance, is followed with this bit of stage business:

And with that word he fell down in a trance
A longe time, and after he up sterte.

At one point Chaucer shows the heroes fighting ankle-deep in their own blood—a circumstance hard to arrange even in a bathtub—and adds "And in this wise I let hem fighting dwelle" (1661). The most famous examples come at the very climax of the story, the death of Arcite:

All is tobrosten thilke regioun;
Nature hath no dominacioun.
And certainly, ther Nature wol nat werche,
Farewell physik! go beer the man to chirche!

(2757-2760)

Obviously the purpose is satiric or parodic. As the Knight tells his perfectly serious tale, an "I" emerges; this "I" selects, condenses, writes. He finds the tale not quite so high-minded—finds it unwieldy, sometimes silly—and he permits some of its most dramatic moments to collapse into moments of irony, even into farce or "camp." Who else can this be but the author? The problem is to decide, if we can, what he may be satirizing and how serious a criticism this satire is meant to be. And the trouble is that we cannot be sure until we have read on—until we have got through the *Melibee*, the Nun's Priest's Tale, the Manciple's Tale—and attained a better sense of the author's frame of mind in its broadest dimensions. To get ahead of myself, I will say that I think Chaucer is satirizing not the Knight himself but the knightly mentality, including its literary tastes, and that he is satirizing it with delicate irony—is satirizing something for which he had respect.

The Knight represents the dominant class in medieval society, and his tale is a composite picture of its mentality. The very form of the tale, with its elaborate symmetry and stately, ritual progression, reflects the medieval knights' love of pageantry and game. And the great emphasis in the tale is upon valor or prowess—the knight's ability to vanquish a foe in battle. This value of the medieval knighthood is symbolically represented in Arcite, the "Martian" character: it is set in opposition to the other knightly value, love. Because Palamon symbolizes this phase of medieval knightly preoccupations (he is Venus's knight) the rivalry of the two heroes represents that bit of knightlore which made the lady's love a reward of knightly valor. The lady herself is a distant and unreal figure: she never speaks except in prayer—to the goddess of chastity. It is probably typical of chivalric idealism that this reward, coming at the climactic moment of the story after Arcite has won the battle, is offered in the exiguous form which knights in romances desired: a friendly look.

> And she again him cast a freendlich eye
> (For women, as to speken in commune,
> They follwen all the favour of Fortune)
> And she was all his cheer, as in his herte.
>
> (2680-2683)

It is probably typical of the chivalric spirit, too, that the changeableness of women is underscored here, for the world of chivalry was a man's world and a lady's favor was a

man's reward, something he won and possessed—she was,
we learn, *his* delight in *his* heart.[24] The other reward of
knightly valor was fame. The "Boethian" speeches at the end
are often allowed to overshadow the fact that after Boethius
has had his say Theseus confers fame upon Arcite, offering
a rationale for dying at the height of one's powers:

> And certainly a man hath most honour
> To dien in his excellence and flowr,
> Whan he is siker of his goode name;
> Than hath he doon his freend, ne him, no shame.
> And gladder ought his freend been of his deeth,
> Whan with honour up yolden is his breeth,
> Than whan his name apaled is for age,
> For all forgetten is his vassellage.
> Than is it best, as for a worthy fame,
> To dien whan that he is best of name.
>
> (3047-3056)

A favorable marriage is part of this chivalric system: at the
end Palamon is "living in bliss, in richesse, and in heele"
(3102). The marriage is a happy marriage without jealousy
"or any other tene" (3106). As a cultural ideal this was a very
secular one: knights strove for victory to attain rewards far
from spiritual—"richesse" is among them.

The operation of the planets, which provides the celestial machinery creaking behind the plot and coming up with
a convenient emergency, is a mirror image of the plot itself:
the planets are gods, and therefore a super-race of nobles—
a ruling class which rules the ruling class. The strife between
Palamon and Arcite (lover and warrior) is reflected in the
heavens by the strife between Venus and Mars. Against
these dazzling figures, the goddess Diana is as shadowy as
her devotee Emelye. A powerful male figure, Saturn, grand-
father of Venus, intervenes and settles things as Theseus

24. I prefer this reading of line 2683, which Donaldson gives, to "And
was al his, in chiere, as in his herte" (Baugh) or "And was al his chiere, as in
his herte" (Manly-Rickert, Robinson). If "chiere" means countenance, not
cheer or delight as I take it, the reading "in chiere" must be adopted, but the
thrust of the passage is undisturbed—the sense would be that she was his in
her appearance or look, as (much as) in his heart.

does below. The two kings who fight for Palamon and Arcite, Lygurge and Emetreus, have been shown to represent the Saturnalian and Martian characters respectively:[25] in them we see the outcome shaping up as we see the armies gather. But the celestial plot is scarcely idealized—the gods bicker and dicker like humans, each has a vested interest, they form alliances, and the outcome depends on power (and seniority) rather than on right.

While this over-plot goes on in the sky, the armies gather below:

> For every wight that loved chivalrye,
> And wold, his thankes, han a passant name,
> Hath prayed that he might been of that game;
> And well was him that thereto chosen was.
> For if there fill tomorrwe swich a cas,
> Ye knowen well that every lusty knight
> That loveth paramours and hath his might,
> Were it in Engelond or elleswhere,
> They wold, hir thankes, wilnen to be there—
> To fighten for a lady, *benedicitee!*
> It were a lusty sighte for to see.
>
> (2106-2116)

This picture of knights coming from all over the world to fight for someone else's lady suggests very strongly that their first love was the fighting. The battle is central, yet the attitudes of the three principals, revealed in their prayers, differ. They belong to a warrior class for whom war is the central action in life, but each *thinks* differently. Palamon does not care whether he has victory or not "so that I have my lady in myn armes" (2247). Arcite can see no further than victory, and the statue of Mars promises him that in a single word (2433). The heroine, like a good medieval lady, wishes first chastity, and, failing that, whoever desires her most. The story presents fundamental passions of love and aggression which reduce the principals to an animal-like state; the imagery used of them, drawn from Boetheus, enforces this conception and reveals a degeneration in

25. Curry, *Chaucer and the Mediaeval Sciences*, pp. 119–149.

them.[26] But the knights are saved from this descent into animal behavior by the ruler's imposition of a code. Theseus demands proper civil conduct: the thing must be done fair and square, and the gods (or planets) join in to bring this about.

It is hard to say whether Chaucer viewed the Knight's tale, despite its mannerisms, sympathetically. The Knight himself was presented in the General Prologue as a noble, indeed ideal figure, though from an older order that no longer examined its assumptions. In the tale, civil virtues give the characters and their actions dignity. But this civility is, as perhaps with all imposed codes, an artifice. And its artificial qualities are what impress the Miller.

The Miller demolishes the civility with which the pilgrimage is meant to progress. Drunk, crying out in "Pilate's voice," swearing outrageously, he proposes a "noble tale" (3126) to "quit" the Knight's tale with. Everyone has agreed that the Knight's Tale was "a noble story" (3111), and when the Host suggests that the Monk tell "somewhat to *quite* with the knightes tale" he has in mind something that will match or reward it, "pay back" its noble quality with something equally noble. The Host spies in the Monk a man of sufficient dignity to do this, a clerk rather than a knight. He evidently means for the game to progress with a stately, measured symmetry like that of the preceding tale. The Miller sees what the Host envisages through different eyes. To him a "noble" story is a raucous, funny one, and "quitting" means paying back in a competitive spirit. The civility and order which would make the pilgrimage go on pageantlike, as the Knight's Tale had, is here abruptly shattered. We leave the world of the nobleman for the world of the "cherl." Through a churl's eyes the ceremonious plotting of the Knight's Tale and the Host's ceremonious notion of the pilgrimage itself are a bore. Of course it is unimpersonated artistry, yet one *can* imagine the Miller listening impatiently and drunkenly to the long tale the

26. Jeffrey Helterman, "The Dehumanizing Metamorphoses of the Knight's Tale," *ELH* 38 (1971):493–511.

Knight tells, picking up a key line here and there, grasping the outlines of the situation and plot without being in the least impressed by its ideas and ideals. Chaucer lets the Miller undress the cast of characters in his mind and reclothe them in country garb. As the cast of nobles in the Knight's Tale reflected the cast of gods (or planets), the Miller's cast of ordinary folk reflects the Knight's cast of nobles. For the two noble rivals we get two clerks in two senses of the word, one a university student, the other a minor functionary in the parish church. The lady who is the object of their longing, far from distant and idealized, is a wench. And the older man, worlds different from noble Theseus, is a "riche gnof," stupid and credulous—he is in one the two greatest stock figures of comedy, the gull and the cuckold. We are going to get love among the common people, and the sympathetic characters are going to be the ones who behave naturally and practically.

In the Miller's Tale knightlore is replaced with folklore. We leave the world of legends and noble deeds, the long ago and far away, for the native countryside and the ordinary people, the world of "funny things that happened." It is very droll that the Miller refers to his tale as a "legend and a life" (3141). It is anything but that. Where the Knight's Tale ends pointing to the fact that noble deeds are preserved in a "goode name" (3049) and "a worthy fame" (3055), the Miller's tale ends pointing to "the folk" laughing, swearing, and chit-chatting to each other, "the man was wood, my leeve brother." Each plot ends in exactly the kind of histori-cal moment at which (in real life) such lore originates: in the Knight's Tale the nobles, hushed and respectful, look back upon the name, honor, and worth of a dead hero; in the Miller's Tale the folk gossip and titter over the humiliation of a dupe—they "turned all his harm unto a jape" (3842).

Everyone knows that the Miller's Tale, a splendid story by itself, is made doubly splendid by its backward look at the Knight's Tale. With repeated lines snatched from key moments in the Knight's story, with fancy love-talk used incongruously, with a parallel situation prompted by motives of a wholly different character, with farts and hot coulters for a tournament, the Miller's Tale parodies the literary qualities of the Knight's and ridicules the circumstance it describes, the resolution it comes to, and the tone in which it is told. But the Miller's Tale is given a further dimension by its forward-looking reference to the Reeve's Tale. We know from its prologue that the Reeve takes exception to it in advance. With cold self-righteousness the Reeve interrupts, "Stint thy clappe!" and tries to shut the Miller up. (The Miller answers with feigned civility, "leve brother Osewold . . ." and taunts the Reeve for a cuckold.) We can be pretty sure how the touchy Reeve will respond.

As the Miller's Tale makes us look back on the Knight's through different eyes, we can suppose the Reeve's will make us look back on the Miller's through different eyes, and we are not disappointed. When we get to the Reeve's Tale we leave the world of the Miller's ebullience for the Reeve's acerb, crabbed view of things. The well-known contrast of their characters is as perfect in its symmetry as anything in the Knight's Tale, but far from ceremonious. The Miller is in the prime of life, robust, sanguine, open and effervescent (he rides at the front of the procession playing a bagpipe); the Reeve is old, thin, choleric, and suspicious (he rides at the rear of the procession). So when the Reeve constructs a plot along the same lines Chaucer lets him reclothe the characters in a suitable way. The two rivals are friends, both university clerks (from Cambridge rather than Oxford), and two ladies are provided for a double cuckolding. Where Emelye was a distant, idealized figure and Alisoun a sexpot, the Reeve produces the priggish, uppity Miller's wife and the pathetic, overprotected daughter whose elders' pretensions have kept her unmarried to the advanced age of twenty. There is nothing spiritually or sexually desirable about either of these women. The wife is "proud" and "pert" (3950), "as digne as water in a dich"; we see her dispense her "hoker" and "bisemare" the first time she speaks:

> Allas! your horse goth to the fen
> With wilde mares, as fast as he may go.

Unthank come on his hand that bond him so,
And he that better shold han knit the reine!

(4080-4083)

The daughter, a fledgling spinster, is described in such a way as to make it plain that she is a stout country girl: one can fairly assume from the four-line description of her (3973-3976) that she is fat, with a flat nose, broad hips, and big breasts (she has, it is conceded, nice hair). When the two clerks hop into bed with these two women, the emphasis is not on healthy pleasure, as in the Miller's Tale, but on the vindictiveness of the situation. The clerks plainly have a good time; so do the women. The Reeve lets us know about the wife "so murry a fit ne had she not full yore" (4230), a low blow to the Miller. The daughter, it is no less plain, enjoys what one may take as her first amorous experience: she cries when her "lemman" leaves her and betrays her father by telling where the stolen grain is to be found. As we move from the world of the Knight into the worlds of the Miller and Reeve the parallels in plot structure simply point up how everything changes—the people, their motives, their conduct, the way they talk and think, even the quality of the sex act itself.

To the Miller, civility is a mask for earthier, and to him healthier, motives; to the Reeve civility is pure sham masking meanness and guile. The civility which Nicholas and Alisoun display to each other in the opening scene is the most perfunctory gloss over their real motives and feelings. Before either has said a word, "prively he caught hir by the queynte" (3276). The courtly love parlance accompanying the gesture is hilarious: "for deerne love of thee, lemman, I spille." The pun on "spille" (a triple pun, it may be) is scarcely out of keeping, and it is no surprise that he holds her by the haunchbones, that she springs as a colt in the trave, and that refusing a kiss she cries, "Do way your handes—for your curteisye!" The traditional hesitancy of the lover and hauteur of the lady are suggested by this kind of language, so that Nicholas's hasty suit and her prompt response seem more earthy by contrast. When Nicholas confronts John, his very civil tone—"John, myn hoste, lief

and deere" (3501)—is funny because it masks a blatantly
sexual purpose and contrasts with John's loutish credulity.

Turn to the Reeve's Tale and you find a more oleagin-
ous civility masking baser motives. The wholesome sexuality
of the Miller's Tale is replaced in the Reeve's by theft,
distrust, and plain malevolence. The two clerks are extraordinarily civil to the miller Symkyn. Everything is hearty
greetings and polite questions:

> Aleyn spak first, "All hail, Symond, in faith!
> How fares thy faire doghter and thy wif?"
> "Aleyn, welcome," quod Symkyn, "by my lif!
> And John also, how now, what do ye here?"
>
> (4022-4025)

The clerks play a charade in which they profess interest in
the marvelous workings of the mill, their purpose to keep an
eye on Symkyn. And Symkyn's thought makes their civility
the more a sham:

> This miller smiled of hir nicetee,
> And thought, "All this nis done but for a wile.
> They wene that no man may hem biguile,
> But by my thrift, yet shall I blere hir eye. . . ."
>
> (4046-4049)

When Symkyn the miller has loosed the clerks' horse, civility
disappears. John puts the blame on Aleyn and calls him a
fool; the miller steals the corn; John knows (4111) the corn is
stolen and that men will call them fools. When they ask the
miller for lodging his reply is venomous:

> The miller said again, "If there be eny,
> Swich as it is, yet shall ye have your part.
> Myn house is streit, but ye han lerned art—
> Ye can by argumentes make a place
> A mile brood of twenty foot of space.
> Lat see now if this place may suffise,
> Or make it rowm with speech, as is your guise."
>
> (4120-4126)

In John's response to this sarcasm ("Ay is thou mirye") the
hearty politeness has now degenerated to the merest masquerade. He knows that he will get nothing except for

money, and he thinks, as he soon says, that he deserves some "esement."

Similarly, the Miller views intellect with a healthy unaca-demic approval as a means to further vested sexual inter-ests; the Reeve sees intellect as trickery. Neither view is anything like the respectful treatment of wisdom and intellect in the Knight's Tale, where the "Boethian" speeches probe the meaning of life and introduce sound morality.[27] In the Knight's Tale we have wise old men and just rulers; in the Miller's and Reeve's tales we get clerks, young college students from the two universities, whose wits are put to practical purposes and who are amusingly outwitted by antagonists of lesser education. In the Miller's Tale, Nicholas's knowledge of astrology is useful: he can foretell the weather. We see him use his reputation as a seer when he fools the old carpenter into believing the flood is to come. In the Reeve's Tale, there is nothing like the elaborate game Nicholas plays. Nicholas makes the boast that "A clerk hadde litherly biset his while / But if he coud a carpenter biguile," but the two clerks in the Reeve's Tale make no such boast. "Him boes serve himself that has no swayn, / Or elles he is a fool, as clerkes sayn," says John. But the clerks plot nothing clever; they only seize an opportunity. Symkyn the miller, in his thoughts and later in open words, sneers at the clerks' learning. When he has succeeded in duping them he openly mocks them—by "arguments," he says, they can make space where there is none. In fact the one bit of intellect or con-ventional wisdom which the Reeve himself offers in his tale has to do with guile:

> "Him thar nat wene well that yvele dooth";
> A guilour shall himself biguiled be.
>
> (4320-4321)

In the Miller's Tale there is a wealth of puns, verbal echoes, and allusions which give it scope and dimension;[28] in

27. See Bloomfield, "The Miller's Tale—An UnBoethian Interpreta-tion," in *Medieval Literature and Folklore Studies*, ed. Mandel and Rosen-berg, pp. 205–211.

28. Cf. Muscatine, "*The Canterbury Tales:* Style of the Man and Style of the Work," in *Chaucer and Chaucerians*, ed. Brewer: "*The Miller's Tale*

the Reeve's Tale there is less of this. The references to the Knight's Tale that occur in the Miller's Tale, the allusions to courtly love, the idiom of popular poetry, and some references to the traditions of biblical exegesis have been demonstrated in detail by various scholars. When we find in this farmyard setting words like "derne," "gent," "rode," "love-longinge," "brid," or "oore" we are aware that a whole tradition of knightlore preserved in love songs is being exploited for its incongruous and comic effect.[29] There is a squinting reference to biblical traditions about Absolon's hair, and there are beyond a question references to the Song of Songs.[30] (Whether the blacksmith suggests the devil,[31] or the three principal characters correspond to the three temptations,[32] I have some doubts.) But these references to religious traditions likewise buttress the humor of the situation and point up the folly of the characters not less than they point up the follies of courtly love itself and the excesses of exegetical interpretation. Obviously the Miller is not up to providing his tale with this substratum of learned and literary allusion: Chaucer himself provides it—he intrudes on the dramatic monologue as he had done in the Knight's Tale. It is unimpersonated artistry—it is in the tale but could not be put there by its teller. But in the Reeve's Tale there is little unimpersonated artistry—we get few allusions to knightlore or clerklore.[33] Chaucer removes himself, makes

manages to remain fabliau, but there was never such a profound one. The tale needs its rich elaboration of courtly conventionalism to make such comic capital of its assertion of naturalness" (p. 111); "The style that supports ordinary fabliau comedy in *The Shipman's Tale* is made specially acerb in *The Reeve's Tale*. The latter has a special sharpness in its descriptions, a special irony created by its use of dialect, which are acutely well suited to the Reeve's attitudes" (p. 105).

29. E. Talbot Donaldson, "Idiom of Popular Poetry in the Miller's Tale," *Speaking of Chaucer*, pp. 13–29.

30. Paul E. Beichner, "Absolon's Hair," *MS* 12 (1950):222–233, and "Characterization in *The Miller's Tale*," in S & T, pp. 117–129; and R. E. Kaske, "The *Canticum Canticorum* in the *Miller's Tale*," *SP* 59 (1962): 479–500.

31. Edmund Reiss, "Daun Gerveys in the *Miller's Tale*," *PLL* 6 (1970): 115–124; my doubts are recorded in "Medieval Poems and Medieval Society," *M&H*, 3 (1972): 104–109.

32. Robertson, *Preface to Chaucer*, pp. 382–386.

33. We do get word play in the Reeve's Tale, but it does not have the

the tale realistic in a straightforward way. It is the only tale whose language imitates speech realistically: the Reeve starts out speaking in the dialect of East Anglia, the clerks speak northern dialect. The language approximates the actual speech of people as they really talked; there is little convergence of a literary or learned language.

What the Cook's Tale would have contributed to this sequence we cannot know. The Cook is a revolting figure; his name, Roger Ware, was the name of a London cook who lived at the time,[34] so perhaps Chaucer set out here to pay off a debt. His "mormal" suggests filthy personal habits and we learn that he serves warmed-over food. He is a minor shopkeeper in business for himself; the fact that he calls the Host by his name, Harry Bailly (which was the name of an innkeeper who lived at the time),[35] suggests that they know each other in a professional way, and that we have here the beginning of a squabble between a cook and an innkeeper based on the same sort of natural enmity that existed between millers and reeves. The byplay between them in the Cook's Prologue results in the Cook's intention to "quit" the Host, but there is no suggestion that the Host will reply in kind. It may be that the Cook's Tale was intended as the last of this sequence. Why it was not finished, even *if* it was not finished, who can say? Possibly it was finished but too scurrilous to be transcribed, and so went underground. Possibly Chaucer or someone else suppressed it, ripped it out of an early copy leaving only what was on the same folio with the ending of the Reeve's Tale. From the fifty-seven lines we have of it we can recognize the beginning of a plot quite like that of the three previous tales. There is an eligible female, the "wife" mentioned in lines 4421-4422; about her we learn the startling detail—it is the last phrase in the fragment—that she kept a shop and "swyved for hir sus-

---

parodic effect of the allusions in the Miller's Tale. Critics have shown echoes of an aube, the service of compline, and various puns; but the word play is scattered, is there for its own sake. In the Miller's Tale it is integrated with the parody of courtly love.

34. See Edith Rickert, "Chaucer's Hodge of Ware," *Times Literary Supplement,* October 20, 1932, p. 761.

35. Manly, *Some New Light on Chaucer,* pp. 77–83.

tenance." There are perhaps to be, for the hand of this "swyving" lady, two rivals: Perkyn Revelour, the sacked apprentice, and his "compeer" who it happens is the lady's husband. It stands to reason that the older man in the picture might be the master vitailler described at the beginning, for the Cook has professed that he will tell a tale about a hosteler (4360). More than that we do not know. The plot never gets off the ground, and there is not a word of dialogue. Since no source is known for the Cook's Tale, it is sometimes thought Chaucer meant here to tell a tale of London low-life out of his own experience, and the story might well have been more unsavory than the Reeve's—the fact that the two young men are not clerks but riotous servants recommends this view, as does the fact that the wife "swyved" for her living.

In this sequence of tales, Knight-Miller-Reeve-Cook, there is a degenerative movement. We begin with something magnificent and end with something gross—how much more gross than the Reeve's Tale the Cook's was meant to be, we can only guess. This degeneration takes place in almost all respects. In social class we move from the behavior of princes and knights to that of minor clerks, peasants, tradesmen, and finally an apprentice. In setting we move from the ancient world, fabled and ideal, to the country, from there to urban low-life. The Knight's vision of the world is one of order, but the tales which follow present an increasing chaos—in the Miller's Tale we get horseplay with farts and hot coulters and cries of "Water," in the Reeve's tale a Faulknerian scene with a runaway horse, a chase, an exchange of beds in the dark, and a general mêlée. The language of the tales proceeds from the high rhetoric of the Knight through the plain talk of the Miller to the dialect of the Reeve. We go from the artificial and literary parlance of the noble life to the natural speech of country folk—perhaps in the Cook's tale we would have got the argot of the gutter. The endings of the tales encapsulate this degeneration of mood perfectly. The Knight's Tale ends:

Thus endeth Palamon and Emelye;
And God save all this faire compaignye! Amen

The Miller's Tale ends:

> Thus swived was this carpenteres wif,
> For all his keeping and his jalousye;
> And Absolon hath kist hir nether eye;
> And Nicholas is scalded in the toute.
> This tale is done, and God save all the route!

The Reeve's Tale ends with less dignity than the Knight's and less buoyancy than the Miller's; the Reeve is more loquacious, detailed, and moralistic, and he is venomous as the others are not:

> Thus is the proude miller well ybete,
> And hath ylost the grinding of the whete,
> And payed for the sopper everydel
> Of Aleyn and of John, that beet him well.
> His wife is swived and his doghter als.
> Lo, swich it is a miller to be fals!
> And therefore this proverb is said full sooth,
> "Him thar nat wene well that yvele dooth";
> A guilour shall himself biguiled be.
> And God, that sitteth heighe in magestee,
> Save all this compaignye, grete and smalle!
> Thus have I quit the Miller in my tale.

In line with this degeneration of mood, the lovers in the tales become more opportunistic: in the Knight's Tale, though the two young warriors act on the principle that all is fair in love, a set of scruples and a principle of justice is imposed by Theseus. In the Miller's Tale, Nicholas throws scruples to one side and plans things to get what he wants. In the Reeve's Tale there is not even planning—the clerks hop into the ladies' beds because they are there. Heaven only knows what might have happened in the Cook's Tale.

As we move from ideals toward realities, Chaucer's voice disappears from the tales: in the Knight's Tale we are aware of the author's intrusive voice providing a running ironic commentary on the tale's elegant symmetry; in the Miller's Tale the parody of love conventions is an intrusion of the author's voice; but the narrative voice in the Reeve's Tale is the Reeve's. We are scarcely aware of the author's presence. He has left us on our own in a world from which civility has disappeared. After two concatenated pairs plus a fragment, the theme is abandoned; and the effect would likely have been the same if the Cook's Tale were complete. As in an interlaced structure we are left at this juncture only with a questioning spirit and are led only to something else.

THE TALES OF DOMESTIC CONDUCT: FRAGMENTS III, IV, AND V

The tales of Fragments III, IV, and V, it has always been understood, deal with marriage or domestic harmony, a subject introduced in the Knight's Tale but not central in it or in the tales following it, where the domestic realm is violated with uncivil shenanigans. Milton saw the Wife's subject as the "discommodities of marriage." In 1908 Eleanor Prescott Hammond christened these tales the Marriage Group; in 1912, Kittredge, renaming the sequence a discussion of marriage, characterized it as a dramatic unit treating a common theme.[36] He proposed that it begins with the Wife of Bath's Prologue and Tale, is interrupted by the tales of the Friar and Summoner, is resumed in the Clerk's story of the patient Griselda and the Merchant's story of January and May, is interrupted again by the Squire's Tale, and is concluded by the Franklin. Kittredge's premise was that the "marriage group" ended with the Franklin's proposing a compromise between courtly love and Christian marriage as a way of establishing domestic concord, and that the solution was "what Chaucer thought about marriage."

36. Hammond, *Chaucer: A Bibliographical Manual* (New York: Macmillan, 1908), p. 256. Kittredge, "Chaucer's Discussion of Marriage," *MP* 9 (1912):435–467; rpt. S & T, pp. 130–159, who add a note (p. 158) on subsequent treatments. Some critics, like Hinckley and Malone, have denied that these tales are a group of any kind; others, like Lawrence, Neville, and Dempster, have argued that other tales—the Squire's, the Nun's Priest's, and *Melibee*—are part of it. To this continuing discussion my own contribution, of which the present section is derivative, was "The Conclusion of the Marriage Group," *MP* 57 (1960):223–232; but as the reader will see I no longer hold the opinion expressed there that the group ends with the Second Nun's Tale.

If the theme of the group is marriage, we need to understand the frame of reference in which the Middle Ages viewed marriage and domestic life: Kittredge did not point this up, though the Wife herself makes it clear. When the Wife speaks of the "woe that is in marriage" she associates marriage at once with the medieval idea of "perfection," which placed the highest value on celibacy; widowhood was second best and marriage third. Accepting this condition with a certain gusto, the Wife proceeds to discuss the question of "sovereignty" in marriage; to this problem the Franklin presents a solution. The big question which the Wife introduces, whether one can marry and still follow Christ's command "Be ye therefore perfect," gets dropped along the way. The Wife's Prologue and Tale present a remarkably integrated conception: we learn first off in the General Prologue that the Wife was "somedeel deef," but do not learn until the prologue to her tale the reason for her deafness:

> Now wol I say you sooth, by Saint Thomas,
> Why that I rent out of his book a leef
> For which he smoot me so that I was deef.
>
> (III:666-668)

The book is the famous Book of Wicked Wives from which her fifth husband read her antifeminist writings and exempla. This body of clerklore haunts her—she is appealing for her *joie de vivre* and wondrous loquacity, but these qualities are energized by the yearning and uncertainty we sense in her. "Alas," she sighs, "that ever love was sinne."

Her ideas are in keeping with orthodox thought. One could command righteousness and obedience to the law of the Church, but one could only "counsel" perfection.[37] The

---

37. Perfection was the goal of the monastic life, and the Wife seems to be thinking of monasticism when she says Christ did not bid every man to sell all that he has and follow Him (107–110), since this text (Matt. 19:21) was the customary scriptural sanction for monasticism. On Christian perfection see the article by Frederic Platt in Hastings' *Encyclopaedia of Religion and Ethics*, 9 (1970):728–737, and that by A. Fonck in *Dictionnaire de théologie catholique*, 12:1219–1251. See also R. Newton Flew, *The Idea of Perfection in Christian Theology* (1934; rpt. Oxford: Clarendon Press, 1968),

result was a notion of "degrees" or "grades." With respect to
sexual matters medieval theologians characteristically
devised a system of three—marriage, widowhood, and
virginity. Using the parable of the sower (Matt. 13:3-23), the
Fathers conjectured that these grades produced different
amounts of return.[38] By this device, St. Paul's view that it is
better to marry than to burn (1 Cor. 7:9) was turned into a
tidy system in which marriage was allowable and righteous
but less meritorious than widowhood or virginity. Marriage
after the death of one's spouse was therefore the least
perfect choice: "widowhood" was the circumstance in which
a person married once and not again—the Wife, now a
widow for the fifth time, has lost her chance. Behind this
system lay the assumption that sexual intercourse for
pleasure is wrong, that even in marriage intercourse performed to satisfy lust is a venial sin.[39] The Parson quotes St.
Jerome to this effect.[40] St. Augustine agreed that remarriage
was allowable but that it was better for a widow not to
remarry. Going on the same principle, Augustine held that it
was more desirable if "even during the life of her husband,
by his consent, a female vow continence unto Christ":[41] the

and Bloomfield, "Some Reflections on the Medieval Idea of Perfection,"
rpt. *Essays and Explorations*, pp. 29–55. On the controversy about women
and marriage, see M. A. Screech, *The Rabelaisian Marriage: Aspects of
Rabelais's Religion, Ethics and Comic Philosophy* (London: Edward Arnold,
1958), pp. 5–27; on the idea that continence is a special gift which not
everyone can expect to attain (the Wife's argument), pp. 68–71.

38. On the three grades of chastity, see Ambrose, *De viduis* IV:23 (*PL*
16:254–255) and *Epistola* LXIII, 40 (*PL* 16:1251). See also Augustine, "On
the Good of Widowhood," 1–5, in *A Select Library of the Nicene and Post
Nicene Fathers of the Christian Church*, ed. Philip Schaff, III (Buffalo, 1887),
pp. 441–443 and passim (this English translation is used in the text). For a
short history of the idea, see Matthäus Bernards, *Speculum Virginum:
Geistigkeit und Seelenleben der Frau im Hochmittelalter*, Forschungen zur
Volkskunde, ed. G. Schreiber, Band 36–38 (Cologne and Graz, 1955), pp.
40ff. And see Bloomfield, "Piers Plowman and the Three Grades of
Chastity," *Anglia* 76 (1948):227–253, as well as his *Piers Plowman as a
Fourteenth-Century Apocalypse* (New Brunswick, N.J.: Rutgers Univ. Press,
1961), esp. chaps. 2 and 3.

39. Augustine, "On the Good of Marriage," 6 (Schaff, pp. 401–402)
and 18 (p. 407).

40. Parson's Tale, X:904f.

41. "On the Good of Widowhood," 13 (Schaff, p. 446); cf. 6 and 15
(pp. 443, 446–447).

chaste marriage of the Virgin Mary was the ideal marriage.[42] Chaucer was familiar with these opinions, for he offered a summary of them in the Parson's Tale (X:915-950), and he offered an example of such a marriage in the Second Nun's Tale.

The idea that there are grades of perfection expresses the very conflict in medieval thought which troubles the Wife. Virginity was the dart set up, as she puts it, for Christians to aim at, but only a privileged few were called to that state. The Wife acknowledges, as was generally believed, that women are less reasonable than men (she uses this as an argument for her husband's having greater patience), but the clerkish estimate of women understandably rankles her:

> By God! if women hadde written stories,
> As clerkes han within hir oratories,
> They wold han written of men more wickednesse
> Than all the mark of Adam may redresse.
>
> (693-696)

Perhaps to this extent she takes issue with received opinion and makes the "first female declaration of independence in English literature," but it is hard to fault her theology. Fallen man, everyone knew, could not be expected to follow the highest counsels of perfection, and those not specially called should not envy those in higher states of perfection than themselves. The Wife accepts this circumstance when she says she "nil envy no virginitee" (142) and "that am nat I" (112). The enthusiasm with which she accepts it, and the astrological determinism by which she palms it off on the stars (609-620) doubtless violate the spirit of medieval morality—she makes it sound inevitable and natural; and the way she speaks about "engendrure," her "quoniam," her "purveiaunce" in husband-seeking, and her having had "my world as in my time" makes it sound like fun. In recent years it has become a habit to berate her as a sinner. This wouldn't surprise her: she herself says

42. "On Holy Virginity," 4 (Schaff, p. 418).

> . . . it is an impossible
> That any clerk wol speke good of wives,
> But if it be of holy saintes lives,
> Ne of noon other woman never the mo.
>
> (688-691)

The Clerk himself grants that "clerkes praise women but a lite" (IV:935). Clerkish critics of the present day respond to her as she expects some at least of the pilgrims to respond—there is a side of her that wants to *épater les bourgeois*.

She *is* a sinner, like the rest of us, of course, but she sins less in deed than in thought and word. Try making a list of her sins and you will hardly find a deadly one among them. When she tells us that her fourth husband had a paramour, she says she "made him of the same wood a croce," but she quickly adds "nat of my body in no foul mannere." We learn she had "swich dalliaunce" with Jankyn in the fields where they walked, and that she earmarked him for her next husband before his predecessor was dead; at the funeral we see her eyeing his "pair / Of legges and of feet so cleen and fair." But we don't really know what sort of "dalliaunce" she had had with him. Chaucer tells us in the General Prologue she had had five husbands "withouten other compaigny in youthe," but the line is similarly ambiguous. We may suspect her of being an adulteress, but it is part of Chaucer's game that we cannot come up with any evidence. In the same way we may assume that she is childless, but we are never so informed. Lecherous pleasure in the marriage bed with her fifth husband—yes, we may accuse her of that; but it was classed a venial sin.[43] What we know of her *deeds* makes her seem a delightfully imperfect adherent of the lowest grade of perfection. She is unambiguously a sinner in thought and word, but her thoughts and her words—her whirlwind stream-of-consciousness and her gift of gab—are what make her one of the richest characters in all of literature.

---

43. See n. 39 above, and Eugene E. Slaughter, "Allas! Allas! That Ever Love Was Sinne," *MLN* 49 (1934):83–86; opinion differed about the gravity of the sin.

Her most serious "heresy" is not any of her opinions about perfection, marriage, or sex, but her opinion that the wife should have the "sovereignty" in marriage. Medieval wives were expected to love, honor, and obey, so her opinion is heterodox. But this very opinion is what delights every reader. Why? Partly because she gives expression to it in such a lively way, but partly, too, because she does not quite manage to convince us: her fifth husband and she had a happy marriage after he resigned "all the sovereignety" to her, but she got it by playing on his guilt and he resigned it willingly. His submission in their marriage is government with the consent of the governed; besides, she is old enough to be his mother. Her quick mind and practiced tongue bring off a brilliant tour de force and start a splendid discussion—it is potentially serious matter, and the men all hear it. "Dame," says the Friar,

> . . . God yeve you right good life.
> Ye han heer touched, also mot I thee,
> In scole-mattere greet difficultee.
> Ye han said muche thing right well, I saye.
> But dame, here as we riden by the waye,
> Us needeth nat to speken but of game,
> And let auctoritees on Goddes name
> To preeching and to scole eek of clergye.
>
> (1270-1277)

The Merchant has his character Justinus, finishing his discourse on the woes of marriage, say

> But lat us waden out of this mattere.
> The Wife of Bath, if ye han understonde,
> Of marriage, which we have on honde,
> Declared hath full well in litel space.
>
> (1684-1687)

The Clerk even introduces his song with a reference to her:

> For which here, for the Wives love of Bathe—
> Whose life and all hir secte God maintene
> In heigh maistrie, and elles were it scathe—
> I wol with lusty herte, fresh and greene,
> Sayn you a song to glade you, I wene;
> And lat us stint of ernestful mattere.
>
> (1170-1175)

She has made a great impression on the men, but they would all as soon brush aside this *mattere*.

It is easy to understand why her opinions about sovereignty generate a "discussion of marriage," but the tale she tells really undercuts her feminist views, reveals something about her we could only have suspected, something she doesn't know herself. Freud is said to have told Marie Bonaparte, "The great question that has never been answered and which I have not yet been able to answer, despite my thirty years of research into the feminine soul, is 'What does a woman want?'" Chaucer managed to understand on instinct something about this question, and he gave expression to that understanding by having the Wife herself pose the question and answer it unwittingly. In one of her digressions she has said why she loved her fifth husband best:

> We women han, if that I shall nat lie,
> In this mattere a queynte fantasie;
> Waite what thing we may nat lightly have,
> Therafter wol we cry all day and crave.
> Forbede us thing, and that desiren we;
> Press on us fast, and thanne wol we flee.
>
> (515-520)

Her tale, if it is an exemplum,[44] exemplifies this point. But it comes closer to being a "queynte fantasie" than an exemplum—a wish-fulfillment fantasy in which an old ugly hag is transformed into a beautiful young girl, a handsome husband provided, male dominance surrendered, and a happy marriage established. What more could any woman want? The Wife's notion in her prologue that women want most what they cannot have is narrowed down in her tale: her "lusty bacheler," guilty of rape, can save his life by going on a quest to find out "what thing is it that women most desiren" (905). She provides a compendium of possible answers to the question, the diverse opinions the knight hears in his quest concluding with a tale from Ovid—an exemplum within an

---

44. See Robert P. Miller, "*The Wife of Bath's Tale* and Medieval Exempla," *ELH* 32 (1965):442–456.

exemplum; when he meets the hag, she demands that he
fulfill the next thing she asks of him, then whispers the truth
in his ear. At court he reports his findings, and all agree he is
right:

> Women desiren to have sovereigntee
> As well over hir husbond as hir love,
> And for to been in maistrie him above.
> This is your most desire. . . .
>
> (1038-1042)

Given the dependency status of women in medieval society,
this bears out the Wife's notion that women want most "what
thing we may nat lightly have." True, she ends asking short
life for husbands that won't be governed by their wives and
for "old and angry niggards of dispence," and prays that
women get "Husbondes meeke, young, and fresh abedde"
plus the grace to outlive them. But this is a coda; the tale
itself has a surprise ending. When the subdued husband and
the transformed hag are united, we learn at the end:

> And she obeyed him in every thing
> That mighte do him plesance or liking.
>
> (1255-1256)

The wife's obedience here is comparable to the "happy
ending" of the Wife's prologue: the fifth husband, having
submitted to her, never had any more trouble. She says:

> . . . I was to him as kinde
> As any wife from Denmark into Inde
> And also trewe, and so was he to me.

What the Wife really wants, and what she unwittingly
suggests women want, is a *token* submission on the part of the
husband[45]—they want the "maistry" in marriage, but when
they have it they want not to exercise it. It is an ambivalent

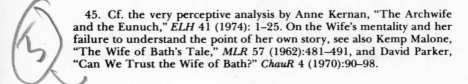

45. Cf. the very perceptive analysis by Anne Kernan, "The Archwife
and the Eunuch," *ELH* 41 (1974): 1–25. On the Wife's mentality and her
failure to understand the point of her own story, see also Kemp Malone,
"The Wife of Bath's Tale," *MLR* 57 (1962):481–491, and David Parker,
"Can We Trust the Wife of Bath?" *ChauR* 4 (1970):90–98.

wish typical of human nature, and as true of men as of women. We want to be dependent and independent both, and much of the time we don't know what we want. Probably happiness in marriage, or in any interpersonal relations, depends on the sorting-out of these conflicting desires; if there is such a thing as mutuality in human relationships it must be based on an *entente cordiale* between the desire for omnipotence and the desire for love. The Wife in her roundabout way gets at such a fundamental truth about human nature that the rest of the "marriage group" seems like sound and fury. She diverts the discussion from perfection to "maistry," and from "maistry" to what a woman wants. You can't read any of the other tales without thinking about what you've learned from the Wife, that neither men or women fully know what they want and most often want it both ways. The structure of the group has the quality of a digression which trails away from the heart of the matter.

The other tales of the "marriage group" fall into three pairs: the Friar's and Summoner's, the Clerk's and Merchant's, the Squire's and Franklin's. Even the manuscript fragments pair them this way. And all relate back to the Wife's discourse.

Friar and Summoner

The Friar's and Summoner's tales are prepared for even before the Wife has launched into her tale. The Friar laughs and makes a harmless comment: "Now, dame, . . . / so have I joy or bliss, / This is a long preamble of a tale" (830-831). Since the Wife has used the friars' methods[46] to confound received values placed on male dominance, virginity, and the single life, it is easy to understand why the Friar would as soon let the matter drop. But there isn't any obvious reason why the Friar's harmless words at the end of her Prologue should trip off such a burst of hostility in the Summoner: we know summoners and friars were naturally in competition

---

46. I.e., "glossing." See Robertson, *Preface to Chaucer*, pp. 317–331.

with each other, that the friars were not under the jurisdiction of bishops and so had immunity from such officers as the summoners, but why does this animosity crop up here after the Wife's rambling prologue and not someplace else? The Wife has just given a testimonial to her own skill at subduing males; on the surface her "confession" is a blow to male vanity. She gets up the competitive hackles of the men and provokes their hostile energy, but she is a formidable opponent, and a woman: no one sets out to refute her arguments, and no one can punch her in the nose. They respond to her as men still often respond to outspoken women, with "repressive tolerance"—with the Friar's gentle put-down ("Perhaps you had better leave these matters to experts"), the Clerk's irony, the Merchant's cynicism, the Franklin's "gentilesse." All the male defenses are up. And for that reason it is a likely moment for the Friar and Summoner to have at each other.

The Friar's attack is deft. He shows a summoner willingly in league with the devil and demonstrates that devils have a better sense of honor. The Friar projects upon the fiend his own training in subtle distinctions—the fiend divines the intentions of the carter's hyperbolic oath against his horse and the old widow's heartfelt oath against the summoner (she curses on her knees!), and so ignores the carter's offerings but accepts the widow's.[47] The Friar cleverly ends his tale by praying aloud that the Summoner repent. The Summoner's reply takes an altogether different tone. He cannot control his anger, and bursts forth with the widespread bit of folklore which would have an enemy's place in Hell in the devil's "ers."

Satire in its most primitive form is a way of cursing;[48] at base the Summoner and Friar wish each other a place in

47. Francis Lee Utley in a paper called "Boccaccio and Chaucer and the International Popular Tale," presented at a conference on Folklore and Medieval Literature at the Ohio State University, 1973, forthcoming in *Western Folklore*, shows that the Summoner is given plenty of chance to repent and obstinately refuses; this was the one great addition to the folktale, Type 1186.

48. Robert C. Elliott, *The Power of Satire: Magic, Ritual, Art* (Princeton, N.J.: Princeton Univ. Press, 1960), chap. 1.

Hell, but the Friar does so with a theologian's subtlety, the Summoner at a level of pre-adolescent filth. His tale of the "glosing friar" ends at the same low level with the absurd conundrum about dividing a fart. As a way of laying down a curse on an opponent it is childish and primitive and shows the Summoner's grossness: his "scatological vision" may get down to the basics of anal aggression, but that only shows the Summoner's infantile level. Yet Chaucer could not so easily let the Friar win the argument. He puts into the Summoner's mouth a picture of a friar in operation: sanctimonious, greedy, self-indulgent, monstrously hypocritical and fraudulent, the friar in the story becomes a compendium of the standard complaints against the begging orders.[49] This is unimpersonated artistry: the gross Summoner isn't capable of such satiric deftness. Chaucer uses his tale as a peg on which to hang a satire of friars, and it is a classic of the genre; but he weaves his own contribution to this literary tradition so subtly into the Summoner's discourse that we manage to overlook its inappropriateness. The ending devolves upon a pun: the friar asks "What is a ferthing worth parted in twelve?" (III:1967) and the rhetorical question plants the idea "farting" in old Thomas's mind. If puns are "the lowest form of humor," if they go back to an infantile or primitive response to experience and language, this unsophisticated pun blends perfectly with the Summoner's unsophisticated aggression. It is impossible to say whether the Friar or the Summoner comes off worse in the clash. The angry outburst ends in a silly quibble. But the two tales gather up with touches of irony such relevant themes as keeping contracts and observing polite forms; and by releasing male competitiveness in a burst of wrath, they soften the blow which the Wife has dealt to male vanity and prepare us for other pilgrims who will respond to her by indirections.

Clerk and Merchant

The Clerk and Merchant, described one after the other

---

49. Arnold Williams, "Chaucer and the Friars," *Speculum* 28 (1953): 499–513, rpt. S & T, pp. 63–83.

in the General Prologue, make a pointed contrast—the Clerk in a threadbare gown, riding a horse "as leene . . . as is a rake," and not so worldly as to have "office"; the Merchant elegantly dressed, sitting "high on horse," much wrapped up in questionable affairs of business. Their tales contrast as vividly. The Clerk's is an ideal narrative of a patient wife, but not without realism.[50] Walter chafes against his people's desire that he give up his freedom in order to marry and produce an heir, asserts male omnipotence by testing his wife's submissiveness, and rewards her when he is sure of her "virtue"—they are not admirable motives, but they are motives. And one can find a progression in the tone of Griselda's speeches—she is lyrically obedient at first, becomes dogged and resigned as her husband's tests become more outlandish. Of course the motives go unexamined; there *is* something demonic about him and something saintly about her. The story is stylized, the manner of its telling rhetorical and intellectual—the Clerk interrupts with philosophical asides, introduces symbols, tacks on a *moralitas*. And the stanzaic form "distances" the narrative by imposing tighter prosodical limits, by parceling out details.

The Clerk begins with a tribute to Petrarch, and we know that the story captivated both Boccaccio and Petrarch, though modern readers have had some trouble understanding why. It is easy to interpret the tale as an allegory of Christian humility rather than a prescription for female conduct, and this is what the Clerk, following Petrarch, does:

> This story is said, nat for that wives sholde
> Follwen Grisilde as in humilitee,
> For it were inportable, though they wolde;

50. The "realism" of the tale has been a subject of much discussion. It is of course an instance of "figural" realism or of the conventional style; see Muscatine, *Chaucer and the French Tradition*, pp. 190–197, who does not however bring Auerbach into the picture. Cunningham, "Ideal Fiction," *Shenandoah*, 19, no. 2 (Winter, 1968):41, reminds us that all characters, especially in a Christian world view, are to a considerable extent "flat." But various critics have shown how the tale has, and especially in Chaucer's additions to his sources, an element of human behavior with which we can empathize in human terms. See for example B. H. Bronson, *In Search of Chaucer*, pp. 103–114; and Donaldson, *Chaucer's Poetry*, pp. 918–920.

But for that every wight, in his degree,
Sholde be constant in adversitee
As was Grisilde; therefore Petrak writeth
This story, which with heigh style he enditeth.

(1142-1148)

But the story must have hit some sensitive areas; it may have touched off the guilt men felt for their position of dominance over women or the tenderness they felt in response to submissiveness. Griselda is not only the constant Christian and the patient wife, but a peasant girl oppressed by an aristocrat[51]—she has the emotionless stoicism of the peasant, accepts the abuse of the lord as something unavoidable, and registers protest only by implication: she could represent the powerlessness of the governed against the governing class. Such conjectures may help us understand why the story appealed so much to the three greatest writers of the fourteenth century, and why it has a curious power to touch us even now. But it is the tale's *un*realistic features that touch us most, its "ideal" qualities. Ideals are after all charged with feeling and have the power to move us; and part of what moves us is our realization that the ideal has never been made to work, is "only an idea," is obsolescent. The Clerk, following Petrarch, lets us know the story is really not meant to teach wives humility but to teach us all to be constant in adversity, to understand that God tests but does not tempt us. This barely squeezes the fruit from the chaff, and the Clerk is left with the fact that he began by trying to rebut the Wife. He has already said "This world is nat so strong, it is no nay,/ As it hath been in olde times yore." Applying this idea of "the world grown old," he tells us there are no more Griseldas, that the gold of such women is now alloyed with brass. His song which follows is superbly appropriate to him (we should ignore the scribal subtitle "L'envoy de Chaucer"). It proclaims with heavy irony—the heavier for its feat of rhyming—that Griselda is dead, that wives should no longer be patient or silent, that they should shoot the arrows of

51. Cf. Howard Rollin Patch, *On Rereading Chaucer* (Cambridge, Mass.: Harvard Univ. Press, 1959), pp. 188–189.

their "crabbed eloquence," bind their husbands in jealousy, let them "care, and weep, and wring, and wail."

"Weeping and wailing," begins the Merchant, "care and other sorrwe / I know ynogh"—his tale tumbles upon the Clerk's last words in as neat a link as Chaucer ever wrote. Having heard the Wife's discourse and the Clerk's idealistic and ironic rebuttal, the Merchant pours forth in outrage his own disillusionment and disgust. The tale is one of Chaucer's best—reams have been written about it. Probably the conception came late: the important fact about the Merchant, that he has had a miserable marriage of two months' duration, is not introduced until the prologue to his tale (which only appears in half the manuscripts), and several lines suggest it may have been intended first for one of the clerical pilgrims. But that is all the more reason why it is a brilliant conception. It works better for a layman who has "fallen in the snare" to be sour on marriage than for a clerk to be; and the choice of a pilgrim from the "middle classes" prepares us for the Franklin's naive idealism. I agree with those who think the Merchant is bitter and the tone of his tale cynical.[52] "Of my owene soore,/For sorry herte, I telle may namoore," he says in his prologue, but the fabliau he tells nevertheless reflects his disgust with himself—he heaps scorn on January with self-lacerating rage. In his prologue he says,

> . . . he that all his live
> Wifeless hath been, though that men wolde him ryve
> Unto the herte, ne coude in no mannere

---

52. This older view, which goes back to Kittredge, is best defended by E. T. Donaldson, "The Effect of the Merchant's Tale," *Speaking of Chaucer*, pp. 30–45. The opposing arguments are based on the workroom estimate of Chaucer's art: because the Merchant's Prologue is a late addition, *therefore* it is unconnected with the tale. Bronson, in "Afterthoughts on the Merchant's Tale," *SP* 58 (1961):596, thought the addition "worked an instant sea-change on the story itself"; Jordan, in *Chaucer and the Shape of Creation*, p. 134, that the interpretation based on the Prologue "has uncompromisingly imposed a prism of bitterness over the tale." Behind such arguments is the premise that diffuse parts cannot have a unified effect; but Donaldson demonstrates that the effect of the tale *is promoted by the language of the tale itself.*

Tellen so muchel sorrwe as I now here
Coude tellen of my wives cursednesse!

(1235-1239)

This remark casts a sidelong glance at single men like the
Clerk, and may explain why Chaucer put—or left—in the
tale two remarks about the "secular estate."[53] The Merchant
would willingly disavow the whole of the secular estate in
which the norm is marriage. He envies the clerks pledged to
celibacy, as modern husbands sometimes envy bachelors. He
has gathered up in memory a thesaurus of ideas and
ideology connected with marriage, and attributes this to
January in a passage of sustained irony, framed at its beginning and end with two vitriolic touches, each flagged with
"and namely":

And certainly, as sooth as God is king,
To take a wife it is a glorious thing,
And namely whan a man is old and hoor.

(1267-1269)

Husbond and wife, what so men jape or playe,
Of worldly folk holden the siker waye;
They been so knit there may noon harm bitide,
And namely upon the wives side.

(1389-1392)

The Merchant here reports January's thoughts, ironically
pretending to agree with them (Chaucer did precisely this
when he spoke of the Monk in the General Prologue—
"What sholde he study and make himselven wood . . .").
Then he lets January express his thoughts in direct discourse. The two passages anthologize everything to be said
in favor of marriage—that it will produce an heir, that it is a
blessed and ordained state, that a wife is God's gift and will
last, that marriage is a sacrament, that woman was made for
man's help, that women are obedient, that Christ was married to the Church. The Merchant has stored up, too, a
supply of allusions to previous tales. The first of these (1342-
1346) echoes the Clerk's Tale (351ff.) and the second (1356-

53. Lines 1251, 1322.

1361) echoes the Wife's. The last two marriage tales are uppermost in his mind, and he harkens back to the Wife's again several times;[54] May's first speech (2189ff.) echoes the Wife's harangue at her husbands. But there are also echoes of the *Melibee* and the Monk's Tale, the Miller's Tale, the Knight's, the Monk's, the Man of Law's, perhaps even the Prioress's.[55] And the outcome of the tale is overseen by a cast of deities, which parodies the Knight's Tale.

This display of acidulous sarcasm directed against every positive opinion about marriage the Merchant can remember reflects his own bitterness, not Chaucer's: the tale is another dramatic monologue in which the pilgrim unwittingly reveals his inner self. And part of what the Merchant reveals is his own blindness and self-centeredness—we don't know if his wife of two months is really such a shrew, but we can suspect he has not given the connubial state a fair try. Doubtless Chaucer would have scorned January's folly; the Parson's Tale gives a few indications of what he might have reckoned sound "doctrine."[56] When January quotes the Song of Songs (2138-2148) and the Merchant calls it "swich olde lewed wordes," we can therefore hardly suppose Chaucer is himself ridiculing the common idea that earthly marriage is a type of the marriage between Christ and His church, but we can't be sure the Merchant is either. The biblical words may *sound* "lewed" to this businessman. Or the comment may reveal a mordant wit. Or the reference may be there to throw January's conduct and the Merchant's frame of mind into relief: the way things should be makes the way they are more vivid.

January's *hortus conclusus* and these biblical echoes can make the final scene in the tree remind us of the Fall of

54. See lines 1427–1430 (cf. WBPro 44a); 1455–1456 (cf. WBPro 112); 1670–1671 (cf. WBPro 175, 489).

55. Lines 1362–1368 echo exempla in the *Melibee* and the Monk's Tale; 1485–1486 echo Miller's Tale 3530; 1942 and 1986 echo Knight's Tale 2808 and 1761; 2280–2283 suggest the Man of Law's heroine Constance. Lines 2055–2057 echo or at least suggest the Monk's "tragedies," and line 2365 may suggest the Prioress's Tale, but these last require that Fragment VII be read before Fragments III–IV–V.

56. X:915–957, esp. 928; 843; 857; 859; 883.

A THEORY OF STRUCTURE 263

Man.[57] But this outcome has a curious turnabout: it makes fallen January at the end seem pathetic. Proserpine gives to May and to "alle women after" a "suffisant answere"—using the Wife's strategy, she harangues Pluto into submission ("I yeve it up," he replies) as May will harangue January into submission. We go away from the tale thinking January a fool, May a baggage, and Damian a traitor. But the bitter story has a wryly happy ending:

> This January, who is glad but he?
> He kisseth hir, and clippeth hir full ofte,
> And on hir womb he stroketh hir full softe,
> And to his palays home he hath hir lad.

(2412-2415)

In his stroking her "womb" one can read a covert reference to her pregnancy.[58] If so, the tale presents at the end a plain fact which answers the Wife's story of woe in marriage and the Clerk's story of adversity better than all the Merchant's bitter irony: the redeeming possibility in the worst of marriages can be the children. But we are left to guess what January is stroking, and whether May is really pregnant or whether, when she said so, she was lying.

The Merchant's Tale is told with a rhetorical flair and a knowledge of Scripture and "auctoritees" which seem inappropriate to its teller. But even if it *was* originally written for the Monk or Friar, Chaucer assigned it finally to the Merchant; and, thus assigned, its brilliant allusiveness is another instance of unimpersonated artistry. The tale answers the Wife with its antifeminism—the Host joins in with a crack at the Wife (2437)—and "quits" the Clerk's idealism with its cynicism. The Merchant's final point seems to be that

57. D. W. Robertson, Jr., "The Doctrine of Charity in Mediaeval Literary Gardens," *Speculum* 26 (1951):43–45, and cf. Alfred L. Kellogg, "Susannah and the Merchant's Tale," *Speculum* 35 (1960):275–279, rpt. *Chaucer, Langland, Arthur,* pp. 330–338.

58. See her reference to "a woman in my plit" (line 2335) and Robinson's note, which refers to Milton Miller, "The Heir in the *Merchant's Tale*," *PQ* 29 (1950):437–440. The line is splendidly ambiguous—lecherous January might well stroke her "womb" (genitalia) as January the expectant father might stroke her belly; see Rossell Hope Robbins, "January's Caress," *Lock Haven Review* 10 (1968):3–6.

happiness in marriage can only be attained by willful blindness: when January's physical sight is restored, he lets himself be blinded to the truth he sees, believes his wife faithful, and thinks her pregnant whether she is or not.

The Clerk's and Merchant's tales complement each other—both are accomplished displays of rhetoric which set realities against ideals. But the Clerk has a feeling for the old ideals and takes an ironic view of present realities; the Merchant heaps contempt on the ideals and takes a bitter view of realities. His disillusionment seems to level all ideals and leave us with nihilism, but then what does the Clerk's irony leave us with?—an ideal no longer followed, a world in decline, gold alloyed with brass. We like the Clerk's tale because we admire his frame of mind, his idealism and irony, his *style*. But the picture itself is not a happier one than what the Merchant offers—it is only that the Merchant's style is less appealing.

Squire and Franklin

The Squire's and Franklin's tales are paired. Kittredge thought the Squire's Tale an interruption in the marriage group, but the Squire's choice, an aristocratic romance which deals with love, fits the previous tales.[59] The Franklin pays him a courtly compliment and offers a romance of his own. The Squire's Tale is "set up" at the beginning to involve the four magical gifts the heroine received; like the Monk, he starts a frame narrative and it runs away with him—he lacks the storyteller's art of knowing when to stop. It is tempting to think that the Franklin politely stops the tale after the first couplet of its third part by pretending that it is over and heaping compliments on it,[60] but we cannot be sure Chaucer

59. See Marie Neville, "The Function of the *Squire's Tale* in the Canterbury Scheme," *JEGP* 50 (1951):167–179, who argued that it answers the Wife's tale by proclaiming the ideal that there is no sovereignty in love, that it furnishes an occasion for the Franklin, and that the Squire attempts to emulate his father's tale but in a bumbling way.

60. Nevill Coghill, *The Poet Chaucer*, 2nd ed. (London: Oxford Univ. Press, 1967), p. 123. Cf. Donaldson, *Chaucer's Poetry*, p. 923. The pros and

meant this. As with *Sir Thopas*, Chaucer did not need to finish the tale; what he wrote accomplishes what he needed to accomplish.

The romance is perfectly suited to the Squire. It describes court festivals and pageantry, involves the traditional appearance at court of a mysterious knight, and if finished would have covered all the "matters" that knights loved—not just fantastical tales about talking birds but tales of "aventures and of batailles" (659). The story reflects the enthusiasms of youthful nobles and is told with the posturing of the "high style." In this it is like the Knight's Tale, but the Squire's expertise is not as great as his father's. It is like the Knight's Tale, too, because we sense Chaucer's presence in various incongruities and absurdities which undercut the tale itself. This satiric or humorous element of the Squire's Tale has only been recognized in recent years;[61] it is not as wild a spoof as *Sir Thopas*—like the Knight's Tale, it is a good story in itself told with some "literary" mannerisms at which Chaucer pokes gentle fun. The Squire is full of protestations about his capabilities as a storyteller and makes an elaborate display of humility. "Have me excused if I speke amiss," he begins, and no sooner has he launched into his initial description than he interrupts:

> I dare nat undertake so heigh a thing.
> Myn English eek is insufficient.
> It moste been a rhetor excellent,
> That koude his colours longing for that art,
> If he sholde hir discriven every part.
> I am none swich, I moot speke as I can.
>
> (36-41)

It is droll that his tale then proceeds with a display of rhetorical attitudinizing. He is full of reverence for the rhetorician's art, and makes the common mistake of talking about it rather than practicing it (for example, 98-109), constantly

---

cons of the Franklin's interruption have become a favorite topic for articles.

61. See John P. McCall, "The Squire in Wonderland," *ChauR* 1 (1966): 103–109, and his n. 1 for earlier such analyses. And see above, chap. 3, nn. 18 and 19.

protesting that it is too much for him. Twice we are reminded that the old grandeur of fabled knights is a thing of the past: the Squire refers to Gawayn "with his olde curteisye, / Though he were comen again out of Fairye" (95-96) and says that no one could describe the court's dances "but Launcelot, and he is deed" (287). The directions that go with the magic horse (314-334), all about twisting wires in the horse's ear and saying secret words which will be told later, are overblown and fantastical. And the beginning of the second part of the tale, in which the drunken guests leave "galping," is ridiculous enough.

In the Squire's Tale, as in the Knight's Tale and elsewhere, we know something is being made fun of but are not sure what. Is it the Squire himself, the tale he tells, the conventions of its genre, the values of his class? In the General Prologue he is presented as a charming young "bacheler" caught up in the aristocratic fads and fashions of his day. The ineptness of his storytelling and the absurdities of his story reflect less on him than on the fads and fashions. The part of the narrative he is allowed to tell is a love story. Like the Nun's Priest's Tale it is about birds who talk courtly lingo; they are, moreover, aristocratic birds, falcons. It takes the Squire four hundred lines to get to this story, and he takes up eight more lines to make the point that he has got to the point:

> The knotte why that every tale is told,
> If it be taried til that lust be cold
> Of hem that han it after herkned yore,
> The savour passeth ever lenger the more,
> For fulsomeness of his prolixitee;
> And by the same reson, thinketh me,
> I sholde to the knotte condescende,
> And maken of hir walking soon an ende.
>
> (401-408)

The lady falcon is, in reverse of the usual courtly situation, languishing for the male, who has deserted her. The male is obliged to leave on unnamed business, and the lady "made vertu of necessitee" (593), as the Franklin's heroine will do, by resigning herself to his absence. At the end of their

courtly parting we are abruptly reminded, as in the Nun's
Priest's Tale, that the characters are birds: the tercelet *flies*
away! We learn that men "of propre kinde" and birds in
cages like "newefangelnesse," and learn how the departed
tercelet falls in love with another, a kyte, so that Canacee's
falcon is "lorn withouten remedie" (629). Canacee brings the
falcon home, wraps plasters on it where it has "with hir
beek . . . hurt hirselve," provides healing herbs, and makes a
coop covered with blue velvet "In sign of truth that is in
women seene" (645)—the coop is painted on the outside with
images of false birds very like the images painted on the
outside of the garden wall in the *Roman de la Rose*. We never
find out what becomes of her or indeed anything else except
what the Squire proposes to continue with.

What has this fantastical fragment to do with anything?
The Squire seems endearing in his earnest but unsuccessful
attempt to match his father's accomplishments as a storyteller—we are delighted by the very thing he claims in his
Prologue, "my will is good." We like his enthusiasm and with
the Franklin admire his earnest efforts. The tale adds
something new to the whole work, for it is the only tale in
which we get the exotic Mandevillian world of oriental travel
which had already captured the imagination of Chaucer's
contemporaries; and it adds something new to the Wife's,
Clerk's and Merchant's discourses. It is as if Chaucer asked
"what has the aristocracy to contribute to such a discussion?"
And the answer is, *nothing*—nothing but fantasy and convention, nothing but courtly clichés and rhetorical posturing,
bromides about love-longing, courtesy, honor, gentilesse,
nothing but hearsay tales of distant princes. I think it is a
moment when Chaucer shows himself out of sympathy with
the knightly classes—it is a glimpse of the "bourgeois"
Chaucer, the "new man" of the fourteenth century. It is
impossible not to think of the *Parliament of Fowls*, which is
also about an aristocratic female hawk absurdly caught up in
a conventional courtly love circumstance. The Squire is as
likeable a character as one will find anywhere in Chaucer,
and one cannot fault him for telling the only kind of story
which the fashions of his day have provided. But Chaucer
suggests that these are empty and jejune.

The Franklin's Tale, linked as it is with the Squire's Tale, seems unlikely to be any kind of model or conclusion, to be "what Chaucer thought about marriage." Kittredge was right that the opening lines of his tale express a compromise between courtly love and Christian marriage, a compromise which manages to include all the points of view hitherto expressed. It satisfies the Wife on the score of sovereignty and incorporates the Clerk's counsel of patience and humility; it responds to the Squire's romantic or courtly view of love and takes issue with the Merchant's denial of happiness in marriage. The Franklin presents his ideas with a buoyancy which makes them sound like a breakthrough, and those ideas were to prevail in time—Chaucer had a good eye for the coming thing. But there are reasons to disagree with Kittredge that those ideas are presented as ideas Chaucer believed in. For one thing, they are not entirely consistent with what the church taught. The Franklin's emphasis on self-denial and patience sounds Christian enough, and he does remove from courtly love what made the tradition objectionable to the church, adultery. But his solution denies the Christian principle of authority: the church believed that a woman should obey and serve her husband—should be, in the Parson's words, "subget to hir husbond" (X:930). The Parson allows that a woman should be "fellaw" (928) to her man and explains that she was not made of Adam's foot because she is not to be held too low. But he does not offer anything like the Franklin's suggestion that the husband should be "servant in love"; he says the opposite, that she should "serven him in alle honestee" (932). The Franklin's notion is a sensible but a worldly one. Its purpose, he says, is to produce bliss, quiet, and rest (744, 760), and these are hardly the goals of the Christian life.

The Franklin's interest in domestic concord is in line with the description of him in the General Prologue. He is "Epicurus owene sone" (336)—he believes that "pleyn delit / Was verray felicitee parfit." Much is made of his desire to entertain lavishly and ostentatiously. He is, in short, an affluent country landowner who has "touched silk" and held office—he is gregarious, affable, sanguine of complexion.

Professor Donaldson does well to compare him, with his red face and white beard, to Santa Claus.[62] There is nothing especially disagreeable in this portrait—those who take him for a sinner, guilty of gluttony or sensuality or some form of cupidity, miss the tone of the passage. Nor is there anything in his tale which reveals gross failings in his character. He is a genial, merry, wealthy gentleman who likes to have everything go right. His tale is perfectly suited to him.

But he is not the sort of character to whom Chaucer would assign a tale meant to settle an issue. In the exchange which precedes his tale Chaucer bears down on his ambitions and pretensions. The Franklin commends the Squire enthusiastically for his eloquence, wit, and virtue: he doesn't seem to realize that the Squire has bungled his rhetoric, or if he does he lets his affability run away with his critical judgment. He compares unfavorably his own spendthrift son, who apparently takes little interest in his father's preoccupations (682-694)—it is amusing that in the speech he unwittingly reveals his lust for "twenty pound worth lond," as it is amusing that the Host responds "Straw for your gentilesse!" We get the old picture of the wealthy landowner, a respectable member of the gentry who has risen by buying (not inheriting) land, and whose greatest wish is to raise his social status.

Kittredge was right when he pointed out that the Franklin's ambitions come out naively,[63] but he didn't see how the Franklin's naiveté is reflected in his tale. That the young squire in it, Aurelius, is naive and literal-minded might well have been a convention found in the sources, but Chaucer makes it plain that the Franklin identifies with the young squire's enterprising and ambitious character. The lady, when she agrees to be his love if he removes the rocks which put her husband's life in danger, does so in the courtly style of ironic badinage. "In play" (988) she sets an impossible quest, that Aurelius remove the rocks. Aurelius, not prepared with the right ironic answer, cries that her request

62. Donaldson, in *The Norton Anthology of English Literature*, rev. ed. (New York: Norton, 1968), I:107.
63. "Chaucer's Discussion of Marriage," 458.

is "an inpossible" and eventually (it takes two years) makes a bargain with an astrologer, compromising himself by accepting an optical illusion. While Dorigen's words catch the style in which courtly ladies spoke, later in the tale she falls into the literal-minded, casuistical spirit with which Aurelius sees such matters as making bargains and keeping agreements. When the rocks have seemed to disappear and the husband has returned, she confesses what has happened; and the husband, no less literal-minded, takes it all in deadly earnest. "Trouth is the highest thing that man may keep," he says, and having said it bursts out in tears. At this point the agreement of mutual concession is amusingly forgotten and he gives his wife orders on pain of death:

> . . . I you forbede, up pain of deeth,
> That nevere, while thee lasteth life ne breeth,
> To no wight tell thou of this aventure.
> As I may best, I wol my woe endure!
> Ne make no countenance of hevinesse,
> That folk of you may deemen harm or guesse.
>
> (1481-1486)

The squire Aurelius, unable to pay the astrologer for making the rocks *seem* to disappear, offers to pay on the installment plan. And the Franklin wraps up his tale by having every character back down a little—agreements are not all exacted because each party is willing to make a deal. The spirit of bargaining here is consistent with that of the initial bargain about marriage; it is the spirit of the businessman, and the joke is that the Franklin thinks it "gentle." He ends his tale by emulating the aristocratic convention of raising a question for debate: "Which was the moste free?" But the "gentilesse" which he attributes to all the characters—to the knight and his wife, to the squire, to the clerk—is nothing like the "gentilesse" of the old nobility. It is a "country-squire" version. Its optimistic, amiable spirit suits the Franklin's temperament as much as it suits his milieu; perhaps in the end such gentlemen behaved themselves better than the intemperate feudal barons of the fourteenth century, but in Chaucer's time they hadn't the prestige of the titled aristocracy and their pretensions could still be viewed with irony by real lords and ladies or by the new men of the age like Chaucer.[64]

If the Franklin's Tale, however admirable, is not the final word on marriage, then the structure of the marriage tales is different from what Kittredge proposed. The points at issue are raised by the Wife, male hostilities are vented by the Friar and Summoner, and other opinions are offered in pairs, but these do not work toward a solution. We get the Clerk's ironic idealism and the Merchant's cynicism; the Squire's aristocratic romanticism and the Franklin's naive optimism. But none presents a recipe for domestic concord. Things do not degenerate as in the tales of Fragment I, but they do not build to a solution either. And none of the tales ever returns to the question the Wife raised first, whether marriage, or marriage more than once, is a desirable state. That question, still a significant issue in Chaucer's day and not without significance in our own, is left open until we come to the last tales. The interlace is broken at this juncture: the structure of the group is one in which an issue is stated at the outset and its ramifications are explored with a questioning spirit in different outlooks, but nothing is concluded; its tales trail off from the central issue and get lost in specialized, highly individual viewpoints—which is just how the group began.

THE TALES OF PRIVATE CONDUCT: FRAGMENT VII

If the groups which have gone before deal with conduct in the civil and domestic realms (in the state or nation, the family or home), one might anticipate a group of stories about some other realm—the church as opposed to the state or the family, the realms of individual moral choice as opposed to those of law or domestic sovereignty. But the tales of Fragment VII, joined by dramatic links which make them a dramatic unit in the story of the pilgrimage, do not appear to have thematic unity the way the tales of the

64. A good analogy to the Franklin's frame of mind is that of Geoffroy de LaTour-Landry; see *The Book of the Knight of the Tower*, ed. M. Y. Offord, *EETS*, suppl. ser. 2 (1971).

"marriage group" do—they are not a debate, do not involve clashes of personality, and have no apparent theme in common. Alan Gaylord,[65] who has suggested that the group be called the "literature group," thinks Chaucer intended the tales to share the theme of storytelling itself, and that the Host is in the position of an editor who manipulates and deletes. He thinks the issue is that raised by the Host in the General Prologue (798), whether a tale should be told for "sentence" or "solace." He finds—and I think he is right—that the first four tales alternate between "solace" and "sentence": the Shipman tells a tale unquestionably of "solace," and the Prioress means to tell a tale of "sentence"; Chaucer's two tales, *Sir Thopas* and the *Melibee*, are respectively "solace" and "sentence." The Monk then tells a tale heavy with "sentence," and the Nun's Priest, in the most effective tale, combines both virtues. Chaucer's tale of "solace" is interrupted, as is the Monk's tale of "sentence." Gaylord points out that the Host addresses the pilgrim with the familiar "thou" for a tale of "solace" and uses the formal "you" for tales of "sentence." The Host's view, he thinks, is a simple-minded one, but a more subtle view is implied: the best kind of story is the one in which the artist responds to the audience and the audience to the artist, and the Nun's Priest succeeds in this better than the others. He might have added that the group is a veritable anthology of medieval genres—a fabliau, a miracle of the Virgin, a parodic tail-rime romance, a prose allegory, *de casibus* tragedies (an anthology within an anthology), and a mock-heroic beast epic.

That Chaucer consciously set out to write in this group of six tales a sequence about the art of storytelling is doubtful. Where he "set out" to introduce a common theme he did so in the most explicit way. The Wife's Prologue begins a

65. "*Sentence* and *Solaas* in Fragment VII of the *Canterbury Tales*," *PMLA* 82 (1967):226–235. Cf. Baum, *Chaucer*, pp. 74–84, who calls it the "surprise group." He thinks the tales after the Shipman's are other than what is expected or requested, and suggests that all are parodies. His argument is for dramatic, not thematic, unity; he is developing the notion advanced by Kittredge, *Chaucer and His Poetry*, pp. 167–185, that the group is an "act in the human comedy" based on interplay of character.

group of tales with a clear statement of theme, and Chaucer was able to introduce a literary theme effectively in the General Prologue, the prologue of *The Legend of Good Women*, and the *Troilus*. In the tales of Fragment VII one can recognize a common theme in retrospect, but there is nothing to show that he set out to do this; it is as likely that the theme emerged as he pieced the tales together.

The fragment begins with the Shipman's Tale and the Prioress's Tale, which have nothing in common: the contrast between them is the noticeable fact about them. That contrast in spirit and intention is what Gaylord points to as the principle of development in the sequence. Whether the six tales share a "theme," it is surely true that they can be broken into three contrasting pairs. The Shipman's Tale is an immoral tale told by an immoral man, and he tells it in full consciousness of its immorality—indeed seems to relish its immorality. The Prioress tells a moral tale, or so she believes, and is altogether unconscious of the immorality which a sophisticated reader of Chaucer's time or of any time would see in it. Taken together, the two tales make a startling contrast and themselves pose a moral issue: which is worse, conscious immorality or immorality perpetrated in ignorance? The following two tales, those which Chaucer himself tells, are a no less pointed contrast. *Sir Thopas* is escapist entertainment at a low level, poorly executed in singsong verse and interrupted for its tediousness; the *Melibee* is told for moral edification and is in prose. The one parodies an altogether mindless entertainment which panders to the naive tastes of drab people; the other is a real allegory with real content, treats significant issues, and is addressed to the ruling class. The remaining pair, the Monk's and Nun's Priest's tales, are a pair in which two clergymen set out to tell moral tales using the principle of the *exemplum*. But the Monk is all caught up in pedantry—he begins pompously with a lecture defining tragedy and then spins out sixteen stories before he is called to a halt. Very like a rooster he is, strutting about with his definitions and running on with his tales; and the Host chaffs him for his roosterlike qualities:

I pray to God, yeve him confusioun

That first thee brought unto religioun!
Thou woldest han been a tredefowl aright.

(1943-1945)

The Nun's Priest appears to pick up this implication and tells his tale of a rooster and hen—you can't say he directs it against the Monk in a personal way, but he gets his licks in at the Monk just at the turning point of his story with a sly reference to Fortune (3403-3404). The Priest's subtle wit contrasts vividly with the Monk's pomposity, his ironic view of the world with the Monk's grimness, his common-sense moral with the Monk's dispirited amorality. And his economy and dramatic verve point up the Monk's failure as a storyteller.

While the six tales in Fragment VII fall into these three contrasting pairs, other contrasts make for concatenation in the pairs. The Prioress tells a tale which she believes is idealistic—she is certain she is telling about innocence and purity and hasn't any notion that her sentimental legend involves a vicious persecution which the Church had, at least officially, condemned. The thoughtlessness of her tale is accentuated by the stanzaic form, which makes it sound like a ballad; the story is very like that of a ballad sung over the centuries.[66] Chaucer's sing-song "rime," whether sung or not, is equally thoughtless. Both pilgrims have committed to memory and can recite tales so stereotyped as to paralyze thought. So the Prioress's Tale and *Sir Thopas* contrast vividly with the *Melibee,* which is nothing if not thoughtful. Two tales in the group are interrupted—the Host stops Chaucer's "drasty riming" because it is dull and the Knight stops the Monk's recitation because "litel heviness / Is right enough" (the Host chimes in, "Swich talking is not worth a butterflye"). Neither tale offers "solace" *or* "sentence," and the two interruptions prepare us for the Nun's Priest's tale which really is a good story and really has a useful moral.

The tales could also be seen arranged in contrasts based on social class. The Shipman owns his own barge and is from

66. See Francis J. Child, *The English and Scottish Popular Ballads,* 5 vols. (1882–1898; rpt. New York: Dover, 1965), III:233–254.

Dartmouth, a major port, so it is fair to call him a bourgeois unless one assumes he is a pirate and hence a criminal. He tells a tale in which he makes a rival bourgeois (a merchant) his gull. His tale is venal, competitive, mean-spirited: it represents all that is worst in the petit-bourgeois mentality, all that leads it into criminality; and that mentality is put down by Chaucer himself in his parody of bourgeois romance. The other tales are aristocratic: the Prioress with her noble airs is ladylike in the worst way, for she embodies characteristics which were and to a degree still are expected of the "lady's" role, empty-headedness and shallowness. The *Melibee* is addressed to aristocrats and deals with problems which they alone confront. The Monk, like the Prioress, is given to aristocratic airs and tells stories about the falls of princes and potentates. The Nun's Priest demolishes this strain of aristocratic pretension with his barnyard fable: his regal cock and hen reduce aristocratic conventions to an absurdity.

All the tales in this group except the last reflect and enhance the portraits of the pilgrims in the General Prologue. This fact contrasts with the vivid impression of the Nun's Priest's mind which his tale gives us, for he was not described in the General Prologue at all. A "faceless" pilgrim, he is the farthest from being mindless. About the Shipman we have learned that he steals wine from his merchant customers and makes prisoners walk the plank; "Of nice conscience," the narrator tells us, "took he no keep." This impression is borne out by his tale—it is no surprise that the butt of his fabliau is a merchant, that the merchant is naively trusting and is made a ridiculous dupe. The tale suits him better than it would have suited the Wife, if Chaucer initially assigned it to her, as some believe. The Shipman seems to take delight in the cynical deviltry of the monk and in the sluttish vanity of the merchant's wife. Her mind is occupied with nothing except clothes, and she is only too willing to sell her body to the monk, and for that matter to her husband, in return for "array." These two self-serving characters manage to rob and cuckold the merchant and keep him in ignorance of his plight. In a series of puns, notably that on "tail," the Shipman connects sexuality and money.[67] The merchant is busily seeking credit for his "chaffare"—we are in the early days of a credit economy—and the sexual bargain is made in the same spirit of borrowing and lending complete with "tokens" and paid debts. It is riotous when the wife tells her husband, about the missing money, that he should "score it upon my taille," but it is part of the process by which the Shipman cynically reduces all values to the most venal ones. The Monk's vows, the "brotherhood" between the monk and the merchant, and the wife's marriage vows are all violated for the sake of "tailling."

This funny but unsavory tale—some think it the most immoral of the tales—lets us see into the mentality of the Shipman, and we are not surprised at what we see. With the Prioress, Chaucer himself, and the Monk, however, we see more about them from their tales than we have been permitted to see in the General Prologue.

Everyone has always been charmed by the portrait of the Prioress—her ladylike daintiness, her affectations, and her negligible infractions against the usual rules of convents, her "conscience and tender heart," her dubious French, her little dogs, her beads and wimple and mysterious brooch are as much beloved by readers of Chaucer as are the details of almost any portrait in the General Prologue. A few prigs fuss at her "sentimentality" and her failure to be a good nun in the strictest sense. But nuns have never been any fun if something of the woman doesn't manage to squeeze through the headdress and petticoats. It takes someone without any personal experience of nuns to be scornful of the Lady Prioress in that initial description of her. Yet Chaucer, having humanized her in this way, having made her interesting and sympathetic, turns the tables in her tale and shows how her simplicity and air of elegance lead her into a frame of mind which is deplorable. No one ought to care if she keeps dogs or wears some jewelry,[68] but we care in retrospect

---

67. See Bernard S. Levy, "The Quaint World of *The Shipman's Tale*," *Studies in Short Fiction* 4 (1967):112–118.
68. The extent to which the details in the description of her constitute

because we see that much the same frame of mind which leads her to these minor infractions leads her to participate unwittingly in something monstrous. People sometimes argue that Chaucer intended no irony in her tale, did not mean it as a criticism of her.[69] True, antisemitism was a way of life in the Middle Ages. True, the Jews had been officially banned from England since 1290. But the Church took a position against the persecution of the Jews, and insightful men saw the base economic motives behind those persecutions.[70] Chaucer was surely an insightful man, and as a Clerk of the Customs he would have known more than enough about base economic motives. As a traveller he would probably have seen and known more of Jews than the average Englishman.[71] And few deny that he was tolerant, open-minded, infinitely capable of empathy. It is out of the question that he could have failed to note the Prioress's moral blindness. The hasty entrance of the Provost is a characteristic bit of Chaucerian irony which underscores the travesty of justice that takes place:

> He came anon withouten tarrying,
> And herieth Christ that is of hevene King,

---

serious infractions of monastic discipline has been the subject of pro-tracted controversy, summarized by Florence H. Ridley, *The Prioress and the Critics*, Univ. of California Publications: English Studies 30 (Berkeley and Los Angeles: Univ. of California Press, 1965), pp. 16–26.

69. Ridley makes the strongest case, and the subtlest, for this point of view. D. S. Brewer, *Chaucer*, 2nd ed. (London: Longmans, 1960), p. 151, thinks "It is an irony which was certainly not realized by the poet, that the gentlest of all the pilgrims should tell what is, from a point of view impossible to the Middle Ages, the only cruel and fanatical story of them all." Since some people were indignant toward the persecution of Jews the point of view was not entirely impossible to the Middle Ages; and even if it was, it does not follow that it was impossible to Chaucer who was in other respects an exceptional man.

70. Richard J. Schoeck, "Chaucer's Prioress: Mercy and Tender Heart," *The Bridge: A Yearbook of Judaeo-Christian Studies*, 2 (1956):239–255, rpt. S&T, pp. 245–258. Cf. the judicious remarks of Donaldson, *Chaucer's Poetry*, pp. 932–934.

71. Ridley, n. 64, reports that about 1375–1380 some Jews were treated with esteem by Charles V of France. It deserves to be added that Chaucer was in France and likely at the king's court probably more than once during this period. See *LR*, pp. 44–53.

And eek his moder, honour of mankinde,
And after that the Jewes let he binde.

(617-620)

And Chaucer emphasizes the fact that the punishment of the Jews falls beyond what is prescribed by law:

He nolde no swich cursedness observe.
"Yvel shall have that yvel wol deserve";
Therefore with wilde horse he did hem drawe,
And after that he heng hem by the lawe.

(631-634)

The reference to Hugh of Lincoln at the end serves to bring the moral close to home. Even the reaction of the company— "every man / As sober was that wonder was to see"—strikes me as the uneasy sobriety of people who know something is wrong but have failed to protest. The recognition that Chaucer would have seen something wrong in his society's treatment of the Jews has led some to suppose Chaucer was denouncing the Prioress as a monstrous bigot and hypocrite; Professor Ridley has dispelled the idea.[72] Madame Eglantine has no idea that there is anything questionable about her tale. She is like those well-behaved ladies who cannot understand why America doesn't just drop its atomic stockpile on the Soviet Union—it is dreadful, but funny too; it is only frightening *en masse*. One can interpret the Prioress's Tale as a droll study in the banality of evil,[73] but it was exactly that banality multiplied *en masse* which produced in Chaucer's time, as in our own, a mass slaughter of the Jews. Banality, in itself usually funny, is only chilling in this abstract way, in retrospect. A single literary character—Christopher Isherwood's "Frl. Schroeder" is a good example—can delight us in the teeth of broader implications; but the broader implications, which are in part what make her interesting,

72. She concludes (p. 29) "Only from the Prioress of the 'General Prologue' could we expect a humorless display of naïveté, ignorance, blind, vehement devotion, and suppressed maternal longing; and that is precisely what we get." I agree with this but not with the notion that her naïveté, ignorance, etc. were lost on Chaucer, on whom very little was lost.

73. The phrase is that of Hannah Arendt, *Eichmann in Jerusalem: A Report on the Banality of Evil* (New York: Viking, 1963).

are what make her chilling. The author may keep his ironic detachment, but the implications aren't lost on everyone. The point at issue is whether they were lost on thinking men of the fourteenth century. They certainly were not lost on the German chronicler Jacob von Königshofen; recounting the slaying of the Jews at Strasbourg in 1349, he wrote "The money was indeed the thing that killed the Jews. If they had been poor and if the feudal lords had not been in debt to them, they would not have been burnt."[74] He added that when the wealth was divided among the artisans, some gave their share to the church on the advice of their confessors.

Chaucer's two tales, like the Prioress's tale, develop his character as it was presented in the General Prologue: we get the pretended naive bourgeois beneath whom lies the thinking man. Everyone knows about Chaucer the Man and Chaucer the Pilgrim. We get first the "elvish" Chaucer, staring at the ground, round in the waist—"a popet in an arm t'enbrace." He recites his foolish rime and when stopped makes a ridiculous apologia (936-966)—it is ill-spoken, meandering, repetitious, and awkward. But in the tale of Melibee Chaucer speaks his prose discourse *in propria persona*, and the side of him we see is very far from elvish. This seriousness (we will come back to it later) is directly relevant to the Prioress's tale which has gone before. Chaucer *shows* us the thoughtful side of himself on which the implications of the Prioress's story couldn't have been lost.

The Monk's tale develops its teller's character too. He was presented in the General Prologue as an "outrider" with aristocratic tastes; he likes horses, fine clothes, and presumably women. The portrait seems to some an allegory of monastic abuse, but it is very particularized—everyone remembers his bald head and his lordly air, his love-knot, his jingling bridle, and so on. Perhaps because of this realism it has puzzled many that his tale is scholarly and stuffy enough to make the courteous Knight interrupt him. It seems

---

74. Quoted from *The Portable Medieval Reader*, ed. James Bruce Ross and Mary Martin McLaughlin (New York: Viking, 1949), p. 176.

inconsistent, but since interesting people are usually inconsistent we should seek a possible explanation for the Monk's
choice of a tale. And there is an explanation: his choice is
prompted by the Host's taunting and hostile speech to him
(1924-1964).[75] The Host's theme is that the Monk is not "like
a penant or a ghost," that he would have been a "tredefowl
aright" if he had not become a religious, that religion "hath
take up all the corn / Of treding" and that women "assay /
Religious folk" because they pay Venus's payments better. It
is a coarse joke, and the Host makes it coarser by ending
"Full oft in game a sooth I have herd saye!" The Monk, we
are told, took it all in patience. He does not answer in kind:
he speaks in a somber way, tells the company he has a
hundred "tragedies" in his cell, defines tragedy bookishly.[76]
It stands to reason that the Shipman's picture of a philandering monk and the Host's sarcasm have hit the Monk in a
sensitive spot; what we learn from the General Prologue
suggests he has good reasons to be embarrassed and feel
guilty. Some people would defend themselves in such a
situation by giving tit for tat, or by getting angry, or by
lapsing into silence, but the Monk's aristocratic demeanor
leads him to stand on his dignity. He plays the detached
scholar.

It reveals something about the Monk that the area in
which he can claim a scholar's expertise is *de casibus* tragedy.
He has made a collection of such stories. On the surface they
seem like the kind of story a monk ought to be collecting;
they deny any value to worldly pursuits and present a stock
moral, that one should have contempt for the world. By
telling them, he can seem to negate the Host's implied
accusation. But there is something worldly about *de casibus*
stories: they are about powerful men, about kings and
potentates, and for this reason they must appeal to the
Monk's obsession with power and dignity. If he is "A manly

75. Cf. Bronson, *In Search of Chaucer*, pp. 72–76.
76. It is perhaps a touch of self-humor on Chaucer's part that he has
the Monk excuse himself for the disorder in his collection (1983–1990) in
the same way that he (i.e. the narrator) did so in the General Prologue.

man, to been an abbott able," if he plays the aristocrat with his horses and hounds and fine clothes, he must have yearnings to be a nobleman, or may be the younger son of a noble family. His tales are a sop to his yearnings: if Fortune casts down the powerful, that is a reason to be satisfied with one's lack of power. But the Monk does not seem to take much comfort from this implication. His stories present a hopeless world in which man is powerless, and the way he tells them reveals his own moral chaos. Only one figure, Nabugodonosor, learns from his mistakes and triumphs. In the end the rest all die or are imprisoned, and most of them suffer their fates as a punishment for their own mistakes. At the center of the Monk's collection are five pure *de casibus* tragedies, those of Zenobia, Peter of Spain, Peter of Cyprus, Barnabo of Lombardy, and Hugolino of Pisa. These chiefly "modern" heroes do not make any mistakes or do any wrongs; each one's downfall comes through the treachery or hostility of others, and capriciously with the turning of Fortune's wheel—one ends in prison, one dies in prison, and the other three are murdered. But the six tales at the beginning and the six at the end present reasons for the heroes' downfall and suggest moral implications. Three (Samson, Hercules, and Olofernes) are brought to their unhappy ends because of women. Lucifer falls because of sin (an oversimplification, since sin began with him), Adam because of "misgovernance," and the rest for pride or presumption or "heigh emprise." The Monk draws a specific moral in only four cases: Samson's tragedy shows us that we should not tell secrets to women; Hercules' tragedy shows us that we should know ourselves and not trust Fortune; Balthazar's tragedy shows us that there is no security in lordship, that one loses one's friends in a fall; King Antiochus's tragedy is said to be the reward of pride. Their punishments are all violent. It is a hapless universe that the Monk reveals, and his obsession with it suggests that Chaucer has given us a study in the psychology of powerlessness. The Monk has the air and manner of a powerful noble but is no more than a "keeper of the cell"; he knows the respect due his cloth, but he seems unsatisfied with this. He rationalizes by dwelling in his thoughts upon the falls of the great.[77] In part he sees the world as a place where there is no justice at all, in part as a place where inscrutable processes punish *ambition*. He does not think much about what punishments may be in store for other vices. He sees life as a hopeless and frightening state in which man has no control over his destiny, and it is perhaps just this sense of his own powerlessness which makes it so easy for him to ignore the monastic rule. There is something cheerless and solemn in the way he goes about it. Why should he study and make himself mad poring over a book, he asks himself, or labor with his hands? How shall the world be served?

If I am right that the pilgrims who tell tales in this group are characterized in greater depth by the tales they tell, this fact prepares us for the Nun's Priest's Tale, where characterization depends entirely on the tale with no help from the General Prologue. Perhaps the Nun's Priest is among the most vivid characters in the work. We do not know what he looks like or how he is dressed, and have no knowledge of his past or his character. He is attached to the retinue of the Prioress, and he rides upon a "jade."[78] But from the style of his tale, from his learning, his wit, his ironical spirit, and his verve, we get as clear a sense of him as we get of the Wife or the Pardoner. Everyone knows how his tale parodies the standard devices of medieval rhetoric, how he draws out his tale with elaborate *descriptio*s at the beginning, prolongs it

77. Cf. Farnham, *The Medieval Heritage of Elizabethan Tragedy*, pp. 129–136. On the Monk's status and demeanor, see Paul E. Beichner, "Daun Piers, Monk and Business Administrator," *Speculum* 34 (1959): 611–619, rpt. S&T, pp. 52–62. And see William C. Strange, "The *Monk's Tale*: A Generous View," *ChauR* 1 (1967):167–180.

78. On his appearance, presumed physiognomy and character, see Charles A. Watkins, "Chaucer's Sweete Preest," *ELH* 36 (1969):455–469, who thought him a sanguine type and therefore strong, healthy, birdlike, and erubescent. For other opinions see Samuel B. Hemingway, "Chaucer's Monk and Nun's Priest," *MLN* 31 (1916):479–483 (that he is young, strong, and lusty); Lumiansky, "The Nun's Priest in the *Canterbury Tales*," *PMLA* 68 (1953):896–906 (that he is scrawny and timid but intelligent and witty); Roy J. Pearcy, "The Epilogue to the Nun's Priest's Tale," *N&Q*, n.s. 15 (1968):43–45 (that he is strong and so aware of the conflict between his libido and his vow of chastity).

with *dilatatio*s, and interrupts it with *apostrophe*s. No one who has read it can forget that the rooster and hen talk the language of courtly love, argue over theories about the meaning of dreams, even get into the mysteries of the medieval pharmacopeia. The Nun's Priest draws in the medieval debate between experience and authority in the argument about dreams; has Chaunticleer provide exempla as they have been provided in previous tales; gets off on the theology of predestination and free will; stumbles into an antifeminist diatribe, retreats, and then dabbles in astrology. Many of these themes have come up in previous tales, but the Priest is not necessarily making fun of his fellow pilgrims. His tale is a kind of universal satire which conceivably refers back to the Knight's Tale (in its courtly parlance, and in its apostrophe on destiny, 3338ff.), to the Prioress's Tale (in its opinion that "murder will out," 3057), and certainly to the Monk's Tale (in the reference to Cresus, 3138, and the reference to Fortune at the climax of the story).

But these backward-looking references to previous tales are subsumed in the Priest's more general spoof of medieval conventions and preoccupations. What is he satirizing? He is satirizing the fads of the medieval intellectual life, the popular subjects that people discussed and argued about; what he finds absurd is not the substance of those fads but the frame of mind with which people approached them. He is satirizing the pomposity and vanity with which people discussed matters of seriousness and the heavy-handed rhetorical forms into which they cast their discourse. You could say he is satirizing "high seriousness" and recommending a spirit not so high and not so serious. His story is directed against "jangling" and "winking": the big mistakes in it occur when Chaunticleer closes his eyes and the fox opens his mouth. What the two of them learn, clearly spelled out, is constantly missed:

> "For he that winketh, whan he sholde see,
> All willfully, God lat him nevere thee!"
>   "Nay," quod the fox, "but God yeve him meschaunce,
> That is so undiscreet of governaunce
> That jangleth whan he sholde hold his pees."

> Lo, swich it is for to be reccheless
> And necligent, and trust on flatterye.
>
> (3431-3437)

Of course it is "flattery" and "vanity" which lead the rooster to close his eyes and the fox to open his mouth, but the heart of the matter is something else: the antidote to those delusions is to keep one's eyes open and one's mouth shut. And the Priest points up the gravity of this moral with some exegetical theorizing which itself might well deserve to be the butt of irony:

> But ye that holden this tale a follye,
> As of a fox, or of a cock and hen,
> Taketh the moralitee, goode men.
> For Saint Paul saith that all that written is,
> To our doctrine it is ywrite, ywis;
> Taketh the fruit, and lat the chaff be stille.
>
> (3438-3443)

The Nun's Priest's Tale sets up a contrast between what is natural and what is intellectual, between what is easily seen by common sense (the common evidence of the senses) and what is easily beclouded by ratiocination. A paradigm is the splendid passage which begins the final scene:

> Whan that the month in which the world bigan,
> That highte "March," whan God first maked man,
> Was complete, and passed were also
> Sin March bigan thrity days and two,
> Bifell that Chauntecleer in all his pride,
> His seven wives walking him biside,
> Cast up his eyen to the brighte sunne,
> (That in the sign of Taurus had yrunne
> Twenty degrees and oon, and somewhat more)
> And knew by kinde, and by noon other lore,
> That it was prime. And crew with blissful stevene:
> "The sun," he said, "is clomben up on hevene
> Forty degrees and oon, and more ywis!
> Madame Pertelote, my worldes bliss,
> Herkneth thise blissful briddes how they singe,
> And see the freshe flowres how they springe!
> Full is myn hert of revel and solas!"
> But suddeinly him fil a sorrweful cas,

For ever the latter end of joy is wo.
God wot that worldly joy is soon ago.
And if a rhetor koude fair endite,
He in a cronicle saufly might it write
As for a sovereign notabilitee.
Now every wise man, lat him herkne me;
This story is also trew, I undertake,
As is the book of Launcelot de Lake,
That women hold in full greet reverence.
Now wol I turn again to my sentence.

(3187-3214)

Everyone knows that roosters can tell time on instinct, and the Nun's Priest says so: Chaunticleer "knew by kinde, and by noon other lore, / That it was prime." But before the Priest gets to that he has ladled on a precise calculation (the date turns out to be the same as that on which Palamon escaped from prison in the Knight's Tale) and an astrological designation. When Chaunticleer crows, he crows an astrological measurement. On top of this the Priest gives us a bit of courtly language ("revel" and "solas") and tells us how a rhetorician would treat the "sorrweful cas" that is about to happen. Simple facts are shot off with Intellect's heaviest artillery. The rooster knows time on instinct; Intellect provides a science of astrology which expresses through the position of heavenly bodies what the rooster already knows. A "sorrweful cas" happens in the barnyard; Intellect provides the figure of Fortune and the theory of animal magnetism to explain why the fox approaches the rooster. The story is a simple everyday occurrence; Intellect gives us rhetoric and learning, and so pads, inflates, bloats.

The Nun's Priest keeps letting the intellectual hot air out by reminding us that the characters after all are barnyard fowls. Common sense, he suggests, isn't good enough: people always want to flesh it out with padding and filler—a dream whose warning is plain has to be argued about with elaborate theories, and the joke is that instinct, the sex instinct, makes Chaunticleer forget about the theories anyway. So when the Priest comes to the outcome of his story he must pause to ruminate whether it is predestined or not. I am not sure if all this intellectualizing and theorizing is really the object of the Priest's irony; I think he has no quarrel with any of the theories, conventions, or ideas which he brings up, but with their capacity to flatter us and becloud our thoughts, to blind us in the realm of private conduct. We would do better to keep our eyes open and our mouths shut.

An amusing feature of the idea of *The Canterbury Tales*, taken as a historical entity, is that the Priest's fable with its simple moral and its fine Chaucerian spirit has seduced ever so many intellectuals into the very flattery which it satirizes. One could almost think Chaucer planned it that way for a super-irony. Dozens of scholars have tried to find a hidden meaning in it—three or four political allegories have been suggested (the poor cock's colors becoming heraldic hints at contemporary personages), and not a few religious allegories have been suggested. The fox has to be the friars, the cock has to be the priesthood, the story has to be about the Fall, or about the efficacy of Man's will in Providence, or about alertness to moral obligation. Common sense is misunderstood almost as often as irony: the poor Nun's Priest has suffered as much as his creator at the hands of academic jangling and flattery. But he has not been misunderstood all the time. One critic has sensibly shown how his tale ridicules the notion of a moral,[79] another that his tale is "a continuously humane suggestion of the relativity of things,"[80] another that it argues "the ultimate uncertainty of any doctrinal point of view."[81] Surely it argues for uncertainty and relativity in intellectual matters, but it also recommends something positive: an ironic, skeptical clear-headedness which is nothing if not Chaucerian.[82]

79. Stephen Manning, "The Nun's Priest's Morality and the Medieval Attitude Toward Fables," *JEGP* 59 (1960):403–416.

80. Muscatine, *Chaucer and the French Tradition*, pp. 240–243.

81. Stanley E. Fish, "*The Nun's Priest's Tale* and Its Analogues," *College Language Association Journal* 5 (1962):223–228.

82. Cf. Muscatine, "The Canterbury Tales," in *Chaucer and Chaucerians*, ed. Brewer, p. 111: "The mixture of *The Nun's Priest's Tale* produces yet another range of effects. It is *The Canterbury Tales* in little; its kaleidoscopic shifts of perspective, exposing a dozen important subjects to the humour of comparison, seems to exemplify Chaucer's basic method in the whole

If the tales of Fragment VII have any kind of unity, that unity is imposed by the Nun's Priest's Tale. It would be impossible to see any theme or development if that final tale were not present. No theme is announced at the beginning and I doubt that Chaucer set out with any in mind, but as he put one tale after another, or juggled them about, a pattern emerged, and the Nun's Priest's tale gives finality to that pattern—it makes a point. We cannot say with certainty that the group is "about" anything—about literature or story-telling or morality. But all the poetical tales in the group show that people do not think much about what they say: the suggestion seems to be that if you ask a group of people to speak their pieces most of what you get is hokum. The *Melibee* is an exception, of course, and belongs to a larger theme developed throughout *The Canterbury Tales*; but per-haps the Nun's Priest would view even that noble discourse as heavy-handed and overly dressed up. The thrust of this group of tales has to do with the way people think or fail to think, with what happens in their heads and how it bears fruit in their conduct. A part of this concern is with the stories they tell; but the heart of the matter lies in their private thoughts.

We said that the first group of tales beginning with the Knight's appears to have a degenerating structure, and that the marriage group begins by stating a problem, views that problem from different perspectives, and "trails off," com-ing to no resolution. The tales of Fragment VII fit the interlace with a different kind of structure. They do not degenerate or trail off; they are not a "discussion" of a common theme; while they are concatenated pairs they do not parody or "quit" each other—only the last does this. The other two groups begin with a tale that makes a strong statement but they end with no resolution; this group begins with three unimpressive tales but does end with a resolution.

---

work." And Donaldson, *Chaucer's Poetry*, p. 944: "in one important respect [the Nun's Priest] is very like his creator: he can survey the world as if he were no part of it, as if he were situated comfortably on the moon looking at a human race whom he knew and loved wholeheartedly but whose ills he was immune from."

The Nun's Priest's Tale looks back upon the previous tales
and finds in them or in their tellers a central flaw. The
group is the only group in *The Canterbury Tales* that has this
kind of retrospective structure, and is therefore the one
most like *The Canterbury Tales* itself. The sequence comes to a
conclusion, and that conclusion is an ironic frame of mind
very like Chaucer's own.

THE CLOSING TALES: FRAGMENTS VIII-IX

References to time and place make it clear that Fragments
VIII and IX come at the end just before the Parson's Tale.
The tales—those of the Second Nun, the Canon's Yeoman,
and the Manciple—are very unlike each other, and no one
has suggested that they make a group or have much to do
with one another or with the work as a whole. Most readers
seem to think they are leftovers, tales Chaucer found no
place for elsewhere, and are among the weaker tales. I will
try to show that they belong where they are, are there for a
purpose, and are among the better tales. If we view *The
Canterbury Tales* as a narrative or sequence of narratives, the
work seems to fall apart at the end. But if we view it as an
assemblage of themes, an interlace, the three last tales may
combine and repeat themes dealt with before.

The Second Nun's Tale is the last of the ideal narratives
and the only saint's legend. It provides a final tale on the
subject of love and marriage, a subject raised as early as the
Knight's Tale. And it does relate back to the "marriage
group."[83] It is not about a state of life higher than marriage
but about a higher form of marriage itself. We said earlier
that even within marriage chastity was considered best so
long as it was maintained with the husband's consent; the

---

83. Raymond Preston, *Chaucer* (New York and London: Sheed &
Ward, 1952), pp. 279–280, thought it a "pious addendum" to the Marriage Group; and see n. 36 above. See also Paul M. Clogan, "The Figural
Style and Meaning of the Second Nun's Tale," *M&H*, n.s. 3 (1972):213–
240. To my knowledge no one has suggested, as I do here, that the last
three tales are themselves a group.

Parson recommends this (X:946) as something of "greet merit" so long as it causes no occasion for the husband to stray. The Second Nun's Tale depicts such a marriage. The Wife of Bath thought it impossible for any clerk to speak well of women "but if it be of holy saintes lives" (III:690), and the Second Nun's Tale is just that—a saint's legend about a married woman. St. Cecile is very different from any of the marriage group wives, but she is like them in selective ways—like Dorigen she is of "noble kinde," like Griselde "full devout and humble in hir corage," like the Wife something of a theologian. She submits humbly to marriage, but gains sovereignty by the husband's consent: she converts him to Christianity, makes him "meek as ever was any lamb," then turns him into a missionary. They remain chaste, devote their lives to the church, and become martyrs.[84]

Like the Franklin's tale, the Second Nun's begins with a vow: in the Franklin's tale this is a vow of mutual concession and courtesy, in the Second Nun's a vow of chastity. Cecile's pagan husband agrees with an improbable lack of resistance, characteristic of saints' legends, to be baptized. But then they are specially called to this vocation—their destiny of purity and martyrdom is announced to them by an angel. Such a marriage is markedly different from the Wife's or Merchant's views on the subject, but it is different from the Clerk's too: it involves not the subjugation of the woman's will to the man's will but the mutual subjugation of both their wills to the will of God. The mutuality in their relationship may be like the Franklin's notion, but the purpose is different: to the Franklin mutuality was a matter of comfort and convenience.

The purpose in the Second Nun's Tale is eternal reward, but Cecile and Valerian practice the active life and live in "the world." They are not ascetics or mystics; their object is good works and the propagation of the faith. Martyrdom and sainthood are the reward, a special vocation the condition: it is not the life for all. In her Prologue the

84. Bernards, *Speculum Virginum*, pp. 43–44, points out that martyrdom was sometimes considered equal to and sometimes higher than virginity in the grades of perfection.

Second Nun says that faith, wisdom, and good works are a guard against idleness and sin. This points up the weakness in the Franklin's "solution" to the problem of establishing domestic concord: it is a way of having "delit," joy, ease, prosperity, convenience—but these are worldly and self-indulgent goals. Her strictures against idleness in the opening lines of her Prologue bear this out, for idleness was conventionally thought a state which led to sin.[85] Her invocation to the Virgin emphasizes virginity and good works, and quotes James 2:17 that "faith is deed withouten werkes" (64). And her interpretation of the name "Cecile" focuses on "chastness of virginitee" (88) and the "Ensample of good and wise workes alle" (105). The emphasis is consistently on the highest Christian ideals of conduct.

While the Second Nun's Tale gives a sort of closure to the theme of love and marriage which runs throughout *The Canterbury Tales*, it is also the last of the "ideal" narratives. These include the Man of Law's Tale, the Prioress's Tale, the Monk's Tale, and the Clerk's Tale. They are the most difficult among the tales for a modern reader; they represent a stylized kind of art which is no longer palatable and an idealism long since out of vogue. The Man of Law's, Prioress's, and Monk's tales give us some reason to question whether the tale is appropriate to the pilgrim who tells it: if we assume it *is* appropriate, we find the pilgrim guilty of misguided moralism or self-righteousness or moral blindness. And the admirable Clerk, whose tale is appropriate, dispels his moral with an ironic envoy. The Second Nun's Tale is different—there is nothing to make us take it less than seriously. The "facelessness" of the Second Nun—the fact that she is not described in the General Prologue—serves an artistic purpose: we have no sense of her personality and so read her tale in a neutral frame of mind. We may

85. In the courtly tradition, owing to the *Roman de la Rose*, Idleness was the guardian of the gate to Mirth's garden; cf. Knight's Tale, 1940. The Parson (X:714–716) says it is the gate of "alle harmes." When the Second Nun says it is the porter of the gate "of delices" the reference may be to the state of *delectatio* which was thought anterior to the act of consent that constituted sin.

extrapolate from it the notion of a simple, credulous nun naive in the ways of the world—but this picture of her only points up the neutral stylized manner of her tale. It is worlds apart from the presumed character of the other "faceless" pilgrim (also of the Prioress's retinue), the Nun's Priest, who is worldly, ironic, witty, as idiosyncratic as the Second Nun is "neutral." Her characters are not real or "round"; they behave in predictable ways and seem impelled by forces outside themselves, a common feature of hagiography. The reader should not expect "motivation" because the characters in a saint's legend are especially called; their motivations do not invite scrutiny.

It is probably important that Cecile comes of "noble kinde" (121), because proper conduct for noblemen has been a theme throughout *The Canterbury Tales*; here we are reminded that the best life for a nobleman, as for anyone, is the highest ideal—purity and sainthood. How seriously a fourteenth-century nobleman would have taken these counsels of perfection must be left to speculation; it's safe to say that some would have taken them less seriously than others. This leads the modern reader to look for irony. Valerian's lightning conversion and Cecile's method of winning him over to chastity (her angel will slay him if he touches her) do not seem a model of tact, and it is hard for *us* to suppress a smile. But Chaucer had these details from his sources, and the only hint of irony I find which is not in the sources is the remark that night came and she must go to bed with her husband "as oft is the mannere" (142). This is not really a formulaic phrase and I doubt that Chaucer used it merely for the rhyme (he used it in a similar context once in *The Legend of Good Women*, 2673). It does sound like the comment of an innocent nun and does have the sly ring of Chaucer's irony, but if so it is the only such intrusion. Otherwise the tale is told in the barebones fashion of a saint's life. Nor is its ending ambiguous; one can't ask for more "closure" than martyrdom and sainthood, yet even here the emphasis remains on the world—the tale ends by reminding us that her church in Rome still stands.[86] It is sometimes thought

86. On the possibility of a topical allusion to Archbishop Easton's

the tale was written in earlier years and put here for want of something better; the Nun refers to herself as a "son of Eve" (62), and while the expression can be explained away it does push along the suggestion that the tale's inclusion in the work, or its assignment to the Nun, was an afterthought, and hence a deliberate choice. The quality of the verse strikes me as up to par with Chaucer's later work; we get a desiccated, stark effect, but this comes from the narrative style, not from the verse. The tale brings to a conclusion many themes by harking back to the days of early Christianity and presenting an ideal in the "figural" style beneath which earlier treatments seem to pale. Its effect is to alter our perspective.

The Canon's Yeoman appears on the scene when the saint's legend is concluded:

> Whan ended was the life of Saint Cecile,
> Er we hadde riden fully five mile,
> At Boghtoun under Blee us gan atake
> A man that clothed was in clothes blacke,
> And under that he had a white surplys.
> His hackeney, that was all pomely grys,
> So swatte that it wonder was to see;
> It seemed he had pricked miles three.
> The horse eek that his yeman rode upon
> So swatte that unnethe mighte it gon.
> About the peytrel stood the foom full hye;
> He was of foom all flecked as a pye.
>
> (554-565)

This spectral figure's unexpected entrance introduces something utterly different from what has gone before. He addresses the company, telling them that his lord wants to ride with them for his "desport" because "he loveth dalliaunce" (592). He praises the Canon in an extravagant way: he could, according to his Yeoman, turn Canterbury town upside down and pave it all with silver and gold (625-626). The Host's reply (he glimpses the Canon at a distance) points to the shabby appearance of the great alchemist—a

---

nomination (1383) as cardinal and priest of that church, see Mary Giffin, *Studies on Chaucer and His Audience* (Quebec: Editions L'Eclair, 1956), pp. 29–48.

notable clerk ought to be dressed appropriately, from the Host's viewpoint, and the Yeoman strangely agrees. He makes an aside to the Host, asking the Host to keep it secret (643): the Canon is too wise, what is overdone is a vice, he misuses his wit. Maybe the first speech is made within the Canon's hearing and the second not, but even if this is so it points up the Yeoman's ambivalence toward his master. He sees from one point of view all that is impressive about the man's intellect, and at the same time sees him as a shabby failure. This negative side of his attitude is what comes out. The Host asks where they dwell and the Yeoman depicts the shabbiest place possible, the suburbs, where robbers lurk "by kinde" and hold their "privee fereful residence" (659-660). The Host then asks why the Yeoman's face is discolored and gets for an answer the beginnings of an exposé: the hopelessly repetitive alchemical experiments leave his face blackened with smoke as they leave his mind blackened with disillusionment. We deceive many, he says, and borrow gold, making them think we can double their money, but we always have hopes of success. He holds out an ideal which seems to have as much allure as any ideal expressed anywhere in *The Canterbury Tales*, but acknowledges it is false:

> But that science is so fer us biforn,
> We mowen nat, although we had it sworn,
> It overtake, it slit away so faste.
> It wol us maken beggers atte laste.
>
> (680-683)

The Canon draws near in suspicion (we get it on Cato's authority that guilty men think everything is spoken about them), and accuses the Yeoman of slandering him. When the Host spurs the Yeoman on, the Canon rides away in shame.

From here on the emphasis is on the Yeoman's attitude. We learn a lot about the methods of alchemy, but what we get is a two-part story describing first a failure, then a fraud. The Yeoman rises to the occasion under the stimulus of the Host's egging and the Canon's flight:

> "A!" quod the Yeman, "here shall arise game!
> All that I kan anon now wol I telle."
>
> (703-704)

Like any good and willing student, the Yeoman is over-whelmed by the possibilities; his head is full of techniques, and he sees the goal of knowledge as bright and shiny as if Canterbury town could really be turned upside down and paved with silver and gold. And yet he knows it cannot. He admires and scorns his master at once: "He is too wise," he says, and "whan a man hath over-greet a wit, / Full oft him happeth to misusen it" (644-649).

The structure of the Yeoman's tale perfectly expresses this ambivalence. The first part is a general description of what alchemists do interspersed with a running diatribe against the hopelessness of it all. The Yeoman is full of information learned by experience, and he can articulate it point for point. He has got the terms down, knows the whole pharmacopoeia of the art, and is imbued with the researcher's enthusiasm. But he hates himself for his own involvement: "our labour is in vain" he complains (777), and his own money is lost too. More than half of the first part is made up of these digressive outbursts, and their intensity mounts. He manages to control himself ("pass over this," 898) and go on, but every bit of information heaps fuel on his wrath and he ends up in a vitriolic spirit characterizing the arguments which alchemists use among themselves to excuse their failures (915-931). He concludes by pointing to his own anger and to the unworthiness of the enterprise:

> We fail of that which that we wolden have,
> And in our madness evermore we rave.
>
> (958-959)

If the tale ended here it would be a tale of enlighten-ment; the Yeoman's disillusionment would make him give it up.[87] But the second part is the story proper. He gets a grip on himself and objectifies: he tells about a crooked London

87. Cf. Bruce L. Grenberg, "The Canon's Yeoman's Tale: Boethian Wisdom and the Alchemists," ChauR 1 (1966):37−54, who sees the Yeo-man as a Boethian figure experiencing a conversion to philosophical and Christian truth. A more subtle interpretation based on the notion that the Yeoman undergoes a conversion and renounces a "wrong way of life" is John Gardner's "The Canon's Yeoman's Prologue and Tale: An Interpreta-tion," PQ 46 (1967):1−17.

canon—we don't really know if it is his master—who performs three tricks, then takes forty pounds from a priest for
the fake recipe. He plumps up all his rhetoric to tell his tale;
it is interspersed with apostrophes of increasing violence,
and with protests about what he is criticizing. He is criticizing
not science but the abuse of science; he is not talking about
honest canons (992-994) or his employer (1088-1090), but is
warning others (1306).

The tone of this dramatic monologue is what makes it so
exciting. The Yeoman continues to believe in the experiments as a possibility, but as with most medieval quests the
goal is so high that it is out of reach. In the background is
the true practice of a Gnostic spiritual alchemy not tainted by
abuse.[88] He only condemns the avarice and falsehood of
deceiving alchemists, not the science itself. His advice is to let
it go, not because it is a fraud or a delusion but because
Christ in His own good time will give the secret to those He
would inspire (1467-1471). Then he contradicts himself by
saying it is against God's will (1472-1475). He really poses the
problem of reason versus revelation: men can struggle with
thought and knowledge, but they cannot conclude anything
unless God wills it. It must have been a dilemma which all
medieval intellectuals felt. R. W. Southern in a splendid
essay has termed this phase of medieval life "scientific
humanism."[89] He thinks that it reached its height in the
thirteenth century, and that the fourteenth century saw a
period of disillusionment and intellectual chaos. (The complex diagrams of the cosmos mentioned in Chapter 4 afford
a glimpse of this scientific humanism.) If this is so, the vain
alchemical experiments were the shabby leavings of an
intellectual idealism which had fallen apart. And the poor
Yeoman is a victim of this historical trend. He is intoxicated

88. See Mircea Eliade, *The Forge and the Crucible*, trans. Stephen Corrin
(New York: Harper, 1962). On the background of the tale in contem-
porary alchemical treatises see Edgar H. Duncan, "The Literature of
Alchemy and Chaucer's Canon's Yeoman's Tale: Framework, Theme,
and Characters," *Speculum* 43 (1968):633–656, who hints at the end that
Chaucer may speak "another message to the true sons of doctrine."
89. R. W. Southern, *Medieval Humanism and Other Studies* (Oxford: Basil
Blackwell, 1970), pp. 29–60.

with the pursuit of knowledge but knows the pursuit can succeed only when God allows it: Milton had a similar way of treating "forbidden knowledge."[90] If you ask what causes the Yeoman's frustration and rage, the answer has to be his own gullibility. But it is not a naive gullibility. He is outraged at the dishonesty of false alchemists—he has the ethics and ideals of committed students, but he has their disillusionment and weariness too. Intellectual pursuit for its own sake or for earthly reward collapses half the time into despair: one is always asking what is the good of it. But this only means that the real reason for the Yeoman's frustration and rage is his inexhaustible hope.

The character of this hope, taken as an aspect of medieval culture (and it did not die until the end of the Renaissance—has perhaps never died), is vastly complex. In the Yeoman himself we experience a tension between the ideals of an eager student and the realities of the laboratory; between the glamor and the wonder of the quest and the abuses and shabbiness of practice; between honest curiosity and exploitation. In medieval and Renaissance society greed was the obvious motive: gold had a physical presence which it was not to have later in a credit economy. You could "make money" in the Middle Ages if you could just find the secret of turning base metals into gold. That was what made alchemy so disreputable. The monks and friars, who esteemed learning and practiced poverty, were forbidden to deal in alchemy.[91] But this was not just because alchemy was regarded as a con game. People believed transmutation was possible. One notion was that the ancients really had the secret but out of avarice had wrapped it in enigmas;[92] perhaps there is just a glimmer of incipient "literary" humanism in this idea that a superior knowledge was hidden in ancient texts. But it was playing with fire.

90. See Howard Schultz, *Milton and Forbidden Knowledge* (New York: Modern Language Assoc. of America, 1955).
91. Duncan, 635–636.
92. Duncan, 643; and 637, n. 14 (quoting the *Icocedron* by Walter of Odington, in Bodleian Ms. Digby 119, fol. 128^r): "Necnon antici sue consulentes avaricie artem enigmatibus involuebant suam potius ignoranciam quam scientiam preferentes. . . ."

The quest of the alchemist had a moral lesson for medieval men: they saw it as a symbol of the great quest of life, so that the philosopher's stone symbolized Christ. Professor Rosenberg thinks that the Canon is therefore a devil or anti-Christ figure,[93] placed here in the eleventh hour of the pilgrimage to remind us that in life's journey we have to know true coin from false. It is one allegorical reading that makes sense. Carl Jung, going on psychoanalytic evidence, believed that alchemy was a projected or externalized spiritual experience which employed archetypal symbols—the pots and pans, the fire, and the pharmacology of the alchemist's trade was all a way of acting out the quest for enlightenment which characterized the spirit of medieval culture. And if this is true then the Canon's Yeoman's Tale does fit nicely with the Second Nun's Tale that precedes it: in both tales an opposition is made between aspects of good and evil.[94]

The Canon's Yeoman's Tale deals with themes which have come up before, among them intellect and idealism. The pilgrims are all great intellectualizers—the Knight himself introduces an intellectual or philosophical element into his tale, and the Miller chimes in with a critique or parody of that intellectual structure. The ideal narratives all impose upon experience an intellectual construct of one kind or another. *Sir Thopas,* considered as a parody, is intellectual; Chaucer's other tale, the *Melibee,* is intellectual in the truest sense. I have tried to suggest that the group of tales in Fragment VII, if they have a common theme, deal with the private basis of conduct, with the problem of how people should think about the things they do and say. The Wife of Bath is an intellectual of sorts, her head full of moral theology and "authorities," and the rest of the marriage group is an intellectual game which pits one opinion against another. The Canon's Yeoman's Tale picks up this intellectu-

93. Bruce A. Rosenberg, "Swindling Alchemist, Antichrist," *CentR* 6 (1962):566–580.

94. The point is made by Bruce A. Rosenberg, "The Contrary Tales of the Second Nun and the Canon's Yeoman," *ChauR* 2 (1968):278–291; cf. Muscatine, *Chaucer and the French Tradition,* pp. 213–221, esp. 216f.

alism and examines it in relief. We see intellectual activity almost in the abstract—knowledge, authorities, books, experiments all applied to an ideal which is a pie in the sky. And what Chaucer lets us see is the emotional component of that intellectualizing, the way it felt. The goal is, ideally, enlightenment—but it is also worldly *curiositas* and wealth. The abuses amount to thievery. Money, thievery, and cheating have been a frequent theme throughout *The Canterbury Tales*—associated with aggression and revenge in the Reeve's Tale, with vanity and sexuality in the Shipman's Tale, with obsessive greed in the Friar's and Summoner's tales. But in the Canon's Yeoman's Tale the quest for money is associated with questing itself, with the great spiritual as well as the intellectual quest at the heart of medieval humanism.

And the Canon's Yeoman's Tale is another instance of "quitting." From the very start the pilgrims pay off debts with one another—the Miller quits the Knight, the Reeve quits the Miller. The Nun's Priest, it might be argued, quits the whole bunch of previous tales. The Friar and Summoner quit one another viciously. The Merchant quits the Clerk, both of them and the Franklin quit the Wife. In the instance of the Canon's Yeoman, the Yeoman quits his master on the spot—we see the Canon retreat in shame. It looks like a triumph of youth over age, of student over teacher; but in the tale itself the Canon is silently allowed to quit the Yeoman back, because the Yeoman remains hopelessly in the grip of his master's obsession. He consigns alchemy to the realm of forbidden knowledge by quoting from old books, and alchemical books at that.

The Manciple's Tale is the last tale before the Parson's discourse; references to place names put it after the Canon's Yeoman's Tale.[95] In the General Prologue we learned that

95. VIII:556 has the pilgrims at Boughton under Blean; IX:2–3 has them at "Bobbe-up-and-doun, / Under the Blee." The latter is normally taken to mean Harbledown, but even if it means Up-and-Down Field in Thannington it comes after Boughton on the Canterbury Road. See Skeat's note on IX:2. The Parson's Prologue and Tale come after the Manciple's (see X:1). The recurring notion that the Manciple's Tale comes on the return journey is based on the notion that "by the morwe" (16)

the Manciple was able to cheat his thirty-odd masters who are wizards at finance—probably they ignore him because he is beneath their notice. In the prologue to his tale he plays a dirty trick on the drunken Cook and has to count on being ignored here too: the Host remarks that the Cook could if he chose betray the Manciple, and the Manciple admits it. The Manciple's mockery of the Cook is awesomely aggressive. After the Cook has fallen off his horse and the company have lifted him back up, the Manciple admits that the Cook could "lightly bring me in the snare" (IX:77). Both belong to a "tightly knit group of city businessmen,"[96] so he endangers himself by provoking the Cook. But he goes ahead and offers the Cook wine, and the Cook drinks and thanks him while the company laugh. The Manciple has put himself in a position where, if any of the company tell the Cook what happened while he was passing out, the Cook might well have a mind to tattle on the Manciple to his masters. So his tale about the tattle-tale crow with its moral about keeping one's mouth shut is suited to his circumstance.[97]

But this realistic estimate of his tale draws attention away from its content. The tale is almost always treated as a throwaway. The prologue is admired for its realistic byplay, but the tale is left out of selections and regarded by most commentators as a slender effort. It is amusing that it suits the Manciple's character and circumstances, that its jeering tone suits his easy-going cynicism, and that his advice might well apply to himself. But it is usually viewed as mechanical and ineffective—a tale written in Chaucer's earlier days and stuck in here for want of something better. I want to argue

means in the morning; but what it means is "on the morning after the night before"—the Host goes on to give two reasons why the Cook might not have slept the previous night. To put the Manciple's Tale on the return journey would require altering the clear statement of X:1, but the workroom critics argue that Chaucer meant to do so; such is the felicity of the house of bondage. For the conjecture that X:1 is a scribal addition see Robert K. Root, "The Manciple's Prologue," *MLN* 44 (1929):493−496.

96. Lumiansky, *Of Sundry Folk*, p. 237, and cf. "Chaucer's Cook-Host Relationship," *MS* 17 (1955):208−209.

97. See J. Burke Severs, "Is the *Manciple's Tale* a Success?" *JEGP* 51 (1952):1−16, who shows how Chaucer adapted his material to suit the teller.

that it is a perfect choice for the last tale: its effect is astonishing, and it prepares perfectly for the Parson's Prologue and Tale which follow.

The tale is neatly structured on principles of medieval rhetoric; it is another instance of unimpersonated artistry. The Manciple tells it in four economical narrative steps, each followed by a digression or "amplification." The narration and digression are about equally balanced—131 lines are given to narration, 127 to digression. The first step (105-147) introduces the characters: Phebus; a white crow who can talk and imitate the speech of any man who "sholde tell a tale" (135); and Phebus's wife, of whom Phebus is jealous. These forty-three lines lay the groundwork of the story and leave us with the stock fabliau situation of a jealous husband afraid of being cuckolded. The second step (155-162) informs us that Phebus does all he can to please his wife so that no man "sholde han put him from hir grace." To this is added a sort of philosophical or scientific observation, that no one can "destreyne" a thing which nature has set in a creature. The third step (196-204) briefly informs us (as we could have guessed) that Phebus's wife deceived him with "A man of litel reputacioun"—in Phebus's absence his wife sent for her "lemman." The fourth step (238-308) is the only protracted narrative sequence: we get dialogue done up with fancy apostrophes, an outcome, and a moral. The white crow sees the lovers doing their "lust volage" and when Phebus returns sings "cokkow!" Asked what the song means, the crow explains that Phebus has been deceived, repeating some lines from the previous narrative sequence, "With oon of litel reputacioun, / Nat worth to thee, as in comparisoun" (253-254). The crow gives further details and "tokens," telling him often that "he sey it with his eyen" (an amusing echo from the Merchant's Tale). Phebus slays his wife, destroys his musical instruments, destroys his bows and arrows, then turns in anger upon the crow. In an apostrophe of operatic proportions (274-291) he laments his wife, the "gem of lustiheed / That were to me so sad and eek so trewe." Deceiving himself after the manner of January, he blames his lack of trust and rash hand, and proposes to slay himself for sorrow. Then, in a classic moment of projection, he punishes the crow: he will "quit" the "false theef" (292) by removing from him his song, his white feathers, and his ability to speak.

This fable about a talking bird teaches tale-tellers the same lesson as the Nun's Priest's Tale, that one is better off to hold one's tongue. The real art of the story is in its four lively digressions. In the first (148-154) we get a bit of folk wisdom, that a good wife should not be kept under observation and that it is in vain to keep a shrew. The conclusion is:

> This hold I for a verray nicetee,
> To spille labour for to keepe wives.
> Thus writen olde clerkes in hir lives.
>
> (152-154)

The second digression (163-195) develops with exempla the theme that none can "destreyne" a quality which nature has put into a creature: one can keep a bird in a cage and adorn it, but the bird by nature prefers the cold forest; a domesticated cat always wants to eat a mouse, because "here hath lust his dominacioun, / And appetite fleemeth discrecioun" (181-182); a she-wolf will take "the lewedest wolf" or "leest of reputacioun" when she wants a mate. He concludes that "Flesh is so newfangel" and that we can have no pleasure in anything that tends "into vertu." This "natural" human quality, applied ironically to "men" (187-188)—oh no, not women—is associated with "flesh" (193) and so with original sin or fallen nature.

The third digression (205-237) comes after we have learned that Phebus's wife has betrayed him. The Manciple, making an apology for his "knavish speche," appeals to Plato, the same authority which the Canon's Yeoman appealed to in rejecting alchemy (VIII:1453ff.), and uses the same Platonic utterance which Chaucer appealed to in the General Prologue:

> The wise Plato saith, as ye may rede,
> The word moot need accorde with the dede.
>
> (208-209)

There is no difference, he says, between a noble woman and

a poor woman if they are dishonest with their bodies, but the noble woman will be called "his lady as in love" and the poor woman will be called "his wench or his lemman." "Men layn that oon," he comments, "as low as lith that other." He clarifies with an analogy: there is no difference between a tyrant and an outlaw—the tyrant has more power, the outlaw only a small following. The difference is similarly *linguistic*: the tyrant is called a captain, the other an outlaw or thief. The Manciple makes what the medievals would have thought a just point, that in matters of moral virtue there are no class distinctions; but he makes a significant addition by showing that the only real difference is a difference of language. This astute observation may not be altogether out of character for the Manciple—as the steward of a "temple" he might have had plenty of opportunity to observe his thirty-odd masters, lawyers and men of affairs, applying subtle distinctions of language to the affairs of the rich and powerful. But it is not hard to find something of the poet's own voice in this meditation on words and things.[98]

The ideal of an accord between word and action is destroyed by the crow's harsh experience with telling the truth. Phebus believes the crow's story, then wilfully disbelieves it and turns against the teller. People do not always want to hear the truth and are not always willing to believe it; the word should accord with the deed, but it has to fall welcome on the listener's ear. This accommodation leads the teller into rhetoric, the art of saying things effectively; and to the extent that rhetoric dresses up the truth to make it more attractive, it goes in the direction of dissembling. Maybe the elaborate rhetoric of the tale illustrates the point. Language used well tells lies—that seems to be the moral. But the tale makes it clear that the fault lies not in language but in values which language reflects: the difference between a "lady" and a "wench" isn't in the words but in our reverence for class distinctions, the difference between a captain and an outlaw in our awe of power. With both examples the Manciple says "There is no difference" (212, 225)—he means that the

98. Cf. Britton J. Harwood, "Language and the Real: Chaucer's Manciple," *ChauR* 6 (1972):268–279.

moral quality is the same but it can be hidden by euphemisms. Perhaps it is a pessimistic or a cynical view, but again it is men's fault, not the "inadequacy" of language.

The fourth digression (309-362) comes after the god of poetry has brought down vengeance on the storyteller. This vengeance is called "quitting" (293) and makes the story like a fabliau. The fabliau figure of the trickster tricked is the crow who can "countrefete" the speech of every man "whan he sholde tell a tale." Since the tale generalizes about language and tale-telling, one could say the trickster tricked is any tale-teller—every one of the pilgrims and Chaucer himself. The Manciple's Tale turns the whole of *The Canterbury Tales* into a super-fabliau in which the storyteller's trickery is tricked. The moral, like the Nun's Priest's, is that one does best to hold one's tongue. The Manciple applies this to the practical circumstance of the tale (one should never tell a man how another man has "dight" his wife because he will hate the teller), but he makes it a general principle of conduct. He tells us that Solomon teaches us to hold our tongues, then protests that he is not "textuel"[99] and turns to proverbs for authority: "thus taughte me my dame," he says, and gives as a sample a collection of proverbs worthy of Professor Whiting himself. This lesson is framed on either side by the immediate application of the exemplum he has told— "think upon the crowe." For the rest, his mother's speech consists of no less than seventeen proverbs all on the theme of keeping one's mouth shut. Twelve of these begin with the address "My son," itself a proverbial or stereotyped utterance which occurs in the biblical proverbs, gnomic verses, and moral Gower's *Confessio*. The repetition of this didactic formula has a thumping effect—we seem to hear the old lady haranguing her son about keeping quiet: it is like what was said of Carlyle, that he praised silence in twenty volumes. We even get "authorities"—Solomon, David, Seneca. The repetition of the one sentiment leaves echoing in our heads the two

---

99. Line 316; he makes the same protestation in line 235. The remarks look forward to the Parson's disclaimer in X:57. Harwood, 279, thinks the Manciple's Tale "a kind of satyr play . . . a moment of verbal Misrule" which prepares for the Parson's Tale.

most frequently repeated words, "jangling" and "tongue," which produce an auditory and a visual image: a disembodied chattering and a tongue wagging, the empty blah-blah of too much talk and the flapping of an open mouth. And with this image the tales of Canterbury are brought to a close.

I hope I have managed to show that the last three tales are not leftovers stuck on at the end but a sequence meant to recapture themes interlaced throughout the work. The movement of this sequence, like that of Fragment I, is degenerative: the Second Nun's Tale enunciates an ideal; the Canon's Yeoman's Tale is about a failed or an impossible ideal; the Manciple's Tale fastens upon fallen nature and makes all ideals—of thought, word, and deed—seem impossible. There are greater disparities among these tales than among those of the other groups. They do not have a theme in common but treat various themes raised earlier. They have no one-for-one relationships with previous tales or groups or with each other, but they are a sequence which has an effect.

And that effect is to destroy. The tales collapse the structure that has gone before. The Second Nun's legend puts before us an ideal so high that all other ideals of civil, domestic, and private conduct vanish before it. The Canon's Yeoman's Tale takes the quest of intellect and makes us see its vanity. The Manciple's Tale lets language itself fall beneath corrupt human nature. The rest, or at least the end, is silence.

The three tales have the effect of an ironical *De contemptu mundi*—they let us see the vanity of earthly pursuits, the mutability of human deeds, the disappointing uselessness of human striving, the corruptness of human nature. They make us change our point of view—we look back on all that has gone before and it looks different. The Knight's vision of the noble life, the Wife's *joie de vivre*, the story-telling game itself, the wit, the intellect, the ironic games, and the fabulous masquerade—what does it all amount to? And this pessimistic effect prepares us perfectly for the Parson, who begins "Thou getest fable noon ytold for me."

This destructive effect makes the Manciple's Tale crucial. And Chaucer leads up to it in a clever way. The group starts with a "headless" tale, and its teller, the Second Nun, is a "faceless" pilgrim not described in the General Prologue. Her personality or "voice" does not color her story. The Canon's Yeoman's personality, though he was not described in the General Prologue either, comes out dramatically in his first appearance. But the Manciple *was* described in the General Prologue. His contretemps with the Cook reminds us of his unsavory character—and makes him more unsavory. And his tale is cynical, destructive: he thinks cuckoldry is natural, truth disprized, moral distinctions masked with words. He thinks deeds *ought* to be virtuous and words *ought* to correspond with deeds, but his tale gives this up as a lost cause. One cannot fault him for theology: when he says "Flesh is so newfangel" (193) he is talking about man's imperfection in his fallen state (and he does add "with meschaunce"). But his style is unsavory like the man himself. His tale destroys everything and does it coldly. The faithless wife is murdered in cold blood; Phebus, presented first as a great archer and musician, destroys his bows and arrows and his musical instruments, threatens to slay himself, then makes the crow black and takes away his song and speech. We are left in a bleak, mean world where the guarded tongue is the best counsel. The Manciple isn't recommending the sort of judicious irony which the Nun's Priest recommended—he levels distinctions of language and condemns jangling because it isn't shrewd. His last words, if taken seriously, would nullify all authors and all "tidings," would nullify speech and story and literature:

> . . . be noon auctour newe
> Of tidings, whether they been false or trewe.

> (359-360)

That is the "sense of an ending" we get at the end of the tales proper; it is almost a mock apocalypse, a final destruction but without the momentous gloom and horror of the apocalyptic *de contemptu mundi*. The wonder of this ending is that it suits what is after all a great humorous work of art. It

negates almost everything set up in the General Prologue—
the word's accord with the deed, the uses of rhetoric, telling
tales or "tidings." But it doesn't negate the common-sense
principle of the General Prologue, that every tale is a bit of
lore selected, preserved, and reshaped by its teller. The
Manciple's conclusion, all blackness and silence, imitates a
feeling everyone knows who has approached the end of a
long, long book: we turn our eyes from the pages and think
"words, words, words." Chaucer lets us have that feeling
before the Parson's discourse; that side of it is unimpersonated artistry. On the other side, we know it is the Manciple's
conclusion; we look back to the General Prologue to see what
kind of man this is. And so it reinvokes the General Prologue
as a principle of form. The interlace in the end brings us
back to its beginning: we are doing what we started out
doing, asking questions about the meanings of tales as they
relate to their tellers. At this last juncture, having glanced
back at the questionable Manciple, we glance forward and
the Parson's Tale looks like an answer.

THE ESTHETICS OF THIS STRUCTURE AND ITS RELATION
TO THE FORM

In these four groups of tales, each a structure in itself, what
kind of larger structure is to be found? The first and last
groups, we have seen, have a degenerating movement—they
start with a noble ideal and end with an unpalatable reality.
The middle two have what could be called a generating
movement: they explore the ramifications of an issue or
cluster of issues in a questioning spirit without settling that
issue. The tales of the "marriage" group begin with the
Wife's specialized view, generate related issues about domestic concord, marriage, fidelity, women's desires, perfection,
"trouthe," and so on; but they only end with another
specialized point of view. The tales of Fragment VII, which
alternate mirth and doctrine, generate issues about how
people think and talk and follow fads, and on them the
Nun's Priest comments ironically or satirically. His tale

comes close to settling an issue by pointing a moral, but the moral recommends detachment and disinterestedness, warns against "jangling" and "flattery." The first three groups are held together by thematic strains: the themes cannot be stated as single propositions, but each group explores a realm of conduct (I've called them civil, domestic, private) from different points of view and so introduces side issues and related issues. The tales of the last group comprise a reiterative narration which raises again themes raised earlier and makes the reader look back on what was said before.

If this interlaced construct of groups and themes is the structure of the tales, however, it means that the *literary* provenance of the structure is the romance. Yet the single self-contained narrative was part of a reaction *against* the interlaced structure of romances.[100] When people began to write discrete tales (*novelle*), each a unit in itself, they were appealing to a taste for something different from interlaced structure. The literary movement we see in Boccaccio and Sercambi, to which Chaucer owed a debt, was such a reaction; it is part of the tendency which led Malory to simplify interlaced structure, Tasso to attack it, Cervantes to parody it. Then, too, the thematic mode of the romance interlace, though it is "above all a questioning one," depends upon characters and situations which recur, not upon themes or content alone. From this point of view, Chaucer and Gower were writing narratives on a set of principles altogether different from that of the romance. And Chaucer often shows himself impatient of romances, especially Arthurian romances; in *The Canterbury Tales* all the romances told on the pilgrimage receive some amount of parodic or ironic treatment—Chaucer's own contribution pokes fun at a romance which, if not stopped because it is boring, would have had an interlaced structure; the same is true of the Squire's Tale. Where Chaucer wrote romances seriously—as in the *Troilus* or the Knight's Tale—he adapted them from Boccaccio and gave them a beginning-middle-end organiza-

100. Ryding, *Structure in Medieval Narrative*, esp. pp. 10–19, 154–161.

tion which does not even resemble the interlace. And he constantly ridicules the tendencies of medieval rhetoric—*amplificatio, digressio, dilatatio*—which encouraged interlaced structure; when we see him, as in the Knight's Tale, using *occupatio* to condense his story, we find him poking fun at the overburgeoning qualities of his original. Surely Chaucer would not have used a structure in *The Canterbury Tales* drawn from a literary fashion he deplored. Isn't it more likely that the model he had in mind was what Gower had in mind, the categorized or subdivided model whose visual emblem (the very antithesis of the interlace) was the *tree*? The "tree of the virtues and vices," which Gower used as a stated model in the *Confessio* and Chaucer used in the Parson's Tale, is a visual emblem familiar to any reader of medieval literature. Isn't the tendency to *group* the narratives so that they fall together and have a common theme much closer to this? Isn't it the idea Chaucer would have shared with Gower? Isn't it what makes *The Canterbury Tales* with its "discussions" different from the *Decameron* with its "days"? And isn't it reflected by its counterpart in the Parson's Tale?

The answer to these questions is, not necessarily. The themes seem to be discrete and therefore seem to be part of a tendency to simplify, to substitute self-contained tales for interlaced narrative. But only in part. The other side of the picture is that the groups of tales are not self-contained but open-ended. Their movement degenerates or turns back upon itself; their tendency is to question, not to answer; their structure does not "lead up" to anything—it is one in which "everything leads to everything else." In the last three tales we look *back* on themes previously treated; the structure itself is collapsed, is turned into a riddle. We are constantly asked to revise our estimate of the work—the Parson's Tale asks that we revise even the frame of mind in which we read.

And, too, there are "metastructures." We see four groups of tales each of which is a unit, three of which explore specific realms of conduct, the last of which explores what has been explored; we see smaller structures of pairs within these groups. But no sooner do we see this than we see loose ends: we look at it another way and we see the Man of Law's ideal narrative, paired with the Knight's tale of chivalry. We then see emerge a group of ideal narratives, variously discredited, which lead up to a saint's legend and then to the final prose treatise on penitence. Similarly, after the Knight's Tale, we see other romances emerge, find everywhere a preoccupation with the prestige group in the society, the "ruling class," which leads up to a prose work addressed to the ruling class. In these two religious and chivalric sequences we have a metastructure which makes the "groups" of tales seem to fall out of focus before a more significant thematic structure which is superimposed.

I must digress here long enough to argue that the *Melibee* is a major structural unit in *The Canterbury Tales,* comparable in importance to the Parson's Tale, and that we cannot understand the structure of the work unless we read it seriously. The point is very important. If the address to the ruling class is one side of a "metastructure," it is not complete without the *Melibee,* just as the religious side of the metastructure is not complete without the Parson's Tale. The reader who does not need to be convinced of this may as well skip the next five paragraphs.

The *Melibee* is, first, elaborately prepared for. Even in the Knight's Tale the audience is made to see the conventions of romance and the ideals and attitudes of chivalry from an amused, an ironical viewpoint. Nothing is "attacked," but the audience is made to think, to question. Here and in later tales Chaucer let his audience view their own conventions through naive, low-class, or bourgeois eyes, and if this widened their perspective it let them laugh at themselves. Thus he has the Miller parody the Knight. If we read Fragments III-IV-V before Fragment VII—this could be a reason for doing so—we see a development from the Wife's tale to the *Melibee.* The Wife's Arthurian romance contains at its end the loathly lady's long harangue arguing that true nobility is of the spirit, not a matter of riches, family ties, youth, or beauty—an argument that carries little conviction given the hapless hero's circumstances. The next romance after the Wife's is the Squire's. The Squire chooses a romance infinitely more fantastical than his father's and tells it in a charmingly youthful but bumbling and long-winded way—the courtly lovers of his tale, like those of the Nun's Priest's Tale, are talking birds! And his tale is followed by the Franklin's—a Breton lay told so as to reveal the Franklin's naiveté and pretentiousness. In Fragment VII, when Chaucer the pilgrim gets to tell a tale, the poet uses a similar joke: in *Sir Thopas* the hero is a bourgeois, his accomplishments are middle-class accomplishments, his dress and weapons are scarcely appropriate to knights—and he is out looking for an elf queen! The parody makes the traditional romance seem debased and absurd—as indeed it had become in many an instance—and even the Host sees its absurdity. He cuts Chaucer off in the middle of his second fit and demands "some mirth or some doctrine." The running joke seems to be at the expense of the bourgeoisie and the lower classes; but when noble ideals become clichés and popular tags they themselves seem silly. By the fourteenth century the knights themselves were probably a bit skeptical about these ideals. Very possibly to the court of John of Gaunt and Richard II the high-minded sentiments of the Knight's Tale would have seemed (to borrow an applicable modern word) a bit Edwardian. And the enthusiasm for "gentilesse" expressed by men like the Franklin would have made such enthusiasm seem a little *infra dig* among those to the manner born.

This questioning spirit is what prepares us for the *Melibee*: interrupted, Chaucer promises a "little thing in prose" which will have more proverbs than usual. Some have suspected that it is deadpan humor, but no one has done more than suspect this—and to suspect it you have to ignore its content. Everything indicates that it *was* taken seriously in its own time.[101] It is about things taken seriously by medieval

101. On its great popularity in some half dozen European languages from the mid-thirteenth into the fifteenth century, see Severs in *SA*, pp. 560–567. Bronson, "Chaucer's Art in Relation to His Audience," *Five Studies in Literature*, p. 42, says Tatlock noted it is one of the tales most often found in incomplete mss. of *The Canterbury Tales*. And of course Chaucer did take the trouble to translate it.

What follows is an explication or "reading" which attempts to show

noblemen—about choosing advisers, making decisions, adjudicating between war and peace or justice and revenge. The name of the central figure, Melibee, means "a man that drinketh hony" (1410): we are told in the first sequence that he is mighty and rich. The honey he drinks appears to stand for two things, *in bono* and *in malo*. At one point he commends his wife Prudence (she is armed with an appalling number of quotations from classical and medieval sources): "words that been spoken discreetly by ordinance been honycombs, for they yeven sweetness to the soul and holsomeness to the body" (1113). At another point she tells him the meaning of his name and adds that he has drunk so much "hony of sweet temporel richesses, and delices, and honours of this world" that he is drunk and has "forgotten Jesus Christ his creator" (1411-1412). This second meaning relates to the three enemies who attack him at the beginning of the work. They set ladders to the walls of his house, enter by the windows, beat his wife Prudence, and kill his daughter Sophie—i.e., his wisdom. Prudence's enterprise is to help him get his wisdom back. Since the daughter is never restored to life in the allegory, it could be thought that the attack of the three enemies and the loss of wisdom symbolize the Fall, or the results of the Fall in the individual life. Dame Prudence tells him that he has sinned against Christ for "the three enemies of mankind, that is to sayn, the flesh, the feend, and the world" (1420). But at the end of the work the enemies are presented as *real* enemies with whom Prudence mediates; she gives Melibee a lesson in peace-making and justice. The enemies repent (in a way hardly characteristic of the world, the flesh, and the devil) and Melibee forgives them as God will forgive us at the time of our dying. The two levels of meaning seem inconsistent, but

---

that it applies religious ideas to political circumstances and not the reverse. For a reading which puts more weight on the religious side see Paul Strohm, "The Allegory of the *Tale of Melibee*," *ChauR* 2 (1967): 32–42. Attempts to pin a political allegory to a particular historical circumstance at a definite date are difficult in a century when the English waged war so often; e.g., see Gardiner Stillwell, "The Political Meaning of Chaucer's *Tale of Melibee*," *Speculum* 19 (1944):433–444.

they are not: Melibee is blinded by drinking too much honey of temporal riches, delights, and honors (which are the "three temptations") and needs to drink the honey of good counsel. The enemies that attack him are the three *sources* of temptation—the world, the flesh, and the devil. But just because of this attack he must learn how to deal with *human* enemies against whom he is (now robbed of his wisdom) tempted to wreak vengeance rather than do justice. The theological side drops into the background as this theology is applied to specific circumstances touching the conduct of rulers. But its lessons are the great Christian lessons of forgiveness, charity, and justice, and these are applied to circumstances which noblemen were always concerned with.

The major issue is whether Melibee should declare war on his enemies. After Prudence has recommended "mesure" and patience, he is approached by a group of advisers: surgeons, physicians, an advocate, young folk, and wise old men. The young folk say that one should smite while the iron is hot and end by crying in loud voices "War! war!" Melibee takes up this view, and his wife (first laying the groundwork for her rebuttal by commending women's counsel) tells him how he should choose counsellors (1114-1230). Her discourse may sound platitudinous five hundred years later, but it's still hard to know whose advice to take seriously and her formula for making decisions is still workable. She says that first one should ask God to be his counsellor, and then take counsel with one's self, driving from one's heart anger, covetousness, and hastiness. Having done this one should keep one's counsel to oneself. She seems to mean that conscience and self-awareness are the best guides, but shared opinions and discussion are useful if one's advisers speak their minds without being led; the great danger is "flatterers." She thinks it important to know who one's friends and enemies are, to trust loyal, wise, and experienced advisers, and to get advice not from one but from many; she rejects the advice of fools, flatterers, old enemies reconciled, one's own servants, drunks, the wicked, and the young. She reminds Melibee that he *can* change his mind, since circumstances alter cases. And she concludes that the greatest and strongest fortification a rich man can have is to be beloved by his subjects and neighbors: a fortification is only as good as those who man it.

There follows a discussion about whether one should take vengeance, test Fortune, or bear adversity with patience (1405-1550). The latter comes out predictably ahead. In taking vengeance one should exercise patience so as not to do "outrage ne excess." One should distinguish between defending oneself and avenging oneself, and one should take no vengeance except "after the order of right, that is to sayn, by the law" (1529). Melibee answers that he has reason to be angry and impatient and can see no harm in taking vengeance since he is powerful and rich: all things, he says, quoting Solomon, "obeyen to money." This leads to a digression about riches, a decent little essay by itself (1551-1670). Like the rest of the *Melibee* it is organized on principles of rhetoric and laced with "authorities." Most medieval moral writings condemn riches as the object of covetousness, point out that riches make men fearful of losing them, or make them vulnerable to flattery or greed or murder; but some allow that riches rightly used are good. The *Melibee* develops this last idea. We need to remember that the audience it was intended for likely included the richest men of the realm (like John of Gaunt) and people like the Franklin or the Man of Law; it wasn't meant to apply to someone with a little pocket change. So it is interesting that it begins by stating a worldly principle: as the body of man cannot live without the soul, it cannot live without temporal goods. The passage supports the Man of Law's opinion that poverty can produce harms and evil (1562-1563) and grants that riches are good to those who get and use them well. Later, Melibee is told "Ye sholden alwey doon your bisyness to get you richesses, so that ye get hem with good conscience." The work doesn't tell the reader what to do with riches but what attitude to take toward them. One should acquire wealth without great desire, gradually and not in haste, for it is the excess desire for riches that leads one into theft and other evils. One should get riches by "wit" and "travail" without doing wrong or harm to others. Hence idleness is to be avoided, in part because it slows down profit, in part because it impedes the proper use of funds. The rich man ought not to be a spendthrift or a miser; he should use his goods with "mesure" and should give to those in need; in getting and using riches he should bear in mind God, his conscience, and his good name. The digression on riches gets back to the main point by urging that one should not begin a war by trusting to one's riches, "for they ne suffisen noght werres to maintene" (1649)—a point relevant enough in any period of Western history.

The rest of the work is about making a just peace. The *Melibee* is sometimes called a "pacifist" work; yet it implies that there *is* such a thing as a just war. The Italy in which its original was written and the England in which Chaucer translated it were both torn with incessant wars; and the ruling class of knights to which it is addressed were a warrior class whose principal occupation was battle. The conclusion of the work applies the Christian message of charity and forgiveness to the universal preoccupation of the medieval knighthood, war. The fable itself is simple: Dame Prudence acts as mediator, the enemies repent their misdeeds, and Melibee is persuaded to forgive them. She says that one of the greatest and most sovereign things in this world is unity and peace (1678); but he, like a medieval knight or a modern statesman, is taken up with questions of honor, of "saving face." Though Prudence says that above all one should make peace between God and himself (1714), she takes a more practical line with the adversaries, pointing out to them the goods that come of peace and the harms and perils that come of war. They repent with stylized willingness, and she, allowing that arbitration is perilous, makes assurances for Melibee's honor. When hotheaded Melibee then dispossesses and exiles them, Prudence reasons that he does not need their goods and need not exile them because they have submitted. Melibee, won over, forgives them. The denouement brushes aside some of the real issues of maintaining peace—an enemy rarely admits so quickly that he is in the wrong, and as often as not wrong can be put on both sides. It is not a practical prescription for ending war or establishing peace, but an ideal circumstance which suggests how wars might be avoided in the first place. Somewhere, somehow, a wrong is done, and the party wronged wants restitution. The wrong itself and the desire for vengeance are owing to the world, the flesh, and the devil; and only prudence can hold this explosive circumstance in check.

I hope this résumé will convince the reader that the *Melibee* contains significant and worthy thoughts which would have given a medieval nobleman pause. Richard II, John of Gaunt, Gloucester, Bolingbroke—all could have profited from it. It is the focal point of an "address to the court" which runs throughout *The Canterbury Tales,* and it is addressed to a social milieu which was changing, during the fourteenth century, from the old feudal values based on self-interest and personal or family ties to a new public-spiritedness devoted to the good of a nation. Shakespeare's great scene in which King Henry rejects Falstaff is the *locus classicus* depicting this transformation of the medieval aristocracy. Chaucer saw it happening, and understood that to make this new nationalism work the ruling class must be moved by the kind of ideals Dame Prudence presents.

The address to the court is not a dramatic unit like the "groups" but a recurrent theme, a "metastructure" which relies on a developed *engagement* between author and audience. The subtle "I" of the Knight's Tale who seems to mock the meat he feeds on, the spectral poet who exists behind romances like the Wife's, Squire's, or Franklin's (which are discredited by the vested interests of their tellers and subtly overblown by the poet), the masquerade figure of the foolish pilgrim who tells the "Rime of Sir Thopas"—all these engage our imagination, make us feel that we can intuit the author's state of mind. In the *Melibee* he appears before us in good earnest and leaves the ruling class among his audience with something to think about. Only again in the Retraction does he appear before us without irony. And in the *Melibee* he addresses himself to fundamental matters of ethics and morality which apply to the civil, domestic, and private realms: we see Melibee as ruler, as head of a household, and as an isolated private man who must come to grips with his conscience.

And yet, what makes the *Melibee* part of an interlaced

structure is the fact that it is not the last word on the subject. It holds up an ideal of conduct, but in characteristic medieval fashion that ideal is set aside and a higher one put forward. This happens at the end: in the legend of St. Cecilia, who was "of noble kinde," we have an aristocrat's life dedicated to chastity and good works, dedicated to conversion—it rises above the level of politics. And in the Parson's tale we have a guide to the Christian life which *every* Christian must lead—it rises above the level of social class. It is characteristic of the interlaced structure, too, that between the *Melibee* and these last tales, the seriousness is dispersed. At once upon the conclusion of the *Melibee* the Host chimes in, having missed the point altogether, that he would rather than "a barel ale" have had his wife hear this story of a patient wife. Then we get the Monk's hapless tales of noblemen who fell from power, and the Nun's Priest's tale of the regal cock with his human foibles.

These thematic structures and metastructures seem to me more comparable to the interlace than to any other kind of medieval structure. If I am right, then Chaucer selected a kind of structure found in the very works against which he was in revolt. And these were foreign works—the interlace did not amount to much as a technique in England until after Chaucer's time. But I believe the selection occurred in the process of artistic creation and came to him unawares from ingrained habits of thought. He set out to do something new, but in doing it he fell back on the old. And it came to him from traditions and conventions more deeply ingrained than those of the romance. The interlace had models of its own. These would be the tendencies in medieval culture which promoted divagation, variety, complexity, ornamentation, inconclusiveness, interrelatedness, effulgence, plenitude; they would be those tendencies which ran counter to, or went beyond, any impulse toward brevity, neatness, symmetry, or simplicity. One doesn't have to fall back on the Gothic cathedral for an analogy; there are analogies much closer to literature, and one of these is rhetoric. Medieval rhetoric was based on the principle of logical development—it recommended a central "heart's line" and parceling out materials by steps. Yet much of medieval rhetoric recommended devices by means of which the artist may develop themes or digress. The principle *amplificatio* was chiefly one of providing exploratory, decorative, or illustrative material. The justification for tale-telling in medieval rhetoric was the exemplum, a story told to illustrate a point and to give it interest and excitement. The tension between mirth and doctrine was everywhere present in medieval rhetoric; the Middle Ages had preserved from Horace and other ancients the principle that an effective literary work should teach and delight, should be useful and entertaining at once—which meant in part that it should hang together and make a point, in part that it should divert and engage the reader's attention. Implicit in medieval rhetoric is the very kind of structure we have been talking about—a visible plan which still wanders and interweaves. The same kind of pattern can be found in the memory-systems which were preserved as an adjunct of rhetoric. The process of artificial memory was one of subdividing and associating, but the actual experience invoked a tendency toward multiplicity and inclusiveness—it was a way of encompassing in consciousness, to the extent that one could, the plenitude of all things that are to be known.

Thus the model of the interlace was supported by models which rhetoric and artificial memory furnished. And the interlace was a model of the mental life itself, of remembered experience and free-floating thought.[102] But if conscious thought as the medievals conceived it lies at the roots of interlaced structure, so does the preconscious or unconscious mental life as they conceived it. The dream-vision, we know, was the literary form which most influenced Chaucer's early development. For years, when it was

---

102. Cf. Northrop Frye, *Anatomy of Criticism*, p. 83: "it is clear that all verbal structures with meaning are verbal imitations of that elusive psychological and physiological process known as thought, a process stumbling through emotional entanglements, sudden irrational convictions, involuntary gleams of insight, rationalized prejudices, and blocks of panic and inertia, finally to reach a completely incommunicable intuition."

customary to do so, critics complained how elements in various dream-visions, including Chaucer's, were extraneous, superfluous, or digressive. It is not that the dream-visions have no story and dramatic excitement, but the story line of a dream-vision is minimal. The events are likely to be as simple as a meeting, a kiss, a marriage, or a death. There is plenty of dramatic excitement in dream-visions, but it is generated by tension, conflicts of ideas or emotions, failures of communication. In *The Book of the Duchess* Chaucer gave dramatic excitement to the vision by having the dreamer befuddled and uncomprehending; he created suspense by withholding a fundamental and obvious piece of information from the narrator's grasp. The successful dream-visions, including the allegorical ones, all have this kind of dramatic appeal, but it is not the kind of drama we are used to—it is not based on a plot or an event or an outcome. In the same way the characters in a dream-vision are intentionally flat and undeveloped—they have the obsessional quality which the figures in dreams often really have; in many dream-visions they are personifications. This does not rob the dream-vision of psychological interest, but we get, rather than psychological realism of the sort we are used to, psychological allegory—the anatomizing of sentiment, feeling, and attitude, as in the *Roman de la Rose*. The Black Knight in *The Book of the Duchess* is very far from a "rounded character" and does not resemble John of Gaunt in the least. He is a figment of the dreamer's inner experience, a faceless knight in mourning who recites a song and tells a story. This abstract quality endemic to the dream-vision gives it an intense realism comparable to "figural" realism, but the comparison rests on the abstraction, the visualization, and the intensity of presentation. We cannot say that dream-visions are all instances of the figural style: *Piers Plowman* is, but *The Parliament of Fowls* is not. The strength of the dream-vision as a literary form was that it permitted the artist to single out in abstraction something of importance and imbue it with an aura of mystery and wonder. The successful dream-visions have the excitement, immediacy, and energy which dreams themselves have. Their organization and development (like that of dreams) is more often thematic than narrative. They present a puzzle, then present a solution.

I said at the beginning of this chapter that interlaced thematic structure is like a grammar, and that the "morpheme" of that grammar is the binary structure, narrative unit + juncture + narrative unit. This is basic in the dream-vision: we wait for some new unexpected development which will explain the puzzle set for us. The Garden of Mirth explains the figures of the Garden's outer wall; the Well of Narcissus explains the Garden of Mirth. There are visual counterparts or "models" of this binary structure: the diptych painting is one, and there are schemata which show units matched in double columns. But the best model comes precisely from the experience which Chaucer points to in the Miller's Prologue, the experience of *turning over a leaf*. In the experience of any literate medieval man the most familiar binary organization would have been the *facing pages of an open book*. There, spread before the reader's eye, are two matching designs which are joined and yet different; and when one reads first the one and then the other, the second furthers our grasp of the first. In the successive turning of pages medieval men would have noted a further binary form: medieval vellum books were made so that the smooth (flesh) side of the vellum faced another smooth side and the rough (hair) side faced another rough side; if books had not been bound this way the rough surfaces would have eroded the smooth. The result was that while two facing pages were different in content but alike in appearance and texture, the next two facing pages were different in appearance and texture. Dante, in a figure altogether puzzling until Elizabeth Hatcher explained it, used this common experience of the medieval reader in a metaphor which shows "a tension between the tight logic of the cosmic system he expounds and the free, associative imagination which governs his figurative language."[103] The very fact that there *were* books with pages (as opposed to the scrolls of ancient

103. Elizabeth R. Hatcher, "The Moon and Parchment: Paradiso II, 73–78," *Dante Studies* 89 (1971):55.

times) meant that two passages could be compared, that one could leaf back to something previously read and refine or alter one's understanding by relating two passages in a work, or two or more chapters, or even two different works bound in the same volume. To read was itself to experience a structure of pairs and concatenated pairs within groups. The process could easily become one in which everything leads to everything else, but the essential experience was that of finding that the second member of a pair alters the character of the first.

This experience of seeing more and thus seeing something else is like an "optical illusion" in which we see one figure and then on closer scrutiny another. One element of a book changes when we read a second element, and the whole experience of the book is an accumulation of these changes in perspective. The prototype of the experience was the Bible. The Old Testament meant something on the literal level, but that meaning was altered when one read the New Testament. The second completed the first, asked the reader then to look back on the first and see a typological or allegorical meaning not apparent before. There, if anywhere, is the real importance of scriptural tradition to medieval "secular" literature: meaning comes out of a book through an act of comparing. And that act of comparing involves groups within pairs and pairs within groups. All of the meanings are part of one truth, but the unity of that truth can only be grasped through multiplicity: only at the end of time will multiplicity be supplanted by unity and meanings by being. So fundamental was this binary or diptych organization to literature and to "bookness" that in written manuscripts it became a fundamental organization of a single page. Very frequently medieval manuscript books are in double columns, so that the open pages of a book present two matching diptych designs, two pairs within a pair. The "morpheme" of this organization, unit + juncture + unit, provided the medieval bookmaker with a fundamental page design. The opening page of the Tickhill Psalter (Figure 13), though some other initial letters occupy a full page, illustrates this diptych structure; it is as though

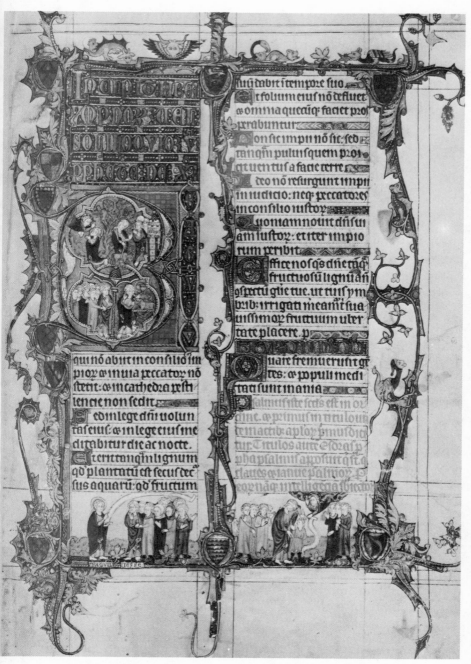

Figure 13. "Beatus" initial of Psalm 1 and beginning of Psalm 2; diptych page design. Tickhill Psalter, Spencer ms. 26, fol. 6ʳ.

the artist wished first to present that "morpheme" on which all else depends.

I am aware that this estimate of structure opens the door to an interpretative chaos which flies in the face of structure itself. A reader approaching the more complex works of "Gothic style," by seeing pairs and observing their similarities and differences, might well see structures taking shape *of whatever sort*. (It is what happened in interpreting the Bible. The result was some work like the *Reductorium Morale* of Bersuire, so full of meanings it is meaningless.) If one imagines a fourteenth-century nobleman listening to or reading *The Canterbury Tales*, it isn't hard to imagine what he would have found of interest. He would have been interested, like anyone, in those aspects of the work which applied to him, which touched on the attitudes and problems of his own milieu. His style of life would have acted like a magnet, drawing details of interest into a pattern of remembrance. We like to say that a book "finds its own audience," but a complex and variegated book finds various audiences; it is as true that the audience finds the book. A clerk or a bourgeois would have found in *The Canterbury Tales* a group of concerns or emphases different from what a nobleman would have found. Each might have extrapolated a thematic structure to suit himself. Chaucer understood this principle and gave expression to it in the General Prologue: when we talk about Chaucer's "breadth of vision" we mean his ability to see the world through others' vision, which is what the General Prologue does and what the tales do. So when we talk about the structure of the tales—the way they are organized or put together—we have to go beyond the principles of linear sequence, dramatic interplay, or thematic grouping. If the audience is free to turn the leaf and choose another tale we have to grant (what is true of any book) that it is going to be different things to different people, is going to be shaped by the way they read and experience it. The reader is going to structure it for himself to some degree. That is what has happened in modern times—we think some tales more "important" than others and so create out of the whole book a structure which suits our frame of mind. Thus some ignore the Second Nun's Tale or the Parson's Tale as negligible addenda; others ignore the fabliaux as "chaff." And the curious thing is, the work allows for this—the author acknowledged it and counted on it. Probably he would have felt that the work would be read best by the reader who read all of it with equal attention and interest. To do so would broaden the reader's vision and multiply his experience of life—would let the bourgeois see through the peasant's or clerk's or nobleman's eyes, would let any of these see through the eyes of the others and so gain distance on his own way of seeing things. If everything leads to everything else, the attentive reader will have been led everywhere and will have seen everything.

If structure in the tales is based on such infinitely convoluted thematic principles, can it be called structure at all? I say yes. The concerns or themes of the linear groups pertain to civil, domestic, and private realms; and other tales, though not in sequence, have such concerns as ideality, tale-telling itself, the right use of language, perfection. This thematic structure, variegated and interlocking, springs naturally from the social conditions described in the General Prologue and produces a thematic effulgence, a variety of concerns which were those of Chaucer's age. One could easily find thematic "metastructures" other than those I have mentioned: the theme of Fortune, for example, is introduced in the Knight's Tale, picked up in the Man of Law's Tale and again in the Monk's Tale, is ridiculed in the Nun's Priest's Tale and is at least mentioned in a number of other tales. Food, money, sex, "quitting" are recurrent themes. A thematic sequence of tales which are parodies might be extrapolated. If there is this multiple structuring, a critic could pick a tale at random and write a whole new book tracing its thematic relationships to other tales—an appalling thought. After all, a socially coherent group telling tales on a journey would gravitate to some themes and not to others; the question is whether thematic structuring is an artistic property of the work, or whether it gets into the work by accident, whether it isn't just part of the random structure of life itself or the world.

I say it is a property of the work. Chaucer acknowledges this random element when he has the first teller chosen by lot: it is a paradigm—the choice is left to chance, but "by aventure, or sort, or cas" the choice is what it should be. The author's guiding hand is acknowledged. This acknowledgment is picked up in the Miller's Prologue: the Miller drunkenly demands to be next and the Host resigns for the time being his position as organizer, but the rightness of the Miller's Tale in the sequence is unchallengeable—everyone agrees it was a stroke of genius on the author's part. The Host has lost control, but not Chaucer. Yet it is just here in the Miller's Prologue that Chaucer permits the reader some control over the book, allows that he can turn the leaves, choose, find enough "great and small," and that what he can find is material of different kinds. If there are churls' tales, there is "storial thing that toucheth gentilesse," "moralitee," and "holiness." These generic distinctions do not themselves point to themes, except perhaps for "gentilesse," but they encourage us to find in the book the book we want, and they are likely to appeal to different social groups. Once we have started to treat the book this way, everything *could* lead to everything else. If the quality of ideas, the quality of the mental life itself, is embodied in *The Canterbury Tales*, it could mean that we have something before us so vast and fluid that there is no point in talking about structure—we will only find such structures as we find in our own experience of the world. We *are* left to go off in that direction, to find out for ourselves how everything that is written can be written for our doctrine. But just at the point when we may thus get lost in the world of story and lapse into ourselves, we are pulled back by the story which contains the stories. They are told by tellers who represent a social order, are rehearsed by a narrator with whom we feel rapport. And there are self-evident, demonstrable juxtapositions, pairs, and sequences which make a complex design. All of it is laid out for us in the General Prologue and the Knight's Tale; if we lose our way we can start back with these, in memory. At any point where structure appears to burgeon into formlessness, into infinite variousness, we are returned in our experience of the work to the principles of form which have admitted multiplicity and formlessness in the first place.

I remind the reader that this long discussion of the way tales fit together is a theory. I hope it is not "idle" theory, but I can imagine a reader who has read this far thinking, "You have claimed to be able to see into Chaucer's mind and describe the 'idea' which informed the whole of *The Canterbury Tales*, but the idea is too complicated and confusing. I can see how what you call 'stated models,' like the narrator's performance or the remembered pilgrimage, existed in Chaucer's mind since they are mentioned in the work; I can even see how the total form of the whole might have resembled in Chaucer's mind the flower-wheel design in which all diverse and mutable things were symmetrically and rationally related as in the mind of God. But now you seem to be arguing that the 'inner form,' the tales themselves, are structured like an 'interlace' in which all things were related *as*ymmetrically and *ir*rationally as in memory. You are telling us that the key element of this interlace design is the 'juncture' between two units—like the double columns or facing pages of a book. And you are telling us that there is a multiplicity of structures in this structure—like that of a Gothic cathedral or an illuminated manuscript. Your theory, with all these 'models,' is too inclusive; it does not fit together."

But I am prepared to argue that as theories go it does fit together. After all, these "models" are only comparisons— we are using them to try to grasp the nature of an art-form, to get the feel of an esthetic. In literature interlaced structure was a way of interrupting a story line with another story line, of entangling many characters and many plots after the manner (in our time) of certain comic strips and soap operas. And the distinguishing feature of such a structure is the interruption or "juncture," the point at which a story line must be held in memory until its later continuation. The interlace as a *visual* design is only a convenient counterpart to this structure, a way of seeing it diagrammatically (and seeing that various arts organized experience similarly). In such a visual design the continuous strand passes over or under itself, and at these points we lose sight of the strand—must imagine it continuing beneath the strand which crosses it. Hence the juncture or interruption is the distinguishing feature of the visual design too.

"Then are you arguing," my objector might go on, "that the tales themselves are comparable *in form* to the inner miniature drawings of an initial capital in a manuscript, but comparable *in structure* to an interlace?" That is exactly what I am arguing. The comparison with the initial capital shows something about the relation of inner and outer form; the comparison with the interlace shows something about the way narrative units are pieced together. Besides, the inner miniature drawings we have seen in the initial capitals of the Tickhill Psalter actually *are* interlaced in a chainlike pattern. These represent serial episodes, but we have to know the rules or theory behind them before we know where the series begins or how it proceeds—before we know how to "read" it.[104] Such rules and such a theory are what I have been trying to uncover in the tales. What I have found is four groups of tales which do seem to fit together thematically, each of which has a different kind of movement, one coming first, one last—three on discrete themes, the last reiterative. And I have found another set of thematic "metastructures" which are imposed upon these groups and seem to offer possible realignments and associations so multitudinous that it is hardly an exaggeration to say that everything leads to everything else. This interlaced thematic structure is like a maze or labyrinth in which it is easy to get lost, but the dominant form of the work—may I say the *idea* of the work—never permits us to come to a dead end. We find our way out of the labyrinth at last.

"Yes, but now," my objector would cry, "you have introduced *another* comparison or 'model,' the maze or labyrinth! You seem to be trying to get inside Chaucer's mind by

104. As it happens, they are read from left to right and top to bottom after the bookish manner, not clockwise; and the drawings at the bottom of the page proceed serially from those interlaced within the initial capital. See Egbert, *The Tickhill Psalter*, who provides abundant evidence.

a series of almost Freudian if not Proustian associations, but they are your associations, not Chaucer's."

But here I play my trump card.

There *was* a medieval visual design called a labyrinth or maze. It was inherited from the ancient world and seems to have reappeared in Italian churches about the tenth century, in French churches about the twelfth.[105] These labyrinths were mosaics set into the stone pavements or sometimes the walls of churches and Gothic cathedrals. It is widely believed (but not proved) that they were used for substitute pilgrimages: a penitent could crawl about the Way on his knees, or if it was on a wall trace it tediously with a finger. Some of these labyrinths are still in existence: the largest (about 40 feet in diameter) is in the pavement of the cathedral at Chartres (Figure 14). The center of such a labyrinth, the destination of the substitute pilgrimage, was called *ciel* or *Jérusalem*; French labyrinths were called *chemins de Jérusalem*. Like any pilgrimage the labyrinth symbolized the Way, the road of life: in the church of San Savino in Piacenza was inscribed a legend along with the labyrinth:

Hunc mundum tipice Laberinthus denotat iste:
Intranti largus, redeunti set nimis artus.
Sic mundo captus, viciorum molle gravatus
Vix valet ad vite doctrinam quisque redire.[106]

In short, the convoluted pattern of the labyrinth symbolized the many difficulties and turning points necessary on life's pilgrimage.

It isn't hard to see a similarity between the interlace design and the labyrinth, but there is an important difference: the interlace was visual, the labyrinth tactile.[107] The

---

105. See W. H. Matthews, *Mazes and Labyrinths: Their History and Development* (1922; rpt. New York: Dover, 1970), esp. chap. 9. There is some additional information in *Dictionnaire d'Archéologie Chrétienne et de Liturgie*, ed. F. Cabrol and H. Leclercq (Paris, 1928), VIII:973–982, including a list of twenty-five known labyrinths.

106. Matthews, p. 57.

107. A difference of less importance is that of shape. There were square and octagonal labyrinths as well as round ones, and these had straight, angular courses rather than curved ones; but while we normally

Figure 14. Pavement labyrinth of Chartres cathedral, with flower-wheel design at the center.

junctures of the interlace are places where the eye must imagine the strand crossing underneath itself. The junctures of the labyrinth are turning points, places where the course turns back upon itself so that one changes direction and seems to retrace one's steps. Medieval labyrinths seem all to have been unicursal; "multicursal" labyrinths or mazes, in which one comes to forks in the path and must make blind choices, were as far as I know a later development. Hence the course of the medieval labyrinth, like the one at Chartres (about 150 yards long), is a continuous way which circles back upon itself in a most tortuous manner, but if you follow the path without getting confused you end up in the center (and otherwise back where you started). It is therefore a good deal like the "endless knot" of the interlace: the major difference is that it does have a beginning and an end. Between that beginning and end, the meandering course of the labyrinth is a single way turning back upon itself; and in this it is comparable to the interlaced "ribbon" or "knot."[108]

Neither the interlace nor the labyrinth is comparable to the "rose" designs which were discussed in the last chapter, for they expressed unity and reason; they symbolized the universal order. The labyrinth and interlace express confusion and puzzlement; they symbolize the world. But the germ of one is always in the other—the one implies or suggests the other. So they are comparable in some respects. The circles-in-circles design displays the complexity of the universal order, the interlace the complexity of the world. Moreover, the flower-wheel design and the labyrinth have one important feature in common: both place a symbol of order and eternity at the still center. This is dramatically so of the

---

think of the interlace as the curling acanthus leaf or knot or chain, an interlaced design can occupy a square or rectangular space and can be comprised of straight lines (as in the design of "Solomon's seal," the six-pointed star made of two interlaced triangles).

108. It would not of course be comparable to those interlaces like "Solomon's seal" comprised of more than one strand, nor strictly comparable to the chain made of separate links, though this is a matter of definition. In fact there are interlace designs where one can see a beginning or end of a strand, as in certain floriated decorations which may end in a leaf or flower.

labyrinth at Chartres. Look again at Figure 14: there at the center, the destination of the pilgrimage, in the very place called "heaven" or "Jerusalem," we find the flower design itself, the ordered circles inscribed within an outer circle and having an inner circle, which symbolized timeless unity.

We observed before that Geoffrey of Vinsauf compared a poem with a house and that Chaucer knew the passage. It is therefore a curious fact, and not necessarily a coincidence, that the labyrinth was called a house, "the house of Daedalus." Indeed one name for the labyrinth in France was *daedale*; and at Lucca, at the entrance of the small labyrinth on the wall of the cathedral there, is an inscription "Hic quem Creticus edit / Daedalus est Laberinthus. . . ."[109] In France the architects of cathedrals placed their names in the center of the labyrinths at Rheims, Chartres, and Amiens; this was a symbolic gesture—the architect traditionally symbolized God himself, the builder of the universe, as the architect was the builder of the house of God and Daedalus the builder of the Labyrinth.[110]

None of this would be more than another scholar's attempt to filch an explanation from "the background" unless we could prove that Chaucer knew about the labyrinth and the "house of Daedalus." It happens that we can. We cannot prove he *saw* a cathedral labyrinth: none are known to have existed in England (there is a legend of one formerly at Canterbury), yet he did travel widely in Italy and France where they were abundant. But we can prove he knew about the conception, because he speaks of it in *The House of Fame*. In the third book of that poem, where he is describing the House of Rumor, he says the house is made as "wonderlych" as "Domus Dedaly / That Laborintus cleped is" (1920-1922).[111] He goes on:

109. Matthews, p. 56.
110. See Ananda K. Coomaraswamy, "The Iconography of Dürer's 'Knots' and Leonardo's 'Concatenation,'" *The Art Quarterly* 7 (1944):118 and n. 38.
111. This is the only occurrence of the word *labyrinth* in Chaucer; elsewhere he uses the word *maze*, twice metaphorically to mean a puzzle (NPT 3093) or a trick (*TC* 5:468), but once when speaking of Theseus in

And, Lord, this house in alle times,
Was full of shipmen and pilgrimes
With scrippes bret-ful of lesinges,
Entremedled with tidinges.

(2121-2124)

The passage is a wild flight of imagination: this "Domus
Dedaly / That Laboryntus cleped us" turns out to be something like a giant wicker cage, in which "tidings" are passed
by word of mouth, growing and becoming distorted in the
process; some of these escape through holes or windows and
proceed to the nearby House of Fame. These "tidings" are
stories or rumors, false and true—"at ones / A lesing and a
sad sooth sawe" (2089). And the poet attributes these tidings
to shipmen and pilgrims, adding "O many a thousand times
twelve / Saugh I eke of these pardoners . . ." (2126-2127).
It will be remembered that "tidings" were what the Manciple
counselled against, "whether they been false or trewe."

This central image of *The House of Fame*, which the poem
leads up to and presents toward its end, is an idea: an idea of
a world of stories or "tidings" like a labyrinth in design,
called a house of Rumor, associated with pilgrims. The
tidings are true or false, the stuff of literary tradition and
history in its raw state before it has arrived at the House of
Fame where prestige will be assigned or not assigned to each
tiding, justly or unjustly, and where each is given a name and
a duration (2110-2117). This image of a labyrinthine house
of Rumor is remarkably like the form and structure of *The
Canterbury Tales*: the labyrinth had a beginning, middle, and
end; was a pilgrimage to the Heavenly Jerusalem; was an
elaborate structure with many turnabouts in which the path
clusters now on one side, now on another, sometimes sweep-
ing past whole areas where it has been before, and yet which
through its overall form and conception encompasses all of its
design and arrives at its end. Professor Leyerle has suggested that this image in *The House of Fame* was the idea of

---

"the hous [that] is krynkeled to and fro,/ And hath so quainte wayes for to
go—/For it is shapen as the mase is wrought" (LGW 2012–2014), a
reference to the Labyrinth.

The Canterbury Tales.[112] I make no such claim. We can never know if, at the time he wrote *The House of Fame,* Chaucer had the idea of *The Canterbury Tales* clearly or even vaguely in his mind. But it is evident that the idea of a convoluted design like the interlace or labyrinth *was* in his mind; that he himself associated the labyrinth with stories, especially the tall tales of "shipmen and pilgrims"; that this design by its legendary character had a beginning, a tortuous middle, and an end; that it was associated in medieval culture with a vicarious pilgrimage, a one-way journey to a destination which was called Jerusalem; and that in Chaucer's mind it was—for he called it this in his translation of Boethius[113]— "the house of Dedalus, so entrelaced that it is unable to ben unlaced."

112. "Chaucer's Windy Eagle," *UTQ* 40 (1971):260: "[The House of Rumour] is sixty miles long and goes round. This is the approximate distance between Southwark and Canterbury, the path that Chaucer's pilgrims were afterwards intended to go round. Many lament that the poet did not finish the *House of Fame,* but where he left off, he possibly began *The Canterbury Tales,* a much finer House of Rumour where 'love-tydynges' are related under a 'man of gret auctorite,' Herry Bailly, the Host. The House of Rumour was to be transformed into the Tabard Inn; throughout Chaucer's poetic career the pressure to turn concepts into actuality continues." Leyerle derives "love-tydyngs" from OE *lof* and suggests the term refers to tidings of fame or glory as well as of love. He cites John M. Manly, "What is Chaucer's *Hous of Fame?*" in *Anniversary Papers By Colleagues and Pupils of George Lyman Kittredge* (Boston, 1913), pp. 73–81, as the origin of this idea, but the statement he quotes is very different in meaning from his own: it was his inspiration, not his source.

113. III, pr. 12, line 156f. The phrase is Chaucer's; Boethius says only "inextricabilem labyrinthum."

VI

THE PARDONER
AND THE PARSON

I N this labyrinthine form, with its component structures and metastructures, there is one juxtaposition
about which we have as yet said nothing. On the
pilgrimage are two preachers, the Pardoner and the Parson.
The Pardoner is the last pilgrim described in the General
Prologue, the Parson the last to tell a tale. Since a final
placement was and is emphatic in rhetoric, this juxtaposition
forces a comparison between them. And both are related in
the most explicit way to the institution of the pilgrimage.
A pilgrimage was at base an act of penance. The Pardoner is
presented as a criminal who grossly abuses the pardon or
indulgence meant only to be given after an act of penance;
the Parson is presented as an ideal parish priest and his
"sermon" is a treatise on penance. The Pardoner's sermon,
intended to sell false pardons, is a thriller, its subject divine
retribution; the Parson's treatise, intended to show us the
Way, is a manual, its subject individual Christian conduct in
the world.

THE "FLOATING" FRAGMENT

The Pardoner's sermon is in a manuscript fragment (Fragment VI) which seems to have no place at all among the

others. It contains the Physician's and Pardoner's tales. They belong to no group, have no link with another tale, contain no reference to time or place. The "alestake" mentioned in line 321 might be anywhere: it is a place abstracted from topography, probably a symbol. Nor do the manuscripts give the fragment any consistent place in the order of tales. Thematic considerations are no help: the Physician's Tale might be part of the marriage group[1]; and since lawyers and physicians were rivals[2] it may be significant that it is a pious story like the Man of Law's Tale. But these are not impressive reasons for placing it after the marriage group or after the Man of Law's Tale. Why Chaucer linked the Physician's and Pardoner's tales is a further difficulty; no relationship asserts itself as one does, for instance, between Miller and Reeve or Clerk and Merchant.[3] The two tales come together but stand apart from the rest.

The Physician's Tale reflects his mentality.[4] If it is one of the ideal narratives (it is not, like the others, in stanzas) it is a dramatic example of misguided moralism: he praises virtue in a tale that is morally revolting. This suits the portrait of him in the General Prologue, which lists generic traits: he loves gold, is in league with apothecaries, has advanced knowledge of astrology, knows old as well as recent medical books. Medicine is not and never was an

---

1. Peter G. Beidler, "The Pairing of the *Franklin's Tale* and the *Physician's Tale*," *ChauR* 3 (1969):275–279.
2. Beryl Rowland, "The Physician's 'Historial Thyng Notable' and the Man of Law," *ELH* 40 (1973):165–178.
3. A linking theme sometimes put forward is the danger of Fortune's and Nature's gifts; the notion is based on the Host's words, VI:294–300. See Ruggiers, *The Art of the Canterbury Tales*, pp. 121–123, who cites the Parson and adds the gift of grace as pertinent to "the entirely Christian context of the Pardoner's performance."
4. Cf. Whittock, *A Reading of the Canterbury Tales*, pp. 179–184. Lumiansky, *Of Sundry Folk*, pp. 195–200, finds in the Host's remarks (VI: 301–313) an acerb put-down of the Physician's hypocrisy. Robert Longsworth, "The Doctor's Dilemma: A Comic View of the Physician's Tale," *Criticism* 13 (1971):223–233, finds the teller's lack of narrative skill a reflection of his impoverished imagination—in other words, he finds it an impersonated lack of artistry, as in *Sir Thopas* or the Squire's or Monk's tales. If this is so, I find the barebones narrative not comic but chilling.

exact science, but Chaucer informs us that he possessed not only learning but the skill or art of healing:

> He was a verray, parfit practisour:
> The cause yknow, and of his harm the roote,
> Anon he yaf the sicke man his boote.
>
> (422–424)

To this he added the proverbial sentiment that his study "was but litel on the Bible." The passage ends with the barbed remark that gold, being a cordial in "physik," was what he especially loved. He is a character still familiar: the perfectly competent physician whose primary interest is money. The most notable detail is his association with pharmacists: "ech of hem made other for to winne—/ Hir frendship nas nat newe to biginne."

The Physician's inordinate love of gold suggests something askew in his motives and ideals. It is not just that he is thrifty; it is that he got rich from the Black Death, for which no physician knew a cure—"He kepte that he wan in pestilence" (442). That many doctors did so was among the scandals of the age. His motive is evidently *pure* avarice—he is not in love with buying land like the Man of Law, nor with airs and pretensions like the Franklin, nor with *making* money like the Merchant, but with gold itself, with *having* it. In a credit economy money has a specterlike quality, but avarice in the fourteenth century would have been more primitive; moralists compared it to idolatry.[5] And gold, that most precious metal, was the principal object of avaricious veneration. This might be seen as a possible link between the Physician's and Pardoner's tales, for avarice is the Pardoner's besetting sin and avarice for gold central to his sermon. But the Physician's *tale* has nothing to do with avarice: it is a

---

5. See for example Pope Innocent III, *De miseria humanae conditionis*, II:15. J. Huizinga, *The Waning of the Middle Ages*, trans. F. Hopman (London: Edward Arnold, 1924), p. 19, remarks of the late Middle Ages that "what haunts the imagination is still the tangible yellow gold. The enjoyment of riches is direct and primitive; it is not yet weakened by the mechanism of an automatic and invisible accumulation by investment; the satisfaction of being rich is found either in luxury and dissipation, or in gross avarice."

pious tale about the preservation of virginity, which Chaucer adapted perhaps from Livy as well as the *Roman de la Rose*. It has no headlink or introduction, but the manuscripts consistently attribute it to the Physician. There is no sure suggestion of a date, though it seems unlikely that it would have been written after 1390, for it shows no influence from the version in Gower's *Confessio Amantis*[6]; one can imagine that it was written in earlier times, when Chaucer was sharing materials with Gower, and attributed to the Physician later. Perhaps it shows the Physician as a sententious moralizer and thus (given the slur on his morals in the General Prologue) a hypocrite. If that is true, he falls into a class with other moralizers who do not practice what they preach, among them the Pardoner.

The way he tells his tale, not its subject, is what reveals his mentality. He is full of high-minded advice for parents and governesses (72–104)—thinks it very important they teach virtue by precept and example. His tale is baldly allegorical: the twelve-year-old virgin is named Virginia, her father Virginius. She is beautiful—Nature, he goes on at length, never created a lovelier. The villain, a false judge named Apius, desires her; with bribes and threats he gets a local churl to appear in court and plead that Virginia is his servant and has been abducted by Virginius. Apius, presiding over this kangaroo court, passes judgment before Virginius has defended himself. Virginius goes home and in operatic fashion addesses Virginia: she has two ways, death or shame, and he ruefully chooses death. She answers "O mercy, deere fader! . . . Is there no grace, is there no remedye?" "No, certes, deere doghter myn," he answers. In her aria that follows she embraces her cruel fate, thanking God she will die a maid. The father then beheads his daughter and brings the head to Apius, who sentences him to hanging. For the finale a thousand people rush in, knowing of the judge's wickedness, and imprison him. He kills himself, and all others "consentant" to the crime are hanged, save only the churl Claudius, who is exiled on

6. *SA*, pp. 398–399.

Virginius's magnanimous plea. "Here," concludes the Physician, "may men seen how sin hath his merite." What he means is that sinners will be struck down *in this life*; it is all very simple, like revenge tragedy or revenge itself. The moral is, forsake sin or sin will forsake you.

That is like the moral of the Pardoner's Tale, and if the two come back-to-back for any reason it is because of the contrast they afford. In the Pardoner's Tale a grim and secret force which punishes evil springs naturally and with a mysterious rightness from wicked deeds themselves. In the Physician's tale this element of wonder and terror is lacking: his is a coldly rational world in which a father can save his daughter's virtue by killing her, in which sinners get killed off mechanically. Underneath it all is a tacit feeling that life is cheap. And who more than an avaricious physician would be likely to harbor this callous estimate of human life? I have been talking as if the Physician made up the tale, but he begins by announcing that it is from Livy. Like Polonius he is keen on the classical background. The tale follows its stoic source closely, not that this makes it the less harsh. The question whether death was preferable to losing virginity by rape was not a new one; Chaucer would have known St. Augustine's verdict that such deaths, however pious their motives, are not necessary because chastity is of the mind not merely of the body.[7] Chaucer's two additions to his sources (35–120, 207–253) emphasize the tale's two most characterizing elements. In the first he adds to the description of Virginia's beauty a passage attributing to her a panoply of virtues, this followed by the address to governesses and parents. In the second he adds the father's final address to his daughter and the daughter's reply. The first highlights the sentious quality of the Physician's moralism, the second the single-minded way he sees the solution. Of course life *was* cheap in the Middle Ages, violence and sudden death

7. *City of God* I:16–19. On Chaucer's way of adapting the tale as retold in the *Roman* to the Physician's character and to the plan of *The Canterbury Tales*, see Anne Middleton, "The *Physician's Tale* and Love's Martyrs: 'Ensamples mo than ten' as a Method in the *Canterbury Tales*," *ChauR* 8 (1973):9–32.

were a part of everyday existence, and people were sticklers for virginity in unmarried daughters. But other tales present alternatives to the Physician's cold moralism; one cannot imagine the Parson subscribing to his view without making plenty of distinctions. That Chaucer himself could view without skepticism the picture of a father beheading his daughter to preserve her virtue and presenting the head to her tormenter is beyond all possibility. But a physician grown rich from the plague would be less sensitive. The grotesque tale and its grisly morality is a suitable prologue to the Pardoner's "moral tale." Simplistic as his tale is, the Physician must really think he loves virtue; but the Pardoner is not so unsubtle.

The Pardoner with his "compeer" the Summoner is a pariah among the pilgrims, and his tale seems to be in a similar position among the other tales—the fragment it belongs to is sometimes called the "floating" fragment. You can put the fragment in any of the gaps in the existing structure (between Fragments I and II, II and III, V and VII, or VII and VIII) and manufacture a literary or thematic relationship, but none asserts itself. I mean to suggest that it belongs in the no-man's land where it is, "floating" on the periphery of the interlaced structure. Doesn't Chaucer suggest this himself by putting the Pardoner last in the General Prologue, like an unpleasant thought nudged out of the narrator's memory as long as possible? The Pardoner's Prologue and Tale get where they belong by a seemingly strange artistic rightness, but this rightness is owing to convention: medieval art had a place for the grotesque, but it was never at the center of things—it was on the outside or the underside. Chaucer lived a century before Bosch and then Breughel isolated this estranged world, nearly a century before the world "grotesque" came to be applied to ancient art discovered in grottos. In his time the grotesque— the disordered, incongruous, and startling element in experience, the *demonic* element—was antithetical to artistic ordering or structuring; its place was at the periphery, but there it was permitted to exist and did exist.[8] There is a right place

8. See Wolfgang Kayser, *The Grotesque in Art and Literature*, trans. Ulrich

for the Parson's "sermon" at the end of the work; the Pardoner's anti-sermon, coupled with the Physician's Tale, belongs in no ordered structure.

THE PARDONER AS A GROTESQUE

To understand the displaced or floating quality of the Physician-Pardoner fragment, we need to understand how the medievals' taste for the grotesque fitted into their *system* of taste, into their esthetic. We know they saw the universe as a hierarchy and saw evil as that part of the universal order which was "upside-down," fallen or perverted from its created goodness. Evil itself was nothing; it was the perversion of something created good. To portray evil in art meant portraying its lure—the artist had to show how attractive it could be in order to show how dangerous it was. The treatises on "contempt of the world" illustrate this problem and may be thought an analogue; Chaucer said he had translated the most famous of them, that of Pope Innocent III, and echoes of it come up in various tales, the Pardoner's among them. Pope Innocent described in detail the terrifying part of life—pain, disease, old age, death; and he described the evils of physicians, lawyers, judges, merchants, rich men, knights, scholars, monks, and parish priests. He described these in such a way that he managed to capture the enticement of evil's snares; it is why his book was such a success. You cannot proclaim the vanity of worldly things if you make them look boring—you have to show how attractive they are to any fallen man (bishops and popes themselves get into Innocent's treatise). In a treatise this poses no problem; Innocent laced his detailed exploration of "the world" with moralizing apostrophes.

But in a work of fiction verisimilitude was thought to be the greater lie; poets spoke the truth through deliberate lies—a story or a play was "a lie designed to tell the truth

---

Weisstein (1963; rpt. New York and Toronto: McGraw-Hill, 1966), esp. pp. 179–189. And see De Bruyne, *The Esthetics of the Middle Ages*, pp. 41, 102, 130.

about reality."[9] Yet this principle doesn't seem to apply to the Pardoner's Prologue and Tale. The Pardoner as a literary character seems all too real; and the Host's rejection of the Pardoner at the end does not turn the episode into an allegory, for the Host's rejection is not a virtuous act—it is "quitting." The Host is as much in the wrong as the Pardoner. It is only that last line—"Anon they kiste, and riden forth hir waye"—that final, ceremonious, and highly stylized kiss of peace, that act of forgiveness, which seems to give a moral meaning, and even then we are not sure whether the two pilgrims are only going through the motions which the Knight urges upon them, only being civil or "curteis." St. Augustine had used an actor as an example of the way a representation must be false in order to be true. But in the Pardoner we are given a representation *of an actor*: the representation is a lie about a lie—it must be true in order to be false. And this reversal of esthetic response, this incongruity or contradiction is grotesque: the grotesque exploits incongruity and distorts what is ordinary, but presents in minute detail what is itself grotesque.

Hence the verisimilitude of the Pardoner's Prologue and Tale. The corruptions the Pardoner embodies were a real part of the world *The Canterbury Tales* represents. Acts of penance were part of the ritual of pilgrimages, and a pilgrimage was itself an act of penance. The act of penance performed with contrition and satisfaction earned the penitent "Christ's own pardon," which the Pardoner grants is best. Pardons—indulgences, remissions of temporal punishment—were decreed and offered to those making the great medieval pilgrimages. The first indulgences were declared in order to support crusades, themselves a form of pilgrimage and one designed to secure Jerusalem for Christian pilgrims. But the Pardoner is a corruption of this institution.[10] The many requirements laid down for the offering of

9. V. A. Kolve, *The Play Called Corpus Christi* (Stanford, Calif.: Stanford Univ. Press, 1966), p. 32. Cf. De Bruyne, pp. 40–41.

10. On the background of pardoners and indulgences, see Alfred L. Kellogg and Louis A. Haselmayer, "Chaucer's Satire of the Pardoner," *PMLA* 66 (1951):251–277, rpt. *Chaucer, Langland, Arthur*, pp. 212–244;

indulgences were directed against false pardoners who in effect gave out a piece of paper for a sum of money. The institution produced a myriad of abuses even among licensed pardoners and a swarm of outright frauds. Behind and beneath the whole tangle of corruptions remained the unalterable fact of the solitary Christian earnestly repenting his sins and gaining Christ's own pardon. So the Pardoner is a hanger-on, a parasite. Yet this figure—corrupt, deformed, extravagant—has the theatrical power to draw attention. And for that reason Pardoners, like Friars, were the bane of parish priests: "with feined flattery and japes / He made the person and the peple his apes" (I:705−706), we learn, and he shows us how he does it.

The Pardoner belongs on the pilgrimage because historically he was a grotesque part of the institution as it really was (and part of the reason for its eventual demise). He is a marginal figure, and his relationship to the form of the work has to be understood as a marginal grotesquerie, like the drawings to which Professor Robertson and others have drawn attention in the margins even of psalters and books of hours, depicting devils, monsters, lechers making lewd gestures; or like the gargoyles and misshapen creatures banished to the outer surfaces of Gothic cathedrals; or like the realistic oddments and bits of misbehavior which cling out of sight beneath the seats of misericords; or like the sports and freaks of nature which Mandeville described in the East, and which came to be pictured on maps about the periphery of the civilized world—as for example on the *mappa mundi* in Hereford Cathedral. He belongs to this *banished world* of the Middle Ages, which is the world of poems and treatises on contempt of the world, or of the *Inferno*, and was to become the world of Bosch and Breughel, looming on the periphery of the ordered world of created goodness—dreadful, vivid, and fascinating.

Arnold Williams, "Some Documents on English Pardoners 1350−1400," *Mediaeval Studies in Honor of Urban Tigner Holmes, Jr.*, ed. John Mahoney and John Esten Keller, Univ. of North Carolina Studies in Romance Language and Literature 56 (Chapel Hill, N.C., 1965), pp. 197−207.

That is why the Pardoner is so much more arresting than the Parson. His tale fascinates and astounds us; the Parson's tiringly instructs. He preaches at a tavern with cakes and ale, the Parson at a "thrope's end" late in the afternoon (that unlikeliest hour for a lecture) at a journey's end. The Pardoner himself is ingratiating and jolly—we are perversely intrigued by him; the Parson is too abstractly good to seem real—we like the *idea* of him, but the man himself, on the two occasions when he speaks, is astringent enough to win a put-down from the Host. The Pardoner's sermon sparkles with Chaucer's art at the height of its poetic and narrative powers; the Parson's is a translation, in workaday prose, divided in parts and with numbered points—no one ever wished it longer. The Pardoner's sermon is a performance, the Parson's a piece of reading matter. If goodness is dull in literature—if Milton's Satan is more interesting than God, Iago more exciting than Desdemona—this is a fact not about goodness or about literature but about ourselves. Take someone to the zoo and he wants to see the snakes. Readers usually end up, like the Host, condemning the Pardoner— Kittredge judged him the one lost soul among the pilgrims.[11] And the curious thing is, the tale *makes* us react this way. Chaucer on this score has nothing to say at all. He sends him on his way, as if telling us to leave him alone; yet that is exactly what we cannot do.

This is the kind of phenomenon the Pardoner is and the kind of effect he has. We are fascinated and repelled. He is meant to haunt us, to hover menacingly over our whole reading of *The Canterbury Tales*, to be central to its idea. Hence we must distrust any reasons (or excuses) advanced for *not* taking him seriously.

It is for example widely believed that the Pardoner is drunk. He takes one draught of ale at line 322 and finishes it at line 456. This and his uninhibited behavior, plus the figure of speech the Wife uses in her prologue (170f.), and perhaps his references to drinking and the drunkenness of the revellers in his tale, have convinced a generation of

11. *Chaucer and His Poetry*, p. 180.

readers that he must be drunk. One critic states as if it were a fact that he is under the influence of *wine*. It seems to me a failure of imagination that instead of "drunk," writers have not thought to use words like "manic" or "compulsive" or "histrionic." For there are things other than drink which can make the Pardoner behave as he does, among them his character.

It is the same with his being a eunuch. It is widely believed that on seeing him the pilgrims all have something go click-click in their heads and come up unanimously with the diagnosis *eunuchus ex nativitate*. He is, as Professor Curry showed,[12] explicitly described as a eunuch in the General Prologue. His piping voice, his beardless face and glaring eyes, his thin waxlike hair hanging in bunches: the symptoms are unmistakable—after you've read Curry. Curry thought the pilgrims "recognize the type immediately and translate his physical peculiarities into terms of character." But the pilgrims were not steeped in the medical treatises Curry was steeped in, and Curry never said they were. They see the symptoms, and the narrator echoes what must be their reaction when he says "I trow he were a gelding or a mare." The line suggests only that he is sexually peculiar— that he *lacks* something: like a gelding the physical equipment, or like a mare the male gender-identity. The pilgrims see there is something strange about him; they do not, like us, hear Chaucer's opinion about this. Nowhere, in the General Prologue or in his Prologue and Tale, is there any

12. *Chaucer and the Mediaeval Sciences*, chap. 3. Curry showed what the Pardoner was from the standpoint of medieval medical lore, with which Chaucer might have been acquainted. More recent attempts to show what he is from the standpoint of modern medicine only obscure the ambiguity of his appearance. Beryl Rowland, "Animal Imagery and the Pardoner's Abnormality," *Neophilologus* 48 (1964):56–60, thinks "gelding" refers to his evident physical abnormality and "mare" to his feminoid and lecherous appearance. She notes that the hare and goat, with which his eyes and voice are compared in the General Prologue, were associated with hermaphroditism as well as lechery. She thinks him a "testicular pseudo-hermaphrodite of the feminine type," a "deviate"—but her argument relies in part on the fact that a true eunuch has no libido, and many take the Pardoner's libidinous conduct as pretense. Cf. Edward I. Condren, "The Pardoner's Bid for Existence," *Viator* 4 (1973):177–205, esp. 189f.

suggestion that his mannerisms are effeminate—if anything, his bravura could be reckoned masculine. The ambiguity about him and the discomfort it produces is the heart of his effect upon others. Among the pilgrims there is only one who could be expected to make an accurate diagnosis of his symptoms, the Physician; this may just be why the Physician's tale is told immediately before his own.

The Pardoner, then, is *feminoid* in a starkly physical way—his voice, his hair, his beard are involved. Critics soften this unnerving fact into "feminine" or "effeminate," and so it is widely believed that he is homosexual. The popular stereotype of the present day holds male homosexuals to be effeminate in appearance and mannerism, though in fact many limp-wristed and reedy-voiced men are heterosexual and many overt homosexuals ostentatiously or ostensibly masculine. Homosexuals are not the same as eunuchs, nor eunuchs necessarily homosexual. The Pardoner travels in the company of the Summoner singing "Come hider love to me," and we are told the Summoner "bar to him a stiff burdoun." This possible pun is always dredged up as evidence of a homosexual relation between the two, but the next line, "Was never trumpe of half so greet a soun," enforces the literal meaning (that the Summoner sings a bass accompaniment), and there is not another line that carries out the sexual suggestion. True, you can find "burdoun" (staff) used in this phallic way elsewhere; but in Middle English you can find the name of almost any elongated object used this way.[13] The real implication is that they are in cahoots: both are criminals, and the Pardoner needs the Summoner to get entree into a diocese. What else they may have to do with each other in a sexual way is at best a faint

---

13. See B. D. H. Miller, "Chaucer, General Prologue, A 673: Further Evidence," *N&Q*, n.s. 7 (1960):404–406; but the evidence is only that the pun occurs in French, as inevitably it should. Any number of common words could be used in a phallic sense given a suggestive context; see for example the lyric "May no man sleep in your hall," *Secular Lyrics of the XIVth and XVth Centuries*, ed. Rossell Hope Robbins, 2nd ed. (Oxford: Clarendon Press, 1955), no. 31. Charles R. Sleeth, "The Friendship of Chaucer's Summoner and Pardoner," *MLN* 56 (1941):138, presents a document showing that false pardoners were in cahoots with summoners.

suspicion that passes quickly in and out of the text, as it should pass in and out of our thoughts.

If the Pardoner is not drunk, not a dead give-away, and not the modern stereotype of a homosexual, what is he? My answer is that he is a mystery, an enigma—sexually anomalous, hermaphroditic, menacing, contradictory. He has a magnetic power of attraction partly because he is frightening and loathsome. We know he is a *eunuchus ex nativitate*, and that eunuchs in exegetical tradition symbolized *in malo* the deprival of God's grace, so that his physical deformity is a counterpart of his moral depravity.[14] The pilgrims, hardly thinking this way, nevertheless turn from him. The Host addresses him derisively, "Thou bel ami" (318),[15] using the familiar "thou." The "gentils" cry out against him, "Nay, lat him tell us of no ribaudye!" (324) The Wife brushes past his genial compliment to her: "Abide! my tale is nat bigunne" (III:169). Even the courteous Knight, peacemaking at the end of the Pardoner's tale, pointedly calls him "thee" (966) though he calls the Host "you." Yet there is something fascinating and irresistible in him. "Tell us some moral thing, that we may leere / Some wit, and thanne wol we gladly heere," cry the righteous "gentils."

The Pardoner has the knack of gauging his audience, and he must see people's ambivalence—must note the snubs and disapproval, the distaste and the glazed eye with which people greet men like him. But he must sense their fascination and curiosity as well. In response, he is courteous,

14. Robert P. Miller, "Chaucer's Pardoner, the Scriptural Eunuch, and the Pardoner's Tale," *Speculum* 30 (1955):180–199; rpt. S&T, pp. 221–244. Implicit is the symbol of the eunuch *in bono* who practices a purposeful chastity; Miller tries to equate the Parson with this *eunuchus Dei* because the Parson is different from the Pardoner, but there is not a scrap of evidence that Chaucer had such a notion in mind when he described the Parson in the General Prologue—in fact he did not trouble to mention his chastity.

15. On its derisive sense, see *MED*. It is comparable to "good fellow" used ironically and so pejoratively. It does not connote effeminacy (if anything it suggests "lover," which is how the Pardoner likes to depict himself) and seems very mildly derisive; the Pardoner ignores the epithet altogether, echoing the Host's "by Seint Ronyan," with its possible phallic pun or perhaps mocking the Host's mispronunciation of Ninian.

ingratiating, cool. "Dame," he replies to the Wife, nothing daunted by her rebuff,

I wolde pray yow, if your will it were
. . . as ye bigan,
Tell forth your tale, spareth for no man,
And teche us younge men of your practike.

The little Falstaffian joke is enough to make the Wife switch from "thou" to "you" in her reply.[16] The speech has an edge of mockery—he is play-acting the young swain about to wed. His trick is to confront, challenge, mock. "I graunte, ywis," he answers the smug gentils, "but I moot thinke / Upon some honest thing while that I drinke." It is done very smoothly— he has already, on the Host's demand for some "mirth or japes," pulled them up at a tavern-sign, thus getting them to hold still and become that many headed monster which he can overpower, an audience.[17]

It is not just his effrontery which inspires awe, it is his histrionic ability, his powers of speech. Everything that he lacks in sexual power he has contrived to regain with the

16. "You" is not plural here, for she then turns and addresses "all this compaignye" (III:188–189); she may pick up the "you" simply from his own use of it (the distinction was a small one, nothing like *tu* and *vous*, let alone *du* and *Sie*), but the switch still shows the Pardoner's power to manipulate others.

17. Cf. Lumiansky, *Of Sundry Folk*, pp. 210–211. My reading of the Pardoner's performance agrees with Lumiansky's in a number of particulars, as will be seen; but I find little evidence to support his idea that the Pardoner has all along planned to try and outwit for the first time a middle-class audience as he has hitherto outwitted "peasant" audiences. Part of the effect is that we do not know any more than his audience does what he has planned. On the Pardoner's performance see the very perceptive argument by James L. Calderwood, "Parody in *The Pardoner's Tale*," *ES* 45 (1964):302–309, that the Pardoner, sensing their uneasiness, "decides to play the role to the limit, to give the 'gentils' the demonic Pardoner of their imaginings" (304), and at the same time wants to gain their approval by ridiculing their stereotype. And see Paul E. Beichner, "Chaucer's Pardoner as Entertainer," *MS* 25 (1963):160–172, who argues that the professional Pardoner entertains the pilgrims with an exposition of his tricks, a sample sermon, and a burlesque demonstration; that the prologue and tale are not a confession, and the relics are funny ones which are part of the entertainment. The notion does not contradict Calderwood's notion of self-parody.

gifts of his tongue. On our first glimpse of him he is singing, the Summoner absurdly accompanying him with a bass burdoun—there may be a hint that the Pardoner calls the tune. Noise-making is his gift and his preoccupation, and "Come hider, love, to me" is the right song: singing and speaking are his substitute for love-making. In the description of him the tone is lewd—the traditional lecherous animals (goat, hare, mare) are associated with him; he is made to seem obscene. His sermon, with its capacity for dominating others and its avowedly rapacious motive is from this viewpoint a kind of monstrous verbal rape. We are told that "alderbest he song an offertorie"—for he knew that when the song was sung he must "affile" his tongue, like a tool or weapon (elsewhere he compares his tongue with the insect's sting and the adder's fang). And his preaching *is* songlike, all memorized and lilting and (as we see for ourselves) lyrical in its sense of rhythm, its forward-rushing flow: "Lordings," he tells the pilgrims,

> . . . in chirches whan I preche,
> I peyne me to han an hauteyn speche,
> And ring it out as round as goth a belle.

He is an extraordinary performer—a natural-born actor with plenty of experience in his "craft." We know this first because the narrator says so:

> But of his craft, fro Berwyk into Ware,
> Ne was there swich another pardoner.
>   . . .
> But trewely to tellen atte laste,
> He was in chirche a noble ecclesiaste.

And we learn in detail the effect he creates. The outrageous "relics" he carries—a pillow-case, a bit of cloth, pig's bones—become under his mesmerizing skill Our Lady's veil, a snip of the sail from St. Peter's boat, the bones of a saint. With these props and some verbal legerdemain he can, when he finds a poor country parson, make him and the whole parish his "apes," getting more money out of them in a day than the wretched parson gets in two months; he has, so he claims, won a hundred marks a year[18] since he became a pardoner. We get a clear picture of his animation, his control of pace and sense of timing, his variety: he takes pains to stretch forth his neck, he says, and bend his head down at the audience from one side to the other like a "dove sitting on a berne." His hands and his tongue "goon so yerne / That it is joy to see my bisynesse." And he has the preacher's aura of righteousness: stern and angered as he denounces evil, clucking over the oaths of his "revellours" and interlacing his exempla with apostrophes and ejaculations borrowed in some instances from Pope Innocent III—"O womb! O belly! O stinkinge cod!" But his greatest trick is arranging his material so that his main point is illustrated by a story—"For lewed peple loven tales olde." When his story has reached its deathly finish, he draws back, feigns a donnish manner with some academic jargon and name-dropping—"But certes, I suppose that Avycen / Wrote never in no canon, ne in no fen . . ." then builds all to an *O altitudo* addressed to the whole human race:

> Allas! mankinde, how may it bitide
> That to thy Creatour, which that thee wroghte,
> And with His precious herte-blood thee boghte,
> Thou art so false and so unkinde, alas?
>
> (900–903)

At last the solemn address—earnest, delicately intimate so that one imagines him looking about "east and west" into their faces, all tranquil solicitude:

> Now, good men, God foryeve you your trespass,
> And ware you fro the sin of avarice!
> Myn holy pardon may you all warice—
> So that ye offre nobles or sterlinges,

---

18. Line 390: grammatically it could mean he has won a total of a hundred marks since he was a pardoner, but he speaks as if he has been at it some time and the sum is not that great. A hundred marks was 66 pounds; Baugh, p. xv, estimates Chaucer's income at an average of 99 pounds a year, something more than $20,000 by the buying power of the dollar in the 1960s. If the Pardoner can, as he says, get more money in a day than a parish priest can in two months, this figure, something like $13,000 per annum, must be what is meant.

Or elles silver brooches, spoones, ringes . . .
Boweth your heed under this holy bulle!
Cometh up, ye wives, offreth of your woole!
Your name I entre here in my roll anon;
Into the bliss of hevene shull ye gon!
I you assoille, by myn heigh power,
You that wol offre, as clene and eek as cleer
As ye were born.

(904–915)

His performance in the role of preacher is the more exciting because we sense the man himself behind it. This comes not just from his frank disavowal of any honest motives but from his unconscious revelation of his own attitudes. It is like watching an actor perform whom we have heard backstage boasting and chuckling over his power to make people laugh and cry—we catch not just the artist's satisfaction showing behind his art, but get a sense of the man himself, the human (and selfish) motives which produce the satisfaction *and* the art. Grotesquely, we see the real face under the greasepaint, see the clown's anguish and the tragedian's smirk.

For Chaucer makes us know the Pardoner better than the Pardoner knows himself. He is proud. The delight he takes in his own skill and success is contagious. His hands and tongue go so "yerne," he proclaims, that it is a joy to see. He makes a great point of the financial rewards. He is pleased with the props and bits of stage business he has worked up—the "bulls" he shows, our liege lord's seal on his patent, the spicy words of Latin he speaks "To saffron with my predicacioun," and the relics, his favorite "gaude." He takes childlike delight in his effectiveness, for he is at pains to remind us that he *can* "stir hem to devocioun," can make them "soore to repente." This is "nat my principal entente," he adds, for he takes equal pleasure in his guile:

For though myself be a full vicious man,
A moral tale yet I you telle can.

That is what shocks us most: he is proud of his own evil, so much so that he cannot keep from boasting of it. At the end he cannot resist a tour de force of the swindler's art.

He is condescending. The poor simple folk he dupes become in his eyes the object of a contemptuous derision. They are the "lewed peple" who "loven tales olde":

I stonde like a clerk in my pulpet,
And whan the lewed peple is down yset,
I preche so as ye han herd before.

For him they are a mass (he uses a singular verb) whom he can treat like a great draffsack—he even absolves them in a lump at the end! The "gaude" he brings off with his relics is the best example of his contempt for them—the shoulder-bone of a holy Jew's sheep which cures animal diseases, makes livestock multiply, heals a husband's jealousy of his wife; the mitten which increases grain; and the warning that anyone who has done a horrible sin, or any woman who has made her husband a cuckold, will have to stay in their seats. It is droll that the "lewed" people fall for this—whether it illustrates his skill or their ignorance is left ambiguous (though we are told he made parsons his apes as well); but it is such a gross, improbable deception that it puts us on his side and makes us share his pleasure. Everyone who has taught the poem knows the little *frisson* of delight which ripples through a class over this passage, and that sets the tone of one's response throughout. *We* are not of the "lewed" people so easily hoodwinked; thus we become party to his tricks and share his pleasure in them. He was trying for the same effect among the pilgrims—his underlying contempt for them only shows at the end; and the Host is the first to see it, or to show he does.

He is intimate. He takes a conspiratorial tone with the assemblage, makes them feel amused and superior as they join in his condescension. It is the oldest trick in the world for gaining audience sympathy—you can always win the sophomores by condescending to the freshmen. That is why his outrageous frankness is so beguiling: he has taken them into his confidence long before he has told them anything. He begins by telling how he preaches as if he preached with the best intentions—tells how he speaks up loud, shows his credentials, throws in a little Latin. "Saffron" is the first suggestion of fraudulency; the next is "Relics been they, as wenen they echoon." Forty lines later he comes out and says it: "By this gaude have I wonne, yeer by yeer, / An hundred mark . . ." and by then their reserve is broken down. Not that a boasting swindler wouldn't still seem offensive to many— one can imagine the nuns clicking their tongues—but he has managed by now to make the tavern or tavern-yard his theater: the gentles who would hear no "ribaudye" are charmed, at least, into silence. From then on, his outright self-revelation never loses interest. His tacit groundrule, "present company excepted," and his disarming openness, are irresistible; and his scandalous confession is followed by the artful sermon itself. When he says frankly that he preaches "again that same vice / Which that I use, and that is avarice," or calls himself accurately "a full vicious man," he paralyzes the audience's indignation: his candor suggests self-knowledge, as if he wishes forgiveness. And his extrava- gance is paralyzing too, perhaps because it terrorizes: he will, Fagin-like, have offerings from the poorest widow in a village "Al shold hir children sterve for famine." (He fol- lows this enormity with a vain boast which somewhat takes the edge off it: he will "have a jolly wench in every town.") And he establishes this intimate tone with the "lewed" people as well. For them he has the little cliché jokes at the clergy's expense ("Al had she taken preestes two or three"), or his farcical parody of the drunken man's breathing ("Sampsoun, Sampsoun!"), or his demonstration-lecture on gamblers' oaths:

> "By Goddes precious herte," and "By his nailes,"
> And "By the blood of Christ that is in Hayles,
> Seven is my chaunce, and thyn is cynk and treye!"

His detailed knowledge of low life (he is a great expert on strong wines) is insinuating and chummy. And his most intimate touch, a *pièce de résistance* of the confidence man, is his last:

> . . . And lo, sires, thus I preche.
> And Jhesu Christ, that is our soules leche,
> So graunte you his pardon to receive,
> For that is best; I wol you nat deceive.

He is ironical. He will, asked for a tale, "thinke / Upon some honest thing." His first point about his preaching, developed at length with a good bit of repetition, is that he preaches always against avarice though avarice is his motive—an idea he expresses in balanced, ironic juxtapositions:

> For myn entent is nat but for to winne,
> And nothing for correccioun of sinne.
>   . . .
> I preche of nothing but for coveitise.
> Therefore my theme is yet, and evere was,
> *Radix malorum est cupiditas.*
> Thus can I preche again that same vice
> Which that I use—and that is avarice.
> But though myself be guilty in that sinne,
> Yet can I maken other folk to twinne
> From avarice and sore to repente.
> But that is nat my principal entente.
> I preche nothing but for coveitise.
> Of this mattere it ought enough suffice.

He relishes the irony that he can stir people to devotion and repentance without intending to. This disparity between motive and act makes much of his discourse ironic—he calls his preaching "Christes holy werk." His tale, too, centers upon an irony—that of the revellers' wishing to have Death die and dying themselves in their pursuit of life. In the end he strives for a *coup de grâce* of irony, to sell the pilgrims pardons they know are false.

He is impudent. There is something bold-faced and grandly daring in all his discourse and behavior. He is a beardless man with a voice like a goat's, but he is able to hold an audience spellbound. It is abundantly clear that he looks odd—his hair alone, hanging in wax-colored colpons, ought to raise an eyebrow—but he rides *dischevelee*, his hood in his "walet," hair spread on shoulders. He sings aloud—and about love. He claims he was about to wed a wife, would have a jolly wench in every town. The text he chooses for his sermon is itself a bare-faced bit of braggadocio. Requested by the gentles to tell some moral thing "that we may leere / Some wit," he thinks a moment, downing a draught of ale, upon some "honest thing," then tells them the most honest thing he can think of: he is a fraud and a scoundrel. Having told all honestly he gets an afterthought—he has pardons given by the Pope's own hand, and if any care to receive,

Come forth anon, and kneeleth here adown,
And meekely receiveth my pardoun;
Or elles taketh pardoun as ye wende,
All new and fresh at every miles ende.

And on top of this effrontery—that they should buy a pardon every mile—he singles out the Host! This is the conduct of a man willing to take extravagant gambles and having an overpowering lust to win, or an unconscious will to lose, or a taste for danger. For beneath all his trickery and daring lies a *knack*: there must have been a time when he knew that such a man as himself, given his voice and appearance, would everywhere provoke the giggle, the taunt, the embarrassed sidewise glance, the surmising look. Most would have kept in the corner; he chose the other way— learned to stare them down, confront and challenge them, *talk* them down. Thus he can forestall the distaste he provokes by calculated insouciance and flair: he rides *dischevelee*, "all of the newe jet," singing. If you *act* on top of the world people will believe it, but you must never for a minute show doubt or fear. And he has the actor's genius, is able to sustain the pose; has the verbal skill; has aplomb. It is a choice which requires bravado, intelligence, a quick wit and tongue, and a will. And what nature did not give him in other respects she gave him in these.

Only, it takes its toll.

He is invidious. The force which energizes his charade is an obsessive lust for power in whatever directions he has a capability—say it is libido necessarily redirected or sublimated, but one cannot miss its most basic force, resentment. He is filled with hate. The "avarice" which moves him is not half so much the avarice of getting or having as that of taking away. His will is to deprive others, his motive antisocial, sheer gloating rapacity: the presentation of him could be considered a study of the obsessional or psychopathic character, of the criminal mind. His condescension, which seems amusing directed against the "lewed" people, is only one symptom of his feeling toward all—*all* are ripe to be his gulls. He has told his audience in detail how he deals with those who do him "displesances":

> Thus spit I out my venim under hewe
> Of holinesse, to seemen holy and trewe.

But he assumes all men are likely to do him a "displesance" and he takes pride in being venomous—actually pictures himself as the adder spitting venom. The poorest widow in a village is not beyond his grasp; her children dying of hunger make no impression on him. So at least he says. But he represents himself in this malevolent picture partly out of self-contempt. His enormous hatred includes himself—it is as if he were demanding of the pilgrims that they excuse his villainy or punish it. Why else would anyone admit in public crimes which by rights he would conceal? Hence the abuse the Host unleashes on him is expected, perhaps invited.

And he is angry. The force of his envy and self-contempt is supercharged with the energy of aggression. The ritual of pardon-selling becomes a habitual fraud, and this becomes a compulsion; he must get more and more because nothing that he gets can satisfy—nothing can unleash upon others the venom he would like to unleash, nothing provide what is missing in him of potency, renunciation, repentance. Hence the energy of detail and of rhetoric with which he catalogues the objects of his evil will—his substitutionary lusts tumble helter-skelter off his tongue: "I will" (which meant to choose) is repeated over and over:

> What, trowe ye, that whiles I may preche,
> And winne gold and silver for I teche,
> That I wol live in poverte willfully?
> Nay, nay, I thought it never, trewely!
> For I wol preche and beg in sundry landes,
> I wol nat do no labour with myn handes,
> Ne make baskettes, and live thereby,
> By cause I wol nat beggen idelly.
> I wol noon of the apostles countrefete;

I wol have money, woole, cheese, and whete . . .
. . . . . .
Nay, I wol drinke licour of the vine,
And have a jolly wench in every town.

(439–453)

So when he turns to the pilgrims he cannot resist a similar catalogue of his greeds:

Myn holy pardoun may you all warice,
So that ye offre nobles or sterlinges,
Or elles silver brooches, spoones, ringes.
Boweth your heed under this holy bulle!
Cometh up, ye wives, offreth of youre woole!

In explaining this compulsion, Professor Kellogg[19] has shown how he progresses through that concatenation of vices implicit in the idea of the Seven Deadly Sins—from pride to envy, from envy to wrath, from wrath to despair, after which the sinner can only wallow hopelessly in sins of the flesh, gluttony, avarice, and lechery, hoping to regain through the flesh what he has lost in the spirit.

This progression in his sinning is why the Augustinian pattern is demonstrably present in the presentation of him—why the exegetical tradition with its "scriptural" eunuch is demonstrably present: because Chaucer, like St. Augustine, could look at those men whom a Christian age called sinners and see in them what we now call a neurotic circle, self-feeding, in which every defeat provokes the motive for a new action and every action provokes a new defeat. The Augustinian conception of evil did not last into and beyond Chaucer's time merely because it was Augustinian. It lasted because St. Augustine was a shrewd and articulate observer of human conduct: what he said squared with the realities of human behavior a thousand years after he wrote it and does still. Hence when I talk about neurosis and compulsion the reader must not think I am "modernizing" Chaucer; it is the opposite—I am using the lexicon of our time to name kinds of behavior which the medievals *already knew*. Psychological

19. Alfred L. Kellogg, "An Augustinian Interpretation of Chaucer's Pardoner," *Speculum* 26 (1951):465–481; rpt. *Chaucer, Langland, Arthur*, pp. 245–268.

realism used to be all any critic saw in Chaucer; now critics want to see Chaucer's characters   "in Chaucer's terms," which means "sources" and "background" and "convention." The Pardoner becomes a copy of Faux-Semblant and a "scriptural eunuch." But such opinions ignore the nature and the meaning of literary tradition; for a literary tradition is nothing more than a set of conventions by which the artist perceives reality—it *is* the artist's "terms." One can argue that medieval men were all reasonable zombies who held identical opinions and saw everything in moral, not psychological, terms; but to argue this one has to ignore everything they wrote about people's motives, their inner states, their dreams, their moral choices, and their souls.

Behind the conventions and the "background" in the Pardoner's Prologue and Tale lies the actual horror with which the Middle Ages viewed guilt. Guilt was produced by misconduct and was a torment; hence sin was its own punishment, leading to a process which is self-punishing and, at a certain secret point, irreversible. Since guilt is a torment, the sinner wishes to flee that torment; and his only choice, unless he repents, is to flee into further misconduct by wallowing in sins and lusts, all of which produce more guilt. Repentance is always a possibility until at a secret moment the scale is tipped; then it was said God had given them up to the lusts of their own hearts.[20] The moment when the scale tipped was the moment of despair. Pride, envy, and wrath produced despair. The anger which surges under the Pardoner's behavior, this charge of aggressive energy fed by frustration and guilt, must at some point break down. Despair (*acedia*) is the failure of hope, and hope—the expectation of God's mercy—is essential to the Christian life. To give up hope is to call into question the mercy of God, to be unable to repent. And at this point the sinner engages in a turmoil of self-indulgence, envy, and frustration which collapses into a state of listlessness and inactivity. The

20. Kellogg, pp. 246–252, offers the clearest explanation of this important Augustinian idea, which he extrapolates from various works by Augustine, and shows that Chaucer would have known the idea.

process is repetitive and cumulative: the sinner does not fall into an irreversible vegetative *acedia*; rather, the *acedia* feeds anew the flames of his wrath, envy, and pride. The only release is from the entrapping chain of cause and effect; and the longer one waits the harder release comes. This self-destroying quality of guilt was, in the thought of the Middle Ages, the ultimate grotesquerie: it was that part of worldly experience which would end in damnation, would be estranged forever.

THE PARDONER'S TALE AS DREAM AND HAPPENING

How do we know the Pardoner experiences this inner torment? Because he projects it unconsciously into his sermon. The medieval sermon normally used exempla as a means of illustrating a point; the Pardoner, knowing that "lewed" people love old stories, bloats up an exemplum so that it subsumes all else, cleverly keeping up interest while he inveighs against other sins in digressions; this organization helps him keep avarice central. Ostensibly the exemplum shows how the rioters brought death upon their heads because of avarice. And it does show this, probably, to the "lewed" people. But from the reader's point of view it reflects the Pardoner's own inner conflict. The three rioters are a projection of himself. They are sinning in a tavern[21] while Death stalks outside: taking the personification literally they attempt to "slay" Death. Told where Death is, they find not a person but bushels of gold florins, and each plots, Cain-like, to kill his "brothers" in order to have more for himself; thus all "find death."

---

21. Line 663. The symbolical value of the tavern is often noted. In Scripture, drunkenness symbolized a loss of rational control, hence sin itself—i.e. all vices and any enslavement to earthly things. It also symbolized exclusion from the Kingdom and was associated with idolatry. See Thierry Maertens, *Bible Themes: A Source Book*, 2 vols. (Notre Dame, Ind.: Fides, 1964), II:361. That the Pardoner has stopped at an alestake (321) should not escape attention, and of course the pilgrimage gathered in a tavern at Southwark.

The events happen in an unaccountable and unmotivated way—characters appear and disappear unpredictably. There are abrupt junctures, as in dream-visions. Many allegorical meanings have been suggested, especially for the old man, but what stands out about him is that he is old (he is depicted with the conventional iconography of Old Age, cloak and staff) and says he desires death. Alfred David[22] convincingly treats him as an archetype. Pinning down such allegorical meanings in the tale involves reading it for content, but the form and tone are what make it so haunting. Its dreamlike quality makes it *sound* like an allegory, but then medieval allegories normally *were* figured as dreams, and it has one quality which makes it far more like a dream than like an allegory: it is an exceedingly personal projection, so much so that everything in it can be related directly to the Pardoner's consciousness. The dream is about three[23] nameless rioters who commit all the same sins as the Pardoner himself; they are "younge folk," and the Pardoner seems to think of himself that way—"teche us younge men of your practike," he has asked the Wife (III:187). Upon them, as inwardly upon himself, he showers down a rain of moral disapprobation. It is not only that they are wicked; their wits

22. "Criticism and the Old Man in Chaucer's *Pardoner's Tale*," *CE* 27 (1965):39–44. For a summary of various interpretations of the Old Man see Christopher Dean, "Salvation, Damnation and the Role of the Old Man in the *Pardoner's Tale*," *ChauR* 3 (1968):44–49, who adds that the Old Man represents God's mercy as well as His justice. John M. Steadman, "Old Age and *Contemptus Mundi* in *The Pardoner's Tale*," *MAE* 33 (1964): 121–130, shows how the Old Man's characteristics contrast with the rioters' and suggest an abstract figure of Old Age which represents the misery of the human condition and so functions as a *memento mori*.

23. The detail is typical. The "young folk" of the tale are introduced at first as "a compaignye" (463); we learn they are three only in line 661. They are not differentiated (they are "this one," "this other," etc.) except by extremes: the proudest (716), the worst (774), the youngest (837). All this is dreamlike, but there are no details which warrant associating them with the three temptations, say, or the three ages of man. If they are a projection of the Pardoner's inner man, it may be significant that man was understood as constituted in three parts because he was made in God's image (see St. Augustine, *City of God* XI:26; *De Trinitate* X:11–12). Kellogg, "Augustinian Interpretation," e.g. p. 262 n. 12 and p. 265 n. 28 shows that the secret punishment is visited upon the reason, the will, and the passions or senses.

are dulled, so that they talk in non sequiturs and repeat
idées fixes as drunks do; and in this they mirror his own
obstinacy, the clouding of his intellect which accompanies
the progressive weakening of his will. He relates their vices
with the same compulsive catalogues he has used to name his
own lusts; puts them in a tavern ("the Devil's temple") like
himself, and in the Devil's service: they

> . . . haunteden follye
> As riot, hasard, stewes, and tavernes,
> Where as with harpes, lutes, and guiternes
> They daunce and playen at dees bothe day and night,
> And ete also and drink over hir might;
> Thurgh which they doon the devil sacrifise
> Within that devils temple, in cursed wise,
> By superfluitee abhominable.

And they are, like himself, vainly boastful of their sins and
eager to encourage sin in others—"ech of hem at otheres
sinne lough" (476).

The events of the tale are a series of dreamlike entrances and exits, unprepared and unmotivated. A bell rings
and a corpse is carried in. A reveller, undistinguishable from
the others, tells a boy to find out who it is. The boy was
already told two hours *before*: it was an old companion of
theirs, slain suddenly sitting drunk on a bench, by a "privee
theef men clepeth Deeth" who (like the boy and the old man)
then "went his way withouten wordes mo." Now for the first
time (679) we learn that a plague is going on (the plague was
sometimes called The Death). At last the boy innocently tells
"what his mother told him" and then disappears:

> Me thinketh that it were necessarie
> For to be war of swich an adversarie.
> Beth redy for to meet him everemore—
> Thus taughte me my dame; I say namore.

The rioters now fall into one of those absurd, literal-minded
arguments familiar in taverns and in dreams. God's arms!
says one, is it so dangerous to meet him? I'll go looking for
him. With curses he gathers the others in a drunken huddle
for ritual oaths of brotherhood: they will slay Death before

nightfall. Now they are off to the village, trailing a babble of grisly oaths whose purport is "Death shall be dead." At the heart of their self-delusion is a trick which language itself plays on them: they misread a figure of speech, taking it literally. Half a mile gone, as they are about to climb over a stile, they meet an "old man and a povre," all wrapped up except his face. The proudest of the revellers asks him why he lives so long: they take his answer no less literally, missing his hints. The old man arrives as suddenly and unpredictably as the young boy; his speeches are as specterlike and pointedly true; and he disappears from the scene as suddenly.

These episodes joined by dreamlike junctures are thematic more than narrative. They single out in abstraction truths which press upon the Pardoner's consciousness; and they are presented with the intensity and visualization characteristic of the dream-vision. Together the boy and the old man suggest youth and age—conceptions of innocence and experience which exist in the Pardoner's mind, each with its own character and its own kind of truth. The innocent boy speaks simple childlike sentences, trails off with simple good sense—"thus taughte me my dame." The weary old man talks in meandering, circuitous sentences, runs on about his plight: however far he wanders he can find none who would exchange their youth for his age, nor will Death take his life, nor will Mother Earth let him in. In two ways the old man's discourse parallels the young boy's, expanding upon the suggestions of the child as experience might be expected to expand upon innocence: (1) As the boy ended with his mother's lesson, the old man ends with the chilling, plaintive address to the ground, his "mother's gate," that is, the grave, which like the womb can offer him peace or let him be born anew. He says he will give his worldly possessions in return only for a haircloth to be wrapped in:

> . . . on the ground, which is my modres gate,
> I knocke with my staff, both erly and late,
> And saye "Leeve moder, let me in!
> Lo how I vanish, flesh, and blood, and skin!
> Alas! whan shull my bones been at reste?
> Moder, with you wolde I chaunge my cheste

That in my chambre longe time hath be,
Ye, for an heire clout to wrap in me!"
But yet to me she wol nat do that grace,
For which full pale and welked is my face. . . .

(729–738)

This awesome portrayal of a soul cast adrift by its mother
into an unwanted life, toward a death wished for and
denied, reflects the Pardoner's spiritual plight—it expresses
his longing for oblivion, for a return to the womb, or for
another birth; and it portrays a circumstance, like his own, in
which no such release is permitted. (2) As the boy's short
discourse is a warning to the rioters, the old man's garrulous
discourse is even more ominous. He twice quotes Scripture—that one should rise before an old man (Lev. 19:32)
and do him no harm (Ecclus. 8:7). This would sound like the
self-centered, querulous murmurings of the very old, except
that it ends with an eerie reverberation of the Golden Rule—
"Namore than that ye wold men did to you / In age"—to
which he pointedly adds "if that ye so long abide." Blessing
them, he concludes "I moot go thider as I have to go," but
they hold him back, demanding to know where Death is. His
directions are equally ominous—he sends them up a "crooked way" where he left Death under a tree (remarking slyly
"Nought for your boost he wol him no thing hide"); the details suggest the Way and the Fall. He blesses them again, then
drops from the picture:

God save you, that bought again mankinde,
And you amend.

This last word, "amend," is hauntingly double-edged: it may
mean "improve," which suggests he knows their evil, or
"make amends with," as is to be the case.

The Pardoner is an ironist, and one can be sure that he
takes some satisfaction in the hidden warnings of this last
scene: it is ironic that the rioters do not get the point. But it is
doubly ironic that in real life the Pardoner is no less
blinded.[24] In what follows, the "amends" brought down

---

24. See Stephen A. Barney, "An Evaluation of the Pardoner's Tale," in
Twentieth-Century Interpretations of the Pardoner's Tale, ed. Dewey R. Faulk-

upon the revellers compound the irony. We see significance everywhere of which the personages in the story are unaware; and we watch an outcome take shape which is the reverse of what they expect. The situation itself generates irony, and the Pardoner capitalizes on this. When the rioters run to the tree and find almost eight bushels of gold florins, the Pardoner adds "No lenger thanne after Deeth they soughte." He has one of them say that Fortune has given them the money to live their life "in mirth and jolitee." Then their greed is turned upon each other—the youngest is knifed by the older two, leaving behind him the poisoned bottles from which his slayers drink in celebration. Thus the gold is their death and good Fortune is ill. It is a fabliau situation in which all three tricksters are tricked by language and Fortune, by each other, and by themselves.

But the trickster Pardoner is ironically tricked by his own story. As his whole tale in its aura of dreamlike unreality reflects his inner turmoil, its outcome is a warning of his own future which he cannot heed. The greed of the rioters turns into destructiveness—they become divided among themselves and bring death upon their own heads; in the same way the Pardoner, divided against himself, is heading into spiritual death. This dreamlike quality makes his tale share in an irony about life from which no one is free—that what we need to know about ourselves is potentially knowable and sometimes known by others, but often lies beyond our grasp. In medieval terms, his tale has about it the quality of the *somnium coeleste*, a warning from on high which he does not heed. That was the case of the spiritually impotent: the self-knowledge which they stubbornly avoided was "repressed" but attainable by an act of will. They could speak true and not heed the truth they spoke. The Pardoner's tale

---

ner (Englewood Cliffs, N.J.: Prentice-Hall, 1973), pp. 83–95. Barney argues (pp. 90–92) that "The Pardoner lends us, through his art, the power of intelligence to discriminate between what the rioters see and what is truly to be seen." He speaks as though the biblical echoes in the passage are put there by the Pardoner, but this could be an instance of unimpersonated artistry: the biblical echoes could be put there by Chaucer to make us see what the Pardoner fails to see.

injects into the presentation of him its most macabre and ironic effect: it makes the *Totentanz* of his inner life dance before us so that we understand how it is possible for him not to see what we see.

The way the Pardoner ends his tale is consistent with everything we know about him, and there is no way of telling whether his attempted joke or trick at the end is an afterthought; he says he forgot to say it, but this could be part of his act, and it would be consistent whether it was an afterthought or not. Not that consistency is necessary in a literary character: an inconsistent or contradictory action is as "real" as any other. When the Pardoner concludes "And lo, sires, thus I preche," he adds a blessing,

> And Jhesu Christ, that is our soules leche,
> So graunte you his pardoun to receive,
> For that is best: I wol you nat deceive.

A blessing is conventional at the end of a tale, but the phrase he chooses is scarcely formulaic or perfunctory. He has made no effort to deceive the company, so there is nothing outrageous in his saying this unless he has already planned the unsuccessful trick which follows. We do not know whether his utterance is sincere or part of his game; likely it is both. "Full oft in game a sooth I have herd saye," says the Host; we can suppose that even if the blessing is part of an effort to hoodwink the company it is sincere at some level of consciousness.[25] Since the Pardoner is an ironist, it is in character that, having said "I wol you nat deceive," he should proceed to deceive them. What does it matter? If they only laugh, he can shrug it off as a joke. Yet he thinks little enough of them to suppose (perhaps rightly) that some at least would be taken in; and he is impudent, dares to confront and challenge them to be his dupes, either by buying his pardons like fools or joining him in an intimate

---

25. Kittredge, *Chaucer and His Poetry*, p. 217, called it a "paroxysm of agonized sincerity," a phrase which most recent critics reject; but Kellogg, "An Augustinian Interpretation," shows how this paroxysm is consistent with St. Augustine's portrayal of the self-punishing nature of evil.

joke against the fools who buy. It is a perfect piece of bravado, for he can pretty well count on the one or the other response. The final speech is another expression of his "method," his bag of tricks, and not a very big risk.

The hiatus between "I wol you nat deceive" and the "afterthought" seems enormous—enough so to make one critic imagine a pause and a hushed silence,[26] and to make editors put a paragraph there. Yet the hiatus is in us, not in the scene: the Pardoner could speak that second line so hard upon the first as to swallow up "deceive." As before, he confronts them with an ironic, mocking challenge. His motive as before is to draw them into his power; and he can do so either by making dupes of them or by making them laugh with him at his own evil. It is a very witty stroke, a gross and exaggerated self-parody: he informs them that they ought to kneel down and meekly receive his pardons, or receive them as they go, anew at every mile's end, so long as they keep offering money—it's a good thing he is there, he adds, because one or two of them might fall off their horses and break their necks, and they are safe in his fellowship since he can absolve them. He lets the specter of Death hover over them again as in his tale; and then he enlists the Host— because he is the leader of the game, because he loves jokes and entertainment, perhaps also because he understands that things said in game are often meant in earnest. The Pardoner may think he sees in him a kindred spirit. Or it may be a self-destructive act on the Pardoner's part—the Pardoner may sense in the Host the one most likely to puncture his moment of triumph—and the Host's anger might be directed at the Pardoner's impulse to spoil his own success.

26. G. G. Sedgewick, "The Progress of Chaucer's Pardoner, 1880– 1940," *MLQ* 1 (1940):431–458; rpt. S&T (see p. 217f. for the imagined hush). Interpreting what follows involves imputing motives; Kittredge thought the Pardoner tried to escape his own conscience with wild jesting, Sedgewick that his effect on his audience tempted him to overreach himself. Calderwood finds the action ambiguous. Barney points out that his tongue and his wallet full of pardons—the tools of his trade—are phallic, so that when he addresses the Host "unbokle anon thy purse" there is a similar phallic reference.

The Host's response is far more of a surprise than the Pardoner's "afterthought," and is harder to understand because we haven't the insight into the Host that we have into the Pardoner. It is sometimes thought that a bluff male figure like Harry Bailly would be offended by the feminoid Pardoner; but this opinion does not square with human psychology any more than it squares with the text. The Host first addresses the Pardoner "thou bel ami," which is mildly derisive, but he goes on to ask for some mirth or japes in a relaxed way without further comment. Compare his response to the hardy, philandering Monk, a "manly man" in whom he seems to see a threat of cuckoldry or competition: he taunts him cruelly for thirty lines about his sexual prowess and his vows of chastity. And he is not less rough-spoken with other pilgrims—"Straw for your gentilesse" he cries at no less a figure than the Franklin. He is not initially rougher to the Pardoner than to others. Besides, for all his appearance of hardy masculinity, the Host is always complaining about his shrewish wife and worrying about cuckoldry. What we need to know is not why the Host "doesn't like" the Pardoner but why he finds this particular speech offensive. One answer is that he is *not* offended—that his retort is a joke of sorts, raucous and overplayed, done without the Pardoner's deft touch; hence it oversteps a bound by hitting at the Pardoner's most vulnerable point. The Host claims he was only "playing" (958) when he sees his outburst greeted by the Pardoner's angry silence; and perhaps, if the Pardoner had answered with some equally extravagant fling, the Host would have taken it in stride. But the Host's language to the Pardoner is very violent: the kernel of his taunt about the Pardoner's "coillons" is framed on either side by images of excrement, and these primitive or infantile expressions of rage are both associated with relics. When he says

> Thou woldest make me kiss thyn olde breech,
> And swere it were a relic of a saint,
> Though it were with thy fundement depaint!

he is probably making a reference to the famous hair breech

which St. Thomas wore, one of the most prized relics of the Canterbury shrine—an object which Erasmus was to find revolting. It is likely that it was thought a particular mortification to venerate this relic; Professor Knapp thinks there might have been an old joke about doing so.[27] The Host appropriately swears by St. Helena, who found the ultimate relic, the true Cross, that he would like to have the Pardoner's coillons in his hand instead of relics or "seintuarie": let them be cut off, he says, and I will help you carry them— they shall be enshrined in a hog's turd. It is too specific to be the stereotyped "shit-on-you" kind of insult; but the degree of its cruelty depends on whether the Host is certain from the Pardoner's appearance that he *is* without testicles. Professor Curry was so convincing about the medical symptoms of anorchism that almost everyone since has taken the Host's words as a calculated insult. Yet part of the realism of the passage lies in the fact that we don't know the Host's intentions any more than we would if we were there. Possibly the Pardoner's extravagance is contagious; possibly the Host is carried away by the ingenuity of his swearing and lets slip out something he has suspected but not allowed himself to think about. That is often what people do when they sense or surmise something best not spoken of. We don't know what the Host *means* to do, only what he says and what powerful feeling is behind it.

What trips this feeling off is equally unclear. I like the explanation offered by Gabriel Josipovici,[28] that the Host wants to play the game by his own rules: "So long as it is he who makes the jokes he is only too eager to invoke the game as an excuse; but as soon as the joke turns on him he forgets all about the game and its rules in his blind anger at the joker. This is just what happens at the climax of the Pardoner's Tale: as the Pardoner finishes, Harry Bailly finds that for the first time the joke is on him, and he does not like it." But we do not *know* that the joke is on the Host. The Pardoner, by asking him to join in a joke on the others, hints that the Host is *not* taken in. The Host recoils from being the

27. Knapp, "The Relyk of a Seint," *ELH* 39 (1972):5–26.
28. *The World and the Book*, pp. 91–92.

Pardoner's accomplice, but after his outburst he *says* he was joking—("I wol no lenger play")—and perhaps he believes it. The earnest feeling beneath his joking does not for that matter have to be anger. Intimacy is part of the Pardoner's bag of tricks, and he uses the intimate tone on the Host— "I rede that our Host here shall biginne, / For he is most envoluped in sinne." But his timing is off: his tricks come too fast, and his hurried commands—"Come forth, sir Host," "Offre first anon," "unbokle anon thy purse"—push too hard. The Host is not the kind of man who likes to take orders. And he must pick up the tense energy of the Pardoner's hasty speech with its self-destructive possibilities. If there is something compulsive or automatic in the Pardoner's last effort to trick somebody or everybody, there is something equally compulsive or automatic in the Host's abusive reply: it is a surge of competitive energy meant to dominate the Pardoner, to keep himself in power. It tumbles out in images of excrement and castration, a possible response whether the Pardoner were a eunuch or not. The remarkable thing about the passage, and the thing that makes it so right, is that it *just happens*—fast and inexplicably. It is a happening, not a story. "Stories have a point and make dramatic sense; their truth is of secondary importance," Christopher Isherwood observes; "happenings do not seem to make any sense at all." One can well imagine Chaucer *had* witnessed a scene like it: almost everyone has.

The aftermath of this happening is reported in only thirteen lines, but there are scarcely thirteen lines anywhere in Chaucer which accomplish more. The Pardoner's angry silence, for such a manipulator of language as he, is the ultimate defeat; it makes him seem mysterious, deflated, and sad. It can be viewed as a kind of martyrdom, or anti-martyrdom. And his silence may be a single ray of hope, the end of his noisy flight from the warning voice within. When he demands that the Host unbuckle his purse and the Host responds by wishing he had the Pardoner's "coillons" in his hand, the two men have in effect exchanged malevolent wishes to castrate each other. The Pardoner thinks of the Host's "purse" (the word had its inevitable bawdy sense).

This is ironic—the purse with money in it is the Pardoner's, not the Host's, surrogate. It is equally ironic that the Host thinks of the Pardoner's "coillons." So it is doubly ironic that what the Host manages to cut off is the Pardoner's tongue, his flow of speech. His paralysis of tongue reminds one of Pandarus after all was lost, "As still as stone, a word ne coude he saye." For Pandarus and the Pardoner are, in all of Chaucer, the two great proprietors of language, glib persuaders who can make others act upon their wills. And the Pardoner's silence is a loss of will: "So wrooth he was, no word ne *wold* he saye." It isn't that he is "speechless," that like Pandarus he *couldn't* speak, but that he has lost the will to—*wold* is the verb used. The Host's reply, as Kittredge pointed out, compounds the injury by calling attention to his wrath; in doing that it calls attention to his defeat. And worse, "all the peple lough."[29]

Then the Knight makes peace between them. It is a courtly gesture which reflects the aristocrat's preference for smooth surfaces; and because the Knight has the highest rank there is good enough reason why he should be the one to step in as keeper of the peace. It is, too, a charitable gesture: if his coming forward "Whan that he saugh that all the peple lough" implies causality, he must feel compassion for the Pardoner. How symbolical the gesture is, I am not sure: if Chaucer meant it for a figure of Christian charity, he would have had the Parson come forward. Nor is the gesture so charitable that the Knight maintains complete impartiality: he seems to side with the Host. "Namoore of this, for it is right enough" could be understood to suggest just deserts, and he calls the Host "ye" and "sir Host," adding "that been to me so deere," while calling the Pardoner "thee." He asks the Pardoner to "be glad and mirrye of cheere" and asks the Host to come forward and make the gesture of peace; this may be a compliment to the Host's sense of justice, but it does treat the Pardoner as the injured

29. Nancy H. Owen, "The Pardoner's Introduction, Prologue, and Tale: Sermon and Fabliau," *JEGP* 66 (1967):541–549, shows how the story to this point is a fabliau situation which frames the Pardoner's sermon.

party. What the Knight wants, as he says at the close of his speech, is for them to laugh and play as before—he introduces no abstractions or ideals. The last line, "Anon they kiste, and riden forth hir waye," is really the only line which seems symbolical or figural. The kiss can be the "kiss of peace" symbolizing Christian charity and brotherhood, but it can also be (since it is the Knight's idea) the upper-class way of symbolizing peaceful relations.

It is hard to say that because of this one line the ending lapses into the figural style and presents a symbolical gesture which unites courtly civility and Christian charity, but I feel that this is what happens. The gesture *was* symbolical, and the brevity of the scene gives it a spectral, abstract quality. After the drama of the Pardoner's sermon and the unpredictable happening which follows, the figures now seem to move fleetingly, as at a distance—there is the Pardoner's silence, the Host's sulky response ("I wol no lenger playe"), the Knight's decorous charge, the ambiguous ritual act. It is a conclusion in which nothing is concluded, yet readers of the poem seem to agree that it is right.

This could be because such ambiguous endings, in which tensions are left unresolved, seem right to modern tastes. When Professor Kellogg says that the Pardoner's evil "is absorbed into the pattern of existence, and the universe goes on undisturbed,"[30] he could be describing the effect produced by a modern novelist. Students of medieval literature often think if a medieval work appeals to a modern taste the appeal must be mistaken, and so scurry off to find an antiquated taste for it to appeal to. But the "modernity" of a passage such as this is nothing more than its power to appeal to subsequent ages, to outlast changes of taste; it may be the first glimmering of a kind of literary effect for which a taste was to develop later. Such effects, and a taste for such effects, are a part of literary tradition, and Chaucer was the principal founder of English literary tradition. There are other medieval works which do not end with a resolution—*Piers*

30. "An Augustinian Interpretation," p. 259; but Kellogg is if anything suggesting the allegorical or figural quality of the ending. On this allegorical quality cf. Bronson, *In Search of Chaucer*, pp. 100–103.

Plowman would be an example—so we could find medieval precedents. If tradition had taken another turn, we would not be able to grasp the "literary" quality of the present passage or respond to its ambiguity. It would only be a puzzle.

But there is another way of responding to the passage which *is* characteristically medieval and not at all modern, and for which we must therefore imagine or acquire a response. The passage takes a circumstance involving psychological realism and permits it to become figural. Throughout the Pardoner's Prologue and Tale there is a tendency in the direction of allegory: the Pardoner's evil has a stark, primal quality, and the dreamlike character of his tale shares with allegory its disembodied, abstract treatment of character and situation. This tendency is now allowed once more to come to the surface; the Knight's decorous speech and the ritual act of peacemaking make the characters seem distant and abstract, where before they had been close-to-hand and lifelike. Emphasis is thrown upon the symbolical act.

The story itself is complete at line 959 where the Host's speech ends. The ending of the Pardoner's Tale is unique in *The Canterbury Tales* because it is the only ending of a tale not told in the pilgrim's own voice. With the Pardoner's ending, "lo, sires, thus I preche," we are returned to the scene of the pilgrimage; beginning at line 956, "This Pardoner answerde nat a word," the narrator reports what I have called a happening. It seems real enough but cannot be explained psychologically. The effect is to put us at a distance from the Pardoner's character and from the final incident itself. This unique "distancing" suggests that the last line is meant to point us further away from the realism of the tale; the last phrase, "and riden forth hir waye," emphasizes the topos of the Way. In the narrator's voice here we catch no attitude, no tone: we may be hearing the naive objectivity of Chaucer the pilgrim or the ironic detachment of Chaucer the man. The mask and the performer behind it harmonize: "Chaucerian" irony becomes identical with Christian charity. There are only a few places in *The Canterbury Tales* where this Chaucerian moment occurs—where we hear a neutral voice which

might as well be Chaucer's own: at the end of the Nun's
Priest's Tale where the priest's own voice seems to merge
with the author's, perhaps in the last lines of the Miller's
Prologue, in the Parson's Prologue, and in the Retraction.
But the possibility of this Chaucerian moment is always
present. The ironic masquerade which produces the narrator makes us aware of the man himself behind it, makes us
intuit his thoughts and feel at one with him. The naive
pilgrim-narrator with his puppyish enthusiasm for everybody, good and bad alike, is a funny charade of charity
which mistakes St. Augustine's dictum to love the man but
hate his evil—the narrator doesn't make the distinction. But
we know Chaucer does. In moments like these there is a
shock of recognition because we glimpse in the writer we are
reading the man we have sensed. They are simple moments
when we seem to come back to a reality already known, like
the moment of waking from a dream or looking up from a
book.

THE TWO SERMONS

If the ending of the Pardoner's Tale brings the reader into
a figural realm and reminds him of St. Augustine's precept
"love the man but hate his evil," this ending is the more
dramatic a reversal because the tale itself prompts in readers
the opposite effect: readers are always amused by the
Pardoner's trickery and by the irony of his preaching against
avarice to gain money—it seems a wonderful game at the
expense of the "lewed" people—but the Pardoner himself is
a grotesque figure for whom we feel repugnance. We hate
the man but take delight in his evil. This is what the Host
does: he listens to the "confession" and then makes an *ad
hominem* attack. The tale lures us into an uncharitable
response, a reversal of St. Augustine's dictum, and then
attempts to reverse or correct our reaction at the end. We
have been teased into laughing at the depiction of evil and
passing judgment on the evil-doer, and the Host's violent
reaction shocks us and makes us draw back. Because his

reaction is directed against the man and not his evil, what it really does is make us think about the man.

If the Pardoner is a *eunuchus ex nativitate* and if this fact has a symbolic dimension, doesn't it symbolize the fact that we are all born in sin? Doesn't it demand that we become involved with his deformity, see ourselves in it? From a realistic point of view the Pardoner was born deformed, and his behavior is an elaborate defense against the extremely uncharitable view which his society took toward such a man as himself. Everyone who has felt repugnance at him, who has thought his peculiarities a joke, a horror, or a disgrace, has played a part in the origin of this defense and owns a share in his evil. The Pardoner, far from being cowed by this, has chosen, has willed, to be what his society assigned him to be. There is something awesome and perversely heroic about him.[31] We have said he is an actor: he acts the role given to him, becomes an embodiment, a charade of evil. And in doing this he reflects back to us the evil we dread in ourselves. The institutions of the Christian life—God's pardon, penance, the veneration of shrines and relics, the pilgrimage—become in his act grotesque representations of themselves. Perhaps that is what the grotesque always does: it parades before us the other side of things, makes us see ourselves by making us see what we think we are not, what we dread to be.

The effect of such a self-parody is itself an astonishing phenomenon, and I do not believe we can understand the Pardoner without understanding this effect. But how? How does one understand what one is meant to *feel*? Yet such an understanding has been reached in modern times. The kind of figure which the Pardoner is has been described by Jean-Paul Sartre in *Saint Genet: Actor and Martyr*. It isn't

31. Cf. Patch, *On Rereading Chaucer*, p. 166, and Whittock, *A Reading of the Canterbury Tales*, p. 194. Edmund Reiss, "The Final Irony of the Pardoner's Tale," *CE* 25 (1964):260–266, remarks that the presentation of him questions the relation of good, evil, and innocence, yet he alone remains unpardoned. Charles Mitchell, "The Moral Superiority of Chaucer's Pardoner," *CE* 27 (1966):437–444, remarks (p. 438) that Chaucer "uses impiety to unmask simulated piety and holds up the Pardoner's evil as a gauge of the evil in others."

necessary to accept Sartre's philosophy to accept his insight into this kind of character or archetype as a phenomenon, and into the effects of that phenomenon. Besides, Sartre's ideas are sufficiently Augustinian; he sees that pride is the root of such a self-realization and perversion, and that its end is nothingness. One could draw from Sartre's book a number of observations uncannily applicable to the Pardoner. "He hangs on," says Sartre of Genet,

> only by power of will. If he pays any attention to the muted sensations which come to him from his organs, he feels impossible and falls into astonishment. He does not find within himself any of those powerful instincts that support the desires of the decent man. He knows only the death instinct. His sexual desires will be phantoms, as his life itself is a phantom. Whatever their object, they are condemned in advance. He is *forbidden from the beginning* to desire. All societies castrate the maladjusted. This castration can be actually physical or can be achieved by persuasion. The result is the same.

And the result: "play acting: he must *play* the male, while knowing that he plays it badly."[32] This playacting is chiefly gesture:

> What is the strange power that makes the gesture gather things about it as does a shepherd his flock? It lies in the fact that the gesture is itself an absence, the simple manifestation of an archetypal gesture. And how can the archetype itself corrode a whole universe? It can do so because it *is not at all*: it is a simple, empty signification which is lost in an abstract heaven. The world exists only to permit a gesture, the gesture only to manifest an archetype . . .[33]

This actor's feeling of standing wholly apart from the natural order defines his relationship to his society:

> He is said to be "contrary to nature." But the reason is that, as far back as he can remember, nature has been against him. We others who issue from the species have a mandate to continue the species. [He] . . . is preparing to die without

32. Sartre, *Saint Genet: Actor and Martyr*, trans. Bernard Frechtman (1963; rpt. New York: Mentor, 1964), pp. 95, 445.
33. *Ibid.*, p. 408.

descendants. His sexuality will be sterility and abstract tension.[34]

Yet it is not fate but will which gives him this relationship to his society.

Just as there is Good only in a will that wills itself unconditionally good, so there is Evil only in an intention that wills itself expressly evil. Evil is then consciousness itself at the height of its lucidity, for an evil mind is all the more perverse in that it is more aware of its damnation and wills it more.

This will, which is bent on denying the evidence and on rejecting being, burns alone in defiance of all, infinitely alone, and feeds on itself. . . . Though rejected by all the forces of the world, crushed and finally annihilated, it did exist, and there is nothing the universe can do about it. It directs its negation against the universe; it shelves the universe. Stranded in failure, error, and impotence, it decides, all by itself, against the world.[35]

Certainly it is true that the Pardoner *wills* the role he plays. He says so: "I *wol* noon of the apostles countrefete." In rejecting the prescribed role-model and playing himself, he decides against the world.

Such a figure, the victim and instrument of "the good citizen," will avenge himself by making the good citizen discover the evil in himself, will make him see his own improper thoughts and "make him experience with loathing his own wickedness."[36] Such a figure is misunderstood if he is understood only as the object of righteous indignation. He has to be understood as what Sartre calls the Other. He exists to reveal to the society its own evil and to the "good citizen" the evil in himself. He makes us question all cultural values and suspect all moral discourse of being cant. This explains why the Pardoner is at once central and parasitic. The explanation, I know, will not fall well on modern ears because it sounds too modern. We like our medieval literature to be "medieval." But Sartre has imaginatively de-

34. *Ibid.*, p. 16.
35. *Ibid.*, pp. 36, 81.
36. *Ibid.*, p. 533.

TREATSEATS®

SPOOKY WORLD®

"AMERICA'S HORROR THEME PARK"

Located at Canterbury Park
Shakopee, Minnesota

October 1-31, 1999

$3 off
Admission

with this coupon.
Coupon valid Wednesdays,
Thursdays and Sundays.

See back for details.

TARGET®

SPOOKY WORLD — JUST BOO IT!

All inclusive admission includes:
- ❏ Hayride of the Un-Dead
- ❏ Four Haunted Houses
- ❏ Monster Mini Golf
- ❏ Booville Children's Play Area
- ❏ Fright-tanic Giant Slide
- ❏ Terror Theatre featuring the Brave New Workshop Performers
- ❏ Special events, promotions and much more!

Spooky World is open Wednesday through Sunday evenings. TREATSEATS valid Wednesdays, Thursdays and Sundays. Gates open nightly at 6:30 pm.

Admission is just $12 with TREATSEATS. Without TREATSEATS, $15. Children age 5 and under are admitted free.

Redeem TREATSEATS coupons when you purchase admission in person at:

Spooky World Box Office
Canterbury Park
1100 Canterbury Rd.
Shakopee, MN 55379

Explore Minnesota USA store
Mall of America N129 N. Garden
Bloomington, MN
For more information, call
(612) 445-8555 or visit web site
www.spookyworld.net.

For TREATSEATS events in your area, or for information on using your Target Guest Card® to receive this discount, call 1-800-4-1-TREAT (1-800-418-7328).
One coupon required for each discount admission purchased. Additional ticket fees may apply. Tickets subject to availability. Prices subject to change. Not valid with group or other discounts or on previously purchased tickets.

THIS IS NOT A TICKET!
FREE COUPON. NOT FOR RESALE.

©1999 Dayton Hudson Brands, Inc.

TR-141692

scribed a phenomenon which is archetypal, which belongs to the human condition. (He has certainly not described Genet as a historical person, and his view of homosexuality has more in common with the Church Fathers than with the twentieth century.) Besides, his philosophical underpinnings are steeped in the Western tradition: the specter of St. Augustine haunts Sartre's pages.

Like Genet the Pardoner puts all about him in perspective—the other pilgrims, the pilgrimage itself, and the complex of social institutions to which it belonged. He unmasks the "good citizen," what Chaucer calls the "gentils." That is why the Host reacts the way he does; why the Knight, the representative of the prestige class, the "good citizen" par excellence, intervenes; and why he is interested in keeping up an aura of good cheer. They are protecting not themselves but their world, their institutions, their roles. The Pardoner throws into relief not only the Christian institutions involved with pilgrimage and pardon, but the realms of civil, domestic, and private conduct. As the Knight's civility is thrown into relief by the final episode, the Pardoner's asexuality throws into relief that whole stratum of the work which touches upon domestic life and sexuality: the two childless female pilgrims, the competition for sovereignty between men and women, the romance fantasies about courtly love, the lusty "swyving," the fear of cuckoldry, the false hopes of January and the dashed hopes of his creator the Merchant, the Franklin's tidy compromise. The Pardoner's admittedly false sermon, able to make people repent but not intended to, throws into relief "moralitee and holiness," recalls the pilgrims' moral tales, which have so often been "misguided moralism." And his "secret" throws into relief the private part of human conduct, reminds us that every one of us has a secret, and so mocks inner motives and vested interests, the tendentiousness which comes out so often in the pilgrims' final blessings. Perhaps it mocks even the ironic frame of mind which is "Chaucerian," for after reading the Pardoner's Prologue and Tale, if one turns to the Clerk's ideal story with its ironical ending, irony seems just a way of resigning oneself: the Pardoner's extravagant attempt at a final swindle is the reverse of the Clerk's ironic withdrawal. The Pardoner with his own irony challenges us to take an ironic view of him, and scarcely anyone has met the challenge.

And if on this account we look skeptically at irony, we look skeptically at Chaucer in the ironical self-image he creates. For as the Pardoner is like a grotesque mirror-image of the institution at the heart of *The Canterbury Tales*, he is also like a grotesque mirror-image of Chaucer himself. Like Chaucer he possesses enormous gifts of rhetoric, of imper-sonation and dramatic flair. Like Chaucer he role-plays himself, and in an ironical spirit. And as with the role-playing Chaucer we get a sense of the man himself behind the role. Perhaps every artist has to be an outrageous liar and role-player, and if we can judge from the Retraction, Chaucer himself may have experienced some amount of discomfort on this score. Yet it is by his success in creating such an illusion that we judge the artist,[37] but by his intentions that we judge the man. So in the Retraction, Chaucer makes a point of quoting St. Paul that all that is written is written "for our doctrine," and says flatly "that is myn entent." The Pardoner's intent is the reverse—he says flatly "myn entent is nat but for to winne / And nothing for correccioun of sinne." The figure of the Pardoner unmasks the role-playing Chaucer, makes us see the man himself as he speaks to us in humble peace and hope of his intent. The ironic stance may give us distance, but the Pardoner's irony gives us distance even from that distance. If in his story we see the inner workings of damnation, its effect *is* apoca-lyptic—it destroys the world and turns us back upon the self.

Turn to the other preacher, the Parson, and the reader is all the more aware of this difference between the world and the self. The description of the Parson in the General Prologue is an interesting and noble passage, but it describes an idea. And it is this abstract figure, the priest rather than

37. Cf. De Bruyne, *The Esthetics of the Middle Ages*, pp. 145–146.

the man, who preaches at the end. He is a "figural" priest who stands for the idea of the priesthood, and his "tale" is a compendium of doctrine which applies to individual conduct. It is a mistake to say that it is dull or too long. It is an amalgam of two estimable treatises, and as such treatises go is mercifully short. It is appropriately divided and subdivided according to set principles, and so is easy to follow. It is translated in English prose which has the virtues we ask of prose: it is clear and forthright, is filled with specific details and examples, and embodies the natural rhythms of speech. It abounds in ideas significant in its day, some of them abstract and difficult ideas over which much controversial ink had been spilt: for example, it sets forth briefly the fraught issue of how sin occurs and when it becomes "actual" (350–357). It uses vivid imagery to clarify abstract ideas: for example, it explains the relation of venial to deadly sin with the traditional figure of a shipwreck, and lets us *see* the wreck happening quickly with a wave or slowly with drops of water seeping through crevices between the boards of the ship:

> For certes, the more that a man chargeth his soul with venial sins, the more is he enclined to fall into deedly sin. And therefore lat us nat be necligent to deschargen us of venial sins. For the proverb saith that "many small maken a greet." And herkne this ensample. A greet wave of the sea comth some time with so greet a violence that it drencheth the ship. And the same harm doon some time the small drops of water that entren thurgh a litel crevace into the thurrok, and in the bottme of the ship, if men be so necligent that they ne descharge hem nat by time. And therefore, although there be a difference bitwix thise two causes of drenching, algates the ship is dreynt.
>
> (361–364)

And this is all *practical* information, applied specifically to details of everyday life. That is why we are reminded again and again of the pilgrims themselves[38]—for example, people's desire (like the Wife's) to "goon to offring biforn his neighebor" (407)—or of the life of their times, right down to

---

38. Cf. Ruggiers, *The Art of the Canterbury Tales*, pp. 251–252.

the paper castles which covered dishes at rich feasts (445).
Some of these references do not appear in sources and may
be Chaucer's additions; they bring into the background of
the treatise the element of timeliness and obsolescence which
was in the foreground of the General Prologue. But the tale
is not a fable. The Parson himself says so. We do not read it
in the same spirit, for it is not a piece of story-telling that we
listen to but a piece of reading matter that we must study and
master. Critics never stop commenting on its importance to
the work as a whole, but who offers—as with the tales—
analysis by the tonnage of its art?

In the General Prologue we learn that the Parson is
"benign" (483), patient, self-sacrificing; that he taught by
good example; that he did none of the things for which
parish priests were criticized, was not "despitous" to sinful
men, not interested in pomp and reverence, had not a
"spiced conscience"; but that if anyone were obstinate, he
would "snybben" him sharply. In later appearances we catch
only this last tendency to chide and reprimand. We never see
him in a kindly or charitable act and do not get an impression of his patient or "benign" qualities. When the Host
first calls on him to tell a tale (II:1164ff.) he cries out
"Benedicite! / What aileth the man, so sinfully to swere?"
The Host answers that he smells a Loller in the wind and
predicts that the Parson is going to preach to them. The
Host likes any tale so long as it is entertaining or instructional; his only requirement is that it be interesting. He stops
Chaucer's "rime" and scorns the Monk's "tragedies" because
they are tedious. He is a pretty good literary critic because at
least he understands that the kiss of death in story-telling is
for the story to bore the audience. Perhaps it is only the
common man's point of view which makes him assume that
the parish priest will preach a sermon and the sermon will be
dull. But obviously he is responding to the astringent,
chiding quality which the Parson shows. The Parson responds irritably to the Host and the Host responds in kind.
When he calls him a Loller he doesn't really mean a
Wycliffite; he only means the kind of priest which presumably the Wycliffites mostly were, a hardnose. Perhaps we

should not chide the Parson for what he does not do, but we
never see him do or say anything kindly—he doesn't inter-
vene when harsh words and insults are exchanged; leaves it
for the Knight to make peace at the end of the Pardoner's
tale; is silent over the abusive treatment which the Friar and
Summoner get at each other's hands; and is not in the
picture at all when the Cook falls from his horse and is
publicly humiliated. But then, he doesn't speak out against
the bawdy tales or act the Puritan in any other way. It
appears that Chaucer meant to leave the real Parson in the
background. Still, in the one other place where he speaks, he
shows the same rigidity. The Host says "Ne breke thou nat
our play" (X:24) and asks for a fable; the Parson answers
abruptly, "Thou getest fable non ytold for me." He thinks
there is an absolute difference between truth and falsehood,
and that all fables are falsehoods; he doesn't understand
about "poetic truth." The tale he tells has got to be wheat or
else it wil be "draf" (35–36). So he proposes "Moralitee and
vertuous mattere" and says that if this can be permitted he
will do them "plesaunce leveful." He cannot "geste" (tell a
story) in alliterative verse or in rhyme, but can only offer
"a myrie tale in prose." He does not make it an exciting
prospect, but the company agree that it is fitting:

> Upon this word we han assented soone,
> For, as it seemed, it was for to doone,
> To enden in some vertuous sentence,
> And for to yeve him space and audience;
> And bade our Host he sholde to him saye
> That alle we to tell his tale him praye.
>
> (61–66)

The audience turns itself by common assent into a congre-
gation.

This means the fun is over; the Host does as the
company tells him, but he adds exactly what we would
expect him to: "Hasteth you," "Beth fructuous, and that in
litel space." The Host has not changed his attitudes at
all—he will go along with what the others think is right, but
he would still just as soon not have a sermon, and if he must
have one he would like it brief. What follows is of course not

brief; if *The Canterbury Tales* were a realistic work the Host, or somebody else, would interrupt the Parson. The pilgrimage on which the pilgrims play a game of telling stories ends here. The Parson's Tale is a part of the work for the same reason that the Pardoner's Tale is—because it shows us something by contrast. It is not a story or fable of any kind, as he himself insists—is different even from the *Melibee*, which has characters and a story. The entire work has been a performance by the narrator of a remembered experience, and now even this is allowed to fade away: when the Parson is through we have only the author's retraction.

This does not mean that the Parson's treatise is unrelated to the whole. It is a book on sin sandwiched into a book on penitence, and its text is about the good way or the true pilgrimage. The Parson gets his discourse off the ground by reminding us that the first cause of contrition is the remembrance of one's sins, and he will shortly add (231) that another cause is the sorrowful remembrance of the good we have left undone on the earth. He ends reminding us that however long a sinner has lain in sin, the mercy of Christ is always ready to receive him (a point especially applicable to the Pardoner). There are dozens of ways in which the Parson's book can be thought a suitable ending, but it is so different from everything else that—like the Pardoner's performance—it tells us something about the whole book that has gone before, makes us turn from the world of that book and look to our selves in the world about us.

THE TWO BOOKS

The Canterbury Tales is a book about the world; "the world" is what "the pilgrimage of human life" refers to and what the Parson's book concentrates on—we get at the end not a vision of the heavenly Jerusalem but an examination of human experience. That examination is given on authority, is a statement of doctrine which the Parson puts "under correction" (X:56). What has gone before is not authority at all; it is tempting to say it is "experience," but it is experience remembered, narrated, performed. It is a story about a series of stories, all of them contingent upon the vested interests of the tellers and the whole contingent on that slippery figure the narrator. From a sober point of view the sound "doctrine" of the Parson must make all the rest seem like so much babble, must make us take seriously the Nun's Priest's and Manciple's injunctions to hold our tongues. Only, the tales are exciting; the Parson's "doctrine" is not. The contrast between the Parson's and the Pardoner's tales is just a more dramatic instance of the contrast between the whole fiction of the pilgrimage and the "sentence" of its conclusion.

The Pardoner's Tale, like the whole story-telling game, is a performance—it is theatrical and arresting; it makes its point because of its art.[39] The Pardoner's silence at the end, what I have called with suitable extravagance his martyrdom, points to something centrally ironic and important in *The Canterbury Tales*: it puts a qualification on art itself. We know that the artist is meretricious, that his art is a bag of tricks, that his intent is to hoodwink. He is a clown and a swindler, and in the end he is silenced like the Manciple's crow. It is going to be the same at the end of *The Canterbury Tales*: the artist is going to silence himself, retract his "enditings of worldly vanities." There isn't any point to all this storytelling if you are looking for the truth, because the truth lies elsewhere—lies in "auctoritee" and finally lies in God. Telling tales on the pilgrimage has only been a way of passing the time, a game; the tales were lies. Compared with the truths of reason and revelation they are nothing; they are only something when we see their point, and we see this only in retrospect, only by thought and memory, in silence, after the tales are told. The teller of tales must therefore be a martyr to a higher truth, a truth known only in retrospect and in silence.[40]

39. Cf. Muscatine, "The Canterbury Tales," in *Chaucer and Chaucerians*, ed. Brewer, p. 112, who remarks that the Pardoner "is the only pilgrim dramatically given literary powers comparable to those of Chaucer himself." Barney, p. 95, remarks that Chaucer raises the question whether writing literature "makes any sense at all from the doomsday perspective or the perspective of natural reason."

40. Cf. De Bruyne, p. 72: "Only silence can equal the Inexpressible; the supreme homage we can pay to Beauty is to fall silent when it appears."

But Chaucer lived at the end of an age in which the attempt to know all things available through reason and revelation had fallen of its own weight. That period of "scientific humanism" was over; there was nothing left but to pick up the pieces. There appears to have been a feeling abroad that one could read anything with profit: it was a matter of "intent." The Squire before his tale says his will is good; Chaucer in the retraction says his intent was that everything written is written for our doctrine. This is what we call humanism—"literary" humanism, the belief that reading a book written by a man, especially an ancient, is a valuable activity, that "truth by whomever spoken comes from God." There were at least two ways of excusing this. One way was to say that everything is "mysteriously meant," that the ingenious or learned reader could extrapolate from all stories a higher truth; that appears to have been the respectable, or at least the intellectual thing to say, and it went on being said into the seventeenth century.[41] The other way has been much less explored in its origins because it is the one that lasted, the one that is still in our blood and that we take for granted: it was the conviction that *to know the world is to know oneself*. Everyone agreed, including St. Thomas and the Parson, that self-knowledge was the first step on the way to knowing the truth. And memory was involved in that knowledge: to know oneself one's past deeds had to be summoned up, one's attachments to the world acknowledged. "For certes," says Lady Philosphy to Boethius (II, pr. 5) in Chaucer's translation, "swich is the condicioun of all mankind, that only when it hath knowing of itself, than passeth it in noblesse all other things; and whan it forleteth the knowing of itself than it is brought binethen all beests"— and it is just then that she reminds him he should have "entered in the path of this life a void wayfaring man" and sings to him of the former age and the world's decline. But it

41. This avenue of understanding literary texts, at least classicial texts by pagan authors, has been chronicled by Don Cameron Allen, *Mysteriously Meant: The Rediscovery of Pagan Symbolism and Allegorical Interpretation in the Renaissance* (Baltimore and London: Johns Hopkins Press. 1970).

was something new to think that reading a book about the world could really be for our "doctrine" because it could present us with an idea of the world against which to measure our idea of ourselves, and so teach us who we are.

Chaucer seems to have been the first literary artist who had this feeling about literary art. One could know *about* the world by authority, but to know the world was not a matter of observing objective reality—it was a matter of observing that inner world of experience where objective reality is registered and retained. This idea was not new; St. Augustine had shown how everything we know, everything we consider as reality, is retained in memory, and that the knowledge of God lies outside memory or in the total experience of memory. But Chaucer was the first to understand that writing down a memory or a memory of others' memories might cumulatively produce the reality by means of which we know who we are—that what is "real" is an interior realm. In our own time we distinguish experience from behavior: behavior is what can be observed and measured, experience what can be known only inside ourselves. It is a mistake to think that Chaucer represented behavior, that he was a "keen observer of human life." He was that, but it is not why we leave *The Canterbury Tales* feeling that we know more about the world than we did before. It is because he understood that dramatic action, the relationships among characters, individual character, plot, theme—all that we take as important to drama, narrative poetry, and fiction—must be re-created for the reader in a mental world which does not represent behavior or "objective reality" but renders experience, the feeling and shape of experience, as it is held in being through memory. He created a world which lived in men's ideas of the world, where the world does live; and he embodied those ideas, through a literary idea, in language. Without that step we could not have had much of the subsequent history of English literature—certainly not the drama and the novel, nor the dramatic and novelistic tendencies in English poetry.

This doesn't mean that Chaucer's art is not a representational or mimetic art, but it means that the object of that representation is not an exterior but an inner reality: an idea. In *The Canterbury Tales* Chaucer did not make a representation of contemporary life or a portrait gallery or a framed series of tales, but a representation of memories and stories, a record of experience. It is mimetic, but that mimesis takes as its object a world within the mind. How did Chaucer learn this? From the dream-vision, perhaps. From medieval esthetics, perhaps. But I believe he may have learned it by learning to write dialogue. He is the first English writer whose dialogue sounds anything like people talking. And it is a curious fact that his first efforts at writing dialogue are in *The Parliament of Fowls* where the speakers are talking birds. They speak, obviously, in a very human way: social class, current fads, and in-group attitudes are reflected in their speeches—the joke is that you can tell from the dialogue what kinds of people the birds are. Now writing dialogue is an extraordinarily hard knack to get, and many still believe that the writer must listen and then imitate on paper the speech he hears people speak. But this is not so. If you listen to a tape-recording of an actual conversation which seemed lively when you participated in it, you discover that it is full of awkward pauses, grammatical lapses, absurd repetitions, dreary silences: what made it seem lively as one participated in it was a nonverbal experience, that of eye contact, gesture, facial expression—and *thought*. Part of what made it seem lively is what one *thought* during it, which probably meant thinking, as one listened, about what one was going to say next or what someone else had said earlier. If you read a transcription of such a tape-recording it does not read like "good dialogue" at all: it doesn't capture the way people talked as we remember it, doesn't capture the "flow" we think we remember, and gives the impression that no one heard or answered anyone else. It is real, but it doesn't *sound* real because the "reality" is in what we selected and remembered, what we experienced. Good dialogue has to catch the vibrancy of spoken language as it falls upon the ear and registers upon consciousness, not as it falls off the tongue. And once a writer has understood this he has understood that representing any "reality" involves the same problem: it must be represented not as it was but as it seems.

For this reason *The Canterbury Tales*, until we get to the Parson's Tale, is "stylized" and "realistic" at once. It has the quality of the mental life. It is structured into disciplined places; it has mobility and multiplicity; its parts are naturally associated but some are interchangeable; it is circuitous and complex; it involves abstractions and ideals as well as detailed memories of the senses; and it is grounded in language—is the story of a linguistic event, a talkfest. But its most significant quality is its ability to recreate the clash of experience with experience, to set one man's reality against another's. It creates within the work a phenomenon which we can only know from introspection: that while we know the world by our own experience, part of that experience is our knowledge of others' experience, and part of this knowledge is attained from books.

And seen this way, the established idea of *The Canterbury Tales* as unfinished is correct—not because Chaucer failed to write more tales but because he created a literary form and structure, a literary idea, whose possibilities were inexhaustible. The idea itself, which is complete, makes the work "unfinished." The Parson's Tale therefore does not "knit up" the work but presents a further knitting, an alternative: it gives a kind of closure, but this closure is esthetically satisfying only from one viewpoint. It settles everything in the manner of a commentary, by authority, but it throws our attention back to the complex experience on which it comments. We have arrived at the center of the labyrinth by a very convoluted progress. What do we do now? If the cathedral labyrinths really were used as substitute pilgrimages, we do not know what the pilgrim did when he reached the center. Would he have retraced his steps from "Jerusalem" back to the entrance, confronting others on the Way as he returned? It is unlikely, because the real pilgrimage to Jerusalem was declared complete at the destination—the idea of a piligrimage was of a one-way journey. So at the center of the labyrinth it seems more likely that the pilgrim would have just got up and walked away, holding the experience in mind.

Such an ending became impossible after the eighteenth century. To end a book with a statement based on authority would not make a modern reader do anything but question the authority and look back on the experience—the effect would be ironic. The Parson's final utterance cannot be read in this modern way; we are meant to read it seriously. And yet, part of its effect *is* like the modern effect; and this effect springs from the most fundamental characteristic of Chaucer's narrative art, contrast. The Parson's Tale sets off by contrast the artistic quality of the whole. And that contrast makes the work complete. Look at it one way and you see a world of story; look at it another and you see the Way.

If it is given to the scientist to record reality so that it can be verified, it is given to the artist to record reality so that it can be known. And it is chiefly to the literary artist, whose vehicle is language, that the profoundest and most puzzling knowledge of reality is available. Chaucer saw this fact before any English writer did; he embodied it in the complex "Gothic" form which his age made available to him, and expressed it in a style which adumbrates the time-bound and mentalistic quality of that reality as it exists in memory. Thus embodied and expressed, it was the idea of his greatest work. He is the father of English literature because through that work he gave that literature its ability to put the reader in touch with a reality he could not know in any other way. The book we read at the end, the Parson's meditation, makes us see this inner reality of the world more clearly in retrospect because it is a reality of such a different order; but we would not see it this way, reading the Parson's Tale, if we had not already experienced what went before. And we return to the unfinished book of tales again and again. It may be a bag of tricks as extravagant as the Pardoner's performance, as spectacular, and as vain; but it is as provocative and astonishing an experience. And its end, too, is silence. As the Manciple's Tale ends with the discredited image of the wagging tongue, the Parson's Tale in its penultimate sentence extolls "the sight of the perfect knowing of

God." Sight, instantaneous vision, replaces time-bound utterance at the end of this most noisy book. So in his final words the author, grave and filled with hope, imposes silence on his feat of impersonation in the work and on his whole performance as a poet, embraces that death and that day of doom which will alone make the world complete, and turns his eye upon the still center.

INDEX

398   INDEX

Norris, Herbert, 105n
Notre Dame Cathedral, 202
Novelle. See Sercambi
Nun's Priest, 106, 122; as "faceless" pilgrim, 275; personal traits, 282, 283,
285, 286
Nun's Priest's Prologue and Tale, 52n,
164–165, 234; ending, 180, 181, 182,
183, 301, 371; irony in, 84, 282–288
passim, 291, 306, 307; morality in,
273, 274, 275, 303; retrospective
structure, 282–288

Obsolescence, 89, 109, 110, 115, 118,
125, 134, 162; clerical group, 98–
101; and concept of time, 167; defini-
tion, 90–92; and General Prologue,
94–105, 378; and idealism, 259; and
irony, 118, 125; literary examples,
92–96; in Parson's Tale, 378; and
social status, 93–97, 102, 103, 130.
See also Memory; "Narrative now";
Time
Original sin. *See* World, concept of
"Origin," 48
"Origenes upon the Maudelayne," 45
Ospring, 163
Ovid, 52, 121, 253, 254
Owen, Charles A., 21n, 25n
Owen, Nancy H., 368n

Painter, Sidney, 97n
Palinode. *See* Endings
Panofsky, Erwin, 20n, 68n, 70n
Paper, 64, 65, 66
"Paperness," 65, 66
Pardoner, 110, 124, 155, 160, 333; in
General Prologue, 97, 150–154;
avarice of, 113, 353, 354, 357; character, 349–357; and Chaucer, 376;
drunkenness of, 164n, 342, 343; as
grotesque, 184, 338–357, 370, 372,
376; income, 348n; and relics, 347,
348, 350, 351, 365, 366; self-hatred,
354, 372–375; sexuality, 170, 343–
345, 366, 367, 368, 372, 375
Pardoner's Prologue and Tale, 52n, 84,
370, 380; concept of death, 164, 165,
183, 357, 359–364; contrast with Parson's Tale, 381; and dream vision,
358–360, 362, 363, 370, 371; ending,
180–183, 363, 364, 369–371, 381,
386; irony in, 121, 123, 183, 352,
361–364, 367–371, 375–376; link

with Physician's Tale, 334–339; location in manuscript fragments, 333,
334
Pardons. *See* Indulgences and pardons
Parker, David, 254n
Parliament of Fowls (Chaucer), 48, 63,
94, 155, 171, 178, 267, 384; dream-
visions, 318; humor, 49, 50; retraction, 58
Parody: of Knight's Tale, 239, 262; in
Pardoner's Tale, 346n; of romance,
310; in *Sir Thopas*, 273; self-, 372;
and "unimpersonated artistry," 231
Parson, 33, 101, 113, 172, 333, 342; on
chastity, 288, 289; and concept of pilgrimage, 68–74; and Host, 175, 378,
379, 380; as ideal figure, 150–153;
376–378, 380; morality, 338, 339; as
realistic figure, 73–74, 378–380
Parson's Prologue and Tale, 21, 28, 30,
45, 122, 212, 249, 308, 371; analysis
of, 376–380; as book, 74; concept of
time, 79, 165–166; contrast with Pardoner's Tale, 381; didactic qualities,
174, 175; as ending of *Canterbury
Tales*, 197, 198, 212, 380, 386, 387;
idealism and morality in, 113, 132,
316; preparation for, 304, 306; in
structure, 58, 59, 216, 217; as treat-
ise, 59
Patch, Howard Rollin, 259n, 372n
Payne, Blanche, 105n
Payne, Robert O., 52, 76n, 137n, 211n
Pearl, 24, 171, 194
Peasant's Revolt of 1381, 102
Pearce, Robert R., 147n
Pearcy, Roy J., 282n
Pèlerinage de la vie humaine, 28
Penance, 113, 132, 197; and death, 172,
173; and guilt, 356, 357; pilgrimage
as act of, 43, 44, 327, 333, 340
Pennaforte, Raymond of, 45
Peraldus, Guillaume, 45
Perfection, 248–250, 291
Performance, 195–196, 233; *Canterbury
Tales* as, 380; Pardoner's Tale as, 381.
See also Esthetics; Form; Narrator
Peter, John D., 48n
Petrarch, Francesco, 37, 39, 40, 66, 110,
258, 259
Philobiblon (de Bury), 62
Physician, 93, 104, 105, 334–336; in
General Prologue, 150–154; irony of,
121, 123, 124

Williams, George, 4n, 22n, 232
Williams, George H., 126n
Wood, Chauncey, 79n, 89n, 165n
Woolf, Rosemary, 132n
Words and phrases in Chaucer's usage: "bel ami," 345; "book," 56–63; "in terms," 147n; "make," 20; "some comedye," 34, 35, 44; "thing," 20; "thrope," 164; "tidings," 305, 306, 331; "treatise," 59; "vavasour," 115; "wandering by the way," 72; "work," 57, 60; "ympne," 57
"Workroom" view of criticism. *See* Criticism
World, concept of: ages of, 89; in decline, 110–111, 133, 259; Fall of Man, 301, 304, 361; labyrinth symbolizes, 329; Pardoner rejects, 374; as pilgrimage, 380; renunciation of, 98; search for, 131–133; secular, 43–45, 145, 173, 229, 289, 291; self-knowledge through, 382–383; as separate from self, 376; as subject of

Canterbury Tales, 44–45, 145, 229; temporal, as province of memory, 173; transiency of, 110, 116, 162, 168, 171, 174; way of the, 67–74; as wilderness, 70, 133, 174. *See also* Golden Age; Way, concept of
World, contempt of the, 33n, 69, 116, 171, 172, 304, 305, 339
Wormald, Francis, 64n
Wrenn, C. L. 139n
"Wrecched Engendering of Mankind" (Innocent III), 44
Wretland, Dale E., 105n
Wright, C. E., 64n
Wyclif, John, 101n
Wycliffites, 378

Yates, Frances A., 140, 146, 151
Yeoman, 21, 149, 151; social status, 101, 103, 153
Young, Karl, 28n

Zacher, Christian K., xii, 28n
Zeno, Saint, Church of, 200, 201